UNSETTLING THE WEST

EARLY AMERICAN STUDIES

Series editors:
Daniel K. Richter, Kathleen M. Brown,
Max Cavitch, and David Waldstreicher

Exploring neglected aspects of our colonial,
revolutionary, and early national history and culture,
Early American Studies reinterprets familiar themes
and events in fresh ways. Interdisciplinary in character,
and with a special emphasis on the period from about 1600
to 1850, the series is published in partnership with
the McNeil Center for Early American Studies.

A complete list of books in the series
is available from the publisher.

UNSETTLING THE WEST

Violence and State Building
in the Ohio Valley

ROB HARPER

PENN

UNIVERSITY OF PENNSYLVANIA PRESS

PHILADELPHIA

Published by
University of Pennsylvania Press
Philadelphia, Pennsylvania 19104-4112
www.upenn.edu/pennpress

Printed in the United States of America on acid-free paper
1 3 5 7 9 10 8 6 4 2

Library of Congress Cataloging-in-Publication Data
Names: Harper, Rob (Historian), author.
Title: Unsettling the West : violence and state building in
    the Ohio Valley / Rob Harper.
Other titles: Early American studies.
Description: 1st edition. | Philadelphia : University of
    Pennsylvania Press, [2018] | Series: Early American
    studies | Includes bibliographical references and index.
Identifiers: LCCN 2017026858 | ISBN 9780812249644
    (hardcover : alk. paper)
Subjects: LCSH: Ohio River Valley—History—18th century.
    | Political violence—Ohio River Valley—History—18th
    century. | Indians of North America—Political activity—
    Ohio River Valley. | Colonists—Political activity—Ohio
    River Valley.
Classification: LCC F517 .H37 2018 | DDC 977/.01—dc23
LC record available at https://lccn.loc.gov/2017026858

For my parents,
Gordon Peacock Harper and Jill Robinson Harper

And in memory of my grandparents,
John Leslie Harper, Marjorie Peacock Harper, John Guido Robinson,
and Pauline Hall Robinson

CONTENTS

In late 1776, Cornstalk and Kee we Tom, both Shawnee, visited a Virginian outpost at the mouth of the Kanawha River. During their visit a third man arrived, a stranger to all. He presented a Virginian commander, Matthew Arbuckle, with a string of wampum, a sign of goodwill, but he spoke a language that none of the others could understand (per Great Lakes diplomatic norms, he likely assumed that his hosts would provide an interpreter). When Arbuckle pressed the Shawnees for an explanation, they disagreed: Cornstalk identified the stranger as a Wyandot, but Kee we Tom called him "a G_d D_n Mingo." The words mattered. At the time, the Wyandot nation was divided on the question of war and might well have sent a diplomatic message to the Virginians. By contrast, the word "Mingo," to Arbuckle's ears, would have denoted the most militant of Ohio Indians: western Haudenosaunees who had recently killed several Virginians and exchanged gunfire with his garrison. Both Wyandots and Haudenosaunees spoke Iroquoian languages, which would have sounded similar—and equally unintelligible—to both Shawnees and Virginians. Soon thereafter unknown Indians captured one of Arbuckle's men; in retaliation he imprisoned the ethnically ambiguous stranger. A few weeks later, Cornstalk negotiated a prisoner exchange, bringing the crisis to a close. He had been correct—the man was Wyandot—but the confusion about what to call him might easily have ended in bloodshed.[1]

Historians, like eighteenth-century diplomats, must choose our words carefully. Like painters mixing pigments, or composers blending sounds, we mix and match ingredients, and assemble them into a larger whole whose import, we hope, amounts to something greater than the inchoate heap we began with. If we choose words well, and deploy them with care, they may conjure up images, bring characters to life, navigate a marketplace of competing and complementary ideas, and—above all—tell stories. It is delicate work, and unlike most storytellers, we must ever remind our audience of the evidence undergirding the stories we tell. Clio is an exacting mistress.

In wrestling our verbiage into some kind of sense, we must reckon with the powers and perils of naming. This is all the more true when contending with the history of colonialism, which functions, in part, by replacing indigenous languages, stories, and names with colonial ones. In the revolutionary Ohio Valley, any given person or place might be named in any number of ways, depending on both the namer and his or her audience. Haudenosaunee people traditionally refer to one Virginian colonist by the name Hanodagonyes, which translates roughly as "town destroyer." His contemporaries variously referred to the same man as "General," "Excellency," "Master," and more. But most English-language histories identify him as "George Washington"— the name he called himself, and the name by which most readers recognize him. According to some sources, the name of Guyasuta (or Kiashuta, or Kayaghshota), a Seneca leader who alternately befriended and fought against Hanodagonyes, translates as "stands up (or sets up) the Cross," but if one visits the Seneca-Iroquois National Museum, one finds it rendered as "Standing Paddles." Perhaps some Anglophone chronicler, seeing Christian symbolism at every turn, heard a description of long, upright pieces of wood and imagined a cross. Similarly, Delaware people referred to one of their leading diplomats by a term—variably spelled Coquai,tah,ghai,tah, Koquethagechton, or Quequedegatha—that means, by one account, "the Man who keeps open the Correspondence between his own & all other Nations." Someone else took the name to mean "man who keeps an eye on Europeans." Others simplified it still further. In consequence, in his own time and since, English speakers have referred to Coquai,tah,ghai,tah by the pseudo-translation "White Eyes."[2] But however bad the translation, White Eyes himself apparently accepted it during his lifetime, perhaps out of convenience: he knew who he was. Clear answers, and perfect translations, are elusive. In the pages that follow I refer to individuals by the names that readers are most likely to recognize. But as you read, keep in mind that such names often hide from view any number of other meanings, misunderstandings, and stories.

Additional problems arise with the names of peoples. The Haudenosaunee, including Guyasuta's Senecas, referred to Washington's people as "Assaragoa," often translated as "Long Knife," in reference to a cutlass that a former governor once wore to a treaty council. The first governor of another province had introduced himself as "Penn"; when the Haudenosaunee asked what this meant, someone showed them a quill pen, earning his successors the name "Onas," or "Feather" (much as Guyasuta's paddles turned into a cross). White Eyes's Delawares called all transatlantic migrants "Schwonnaks," which translates roughly as "salt beings," alluding to their journey across the ocean. But Anglophone readers will more readily recognize the terms Virginians, Pennsylvanians, and Europeans. Similarly, the people whom English speakers call "Delaware" refer to themselves as the Lenne Lenape, or "real people." Guyasuta's nation calls itself O-non-dowa-gah: the term "Seneca" originally referred to a single village. They belong to a league of Six Nations known to themselves as the Haudenosaunee, or people of the Longhouse, but referred to by others as "Iroquois," a term of uncertain, but decidedly non-Haudenosaunee origin. Similarly, those who call themselves Ani-Yunwiya are known to English speakers as Cherokee, and those who call themselves Wyandots are sometimes referred to as Hurons. The dangerous word "Mingo," used at times to identify all western Haudenosaunees, derived from a Delaware root that translates roughly as "untrustworthy." The list goes on. But a people's use of one name to refer to itself does not necessarily entail the rejection of familiar alternatives: Senecas, Cherokees, and Delawares, among others, generally accept these names, despite their nonnative origins.[3]

I refer to all such groups by the names with which they most commonly identify themselves to others, using the most widely recognized spellings: hence Virginians, Pennsylvanians, English, Irish, Haudenosaunees, Senecas, Delawares, Cherokees, Shawnees, Wyandots. As much as possible, I favor these specific terms to misleading generic ones. When referring generally to the indigenous peoples of the place Senecas call Hah-nu-Nah, or "Turtle Island"—known to English speakers as North America—I regretfully fall back on Columbus's mistake: "Indians."[4] To identify native nations living in and around the present-day state of Ohio—Delawares, Shawnees, Senecas, Wyandots, and more—I use "Ohio Indians." Today's Allegany Indian Territory—part of the Seneca Nation of Indians—is located on the Allegheny River, a name of Lenape origin. I use Allegheny throughout. Senecas consider the Allegheny part of the much longer river they know as Ohi:yó, but Anglo-American maps came to reserve the name "Ohio" for the portion downstream from Pittsburgh. Similarly, in eighteenth-century sources, Tuscarawas was a village site located on the Muskingum River; on today's maps, the river itself is called Tuscarawas, a tributary of the Muskingum. I stick with the earlier version. Chronology presents another difficulty: in the midst of the revolutionary period, many Schwonnaks stopped calling themselves British and instead took up the name "American." My text broadly follows this shift: I refer to Britons as Americans only after they themselves came to identify with a new confederation, and later republic, they called the United States of America.

I make one major exception to this rule of naming by self-identification. As Schwonnaks ceased being British, they also stopped calling themselves colonists. Following their lead, American historians conventionally reserve the term "colonist" to the period before 1776, when the Continental Congress then declared Britain's seaboard colonies "free and independent states." But at the time, the colonization of the Ohio Valley had only just begun and would soon accelerate. I therefore use "colonists" to refer to all non-Indians who colonized the region, both before and after American independence. In doing so, I jettison "settlers" and "settlement": words that suggest peacemaking, compromise, and the benevolent ordering of the land. These connotations elide the brutality of dispossession, the tumultuous politics of colonization, and the attendant bloodshed and misery. These transformative processes, along with subsequent mythmaking, together comprise Anglo-American colonialism: the process that turned much of Hah-nu-Nah into the United States.[5]

ABBREVIATIONS

AA4 and 5
: *American Archives: Consisting of a Collection of Authentick Records, State Papers, Debates, and Letters and Other Notices of Publick Affairs.* Fourth and fifth ser. Washington, DC, 1837. http://amarch.lib.niu.edu/.

Butler
: Butler, Richard. "Journal of General Butler." Edited by Neville B. Craig. *The Olden Time* 2, no. 10–12 (Oct.–Dec. 1847): 433–64, 481–527, 529–31.

C&M
: Heckewelder, John. "Narrative of the Indian Mission on Muskingum: Captivity and Murder," [1786?]. Box 213, folder 16. Records of the Moravian Mission Among the Indians of North America. Archives of the Moravian Church. Bethlehem, PA. Microfilm.

Chalmers
: Papers relating to Indians, 1750–1775. George Chalmers Papers, 1606–1812. New York Public Library. Microfilm.

CO5
: Colonial Office. CO5: America and West Indies, Original Correspondence, Etc., 1606–1807. 119 microfilm reels. Public Records of Great Britain, ser. 4. White Plains, NY: Kraus-Thomson, 1987.

Connolly
: Connolly, John. "Journal of My Proceedings &c. Commencing from the Late Disturbances with the Cherokees Upon the Ohio." Papers relating to Indians, 1750–1775, George Chalmers Papers, 1606–1812. New York Public Library. Microfilm.

CRBJ
: Butler, Richard. "Captain Richard Butler's Journal." Historical Society of Pennsylvania.

Cresswell
: Gill, Harold B., Jr., and George M. Curtis III, eds. *A Man Apart: The Journal of Nicholas Cresswell, 1774–1781.* Lanham, MD: Lexington, 2009.

CRP
: *Colonial Records of Pennsylvania.* 16 vols. Harrisburg, PA: Theo. Fenn & Co., 1838–53.

DAF   Darlington Autograph Files, 1610–1914. DAR.1925.07. Dar-
              lington Collection. Special Collections Department, Uni-
              versity of Pittsburgh, http://digital.library.pitt.edu/d/darling
              ton/index.html.

DBP   Daniel Brodhead Papers. DAR.1925.04. Darlington Collec-
              tion. Special Collections Department, University of Pitts-
              burgh, http://digital.library.pitt.edu/d/darlington/index.html.

DDZ   *Diary of David Zeisberger a Moravian Missionary Among the
              Indians of Ohio.* 2 vols. Edited and translated by Eugene F.
              Bliss. 1885; St. Clair Shores, MI: Scholarly Press, 1972.

Denny   Denny, Ebenezer. *Military Journal of Major Ebenezer Denny,
              an Officer in the Revolutionary and Indian Wars.* Edited by
              William H. Denny. Philadelphia: Historical Society of Penn-
              sylvania, 1859.

DGW   Jackson, Donald, and Dorothy Twohig, eds. *The Diaries of
              George Washington.* 6 vols. Charlottesville: University Press
              of Virginia, 1976–79.

DHDW   Thwaites, Reuben Gold, and Louise Phelps Kellogg, eds.
              Documentary History of Dunmore's War, 1774. Madison:
              Wisconsin Historical Society, 1905.

Draper   Lyman C. Draper Manuscripts. Wisconsin Historical Society,
              Madison.

EHP   Hand, Edward. Papers, 1771–1807. Historical Society of
              Pennsylvania.

FAUO   *Frontier Advance on the Upper Ohio, 1778–1779.* Edited by
              Louise Phelps Kellogg. Publications of the State Historical
              Society of Wisconsin, vol. 23. Madison: State Historical So-
              ciety of Wisconsin, 1916.

FDUO   *Frontier Defense on the Upper Ohio, 1777–1778.* Edited by Reu-
              ben Gold Thwaites and Louise Phelps Kellogg. Publications of
              the State Historical Society of Wisconsin, vol. 22. 1912; Mill-
              wood, NY: Kraus Reprint, 1973.

FRUO   *Frontier Retreat on the Upper Ohio.* Edited by Louise Phelps
              Kellogg. Publications of the State Historical Society of Wis-
              consin, vol. 24. Madison: State Historical Society of Wis-
              consin, 1917.

GCP   George Croghan Papers. Cadwalader Collection, ser. IV.
              Historical Society of Pennsylvania.

GD   Schmick, Johann Jacob, and Johann Roth. Gnadenhütten di-
                      ary, 1773–77. Translated by William N. Schwarze and Robert
                      H. Brennecke. Box 144. Records of the Moravian Mission
                      Among the Indians of North America, 1735–1900. Archives
                      of the Moravian Church, Bethlehem, PA. Microfilm.

Gratz   Gratz Collection. Historical Society of Pennsylvania.

GRC   *George Rogers Clark Papers.* Edited by James Alton James.
                      Collections of the Illinois State Historical Library, vols. 8, 19.
                      Springfield: Illinois State Historical Library, 1912–24.

GWP   George Washington Papers. American Memory, Library of
                      Congress, https://www.loc.gov/collections/george-washing
                      ton-papers/.

Harmar   Josiah Harmar Papers. William L. Clements Library, Ann
                      Arbor, MI.

HSP   Historical Society of Pennsylvania.

INF   Irvine-Newbold Family Papers, ser. 1. Historical Society of
                      Pennsylvania.

Jones   Jones, David. *A Journal of Two Visits Made to Some Nations
                      of Indians on the West Side of the River Ohio in the Years 1772
                      and 1773.* 1774; New York: Arno, 1971.

McClure   McClure, David. *Diary of David McClure, Doctor of Divinity,
                      1748–1820.* Edited by Franklin B. Dexter. New York: Knicker-
                      bocker, 1899.

McKee   [McKee, Alexander]. "Extract from My Journal from the 1st
                      May 1774 Containing Indian Transactions &Ca." Papers Re-
                      lating to Indians, 1750–1775, George Chalmers Papers,
                      1606–1812. New York Public Library. Microfilm.

MMD   *The Moravian Mission Diaries of David Zeisberger, 1772–
                      1781.* Edited by Herman Wellenreuther and Carola Wessel.
                      Translated by Julie Tomberlin Weber. University Park:
                      Pennsylvania State University Press, 2005.

Morgan   Morgan, George. George Morgan letterbooks, 1775–79.
                      P-410. Carnegie Library of Pittsburgh. Microfilm.

MPHS   *Historical Collections: Collections and Researches Made by the
                      Michigan Pioneer and Historical Society.* 40 vols. Lansing,
                      MI: Wynkoop, Hallenbeck, & Crawford Co., 1874–1929.

PA   *Pennsylvania Archives.* 12 vols. Edited by Samuel Hazard.
                      Philadelphia: Joseph Severns & Co., 1852–56.

PA2–PA6	*Pennsylvania Archives*, 2nd to 6th ser. Harrisburg, 1879–1935.
PFH	Correspondence and Papers of General Sir Frederick Haldimand, 1758–1784. London: World Microfilm, 1977.
Prevost	Wainwright, Nicholas B., ed. "Turmoil at Pittsburgh: Diary of Augustine Prevost, 1774." *Pennsylvania Magazine of History and Biography* 85, no. 2 (1961): 111–62.
PWJ	*The Papers of Sir William Johnson*. 12 vols. Albany: State University of New York, 1921–63.
RPRG	Records of Pennsylvania's Revolutionary Governments, 1775–90. RG 27. Pennsylvania State Archives, Harrisburg. Microfilm. Page reference indicates reel:frame.
RUO	Thwaites, Reuben Gold, and Louise Phelps Kellogg, eds. *The Revolution on the Upper Ohio, 1775–1777*. Madison: Wisconsin Historical Society, 1908.
RVRI	Van Schreeven, William J., Robert L. Scribner, and Brent Tarter, eds. *Revolutionary Virginia: The Road to Independence*. 7 vols. Charlottesville: University Press of Virginia, 1973–83.
SCP	*The St. Clair Papers: The Life and Public Services of Arthur St. Clair*. 2 vols. Edited by William Henry Smith. Cincinnati, OH: Robert Clarke & Co., 1882.
TGP	Thomas Gage Papers. William L. Clements Library, Ann Arbor, MI.
VSP	Palmer, William P., ed. *Calendar of Virginia State Papers and Other Manuscripts*. 11 vols. Richmond, VA: R. U. Derr, 1875–93.
WIC	*Washington-Irvine Correspondence*. Edited by C. W. Butterfield. Madison, WI: David Atwood, 1882.
Yeates	Jasper Yeates Correspondence, 1762–86. Box 740. Yeates Papers. Historical Society of Pennsylvania.

UNSETTLING THE WEST

Introduction

In the summer of 1772, a recent Dartmouth graduate, David McClure, set out to bring Christianity to the Indians of the Ohio Valley. As he trudged across the Alleghenies, he met fifteen packhorses headed eastward, hauling cannonballs. The British empire, McClure learned, could no longer afford its garrison at Fort Pitt, and so the imperial ordnance now marched away from the frontier he hoped to civilize.[1] As he watched the horses pass, the young missionary likely wondered what he had gotten himself into. British influence over the Ohio Valley—tenuous to begin with—was waning further, leaving the region's peoples free from imperial oversight. The West was becoming wilder—or so it seemed.

Like McClure, many histories of the Ohio Valley maintain that imperial weakness bred frontier wildness. The region's ensuing colonization, one suggests, unfolded "from the bottom up," driven by the dreams of ordinary colonists who hungered for land and bristled at government meddling. An array of medical and aquatic metaphors conveys the organic force of this migration: tens of thousands succumbed to a "land fever" that made them pour, flood, and surge across the Appalachians. Attitude and impulse also seem to explain intercultural violence: Indians and colonists hated one another, and with no state to restrain them they slaughtered at will. But a closer look calls these explanations into question. Colonists coveted Indian land, but they colonized new areas only where they had some hope of gaining legal title. Horrific violence ensued, but its scale varied sharply over time. When governments ignored the region, relative peace prevailed. When they tried to control it, hostilities escalated. Intercultural hatred persisted throughout but led to war only when government initiatives empowered the region's inhabitants to fight. Rather than springing from state absence, the horrors of the period stemmed from governments' intrusive presence.[2]

A gaggle of polities contended for power in the revolutionary Ohio Valley. The Six Nations of the Haudenosaunee in the north and the Cherokee nation in the south claimed large and overlapping territories, while

Wyandots, Delawares, and Shawnees insisted they owned much of the same land. A series of legally dubious treaties with Europeans complicated matters further. The proprietary government of Pennsylvania and the royal government of Virginia bickered over ill-defined borders, even as imperial officials vetted proposals for new western colonies. In 1774, Britain declared Ohio to be part of Canada. In 1775 and 1776, the colonists of the Atlantic seaboard toppled their old regimes and declared themselves "free and independent states," while a Continental Congress struggled to coordinate a united struggle against the empire. In 1783, Britain surrendered all territory south of the lakes to the newly independent United States, but the region's Indian nations pointed out that they had never ceded the land to anyone. The British at least intermittently encouraged native claims, and refused to hand over their Great Lakes forts until 1796. Meanwhile, the late 1780s and early 1790s brought a new "Northwest Territory" north of the Ohio, new constitutions for Pennsylvania and the United States, and the separation of Kentucky's government from Virginia. Throughout, agents of different governments argued and sometimes fought over their competing claims to authority.[3]

These ubiquitous disputes suggest Hobbesian chaos, but they can be better understood as part of a process of state building that transcended the rise and fall of specific governments. Rather than clearly defined institutions set apart from civil society, governments in the Ohio Valley comprised "extensive, fluid networks of people" pursuing a wide range of dissimilar and even contradictory goals. In this world, modern distinctions between state and nonstate actors, or between government and civil society, had little meaning. Policies approved in London, Williamsburg, or Philadelphia had little effect without the cooperation and influence of local allies, creating ample room to resist, negotiate, or reshape state authority. Specific governments came and went, but their diverse constituents usually continued their work under the aegis of a different government, in hopes of building a more advantageous political order. Ohio Valley inhabitants' visions for that future varied immensely but generally involved some sort of composite polity that balanced local self-rule with the protections of a larger empire. Rather than either resisting or submitting to state authority, Indians and colonists pursued "advantageous interdependence." They cherished local autonomy, yet wanted to participate in a political system strong enough to effectively regulate trade, resolve disputes, enforce boundaries, and guard against attack. Though they decried unwelcome government meddling, few Indians or colonists savored the thought of pursuing these goals independently. Far from "car[ing] little for states," they sought to shape the emerging state to suit their own ends.[4]

Understanding state building in the Ohio Valley requires close attention to both intracultural divisions and intercultural alliances. Both Indian and colonial societies comprised a mosaic of distinct geographic and cultural communities, in which individuals responded to conflicts in myriad ways. Though Ohio Indians broadly shared a commitment to some kind of territorial sovereignty, individuals adopted diverse and often conflicting strategies in order to secure it. Most colonists in the region aspired to own land, but when, where, and how they tried to do so varied substantially, and their ambitions fueled internecine conflict at least as often as unity. Lacking either strong coercive institutions or broad political consensus, Ohio Valley inhabitants could wage war, make peace, and pursue their various goals only by building coalitions. As in modern states, coalition politics often made strange bedfellows, as individuals and communities with different and even contradictory long-term goals joined to pursue common short-term objectives. It entailed searching for allies with overlapping interests, articulating those interests effectively, and continually finessing divergent aims. To unify amid so much diversity, the coalition builders, or brokers, often manipulated or distorted information in order to obscure or downplay differences among allies—at least enough to permit cooperation, for a time.[5]

More durable alliances linked such brokers with influential patrons: investors, military commanders, or political authorities, usually based outside the region. Brokers provided patrons with information and promoted their interests in exchange for credit, influence peddling, and official appointments. Rather than a zero-sum game, in which state institutions gained power at the expense of their subjects, such relationships tended to be symbiotic, with both patrons and brokers gaining advantages through collaboration. Thanks to patronage, brokers gained influence in their communities, enabling them to both better serve patrons and cultivate clients of their own. Representatives of colonial governments were especially attractive patrons, despite their lack of effective authority, because they could offer a wide array of resources: trade goods, food, weapons, teachers, soldiers, and land titles. Patronage networks tended to be more stable and durable than other coalitions, but as interests, strategies, and opportunities shifted, brokers might switch patrons or cultivate competing patrons simultaneously. Patrons, too, might abandon brokers when they found other, more useful allies.[6] But during the Revolutionary War, as British- and American-allied coalitions spawned mounting intercultural violence, Ohio Valley communities grew more dependent on government patronage, limiting their ability to resist state demands.

Scholarly explanations of those horrors understandably emphasize cultural and ideological factors. Competition for land, as well as the traumas of recent wars, fueled hatred between Indians and colonists, offering ample motive for murder. Contrasting beliefs about violence deepened the antagonism. For many Ohio Indians, permissibility of killing hinged on collective identity. They broadly accepted violence against communities with whom the perpetrator's own people were at war, while condemning the killing of those with whom one's people were at peace. In the latter case, the killer's extended family and nation were expected to atone for the injury or face collective retaliation. Captured enemies could be ritually adopted—absorbing their physical being into the captors' community—or ritually killed to secure their spiritual power. By contrast, European and colonial ideas about violence depended—at least in theory—on the attributes of the specific victim and perpetrator. Individuals who appeared dangerous—enemy combatants, rebellious slaves, or other threatening figures—could be killed, but noncombatants, especially women and children, were ordinarily to be spared. Wrongdoers were subject to personal punishment; their families and communities, generally speaking, were not. By the late eighteenth century, Indians and Europeans in the Great Lakes region and Ohio Valley understood these differences and accommodated them out of necessity, but few recognized the other's value system as legitimate. Above all, many colonists denied that their prohibitions of murder applied to Indians at all. Citing the Israelites' extirpation of Old Testament foes, some described the indiscriminate killing of native people as a holy calling. Because of such attitudes, colonial courts almost invariably failed to convict murderers of Indians.[7]

But while cultural differences and hatreds help explain violence, they do not account for the full range of intercultural bloodshed, or its ebbs and flows. Violence often sprang from everyday interactions like tavern bickering or haggling over trade, circumstances that jar with the presumption of ubiquitous intercultural hostility. Motives for premeditated killing varied: many acted on hatred and vengeance, but some also aimed to impress an audience, to serve a spiritual purpose, to comply with orders, or to facilitate theft. Equally important, the scale of violence shifted dramatically over time, ranging from sporadic and isolated murders to wars of attrition. Noting these ambiguities and variations does not deny that categorical hatred made everything worse. But hatred alone does not suffice to explain how, when, and why Ohio Valley inhabitants killed one another. The story of these atrocities hinges on what happened between "acquisition of a violence-promoting idea and direct participation in mayhem."[8] In this case, the escalation and de-escalation of hostilities correlates closely with the ever-shifting influence of governments. When those disposed to violence enjoyed access to government patronage, or had reason to expect official backing, bloodshed escalated. When government support diminished, violence lessened apace.

Unstable and ineffective governments exerted so much influence because both Indians and colonists sought to use government resources for their own ends. Competition for state patronage magnified the influence of government officials, while conflicts between rival governments forced officials to collaborate with the region's inhabitants. The results of such collaborations often disappointed most or all of those involved. Ohio Indians found that formal relationships with the Anglo-American state could facilitate dispossession, rather than prevent it. Many colonists failed to obtain the legal land title they sought, or they soon lost it through litigation or bankruptcy. For their part, government officials incessantly complained about the unruly willfulness of even nominal friends and allies. But if such partnerships often failed to yield desired results, they also profoundly unsettled the Ohio Valley, ultimately subjecting its peoples to the authority of an increasingly potent federal state.

These findings point to a new and more nuanced understanding of revolutionary Anglo-American colonialism. Scholars of the nineteenth- and twentieth-century trans-Mississippi West have long emphasized the centrality of state power in that region's transformations, calling into question deep-seated popular myths of an individualistic frontier. The eighteenth-century state, fragmented and unstable as it was, lacked the resources and technologies that made its successors such effective tools of conquest and dispossession. Nonetheless, the story of rugged frontier independence, of colonists marching west with no regard for political authority, proves as fallacious for the revolutionary Ohio Valley as it is for Montana or California.[9] At the same time, the eventual colonial regime, like emerging states around the world, grew through a nonlinear and often unplanned process, driven by internecine rivalries as much as by intercultural antagonism. Politically influential speculators pressed governments for western lands. Official initiatives—land grants, road and fort building, treaties, and wars—as well as competition between rival claimants, spurred colonists to move west. Indian communities, often at odds with one another, angled to preserve their territory and sovereignty by cultivating both native and colonial allies. The resulting pattern of coalition building alternately facilitated both peacemaking and violence. Governments, meanwhile, pressed their competing territorial claims by arming the region's inhabitants, and militant Indians and colonists exploited such support to mobilize for war. The ensuing devastation deepened dependence on government patronage and bolstered the influence of leaders who could obtain it. All told, this brand of colonialism reflected the interplay of state influence and state weakness, of intracultural divisions and intercultural violence, of individual agency and community dependence. This is a story of negotiation, accommodation, and coalition building, as well as a story of the emerging power of a colonial state.[10]

Most of the Ohio Valley's Indian peoples had entered or reentered the region less than half a century before McClure's encounter with the cannonballs. A series of seventeenth-century wars had temporarily driven the region's inhabitants, including Shawnees, to other areas. In the first half of the eighteenth century, many of their descendants moved back to the rich farmland of the Scioto Valley. Around the same time, Haudenosaunee and Delaware migrants from the east made new homes in the Allegheny and Muskingum valleys, while peoples from the north and west, including Wyandots, Odawas, and Miamis, repopulated the Maumee and Sandusky valleys. Many of these nations—to whom I refer collectively as Ohio Indians—had interacted regularly with European colonists since the early 1600s. Now they came to Ohio for its fertile soil, burgeoning deer population, and distance from the growing seaboard colonies. But distance did not mean disconnection. Though some spiritual leaders called on their people to reject colonial trade, such preaching did little to slow the exchange of beaver pelts and deerskins for European-manufactured textiles, tools, weapons, and rum. Living between French and British colonies allowed Indian peoples to leverage imperial rivalry for commercial and diplomatic advantage. To many, moving west and trading for European goods were complementary tactics that promoted both autonomy and prosperity.[11]

   After bidding the packhorses farewell, David McClure pressed on with his journey, eager to see the peoples he called "those distant & savage tribes beyond the Ohio." A few days later, he learned that Ohio Indians were neither as distant nor as savage as he had imagined. As he traveled west to Pittsburgh, an Allegheny Seneca leader named Guyasuta was journeying east to visit imperial officials in Philadelphia and New York. The Seneca impressed the missionary with his "martial appearance," but rather than paint and a breech-clout he wore scarlet and lace. His head likely bore a long, braided scalp lock, but it was hidden under a "high gold laced hat." McClure also praised his "very sensible countenance & dignity of manners," as well as his thoughtful comments on religion and politics. The missionary was not alone in his admiration. Colonial newspapers fawningly reported Guyasuta's tours of the eastern port cities, noting that while pursuing business "of the greatest importance" he also made time to observe public "electrical experiments."[12]

This scientifically curious, scarlet-dressed diplomat had followed a long and circuitous political and military career. In 1753, he had guided a young George Washington into the upper Ohio Valley. The Virginians wanted to drive the French from the region; they failed but, in doing so, started a world war. For most of the following decade, in a conflict misnamed the Seven Years' War, the forces of Britain, France, and their respective allies clashed repeatedly around the globe, from Saxony to Senegal, Madras, and Havana. Back in North America, Guyasuta switched sides, joining a large Franco-Indian alliance that ambushed and destroyed General Edward Braddock's army in the Battle of the Monongahela, just upstream from present-day Pittsburgh. Their victory, and the alliance, proved short-lived. French-allied Indians, eager to reverse British colonial expansion, terrorized the outer reaches of Pennsylvania and Virginia, but British and colonial forces retaliated by burning Indian towns and crops. Both sides slaughtered noncombatants in raids that had more to do with territorial dispossession than imperial alliances. By the late 1750s many nations, including most of Guyasuta's Senecas, had abandoned the French in exchange for concessions from the British, who subsequently captured the Forks of the Ohio, Niagara, and all of French Canada. In the eventual treaty, France surrendered all its claims to North America. At Detroit and elsewhere, French colonists and trading networks remained, but Great Lakes and Ohio Valley Indians could no longer leverage interimperial conflict for diplomatic and commercial advantage.[13]

These momentous changes soon exhausted Guyasuta's hopes for peace. Victorious British commanders quickly forgot their promises. They abandoned long-standing diplomatic protocols, refused to remove forts and soldiers from native land, and showed little interest in curbing colonization. In 1761, Guyasuta urged Great Lakes nations to strike back, likely hoping that their erstwhile French allies would support them. Few heeded his call, but two years later a far-flung alliance of Great Lakes Indians captured nine

British forts, spread hundreds of miles apart. Guyasuta personally helped capture the Allegheny Valley outpost of Venango and later joined an ultimately unsuccessful siege of Fort Pitt. The region plunged into a conflict known as Pontiac's War, after the Odawa leader who led the assault on Detroit. The reciprocal raids, town burning, and killing of noncombatants resumed, setting a pattern that became all too familiar in years to come. After two years of fighting, Guyasuta led a peace delegation to Fort Pitt, where the heavily indebted British empire welcomed him. He and his allies, having destroyed most of the region's forts, pledged to stop attacking the ones that remained. The empire, in turn, banned colonization west of the Appalachians, though the Six Nations tentatively agreed to a future cession of lands south and east of Pittsburgh. Many colonists and Indians had little use, or respect, for these concessions, but large-scale fighting nonetheless ground to a halt. On both sides, the human and economic costs of war had proven too much to bear.[14]

Guyasuta, accordingly, reinvented himself as an Anglophile. A few years after besieging Fort Pitt, he publicly defended the British army's right to stay there. In championing first the French and then Pontiac's alliance, he had defied the more moderate Six Nations council, including many of his fellow Senecas. Now he insisted on the Six Nations' political supremacy over his erstwhile western allies and welcomed the anticipated land cession. During an autumn 1770 hunting trip, Guyasuta learned that his old friend—and sometime enemy—Washington was journeying down the Ohio. He welcomed the Virginian with open arms, presented him with "a Quarter of very fine Buffalo," and insisted that his party join the Seneca camp. In their ensuing conversations, Guyasuta vividly described the rich bottomland west of the Kanawha River. Washington took copious notes.[15] Guyasuta had spent the better part of ten years trying to drive the British out of the Ohio Valley. Now he encouraged them to move in.

At first glance, this reversal might look like cynical opportunism, and perhaps, in some measure, it was. But in shifting between pro- and anti-British strategies, Guyasuta adhered to a broader goal that guided his long political and military career: the security and sovereignty of Allegheny Senecas. In 1753, collaborating with the Virginians promised to bolster his people's power against the increasingly aggressive French and their western allies. Over the next two years, Washington's and Braddock's defeats shattered British credibility. Allegheny Senecas rationally embraced the seemingly victorious French, then abandoned them as the fortunes of war turned: a series of maneuvers that mirrored the ever-shifting alliances of eighteenth-century Europe. After the war, a string of British outposts directly threatened Guyasuta's people. When Britain refused to evacuate them, he helped build a new alliance that leveled all but Fort Pitt. That garrison's survival, however, dictated a new approach. By befriending Britain—for the third time—Guyasuta ensured Seneca access to Pittsburgh trade and imperial patronage. In 1771, when his people faced food shortages, he persuaded British agent George Croghan to give them "two hundred Bushels of Corn." Meanwhile, he seized the opportunity to divert colonists westward down the Ohio, away from the Seneca towns on the Allegheny.[16]

Along the way, Guyasuta crafted the genteel persona that so impressed McClure. The patronage of prominent colonists, he recognized, could help win commercial and political concessions: hence his courtship of Washington. Colonists and imperial officials came to see him as the "head" of the western Haudenosaunee, an essential intermediary who wielded "great Influence" over the troublingly independent Ohio Indians. By the time of his meeting with McClure, he had won the confidence of William Johnson, Britain's top frontier diplomat, who shared his eagerness to strengthen Six Nations authority. During his trip east, Guyasuta insisted on meeting personally with Commander-in-Chief Thomas Gage, to assure him that "the true situation of Affairs" in Ohio was "quiet and peaceable." As he cultivated these connections, Guyasuta increasingly emulated the appearance, demeanor, and language of British officers. In his meetings with McClure and Gage, he still spoke through an interpreter, but by 1775 he translated for colonial emissaries himself.[17]

Guyasuta was an outlier: few traveled, or hobnobbed, so widely. But his cultural flexibility, his penchant for coalition building, and his shifting political strategies exemplified common characteristics of the Ohio Valley's diverse native peoples. These were nations in flux, adapting to new and often changing external pressures, most notably colonial demands for land, while also constantly negotiating political divisions among and within their communities. Europeans and colonists who knew of Indians only slightly, including McClure himself, tended to categorize them either as friendly or antagonistic, and behave accordingly, but many, like Guyasuta, moved back and forth between peacemaking and militancy, and any number of points in between, as ever-shifting circumstances warranted.

When he crossed the Ohio, McClure found a forest "clear from underbrush," contrasting sharply with the dense thickets east of the river. In this open woodland, he found it easier to hunt and gather food: deer, turkeys, geese, pigeons, fruit, nuts, and berries. Ohio Indians had created this cornucopia. McClure described how they periodically burned the ground cover, "that they may have the advantage of seeing game at a distance among the trees." In doing so, the burners also controlled insect pests, promoted the growth of edible plants, and created a favorable environment for deer and turkey. A similar landscape had once flourished east of the river, but it had reverted to an overgrown tangle after Indians fled west during the midcentury wars. Now, as eastern game populations fell, colonial hunters from Pennsylvania to the Carolinas ventured farther into Indian lands. By the early 1770s, Delawares complained that "game grew scarce"; in Gekelemukpechünk, a visiting missionary noted that "no meat could be had here for love or money." Not long after singing the praises of the managed open woodland, McClure feared for his safety because of Delaware hunters' "extreme resentment at the encroachments of the white people."[18] The region's growing human population took a heavy toll on its deer and bison, setting the stage for greater subsistence crises to come.

As the missionary moved west, the upper Ohio Valley's steep ridges gave way to rolling terrain and lush farmland. At Gekelemukpechünk, McClure found hundreds of Delaware people living in a mix of bark wigwams, log cabins, and English-style homes made of "hewed logs, with stone chimneys." Across the river, Delaware women planted "a large corn field, in rich low ground," in which each matrilineal household worked its own plot. Other Ohio Indians lived in similar towns, clustered in the region's sinuous river valleys, surrounded by fields, orchards, and managed forests. In contrast to scattered colonial homesteads, they generally lived in larger communities and farmed collectively. Many colonists overlooked or denigrated Indian agriculture, partly because they discounted the labor of Indian women, but even the most chauvinistic visitors praised their prolific harvests. By the 1770s, many Ohio Indians had diversified their economies further. Gekelemukpechünk impressed McClure with its "regular & thrifty peach orchard." The Shawnee town of Wockachaali raised fine herds of horses and cattle. The prosperity of Anipassicowa, a Shawnee woman, impressed visiting colonists, who noted that she kept and milked cattle to complement traditional maize-based agriculture. Once or twice in each generation, as soils grew depleted, Ohio Indians moved their towns and fields to new sites, but they continued using the surrounding woodlands and streams for hunting, fishing, and other subsistence activities.[19]

Ohio Indian women also played a pivotal role in intercultural trade. Since the mid-seventeenth century, indigenous peoples across North America had exchanged animal skins and other commodities for European manufactures like tools, weapons, fabrics, and liquor. To facilitate this commerce, Indian women often partnered with male colonists in relationships that were both commercial and sexual. In 1775, a young Ohio Mohawk woman took a neophyte trader, Nicholas Cresswell, under her wing, despite knowing only a little of his language. When he lodged with her family in the town of Old Hundy, she slept with him and, the following morning, persuaded him to bring her along on his journey. Their relationship brought tangible benefits to both. He needed someone to guide him to customers, cook his food, nurse him when he got sick, and keep track of his horse, which he had a habit of losing. For her part, she brought his business to her kin. Real affection developed between them, culminating in a teary-eyed goodbye. Over decades, countless similar partnerships created elaborate trading networks, in which Indian women and colonial traders linked indigenous kinship groups to merchants in Philadelphia, Montreal, and London. Trade with colonists was not always beneficial: liquor brought a host of problems, and male elders sometimes complained about young women selling rum in their communities. But for good or ill, such entrepreneurship reflected a long-standing pattern of exchange that forged lasting commercial and familial relationships.[20]

Some Ohio Indians' distant ancestors had lived in large and relatively centralized city-states, but centuries of climatic cooling, together with the more recent ravages of European pathogens, had encouraged political and social dispersal, creating a landscape of politically autonomous towns. By the mid-eighteenth century, it became clear that small and scattered communities were all the more vulnerable to land-hungry British colonists. Many Ohio Indian leaders thus began promoting consolidation: clustering towns near one another, inviting distant friends and allies to become neighbors, and leveraging demographic density for political advantage. The Wyandots invited the Delawares to settle on their land in eastern Ohio, and the Delawares in turn recruited other easterners to join them, including Delawares and Mohicans who had embraced the German-led Moravian Church. The Six Nations urged Ohio Indians to move closer to the Haudenosaunee homeland, while Shawnee leaders invited western Haudenosaunee to move to the Scioto Valley. These efforts garnered mixed results. Many Shawnees opted instead for an older strategy of mobility and dispersal. Even so, the migration of far-flung Indians to a shared Ohio homeland added still more diversity to an already complex mix of peoples. The Muskingum Valley became home to both traditionalists who decried European influence and Christians who played a spinet piano during Sunday services.[21]

Widespread intermarriage, adoption, and migration ensured that many towns were multiethnic and multilingual. Native families commonly adopted wartime captives to replace deceased loved ones; demand for such adoptees constituted a major motive for going to war. A Cherokee captive was adopted into one Delaware family, married into another, and subsequently joined the Moravian Church. Somewhere along the way, he learned to "speak the Wyandot language pretty well." When Cherokee and Wyandot emissaries visited the Muskingum Valley, he volunteered his services as interpreter. Anipassicowa's town was home to Shawnees, Delawares, and descendants of both Africans and Europeans. In the early 1770s, nearly twenty light-skinned people, most of them childhood captives adopted into Shawnee families, lived in the Shawnee town of Chillicothe. Shawnee and other Indian women commonly married resident white traders. Some captives eventually returned to colonial society but remained close to their adoptive families. During a trip through Ohio, a colonist named Joseph Nickels went out of his way to visit "his indian acquaintance, for whom he had a friendship, from his early days of captivity among them."[22]

Adoptees entered complex social and political systems that defy popular stereotypes of "tribes" and "chiefs." The *šaawanwaki*, or Shawnee people, for example, includes five major patrilineal divisions or "society clans": the Chalaakaatha (or Chillicothe), Mekoche, Kishpoko, Pekowi, and Thawikila. Though these groups share a common language and culture, they traditionally lived in separate towns with distinct sets of female and male leaders. The Delaware include two major ethnolinguistic divisions, the Munsee and Unami, as well as three matrilineal phratries associated with the turtle, the wolf, and the turkey. They also enjoy close historic, geographic, and linguistic ties to the Mohican nation, evident today in the Stockbridge-Munsee community of Wisconsin. The Wyandot originated as a confederacy of several nations, similarly divided among three phratries. The Six Nations of the Haudenosaunee, commonly known as Iroquois, include the Seneca, Cayuga, Onondaga, Oneida, Mohawk, and Tuscarora. To the north, the Ojibwe, Odawa, and Potawatomi nations share a common identity and cultural heritage as the Three Fires of the Anishinaabeg. To the south, the Cherokee nation was historically divided among several regions, each of which possessed, to some degree, a distinct political identity.[23] The nature and significance of these unions and divisions varied, and varies, a good deal. In eighteenth-century politics such extranational or subnational affinities often mattered at least as much as one's identification with a specific tribe or nation.

These divisions and confederacies often paled in importance compared to kinship systems that Shawnees call *m'shoma*, Anishinaabeg call *doodem*, Wyandots call *,entiok8ten*, German missionaries called *Freundschaften*, and modern English speakers call clans.[24] Clan membership stemmed from descent, either matrilineal (for the Delaware, Wyandot, Haudenosaunee, and Cherokee) or patrilineal (in the case of the Shawnee and Anishinaabeg). Clans (and sometimes phratries) were traditionally exogamous, so while individuals inherited clan membership from one parent, they enjoyed kinship ties with the clans of both. Such ties played a critical role in both daily life and regional politics. When Joseph Peepy, a Christian Delaware from New Jersey, escorted McClure to the Muskingum Valley town of Kighalampegha, they found a warm welcome from Peepy's kin despite widespread distaste for their religious message. Israel Welapachtschiechen, a prominent leader of the Delaware turkey phratry, exerted considerable influence across the region in part because his clan was "very widespread." When he adopted Christianity, many fellow clan members followed his example. Others protested his decision, but bonds of kinship continued to link them and facilitate coalition building despite their religious differences.[25]

Political leadership reflected these ethnic and kinship relationships. Among Shawnees, male *hokimas*, or civil leaders, derived their authority in part through their patrilineal clan inheritance, as well as from personal virtues and accomplishments. Hokimas of different clans had distinct responsibilities, according to the spiritual attributes of each lineage. Their mothers, known as *hokima wiikwes*, oversaw agriculture, the adoption of captives, and other traditionally female responsibilities while also advising hokimas on political and military matters. Similarly, the Six Nations' ancient Great Law of Peace specifies that clan mothers choose and advise male civil leaders. Among all Ohio Indians, civil leaders usually deferred military authority to war captains. Many of the region's peoples chose still other individuals as spiritual guides.[26]

With authority so decentralized, leaders of all kinds had to seek consensus rather than impose their will. One missionary wrote that Shawnees were "strangers to civil power and authority," believing that "one man has no natural right to rule over another." Formal leaders spoke first in meetings but otherwise had "no more honor or respect payed them than another man."

Political prestige depended less on wealth or status than on generosity. Netawatwees, the preeminent civil leader of the Delaware turtle phratry, lived in
"a poor house" and bore "no emblem of Royalty or Magesty about him."
Rather than accumulating personal wealth and tangible markers of authority,
he maintained his influence by redistributing resources around the community. Ohio Indian communities could "Never Suffer for want," one Irish trader
observed, because their "hospitality is so grate." When McClure offered his
spiritual guidance to the Delaware council, he expected a prompt and decisive reply. Instead, they spent two full weeks debating his proposals and solic-
iting input from other towns before Netawatwees rejected his proposals.
Rather than introducing European customs to his hosts, McClure had to accept a Delaware process of discussion and consensus building.[27]

McClure's impatience with Delaware politics reflected how much the
Muskingum Valley towns remained a "native ground" where Indian customs
prevailed and European visitors had to adapt accordingly.[28] But at the same
time, proximity to the British colonies and the benefits of intercultural trade
challenged Ohio Indians to build relationships with Anglo-American governments. To do so, some sought to centralize decision making. Six Nations
leaders, including Guyasuta, increasingly, albeit ineffectually, claimed authority over Ohio Indians. Delaware leaders answered by asserting their independence. Colonial officials, meanwhile, increasingly demanded that
Indian emissaries sign binding agreements prior to building consensus
among the affected peoples.[29] To maintain hard-won agreements with colonists, Indian leaders had to claim and somehow uphold a kind of central authority that their peoples had never permitted before. Doing so brought civil
leaders and diplomats into repeated conflict with members of their own nations, threatening to undercut the national unity they sought to create. But
the alternative was daunting. To maintain prosperity and sovereignty, Ohio
Indian leaders had to protect their peoples against colonial violence, secure
their territory against colonial land grabbing, and maintain a reliable trade
for European imports. Many concluded that they could achieve these goals
only by winning both respect and formal recognition from colonial
governments.[30]

Both before and after the American Revolution, Anglo-American officialdom delegated relations with Indians to two distinct sets of people: "Indian agents" and army officers. Though their specific titles, responsibilities,
and influence varied considerably over time, Indian agents were broadly
charged with diplomacy: hearing Indians' grievances, distributing gifts, regu-

lating trade, and, at times, mobilizing them for war. Armies were charged variously with protecting colonists from Indians, protecting Indians from colonists, enlisting Indians as allies, evicting colonists from Indian land, and burning Indians' towns and crops. Indian agents typically had extensive experience in western trade, politics, and land speculation. They did not necessarily know Indians well, but they understood the protocols of regional diplomacy. Army officers typically knew far less about a region and its peoples. British military culture prized hierarchy, uniformity, and harsh discipline: values antithetical to those of both Indians and many Ohio Valley colonists. Nearly all of Fort Pitt's commanders detested the region's inhabitants, though some concealed their contempt better than others.[31] Imperial and United States officials repeatedly reorganized the relationship between the "Indian department" and the army, muddying the chain of command. The governments of Pennsylvania and Virginia, meanwhile, sometimes appointed agents of their own. The colonies' war for independence then threw all such arrangements into disarray.

Notwithstanding such upheavals, the friendship and support of officers and agents brought tangible benefits. They controlled trading centers at Pittsburgh, Detroit, and Niagara, making them gatekeepers between Ohio Indians and transatlantic commerce. They periodically received funds to hold treaty councils, enabling them to pay colonial contractors to feed and supply hundreds or thousands of Indians. Equally important, agents and officers could present Indian grievances to their superiors, or not, enabling Indians to win, or lose, military protection, favorable terms of trade, or recognition of territorial sovereignty. To win agents' and officers' sympathies, Ohio Indians used familiar diplomatic tactics, such as ritual adoption and gift giving. But revolutionary upheaval made it difficult to forge enduring relationships, and both agents and officers coveted Indian land. Meanwhile, shrinking deer and bison herds, and colonial armies' destruction of towns and crops, created serial subsistence crises that deepened native dependency on government patronage. Rather than pulling government officials into native systems of kinship and reciprocity, Indian leaders' efforts tended to draw their own peoples more fully into the emerging Anglo-American state.

On a cold December day in 1772, McClure made his way to a large log house to join two Virginians in holy matrimony. On entering, the staid New Englander found a raucous scene. Wedding guests packed the building, their attention fixed on a fiddle player and a crowd of dancing couples. No one noticed the minister's arrival, so he sat next to the fire and seethed in sullen disapproval. When he had seen all he could endure, McClure called a halt to the dancing and began the ceremony. The happy couple stepped forward, "snickering and very merry," and the spectators laughed until McClure urged them all "to attend with becoming seriousness, the solemnity." As soon as "the solemnity" ended, the fiddler struck up a new tune and the party resumed. One of the women repeatedly invited the minister to join her for a dance, but he steadfastly refused, and instead sat quietly, marveling at the Virginians' "wild merriment."[32]

The community that so offended McClure was less than a decade old. Until the end of Pontiac's War, the upper Ohio Valley's white population amounted to a scattering of fur traders, but the midcentury wars spurred rapid change. Though a royal proclamation banned colonization west of the mountains, provincial and military policies—often unintentionally—sent the opposite message. Beginning in the mid-1760s, Marylanders and Virginians moved to the river valleys south and southeast of Fort Pitt, while others, like McClure, came west from Pennsylvania. By one estimate, within a decade the region's colonial population reached tens of thousands. The town next to the fort grew more slowly: in the early 1770s Pittsburgh boasted only thirty-odd houses, whose inhabitants had little to do with the farmers of nearby valleys. But the presence of both town and fort encouraged homesteading in the surrounding area. As one Shawnee noted, "wherever a Fort appeared in their Neighbourhood, they might depend there would soon be Towns & Settlements."[33] The empire tried to halt colonists with one hand while waving them onward with the other.

Indians and imperial officials often described these colonists as an undifferentiated mass of troublemakers, but McClure's complaints about the wedding party reflected wide social and cultural divisions. One set of travelers included "two Englishmen, two Irishmen, one Welshman, two Dutchmen, two Virginians, two Marylanders, one Swede, one African Negro, and a Mulatto." Amid this diversity, McClure identified three major cultural groups: Scots-Irish Presbyterians, Germans, and Anglo-Virginians. The missionary found the Germans sullen and grasping, and he scorned the Virginians' penchant for "drinking parties, gambling, horse race[s] & fighting." By contrast, he praised the piety and hospitality of the Scots-Irish, though some of them doubted his New England credentials. They had little use for their non-Presbyterian neighbors. An English traveler found a cold welcome among them until he began "acting the Irishman." For his part, McClure dismissed the region's few Baptist clergy as "illiterate preachers." Steep and sinuous ridges discouraged communication and cooperation between inhabitants of neighboring valleys. Geographic isolation brought a vulnerable independence, fostering both antigovernment resistance and pleas for state protection.[34]

Economic troubles divided colonists still further. The rugged Alleghenies cut off farmers from Anglo-American markets, while uncertain relations with Spanish Louisiana—as well as fluctuating river levels—hindered trade downriver to New Orleans. Many distilled their grain into whiskey, a more portable and profitable commodity, but most of the region's colonists remained chronically cash-poor. Colonial farmers largely neglected both the agricultural expertise of Indian women and recent European innovations like crop rotation. One son of England's landed gentry found it necessary to teach his hosts a modern method of stacking wheat. These deficits of skill and technology, combined with the region's frosts, floods, and pests, fostered widespread indebtedness, driving many into bankruptcy. Within a generation of colonization, landownership among upper Ohio colonists dropped sharply, as absentee landlords acquired an ever greater percentage of the region's farmland. Living conditions and disparities of wealth worsened throughout the revolutionary period.[35] Colonists increasingly found themselves in economic straits as bad as or worse than those they had left behind.

Contemporary observers, including McClure, argued that Ohio Valley colonists despised state authority. The region's "Unruly Settlers," they alleged, sought to escape "from Justice & from Creditors" by moving "beyond the arm of any government." Colonists often resisted government policies, especially when they expected a competing government to treat them more favorably, but they largely lacked the resources and cohesion necessary to pursue self-rule. They looked to governments to resolve disputes, guard against attack, and build roads, jails, and arsenals. They fiercely opposed officials who favored competing land claims, but coveted validation of their own, so systems of land distribution attracted both resistance and customers. In 1769, Pennsylvania opened an office in Philadelphia to sell land within its still-undetermined western boundary. In 1773, Virginia appointed county surveyors for much of the same territory. In either case, prospective landowners had to locate and survey desired tracts, obtain paperwork from provincial officials, and pay either in cash or, in Virginia, by redeeming land certificates issued for wartime service. Those who could not afford the requisite time, travel, and expense often embraced speculative schemes that promised to circumvent formal procedures. Others sought title by preemptively occupying land shortly before a government began selling it, hoping that their physical presence would outweigh their relative poverty.[36] But rather than rebelling against state authority as such, these quasi-legal colonists sought to manipulate the system in order to win legal title for themselves.

Disputed land claims magnified the influence of county courts and the individuals who presided over them. In 1773, Pennsylvania established West-moreland County, the first seat of British government west of the Appala-chians. Virginia countered by establishing an overlapping "District of West Augusta" and in 1776 added an immense "Kentucky County" farther west. Both governments subsequently subdivided these jurisdictions into smaller counties, each of which boasted appointed or elected judges, a sheriff and constables, various administrative officials, and militia commanders. Local courts provided a venue for dispute resolution and a means of dealing with refractory servants, impoverished orphans, and belligerent neighbors. County officials also raised the funds, labor, and supplies necessary to build public infrastructure, most notably roads. Rather than undertaking such projects independently, colonists petitioned the infant court of West Au-gusta, which vetted proposals, assigned individuals to oversee construction, and taxed nearby inhabitants to cover costs. The court records do not reveal how well or how quickly local inhabitants carried out the court's instructions, but nonetheless they demonstrate that communities looked to local govern-ment to undertake collective projects.[37]

At least in theory, county militias similarly marshaled the time and en-ergy of fighting-age men for the common good. Rather than independent, self-organized associations of neighbors, colonial and revolutionary militias were arms of the state, organized and funded through official regulations. Virginia had required militia service since its founding, while Pennsylvania enacted its first formal militia law in 1777. In both cases, the government ap-pointed county commanders who chose or supervised the election of subor-dinate officers. According to law, militia companies had to periodically muster and drill, and militiamen could be drafted into active service at the governor's orders. When drafted, men were to be paid wages, fed, and sup-plied much like regular soldiers; delinquents faced stiff fines. In a cash-poor region, the resulting redistribution of funds profited both militiamen them-selves and those who supplied them. For the emerging elite, serving as a mi-litia officer brought control over official funds and signaled higher social and political status. But the system often failed to work as planned. Colonists rou-tinely refused to serve or disregarded orders while on duty, and those who complied often had negligible military training. When threatened with attack, communities readily built and defended makeshift stockades, but they often declined to help defend neighboring valleys, let alone march farther afield.[38] Even so, militia laws created an institutional structure necessary for mobilization. When armed colonists assembled in dozens or hundreds, they almost invariably did so through the formal militia system.

In his travels, McClure repeatedly lodged with Arthur St. Clair, a Scottish army officer who had acquired "a good farm and Grist mill . . . & large tracts of wild lands" in western Pennsylvania. McClure found him a prosperous country gentleman, enjoying ample "ease, & good cheer," despite his chronic gout. As a landlord and mill owner, St. Clair belonged to the emerging frontier elite. Mills like St. Clair's hosted political meetings and religious services, giving their owners a measure of political as well as economic sway that made them valuable agents for eastern governments. St. Clair himself received a long series of local government appointments and commanded a small army outpost on the road to Fort Pitt. This fusion of economic, political, and military status typified the aspirations of the upper Ohio elite. Local judges and administrators could augment their wealth with fees and bribes, as well as secure their land against rival claimants. But such appointments also invited controversy: some in the region would continue defying Pennsylvanian jurisdiction, and St. Clair's authority, for over a decade to come.[39]

Because of such conflicts, St. Clair and other members of the nascent frontier elite enjoyed only a tenuous grasp on the status they craved. Britain's North American colonies broadly replicated the home country's division between the gentry (who lived on the labor of tenants, servants, and slaves) and the "common folk" (who might own land but worked it themselves). Upper Ohio Valley landlords and mill owners considered themselves (and wanted others to consider them) gentlemen, and they thus set themselves above most of their neighbors. But their recent arrival in the region, as well as chronic jurisdictional uncertainty, deprived them of the social and political capital that protected the better-established eastern gentry. Their insecurity raised the stakes of factional disputes, as gaining or losing control of local government posts could make or break an individual's fortune. With so much hanging in the balance, Virginia's and Pennsylvania's dueling sets of magistrates, sheriffs, and militia commanders fiercely denounced one another's authority, even when the governments they represented urged calm. In the process, they competed for the loyalty and cooperation of ordinary colonists, many of whom resented policies the officials were expected to enforce. Gaining credibility as a local leader could even require denying one's aspirations to leadership. At a 1770 meeting with Haudenosaunee leaders, a Monongahela colonist, Van Swearingen, stressed that though his neighbors had chosen him as a spokesman, he claimed no formal authority: their community had "no head Man amongst them." In fact, Swearingen was a relatively affluent slave-holder who had formerly served as a Virginian official and subsequently became a magistrate and army officer in Pennsylvania. His social status qualified him for such posts, but maintaining his position required embracing his neighbors' relatively egalitarian political culture. The aspiring elite thus occupied an awkward intermediary position, from which they attempted to persuade both eastern officials and upper Ohio colonists to accept each other's demands.[40]

The west that McClure visited in 1772 was considerably less wild than he imagined. The Indians and colonists who lived there had little love for one another, but neither did they kill each other as frequently or as indiscriminately as their detractors alleged. Ohio Valley inhabitants navigated regional politics by building tenuous coalitions and manipulating eastern and imperial patronage. The resulting networks, together with the containment of intercultural violence, enabled a naive and arrogant young missionary to traverse the region safely for months.

This troubled but stable order would soon collapse, but its demise resulted less from state absence than from exertions of government influence that accelerated colonization and encouraged intercultural conflict. Following Pontiac's War, peace prevailed for ten years, thanks in part to an imperial pledge to reserve Kentucky for Indians. In 1774, Virginia's royal governor tried to seize Kentucky for colonization, triggering a land rush and a brief war. The Virginians' victory spurred hundreds of colonists westward, even as revolution unfolded in the seaboard colonies. Rather than triggering bloodshed, the collapse of imperial authority brought two years of relative peace. But in 1777, both revolutionary and imperial governments began recruiting, organizing, and supplying fighting forces that ravaged one another's communities. In the ensuing years, British-allied Ohio Indians repeatedly pressed for peace with the newborn United States, but American commanders spurned their offers. Years of horror ensued, as militant Indians and colonists carried out atrocities with government-supplied weaponry, leaving their respective peoples desperate for state protection. The 1783 Treaty of Paris brought the fighting to a halt, for a time. Some Indian and colonial leaders tried to hammer out a durable peace, but their efforts could not overcome Congress's insistence on colonizing Ohio. Meanwhile, leaders among both Indians and colonists forged ever stronger ties to British and United States officials. Rather than preserving local autonomy, the emerging political order brought a new federal government determined to squash western resistance.

The case of the Ohio Valley thus illuminates how diverse groups of people attempted to attain, contest, and manipulate power in a place where competing governments wielded some influence but little actual authority. Instead of Hobbesian anarchy or a two-sided clash of opposing cultures, the region exhibited a complex pattern of coalition building, in which an array of political brokers pursued disparate aims through informal and often ephemeral collaborations. Individuals and communities built coalitions to reap profits, to gain diplomatic leverage, to acquire and dispense patronage, to defend or contest claims to land, to make peace, and to wage war. These efforts often brought unintended and unwelcome results, but even when coalition builders failed to achieve their goals, their work still shaped the region's transformation. Partnerships with colonial governments repeatedly spurred new waves of colonization and violence, which in turn deepened Indians' and colonists' reliance on government resources and the brokers who could deliver them. Rather than proceeding "from the bottom up," Anglo-American colonialism was joined at the hip with the unsettling process of state building.

CHAPTER 1

Containment, 1765–72

Peter was dead; that much was certain. The Delaware war captain died in early 1767 near the mouth of Redstone Creek, where a Virginian, John Ryan, fatally shot him. Ryan then fled into the mountains, never to be heard from again. Pittsburgh traders, British Indian agents, and other imperial officials all blamed Peter's death on the hundreds of colonists who had recently occupied land around Redstone and on the slippery land speculator Thomas Cresap. According to the officials, the Redstone colonists considered killing an Indian "a meritorious act" and "wish[ed] for nothing more than an Indian War."[1] Modern historians generally echo this view, citing a long parade of horrors—the Paxton Boys massacre of 1763, the Middle Creek massacre of 1768, and others—in which ungoverned and ungovernable colonists routinely lashed out at Indians they hated. One landmark study describes those at Redstone as "ragtag refugees" who "despised Indians and abused them." Their abuses brought about "a state of war" in which "almost any encounter . . . could end in death and open the door to a bloody cycle of retaliation."[2] Small wonder, then, that Ryan killed Peter.

A closer look, though, complicates the story. The fatal encounter began when Peter seized Ryan's kegs of rum. Nor was the killer a Redstone colonist: he had only just arrived, kegs in tow. Rather than taking Indian land himself, Ryan was selling liquor to those who were. Peter tried to seize the kegs at the request of Cresap, who sought to monopolize the lucrative rum business for himself and his sons. "If he met with any Traders in the Country or going to it," Cresap reportedly told Peter, "he should take their Liquor from them & cause the Kegs to be staved." Rather than being a victim of Redstone's rapid colonization, Peter had worked for the man responsible for it, providing, in the parlance of another era, muscle to protect Cresap's turf.[3] This partnership echoed a regional trend. In the ten years after Pontiac's War, Ohio Valley

Indians and colonists interacted peacefully much more often than they killed
one another. Internecine divisions, and memories of wartime horrors, encouraged them to seek allies and trading partners across the cultural divide.
When tavern brawls and trade disputes ended violently, both Indians and
colonists hurried to contain hostilities. Distrust remained strong but did not
preclude cooperation.

Amid this relative stability, Ohio Valley inhabitants sought to reshape their
relationships with the multifaceted British state. After a decade of war and the
decisive defeat of France, few could envision a future wholly separate from the
British empire. Having failed to expel the British in Pontiac's War, western Indians now sought imperial recognition of their political and territorial sovereignty, along with ongoing trade and diplomacy. Their diverse strategies for
obtaining these goals often caused tensions within and between their own nations. Colonists, meanwhile, raced to occupy and obtain legal title to upper
Ohio Valley land. Rather than either accepting or defying imperial authority,
colonists more often debated which manifestation of the imperial state ought to
prevail in a given time and place. An array of uncertainties—the merits of
decades-old Virginia land grants, the precise western boundary of Pennsylvania, and more—fueled lasting disputes in which all sides claimed to respect and
uphold some version of tangled and contradictory imperial policies. Such feuds
gummed up the workings of nascent governing institutions, but also fostered
coalitions and patronage networks that in themselves created a tenuous order.

This story of the interwar Ohio Valley begins with the creation of two
new communities: the Seneca town of Two Creeks and the cluster of colonists around Redstone. From the mid-1760s into the early 1770s, the people
of these communities traded, talked, fought, and made peace. Both groups
often exasperated nominal authorities in the Six Nations and the British empire, sometimes finding common cause as they grappled with imperial demands. In 1768, a massive new land cession threatened to bring on a new war,
but British officials responded with a compromise boundary that most of the
region's inhabitants seemed to accept. Throughout, Indians and colonists met
and interacted often, usually peacefully. When they fought, they did so in this
context of everyday encounters. Animosity endured, and sometimes led to
bloodshed, but through the early 1770s the region's peoples contained such
violence. Rather than a virtual state of war, they preserved a tenuous peace.

On a Sunday morning in March 1768, the Reverend John Steel delivered a
sermon and a death threat. The governor of Pennsylvania had sent him and

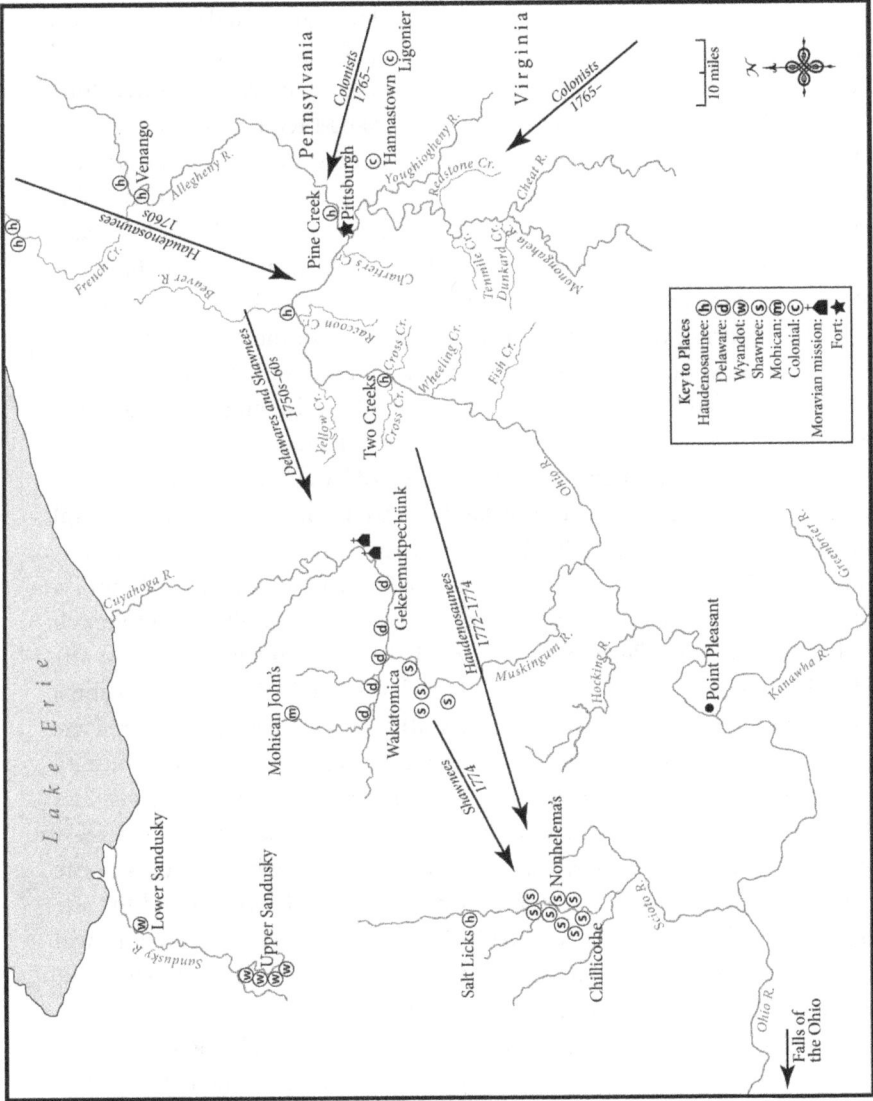

Figure 1. The Upper Ohio Valley, 1765–74.

three companions to Redstone Creek to order the unauthorized colonists there to leave or face execution. The errand seemed urgent. Just two months before, two white men had murdered ten Senecas and Mohicans in the Middle Creek massacre, 170 miles to the east. The local sheriff jailed the culprits in Carlisle, but nearby colonists rioted and set them free. To atone for this failure of colonial justice, provincial officials aimed to drive off the Redstone colonists, about whose presence the Six Nations had repeatedly complained. When Steel arrived, the trespassers insisted that their native neighbors "were very Peaceable" and wanted them to stay, but the minister insisted that "a few straggling Indians" could hardly represent "the mind of the Six Nations" as a whole. Amid heated discussion, most of Steel's audience agreed to leave. Then eight Senecas arrived from the town of Two Creeks, about seventy miles to the west, bearing wampum to affirm the integrity of their words. Steel and his companions hoped they would persuade the holdouts to move, but instead they insisted that the colonists stay. All talk of leaving ceased and the Pennsylvanians headed for home, their mission a failure.[4]

Like the Redstone colony, the Seneca town of Two Creeks was only a few years old. The historic Seneca homeland lies south of Lake Ontario, several hundred miles northeast, but by the 1740s many Senecas and other Haudenosaunees had built new towns on the upper Ohio River and its tributaries. During the Seven Years' War, a group of Senecas left their villages on French Creek, between the Allegheny River and Lake Erie, and moved down the Ohio River, hoping to find "plenty of Game." They built about twenty cabins on the river's west bank, just above the mouths of two creeks that entered the Ohio from opposite sides. Colonists subsequently referred to the community by various names: Two Creeks, Cross Creeks, Crow's Town, or simply "the Mingo town." In 1761, other Senecas built a town at the mouth of Pine Creek, just a few miles from Pittsburgh and directly across the Ohio from the home of the British Indian agent George Croghan. They likely abandoned the site during Pontiac's War but reoccupied it soon thereafter. In early 1767, a third group of Senecas occupied an abandoned Shawnee and Delaware village at the mouth of Beaver River, thirty miles downstream.[5]

By settling on the region's aquatic thoroughfare, these Ohio River Senecas gambled on a peaceful and commercially vibrant future. Their new towns positioned them to profit from colonial trade, but also left them vulnerable to attack. During the Seven Years' War many Delawares and Shawnees had moved from similarly exposed locations to new sites northwest of the Ohio, farther from British garrisons. By contrast, the people of the Pine Creek,

Beaver River, and Two Creeks towns aimed to capitalize on proximity. In 1765, as western Indians assembled at Fort Pitt to end Pontiac's War, about eighty Two Creeks Senecas showed up with loads of peltry, "expecting to Trade." The politically nimble Guyasuta, now a prominent leader at Pine Creek, urged "our Brethren, the English," to "Open the trade, and let us sell our skins." This enthusiasm for economic connectedness accompanied an equally fervent political independence. Ethnic and linguistic ties linked the three towns to one another, and to the Six Nations league as a whole, but like other Haudenosaunee communities they governed themselves locally. In 1765, when Croghan led an intercultural embassy to Illinois, a Two Creeks leader insisted on joining him to represent his community, marking it as an autonomous entity rather than a mere satellite.[6] Their subsequent defense of the Redstone colonists thus reflected a shared ambivalence, if not indifference, toward national and imperial authorities.

A well-worn path stretched southeastward from Two Creeks to the Redstone country, where John Ryan killed Captain Peter and the Reverend Steel gave his ineffective sermon. In the eyes of imperial officials, the Redstone colonists had flagrantly violated a royal ban on trans-Appalachian colonization. Colonists could move there, they argued, only after the Six Nations sold the region to the Crown, and then only under imperial and provincial oversight. One described the colonists as "idle Persons" looking to avoid the demands of either "Landlord or Law."[7] People with so little regard for their king, they reasoned, would hardly tolerate other aspects of social order.

The officials failed to recognize, or conveniently forgot, how imperial and provincial policies had spurred Redstone's colonization. Twenty years earlier, land-hungry Virginia had issued a series of vast upper Ohio land grants to well-connected speculators, who surveyed, established trading posts, and brought colonists to live there. The colonists fled during the midcentury wars, but the fighting created new means and incentives to move west. Virginia promised western land to those who fought to defend its claim, while the British army built two roads linking the region to the seaboard colonies. After expelling the French and building Fort Pitt, many soldiers and camp followers liked what they saw of the region and chose to stay. By the early 1770s, thousands had joined them. Such migrants plainly violated the royal ban on western colonization, but Fort Pitt's commanders muddied things by inviting farmers, traders, and craftsmen to settle nearby to help feed and supply the garrison. Citing such arrangements, some colonists insisted they had built homesteads on "the King's orders." Others asserted that Virginia's prewar grants—including a 100,000-acre spread issued to William Russell and partners—trumped the royal prohibition. Rather than a spontaneous flood of independent pioneers, the colonization of the upper Ohio Valley stemmed from the expansionist policies of Virginia, wars that those policies brought about, and the British army's determination to hold on to the region after the wars were won.[8]

The Redstone colony combined all these elements. In the 1740s Thomas Cresap helped establish the Ohio Company, the most ambitious and influential of the Virginia grantees. He became one of the company's foremost agents, surveying land, reaching out to nearby Indians, and fending off rival speculators. The company built a small trading post at Redstone, cleared a rough path to the Potomac, and recruited eleven families to settle nearby. The colonists fled during the Seven Years' War, returned in the early 1760s when the British built a small fort there, and fled once more at the outbreak of Pontiac's War. When hostilities ended, Cresap sought to revive his dormant claim despite the new ban. He offered land around Redstone on easy terms, aiming to populate the area with people whose right to the land depended on his own. In the spring of 1766, after the Six Nations complained about the trespassers, both the army and the governor of Virginia threatened to drive them off by force. Cresap promptly met with a few dozen Haudenosaunee, who allegedly "ceded to him a large Extent of Land." Neither the Six Nations nor British authorities considered the sale valid: Cresap likely met only with passing travelers, rather than anyone empowered to sell territory. But he found many customers willing to gamble on his dubious title: within a year, hundreds of families had built homesteads on his claim. When an army detachment burned all the houses they could find and urged the colonists to leave, they quickly rebuilt, and more joined them. Within a few years of Pontiac's War, colonists had occupied nearly all the good farmland east of the Monongahela.[9]

Rather than illegal squatters with no regard for authority, these migrants are better understood as quasi-legal colonists seeking to manipulate the law for their own ends. From long experience in the seaboard colonies, they had learned that the imperial state's many arms often promulgated contradictory policies, and that local interpretations of the law usually mattered more than imperial ones. They also knew that wealthy and well-connected colonists often exploited such contradictions to their own advantage, particularly in matters of land tenure. These circumstances, together with the vicissitudes of the Atlantic economy and the perennial scarcity of cash, had dashed many people's aspirations to own farms east of the mountains, even as the royal proclamation denied them the chance to obtain legal title in the west. But the "fluid constitutional environment" of British North America offered fuzzy and malleable lines between legality and illegality. The quasi-legal claims of Russell and Cresap, as well as the army's need for farmers to supply Fort Pitt, suggested plausible routes to circumvent London's disapproval. Far from indifferent to government authority, the Monongahela colonists aimed to finesse murky imperial policies to gain a title that might someday prove good.[10]

The colonists' persistence reflected a mutually advantageous relationship with nearby Indians like the Two Creeks Senecas. A decade of war had disrupted trade networks and inflated prices. Meanwhile, postwar imperial policymakers tried to restrict frontier trade to established posts like Fort Pitt, under army and Indian Department supervision. Agents who stood to profit from the new system insisted that it would prevent fraud and abuse, but it forced Indians to travel farther to buy goods and limited competition among merchants. Many simply ignored the policy. Shawnee and Delaware towns in Ohio soon hosted many resident traders, often working for prominent Pennsylvania merchants, who trucked and bartered at will. On the Monongahela, Cresap regularly traded with Haudenosaunees from the Ohio River towns, as well as others passing through the region, and asked Virginia's governor to help squeeze out Pennsylvanian competitors. After the governor rebuffed him, Cresap and his colonists waged a price war, inviting Indians to buy goods "at one half the Rates" charged by Pittsburgh merchants. The Pittsburghers howled in protest. In 1770, Croghan complained that "every Farmer [wa]s a Sutler," foiling all his attempts to police trade. Cresap's low prices helped reconcile his customers to the growth of his colony. As a rival speculator noted, Indians were "more oblidging" to colonists "[w]ho Trade[d] with them."[11]

The Redstone colonists also paid at least some respect to Indian territorial rights. They built homesteads only east of the Monongahela River, "for fear of Disturbing" their native neighbors. This discretion likely reflected an agreement with nearby Senecas. When provincial officials surveyed the southern border of Pennsylvania, Indians stopped them at the Monongahela, insisting that the survey proceed no farther until they were "paid for the Land." They did not object to the survey east of the Monongahela, even though Britain had not yet paid for that land either, suggesting that they, too, recognized the river as an intercultural boundary, even if the British empire did not. This common understanding likely emerged during informal discussions, probably in the course of trade. Ohio Indians fully expected the Six Nations to sell the Monongahela Valley within a few years—in 1765, William Johnson and Six Nations leaders had demanded that they acquiesce to the planned cession—and so the premature arrival of Cresap and his colonists deprived them of nothing they did not already expect to lose. This expectation, together with their shared understanding of a Monongahela boundary, deterred nearby Indians from opposing the colonization of Redstone, even when British officers encouraged them to do so.[12]

For one Haudenosaunee family, the Redstone colonists were literally neighbors. Like many others of his nation, Mohawk Peter moved west from Kahnawake, near Montreal, but while most of the migrants settled in central and northern Ohio, Peter, his wife, and their children made their home near the mouth of Redstone Creek. They may have done so to be close to his wife's British family: when Pontiac's War began, they took refuge among her relatives east of the mountains. Prior to that conflict they had lived alongside Redstone's small British garrison, on the site of Cresap's earlier Ohio Company settlement. After Pontiac's War, Peter's family reoccupied their home alongside the rapidly growing colonial population. When Six Nations spokesmen demanded that the Redstone colonists be evicted, they stressed that Peter and his family could stay. In 1768, when the Two Creeks delegation came to the Redstone colonists' defense, they stayed at Peter's home. The following year, when a Pennsylvania land office began selling upper Ohio Valley land, Peter obtained a warrant for over three hundred acres across the Monongahela from Redstone. His widow and son sold the land in the mid-1780s, perhaps to escape growing anti-Indian sentiment. But in the 1760s, trade, cooperation, and intermarriage remained possible, even amid wartime upheaval.[13]

Two months after Steel's mission to Redstone, perhaps two thousand Ohio Indians met with Pennsylvania officials in Pittsburgh. Six Nations spokesmen once again demanded that the British "remove the people from our Lands" until "you have purchased them." In reply, the Pennsylvanians detailed their attempts to do so and griped about interference from Two Creeks. A prominent Pine Creek leader agreed to accompany Pennsylvanians John Frazier and William Thompson to Redstone to drive off the offenders once and for all. The next morning, Frazier and Thompson woke early, saddled their horses, and waited. After some time the Senecas appeared and declared they could not undertake such a "disagreeable" task. The English, they argued, ought to take full responsibility for their own people's misbehavior: if the Pennsylvanians wished to confront the Redstone colonists, they would have to do so on their own.[14] Knowing they could do nothing without Six Nations support, Frazier and Thompson gave up their plans.

This sudden reversal reflected divisions among the western Haudenosaunee. To the Six Nations council hundreds of miles away, and even to Guyasuta at Pine Creek, the Redstone colonists were an abstract impediment, but Two Creeks hunters knew them as neighbors, trading partners, and potentially deadly enemies. In a private meeting with the Pennsylvania commissioners, Guyasuta explained that "all our . . . young Men" refused to help, unwilling to risk earning "the ill Will of those People." Noting that the Six Nations would soon sell the land around Redstone to the British, and that the evicted colonists would then return, Haudenosaunee men had argued against giving them "Reason to dislike us, and treat us in an unkind Manner when they again become our Neighbours."[15] Guyasuta could have aided the Pennsylvanians anyway, but the tenuousness of his authority gave him pause. He and his fellow Senecas sought a secure position in the region's future political order, and this pursuit led them, in this instance, to refuse to help Pennsylvania's proprietary government. The outcome foiled the plans of Pennsylvania officials but preserved the informal relationships that upheld the region's tenuous peace.

The Six Nations' ensuing treaty with Britain threatened to undo that peace, but intracultural divisions and intercultural compromise still fended off hostilities. At Fort Stanwix, hundreds of miles northeast of Pittsburgh, the Six Nations planned to sell the upper Ohio Valley, but Britain's Indian superintendent, William Johnson, instead negotiated a much larger cession that encompassed nearly all of Kentucky as well. The Six Nations made little use of Kentucky's resources, but their leaders nonetheless argued that their ancestors had conquered it over one hundred years earlier. To them, the extended cession promised to protect more vital Haudenosaunee territory by directing colonial migration into the west. But Shawnees, Cherokees, and others relied heavily on Kentucky's prolific deer and bison herds. Western nations immediately denounced the treaty, insisting that Kentucky was "as much theirs" as the Six Nations'. Upper Ohio Senecas protested that they had received no share of the purchase price; when the British ignored their complaints, they shot the cattle of nearby colonists. From London, Colonial Secretary Lord Hillsborough berated Johnson for deviating from his instructions. Though the Crown nominally accepted the larger purchase, Hillsborough prohibited any colonization west of the Kanawha. A separate treaty with the Cherokees similarly established a Kanawha boundary. Virginian speculators fumed, but the plan delighted George Croghan, who had joined a coterie of investors backing a proposed new western colony called Vandalia. The Kanawha boundary promised to rein in rival speculators until the Vandalia backers could secure Kentucky for themselves; in return for Croghan's diplomatic aid, they promised to confirm his legally dubious land claims. Anxious to appease the peoples whose land he coveted, Croghan repeatedly announced the new policy to Ohio Indian leaders.[16]

Ohio Indians broadly accepted the Kanawha boundary and set about enforcing it. British officers had repeatedly assured them that trespassers on Indian land were "Lawless Raskals" and "no part of us." Now, British officials advised Cherokees to seize the possessions and burn the houses of "any People Hunting or Settling beyond the line." Ogayoolah, a Cherokee leader, received a written pass authorizing him to take "all the Deer Skins . . . Guns and Horses" found "in possession of the Tresspassors." Shawnee and Cherokee hunters complied. In the second half of 1770, they reportedly confiscated at least 1,400 deerskins. In contrast to their counterparts in England, where convicted poachers suffered death, these Indian game wardens only rarely resorted to lethal force. When one Cherokee hunting party killed a few Virginians, they met with scorn and censure in their own community. More often, the captors freed the interlopers and warned them not to come back.[17] Many colonial hunters ignored the warnings, but through the early 1770s they remained only transient visitors, bringing no families and building no permanent homesteads. As imperial officials despaired of controlling an unruly frontier population, Cherokees and Shawnees did so for them.

While some Indians drove off colonial poachers, others forged new alliances. Pontiac's War had failed to expel the British or bring back the French, leaving many to dread renewed hostilities. Ohio Indian leaders still aimed for the same goals that had led them to war—physical security, territorial sovereignty, and flourishing trade—but now pursued them through diplomacy. In particular, many labored to unite western nations to oppose further land grabs. These proponents of pan-Indian unity sought to counter the influence both of the Six Nations, whose land cessions had forced thousands of Delawares and Shawnees to move west, and of their ally William Johnson. The alliance they envisioned would command imperial respect where scattered independent towns did not. Some continued to press for a new anticolonial war but found it necessary to rein in their rhetoric and seek common ground with moderates.[18]

In 1769, two Shawnee leaders brought a curious account of the Fort Stanwix treaty to a council of Great Lakes nations at Detroit. After explaining the
sale of Kentucky, they reported that William Johnson worried that the Six
Nations "perhaps had not power to make ... such a gift," as "all that Land
does not belong to them." They claimed he had asked them to discuss the
matter with other western Indians, urging them to "Be always united" and
"Have only the same mind, all of you who Inhabit the same Continent, and
are of the same Colour." Johnson had said nothing of the kind. He had insisted that the Shawnees had no say over the treaty, and he dreaded the
thought of pan-Indian unity. The Shawnee spokesmen had exploited their position as intermediaries to promote a starkly different agenda. Even so, their
performance was markedly moderate. Rather than openly promoting war, or
obsequiously allaying British fears, they tried to bolster their call for pan-
Indian unity with the stamp of imperial approval, at least partly to reassure
Indians who feared renewed fighting. Western nations could stand together
against the Stanwix cession, they suggested, without unduly antagonizing
their colonial neighbors. The deception reflected sharp divisions. Some hoped
to exploit resentment of land cessions to rally support for war. Others sought
greater diplomatic leverage by presenting a united front.[19] Achieving unity
among such diversity required finessing sharp disagreements about means
and ends. Proponents of unity broadened their coalition by muddying its
purpose.

Throughout the interwar period, western Indians labored to rebuild and
expand the multiethnic alliance of Pontiac's War, but they downplayed its
potential militancy. In 1765, western Senecas began forging what Croghan
later called "a Gineral Union" to stop colonists from "Coming into thire Cun-
try to Setle any further." In the summer of 1767, hundreds of Indians from
thirteen nations met at the Scioto Valley Shawnee towns to pursue this project. After Fort Stanwix these efforts accelerated. In May 1769, at a new Scioto
council, Delawares, Shawnees, Senecas, and members of several Wabash Valley nations announced a new multiethnic alliance separate from the Six Nations, pledging to "Defend themselves against any Enemy that may hereafter
Quarrel with either of them whether English or Indians." Before year's end,
Shawnee messengers had visited the Chickasaws, Cherokees, and Creeks in
the south "to form a General Confederacy on the principle of defending their
Lands." Cherokee and Creek leaders rebuffed their proposals, but at a 1770
Scioto council a number of Cherokees pledged to make peace with the west-
ern nations. Throughout, they stressed the need to counterbalance the Six

Nations and prevent a repetition of Fort Stanwix. By late 1772, some western Haudenosaunee flatly refused to attend the league's Onondaga council fire because of "the [Co]ntempt and Neglect shown them." The Six Nations' domination of neighboring nations, a decades-old presumption of regional diplomacy, seemed increasingly flimsy.[20]

While more militant coalition partners aimed to keep preparations for war secret, moderates publicized their activities to press for further British concessions. In 1769, a delegation told British agents that they had "great trouble in preventing some of our rash unthinking young Men" from retaliating violently for the Stanwix cession. In a private conference with the Indian agent Alexander McKee, a Shawnee leader explained that if the British failed to respond satisfactorily to the westerners' demands, "they are then to pursue their own measures."[21] In effect, moderate pan-Indian leaders sought to build two distinct coalitions: one of western Indian nations to gain diplomatic leverage with the British, and another with British officials to squash militant calls for war. By unifying western nations, and serving as an internal bulwark against militant schemes, they forced the British to take them seriously. By winning concessions from the British, they strengthened their own authority and lessened the appeal of military action.

In March 1771, John and Joseph, two Stockbridge Mohicans who had settled among the Shawnee and Delaware, warned British Indian agents that a large gathering of Ohio, Wabash, and Great Lakes Indians had agreed to "Strike the English" that spring. Other moderates soon confirmed the report. The informants were themselves part of this new alliance—John had sat "at all their Councils" but "dread[ed] being forced into" war. To end the plot peacefully, they invited British agents to the next Scioto conference. The militants had claimed Six Nations and Cherokee support, but a subsequent Six Nations delegation flatly denied it and demanded that the western Indians "Confirm a lasting peace." The refutation threw "the Western Nations into great confusion" and doomed any hope of a broad pro-war coalition.[22] Both moderates and militants continued to pursue a pan-Indian alliance, but the moderates had blunted its militant potential, while reminding British officials of their value as allies. And with Shawnee and Cherokee game wardens guarding Kentucky, they could persuasively argue that "a lasting peace" with the composite, interdependent empire might preserve remaining Indian land from colonization.

Other Ohio Indians offered alternative visions. In the spring of 1773, the Delaware White Eyes arrived in New Orleans with 1500 deerskins, 300 beaver pelts, and "other small furrs." He traded them to a Louisiana merchant house, then sailed to Philadelphia with £200 in hard currency and credit for the purchase of a "small Cargo" of high-demand European imports, which he then shipped west to the Ohio Valley. Like many eighteenth-century entrepreneurs, White Eyes found himself in legal squabbles with his trading partners for years to come. Nonetheless, his long journey marked an impressive commercial debut.[23] The year before, his Seneca counterpart, Guyasuta, had toured the eastern colonies dressed in the style of a British army officer. White Eyes, by contrast, had turned himself into an Atlantic merchant. But where most merchants reinvested their profits in new enterprises, he planned instead to finance a Delaware embassy to the court of George III.

These plans reflected long-standing efforts to turn a collection of autonomous towns, scattered from New Jersey to Ohio, into a unified ethnic nation. Over several decades, the Six Nations had repeatedly sold Delaware land out from under them. Now, in the wake of Pontiac's War, many Delawares favored peace with Britain; even the nativist prophet Neolin now declared that "all the people which inhabit this Continent" ought to be "one people, having but one Father." Nonetheless, the Fort Stanwix treaty reminded them that children of the same father might still steal one another's land. To forge a more unified nation, White Eyes and his allies recruited eastern Delawares to settle in the Muskingum Valley on land the Wyandots had gifted them, making it a country "which the Six Nations can not Sell to the English." They also tried to centralize decision making in a new council of leaders from different villages, led by Netawatwees, the preeminent civil leader of the nation's turtle phatry. Simultaneously, Delaware leaders petitioned British officials to recognize their territorial claims, offering in exchange both political loyalty and cultural reform. During a 1771 visit to Philadelphia, Bemineo and Gelelemend, the son and grandson of Netawatwees, explained that they wanted British help to "Establish Schools . . . for . . . Educating their Children, & Ministers to preach the Christian Religion." They also sought training in "the Mechanical Branches among the White people." White Eyes similarly pledged "to be religious, and have his children educated," and argued that declining game populations would force Delaware men to abandon hunting in favor of European-style commercial agriculture. To secure sovereignty and prosperity, White Eyes argued, the Delaware needed to integrate themselves more thoroughly into the colonial world around them. Doing so, Delaware leaders assured colonists, would "annex them by the Strongest ties to the English Interest."[24]

Among themselves, Delawares strenuously debated such plans. While some had already embraced Christianity, one member of the new council insisted that he could consider the colonists' religion only when they stopped trespassing on Delaware land. Others insisted that the Creator wanted Indians to remain on their own path, rather than attempting to follow that of Europeans. Many Delaware leaders, though, saw religious conversion as a bargaining chip to serve their broader agenda. When a missionary, David McClure, offered his services, he got council members' attention by mentioning that his sponsors would send a schoolmaster, tools, and a grist mill "to promote their comfort in this world." The council ultimately sent McClure packing, but they objected less to his theology than to his fellow Presbyterians' history of murdering Christian Indians. Moravian missionaries enjoyed greater success, but many scorned them as well for failing to protect their converts from Presbyterian attacks. Bemineo suggested leaving the choice of missionaries to the British Crown, reasoning that the king's favor would better "protect them in war time." His plan showed a sophisticated understanding of the eighteenth-century English world, in which Presbyterians and other dissenters claimed many adherents but wielded scant influence in provincial or imperial government. Recognizing the political implications of denominational affiliation, Delaware leaders aimed to barter their religious loyalties to bolster security and sovereignty.[25]

The Delaware thus offered Britain both temporal and spiritual allegiance in exchange for both territorial sovereignty and help adapting to a new colonial economy. But building such a relationship required circumventing William Johnson, who insisted that the Delaware and other Ohio Indians remain subordinate to the Six Nations. Bemineo thus asked the governors of Pennsylvania, Maryland, and Virginia to record his speech in writing and "send it to the Great King" directly. The governors, wary of antagonizing Johnson and his Haudenosaunee allies, repeatedly spurned Delaware overtures. Lacking official sanction, Delaware leaders resolved to send an embassy to London at their own expense, by raising funds through the fur trade: hence White Eyes's visits to New Orleans and Philadelphia.[26] Johnson's opposition and the mounting imperial crisis frustrated their plans, but these years of interwar activism nonetheless prepared White Eyes and others for more ambitious projects in the years to come.

White Eyes, Guyasuta, and pan-Indian alliance builders all sought to establish a new political order that affirmed some form of Indian sovereignty and territorial integrity. They disagreed sharply about both means and ends: Guyasuta encouraged the colonization of Kentucky while the pan-Indianists staunchly opposed it; Delaware leaders labored to win British recognition of a distinct and sovereign Delaware nation. But despite these differences, their work reflected a common disillusionment with military resistance and hope for creating a more fruitful relationship with the multifaceted imperial state, whether through pan-Indian unity, Guyasuta's clientelism, or White Eyes's program of cultural adaptation. None of them called for submitting whole-sale to British authority, but neither did they advocate the stark political and cultural separation that nativists like Neolin envisioned. Instead they sought more advantageous terms of interdependence with a colonial empire that had seemingly come to stay.[27]

As Ohio Indians pursued that interdependence, upper Ohio colonists wrangled with other facets of the composite imperial state. On a September day in 1771, Abraham Teagarden learned that a Pennsylvania sheriff planned to evict a nearby colonist from a Monongahela Valley homestead. Teagarden had butted heads with Pennsylvania before: in 1768 he had heard and ignored the Reverend Steel's plea for the Redstone colonists to leave. Soon after the Fort Stanwix treaty nominally empowered the provincial government to sell upper Ohio tracts and evict—or exact payment from—quasi-legal colonists. Before Stanwix, the Two Creeks Senecas had helped protect Teagarden and his neighbors, but now the colonists took matters into their own hands. Tea-garden rallied nearly thirty men "armed with guns, clubs, and tomahawks" to defend their neighbor. The sheriff backed down. Teagarden's band let him go unharmed, but they warned that if he attempted to enforce Pennsylvania law against them again, he would meet with "the height of ill usage."[28]

Like Ohio Indians, many upper Ohio colonists resented the Fort Stanwix treaty, though for different reasons. And like Indians, rather than rejecting imperial authority, Teagarden and his neighbors aimed to reshape and ma-nipulate it to serve their interests. In particular, they exploited the region's chronic jurisdictional confusion. Quasi-legal speculators like George Croghan and Thomas Cresap encouraged them, seeking support for shady land titles. Croghan had once served Pennsylvania, but he turned against the proprietors when they refused to endorse a massive, and legally dubious, private land purchase from the Six Nations. He now insisted that the chartered breadth of Pennsylvania—"five degrees of longitude"—could not possibly reach as far as Pittsburgh. When the proprietors demanded that upper Ohio colonists pay for their land, Teagarden and his neighbors resisted, just as Croghan had hoped. In 1771, they formed an association to "Keep off all Officers belonging to the Law," threatening a £50 fine for anyone who failed "to appose Everey of Pens Laws." Provincial officials repeatedly arrested Teagarden himself, but each time his supporters broke him out of jail. Croghan's pronouncement that Pennsylvania lacked jurisdiction helped mobilize resistance for years to come. Neither Croghan nor Teagarden opposed state authority in general—both coveted legal confirmation of their claims—but they sought to replace Pennsylvanian rule with a manifestation of the state that better served their ends, such as the proposed new colony of Vandalia.[29]

Other colonists eagerly patronized the new land office, including a surprisingly well-funded Virginian named William Crawford. A veteran of the Seven Years' War, Crawford had subsequently built a homestead at a critical river crossing on an army road tying Pittsburgh to the east. He knew the region well but, like most upper Ohio colonists, lacked the ready money the new land office required. But Crawford had a patron: his former comrade-in-arms George Washington. In 1767, the two men worked out a mutually beneficial arrangement: Crawford quietly explored the region identifying desirable tracts, and Washington fronted the money to purchase them as soon as they became legally available. Their plan flouted royal restrictions on colonization, but they gambled that the king's order was, in Washington's words, merely "a temporary expedient to quiet the Minds of the Indians." Sooner or later, they expected the ban would be lifted, prompting a land rush. By identifying desirable tracts in advance, the two Virginians gained a head start on the competition, enabling Crawford to appear in Philadelphia, cash in hand, when the new land office opened.[30]

The Washington-Crawford collaboration scorned imperial policy but bolstered the tenuous authority of the provincial government. In acquiring Pennsylvanian title, they gained a vested interest in defending the proprietors' jurisdiction, just as colonists who bought from Cresap and Croghan came to oppose it. Pennsylvania rewarded well-connected customers with lucrative local government appointments, giving them and their friends still more reason for allegiance. Crawford and Dorsey Pentecost, another Virginian who bought Pennsylvania land, found places for themselves in the new western Pennsylvania courts. For these aspiring members of the upper Ohio elite, collaborating with Pennsylvania offered a means to obtain landed wealth and political power. Such ambitions did not necessarily foster loyalty: Crawford and Pentecost later abandoned the Pennsylvania camp when it suited their purposes. But the combination of land sales and political appointments nonetheless created networks of patronage that gave socially prominent colonists a stake in provincial authority.[31]

Competition for land thus fostered coalitions that linked a wide range of colonists to some manifestation of state power. Small-scale homesteaders like Teagarden based their ownership claims on purchases from quasi-legal speculators like Cresap and Croghan, who offered favorable terms of sale to build support for their claims. They, like Crawford, cultivated patrons in Philadelphia, Williamsburg, or London. Access to the coveted resource—legal land titles—varied with social and political status. Teagarden's hopes depended on those of Russell and Cresap, just as Crawford's plans hinged on the favor of Washington. In turn, these patrons lobbied imperial officials to support their various schemes. At the same time, distant patrons required local allies to help make their claims good. Rather than the rugged individualism of national mythology, ordinary colonists' aspirations for economic security rested on their reciprocal relationships with both members of the emerging regional elite and, increasingly, provincial and imperial officialdom.

The midcentury wars left lasting distrust and antipathy between Indians and colonists. In the years that followed, thousands of colonists moved to the Monongahela Valley, Indians complained frequently about the loss of land and deer, and imperial officials repeatedly warned of imminent hostilities. Not surprisingly, intercultural encounters were often tense and sometimes ended with bloodshed. But for nearly a decade, Ohio Valley inhabitants successfully contained such violence. Although Indians and colonists usually distrusted and sometimes killed one another, they nonetheless averted renewed warfare, for a time.[32]

Between 1765 and 1773, intercultural violence followed markedly different patterns on each side of the Alleghenies. East of the mountains, both during and after Pontiac's War, large bands of Pennsylvanians and Virginians repeatedly assembled to kill defenseless Indians or to free murderers of Indians from jail. In 1763, a large gang dubbed the Paxton Boys slaughtered the men, women, and children of Conestoga Manor, near Lancaster, then marched on Philadelphia in defiance of the provincial government. Two years later in western Virginia, another group of colonists fell upon a party of traveling Cherokees, killing five. Officials briefly jailed some of the killers, who called themselves the Augusta Boys in imitation of their Paxton counterparts, but a mob soon freed them. Then, in early 1768, Pennsylvanians Frederick Stump and John Ironcutter murdered ten Senecas and Mohicans, including three women and three children, on Middle Creek in Cumberland County. The local sheriff arrested and jailed the men, who admitted their guilt, but more than seventy armed men soon descended and "carried off" the culprits "in open Triumph, and violation of the law." In each case, eastern colonists displayed a shocking readiness either to murder Indians indiscriminately or to assemble en masse to aid those who did.[33]

West of the mountains, colonists who attacked Indians similarly evaded punishment, but the pattern otherwise differed in both scale and context. Instead of rallying in large groups, western killers of Indians usually acted alone or in pairs. Rather than enjoying the backing of their communities, most were marginal individuals like runaway servants or deserting soldiers. They eluded justice thanks to stealth, incompetence, or corruption, with no mobs appearing to rescue them. Rather than indiscriminate attacks on strangers, these western murders more often arose out of everyday interactions: brawling in taverns, haggling over trade, or feuding with coworkers. Western violence was also less one-sided: Indians killed colonists as well. Above all, retaliation remained rare, as both Indian and colonial leaders acted quickly to prevent escalation. Viewed apart from the horrific massacres east of the mountains, the murders of the interwar Ohio Valley underscored that Indian and colonial lives remained enmeshed.[34]

A brief catalog of bloodshed illustrates the western pattern. In the spring of 1765, near Pittsburgh, a white trader sexually assaulted a Seneca woman, perhaps one of his customers; her husband killed him. The following year, when a group of Shawnees sheltered two colonists, the guests killed three men in their sleep and stole their canoe. The murderers turned out to be deserters from Fort Pitt: knowing the Shawnees were on good terms with the army, they likely feared being returned to the garrison. In the summer of 1767, British officers arrested two Saginaw Ojibwes near Lake Huron; in retaliation, another Saginaw party attacked two traders' boats on the Ohio, killing ten colonists and stealing their goods. That September, a Shawnee man killed Thomas Mitchell, one of many traders then living and trading, otherwise peacefully, in the Scioto Valley Shawnee towns. Three months later, a Delaware man killed John McDonald and wounded another colonist on the Monongahela. A farmer had hired both the victim and his killer, it turned out, to watch his fields over the winter. The killer complained that McDonald had given him "Ill treatment." Whatever the cause of their dispute, the conflict once more erupted out of the closeness of Indians and colonists, rather than the cultural distance between them. When Pennsylvanian officials complained about McDonald's death, White Eyes replied that his killer "was half a white Man, and the other half an Indian," making the colonists "equally concerned with us in that Breach of Friendship."[35]

The marked differences between violence east and west of the mountains reflected other regional distinctions. The Paxton and Augusta mobs came from young but well-established communities. Many of their inhabitants had lived, worked, and fought together for a full generation before and during the recent wars. Those wars had driven most Indians out of the region, giving colonists east of the mountains a massive demographic advantage even in frontier areas. Trade continued—Stump and Ironcutter murdered their victims after selling them rum—but was becoming an increasingly marginal part of the local economy. By contrast, colonial communities west of the Alleghenies remained in their infancy. Because of their recent arrival and dispersed pattern of settlement, many early Ohio Valley colonists knew their neighbors only slightly. Until the mid-1770s, they largely lacked civil institutions like churches, courts, and militias. The difficulties of transmontane transportation left them few opportunities to trade with, or seek aid from, the seaboard colonies. In addition, at least three Haudenosaunee towns stood within one hundred miles of Redstone, and many more Indian communities dotted rivers to the north and west. Monongahela colonists thus had much more to gain from trade, and lose in war, than their counterparts in Paxton and Augusta. In the spring of 1771, Bemineo and Gelelemend learned the difference firsthand. In the Ohio Valley they and other Indian diplomats moved freely, but when they traveled east to Philadelphia they required an armed guard to protect them from murderous colonists.[36]

In early September 1769, a Cheat River colonist named Charles Haningam and two other men murdered a Delaware man named Jacob Daniel and his two sons at the victims' hunting cabin on Dunkard Creek. Within days, two other colonists, Charles Martin and Henry Tracks, publicly accused Haningam of the crime and pledged to provide evidence against him. A third colonist, James Booth, arrested the culprit and handed him over to two traders, David Owens and John Williams, who brought him down the Monongahela to Fort Pitt, where the British commandant jailed him. In sum, five different colonists worked together to arrest and transport Haningam over one hundred miles, a journey of two or three days, through the heart of the growing Redstone community. In contrast to similar cases east of the mountains, no one interfered with Haningam's arrest or imprisonment. Haningam eluded justice all the same: after sitting for ten days in the Fort Pitt guardhouse, chained hand and foot, he managed to slip out of his leg bolts and escape in the night, reportedly "through the Negligence of the Sergt. of the Guard." He probably had help, especially with the leg bolts and the guard, but this flight in the dark bore little resemblance to the Carlisle mob's midday rescue of Stump and Ironcutter.[37]

About two years after Haningam's escape, an indentured servant, Mathew Haley, ran away from his master, Richard Brown. Two Seneca men found the fugitive in the woods and turned him in, but Haley soon escaped again, only to stumble upon the two Senecas once more. According to Haley's subsequent confession, the Senecas this time "gave him a Tomahawk and one pr. of Macosons" and promised to let him stay if he helped them "Steal Horses from the white people." Instead, Haley killed them with the tomahawk and fled into the woods with as many of their possessions as he could carry. Later, after Brown recaptured Haley, the servant confessed his crime. Allegheny homesteader John Miller and his wife, who had sheltered Haley in exchange for stolen goods, later confirmed the story. Guyasuta came to Fort Pitt to report the victims' disappearance; soon thereafter, Haley's master turned him in. Both colonists and Senecas acted quickly to prevent further violence. The British commandant invited Guyasuta to see the imprisoned murderer, explaining that he was "a foolish boy" who had murdered the Senecas because he feared "being delivered up" to his master. Guyasuta thanked the British for their efforts, though he may well have doubted whether Haley would face further punishment. If so, he had good reason: Haley soon recanted his confession and was sent across the mountains for trial. Pennsylvania's Bedford County court extended Haley's term of service for eighteen months to compensate his master for "gaol fees and loss of time," but did not charge him with murder. The events further underscored transmontane differences. In the upper Ohio Valley no one objected to putting Haley in chains, but across the mountains in Bedford the court did not even prosecute him. Brown and his neighbors did not necessarily like Indians any more than the people of Carlisle and Bedford, but they hesitated to defend those who killed them.[38]

Amid these periodic murders, Redstone colonists and Two Creeks Senecas continued to meet, drink, and trade, notwithstanding occasional disputes. In 1767, men from Redstone and Cheat River reportedly took up arms after Beaver River Seneca hunters took some of their horses. In response, the "Whole People" of the Senecas' town brought the horses to Fort Pitt. The commandant assured the Senecas that the Redstone colonists lived outside of British protection, but they returned the horses anyway, bringing the crisis to an end. At a 1768 council, British officials complained that the Two Creeks Senecas took "Rum and other Things" from traders traveling to other towns downriver. The Senecas likely considered the goods a toll exacted for the privilege of conducting business on their river, but they apparently stopped the practice after the British complained. Their trading visits to Redstone and Cheat River continued.[39]

During the early 1770s, though, imperial politics disrupted upper Ohio commerce. Colonial protests against British policies cut off merchants from European manufactures, including the cloth, jewelry, and metal tools that Ohio Indians expected in trade. Colonists who wished to buy their deerskins increasingly offered a more abundant commodity: rum. Indians soon complained about both the lack of goods they wanted and the problems caused by the influx of liquor. In April 1771, Shawnees reported that in the past year, nine of their people had died because of alcohol. In the four months that followed, eight more Indians died in alcohol-related violence in the Pittsburgh area alone. In September, a Delaware leader noted that drunkenness had caused eleven deaths in his town and that there was "not a Village any where thro' the Country but what has had some People killed by drinking Rum." Not surprisingly, the influx of rum also launched a new wave of intercultural violence. In early July 1770, a Fort Pitt soldier shot and gravely wounded a Seneca man, sparking rumors that the British army had gone to war against Indians. Instead, the soldier and the Seneca had been drinking together in a cabin—likely a makeshift tavern—across the river from the fort. They argued. They came to blows. The soldier, "A young Unexperienced Lad," grabbed a gun and fired a load of buckshot into the Seneca's side. After the Seneca recovered—with the aid of an army surgeon—a Two Creeks delegation visited Fort Pitt to ask that the soldier be spared from punishment.[40] The shooting showed not only the dangers of mixing alcohol with firearms, but also the ubiquity of intercultural drinking.

A few days after the shooting, about sixty miles to the south, two men, two women, and a child from Two Creeks stopped to trade at the Cheat River homestead of a colonist named Wilson, then paddled away in Wilson's canoe. The Senecas probably believed Wilson had sold them the canoe in exchange for their deerskins, but Wilson claimed they had robbed him. He and several neighbors pursued and attacked them at their camp farther down the Monongahela, killing one man. The survivors fled, leaving all their deerskins and other possessions behind. Some of the attackers pursued until a Seneca shot back and killed one of them. After the shootout, Wilson hurried downriver to explain the events to George Croghan. When the news reached Two Creeks, the townspeople sent a large delegation to Pittsburgh to explain that their people had fired in self-defense. In a series of condolence ceremonies, all involved reiterated their desire to keep the peace. In the midst of their meeting, another Haudenosaunee man appeared with news of further skirmishing, this time at Redstone. Two separate groups of Indian hunters had camped nearby to trade deerskins for blankets and other supplies. The colonists, at least some of whom knew their visitors personally, had little to sell except rum. Loud reveling ensued. At one camp, the Haudenosaunee invited two white hunters to join them, but the white men fled amid the carousing and later complained that the Indians had robbed and "abused them." Somewhere nearby, another group of Haudenosaunee hunters reportedly ransacked the homes of rum-selling colonists. As Wilson had done less than two weeks before, the colonists pursued the Indians on horseback, overtaking first one group of hunters and then the other. One pursuer called out in Delaware that they intended no harm, but others fired their guns as soon as they caught sight of Indians, who fled. No one was harmed, but the Haudenosaunee hunters lost all their deerskins as well as other valuables.[41]

News of these assaults spawned rumors that Virginia had declared war on Indians. Delaware, Shawnee, and Haudenosaunee communities "call'd in all their hunters . . . [,] kept night watches about their Towns," and dispatched delegations demanding an explanation. In a short council, Croghan blamed the recent shooting on rum and insisted that no one wanted war; White Eyes and a Shawnee messenger promptly left to spread this version of events throughout Ohio. Meanwhile, at the Indians' invitation, a delegation from Redstone arrived to help clear the air. Their spokesman, Van Swearingen, freely admitted to selling the liquor that precipitated the latest incident, and he pledged in the future to sell it only in smaller quantities. While faulting his trading partners for drunken carousing and theft, he acknowledged that his own companions had fired on the Haudenosaunee against his orders, and he pledged to return the goods they had abandoned when they fled. Swearingen and Guyasuta exchanged mutual pledges of goodwill and promised to spread news of their agreement among their respective peoples. Not for the last time, this seeming consensus among Indian and colonial spokesmen belied sharp divisions within their respective constituencies. According to Croghan, many Indian leaders at the council with Swearingen initially called for "revenging the many insults they had received" by "attacking and driving the Virginians over the Mountains." Similarly, not all Redstone colonists shared Swearingen's desire for reconciliation.[42] Trusting in the peacemakers' promises demanded a leap of faith.

For the Two Creeks Senecas, such faith was running out, bringing an end to their ambivalent friendship with Redstone. When the town's leaders visited Pittsburgh to help patch up the crisis, they assured Croghan they would no longer visit the Monongahela colonists to trade. The next spring, a Shawnee delegation invited them to move to the Scioto Valley. Increasingly wary of their colonial neighbors, most of the townspeople began moving west in the fall of 1771. Others moved upriver instead, likely to the Beaver River or Pine Creek towns. By the spring of 1772 only a few families remained at Two Creeks, and they soon departed for the Scioto as well. From their new homes, the migrants brushed off Guyasuta's and Johnson's pleas to return, reiterating their independence from the Six Nations. They also rejected Guyasuta's policy of territorial concession and embraced the contentious pan-Indian movement. Meanwhile, the deadly violence on the Monongahela likely heightened Ohio Indian militancy. In the spring of 1771, unknown attackers killed a white woman and her four children at a new homestead near the Kanawha boundary. In 1772 the British army evacuated Fort Pitt, shuttering the region's only semblance of imperial authority. British officials, clearly, would punish neither Indians nor colonists for intercultural murder.[43]

And yet peace endured. The sporadic violence of 1770 and 1771 failed to trigger wider hostilities. Divisions within both Indian and colonial societies, as well as the remaining alliances between them, continued to mitigate against large-scale violence. Without Six Nations and Cherokee backing, Indians who favored war had little hope of winning over others. Neither Guyasuta nor his militant rivals could credibly speak for all or even most Ohio Indians, but Guyasuta's case for peace was an easier sell. Similarly, Swearingen's promises of goodwill rang hollow, but his Redstone neighbors carried out no further attacks. Upper Ohio colonists might sympathize with the Paxton Boys, but they lacked the unity and cohesion necessary to emulate them. Above all, the unavailability of even quasi-legal land title in Kentucky, together with Shawnee and Cherokee policing, confined trans-Appalachian colonists to the upper Ohio Valley. Despite widespread intercultural suspicion, fear, and even hatred, intercultural violence remained sporadic. To bring about the war that so many dreaded, something would have to change.

CHAPTER 2

Patronage, 1773–74

In early June of 1773, the Hardman, the Shawnees' preeminent civil leader, faced a diplomatic dilemma. Several Virginians had appeared at Chillicothe, claiming to bring a message from Virginia's governor. A veteran peacemaker, the Hardman had negotiated several treaties and championed the British alliance, but these Virginians presented a puzzle. They had failed to send news of their coming in advance or bring wampum to validate their words: standard protocols that British emissaries had observed for decades. Moreover, they had circumvented the Indian agents at Pittsburgh, the usual bearers of imperial speeches. The Hardman thus doubted the visitors' credibility, but he worried that turning them away might antagonize Virginia. Instead, his people followed the standard protocol for greeting other nations' spokesmen when they "first [came] to make peace with them." The Hardman and other civil leaders stayed away: they had no business with not-yet-allies. Instead, more than one hundred armed and painted warriors demonstrated Shawnee prowess with shouts, threats, and brandished weapons. Then the nation's military leaders welcomed their guests to a cordial council to exchange speeches. But the strangers' message muddled matters even more. With a trader, Richard Butler, interpreting, Thomas Bullitt, the Virginians' leader, explained that his governor had sent them to colonize Kentucky. The announcement made no sense. British agents had repeatedly declared that the king had forbidden colonization west of the Kanawha River. The Virginians clearly misunderstood imperial policy, but setting them straight was the job of imperial officials. So the Shawnees replied amicably, sent the strange delegation on its way, and dispatched messengers to Pittsburgh for answers.[1]

The meeting had gone smoothly enough, but the participants interpreted it in ominously different ways. Bullitt believed that Ohio Indians had endorsed his plans. But as Butler pointed out, the Shawnees "claim[ed] an absolute rite to all that country" and looked to British authorities to set the Virginians straight. Butler urged Bullitt's men to win the Shawnees' trust by not "destroying the game."[2] Instead, the visit began a dizzying series of events leading to a series of brutal murders, the burning of Ohio Indian towns, and a pitched battle involving over 1,500 combatants. Ultimately a Virginian army, led by Governor John Murray, the Earl of Dunmore, marched on Chill-icothe, demanding that Shawnees acquiesce to Kentucky's colonization.

Some accounts of these events portray Dunmore as a greedy schemer, while others credit him with attempting to bring order to a lawless region, but nearly all trace the conflict's origin to Ohio Valley colonists' unruliness and impulsive violence.[3] By contrast, beginning the story with Bullitt's visit to Chillicothe blurs the distinction between bloodthirsty frontier folk and the gentlemen who aspired to govern them. Rather than a Hobbesian nightmare, the Ohio Valley remained largely peaceful until Bullitt's surveyors moved into Kentucky. Their widely publicized venture signaled Dunmore's new pol-icy of aggressive expansionism, which triggered a land rush the following spring. Far from reflecting disregard for state authority, the initial wave of killing in April 1774 resulted from colonists' close attention to Dunmore's plans. Nor did Indians retaliate impulsively. The victims' friends and relatives attacked no colonial homesteads until weeks after the initial murders, when Dunmore's agent blamed the bloodshed on Shawnees and reiterated Virgin-ia's claim to Kentucky. Indians and colonists had disliked one another long before Dunmore arrived on the scene, but it took the governor's pursuit of land—and countless others' pursuits of the governor's patronage—to plunge the region into chaos.

Beginning in October 1772, advertisements in Virginia and Pennsylvania newspapers announced that Dunmore had appointed Bullitt "surveyor on the Ohio" and that he planned to set out "early next spring" to "locate . . . claims." News of Kentucky's imminent colonization spread quickly. In far-off Pittsburgh, it reached Pennsylvanian John Connolly, a onetime surgeon's mate who had received land certificates for serving in Pontiac's War. Con-nolly had since met and married Susanna Sample and became "intimately associated" with one of her relatives: the Indian agent and land speculator George Croghan. The older man had repeatedly rescued Connolly from debt, then got him a job as an army surgeon in Illinois. The journey west brought the young doctor to the miles-long portage around the Falls of the Ohio, where he saw visions of future wealth and power. A man who owned land around the rapids, he saw, could reap immense profits from the passing traffic. Over the following years, as he dodged creditors and set broken bones, Connolly sought patrons to help him become that man.[4]

In 1770, Connolly finagled a meeting with Virginian George Washington, who avidly recorded his glowing descriptions of Kentucky. The future president spurned Connolly's proposals but returned to Mount Vernon determined to acquire such land himself. With the help of William Crawford, Washington had already bought desirable tracts in the upper Ohio Valley, but that region's jurisdictional disputes and quasi-legal speculative schemes left no commonly recognized authority to resolve the tangle of overlapping claims. "As soon as a mans back is turnd," Crawford complained, "an other is on his Land." The mayhem left scant chance for profit, so speculators increasingly looked west to Kentucky, a region filled with rich soil and empty of colonists. Their hopes required a change in imperial policy. In 1768, the Six Nations had sold most of the region to the Crown, but British officials had quickly prohibited colonization west of the Kanawha. In 1772, London explicitly barred Virginia from issuing new western land grants. Instead, the ministry entertained a proposal to establish a new Ohio Valley colony, called Vandalia, to be run by a coterie of British and American investors.[5]

To overcome such obstacles, Virginia speculators turned to their new governor, an ambitious and well-connected Scottish nobleman. Starting in 1771, Washington repeatedly pressed Dunmore to grant Kentucky lands to the holders of military certificates, like himself and Connolly, or risk losing hold of the region completely. Westering colonists, speculators argued, poured uncontrollably into new lands. "Not even a second Chinese wall," one wrote, "unless guarded by a million of soldiers," could prevent Kentucky's colonization. Imperial officials could avert disaster only by granting land to Washington and his ilk: reliable gentlemen who could be trusted to manage colonization wisely. This self-serving logic had little basis in reality: by 1773, reports of Kentucky's fecundity had circulated for years, and yet the documentary record yields negligible evidence of colonial homesteads west of the Kanawha. But Dunmore sympathized with the speculators—he himself coveted a 100,000-acre western estate—and slowly embraced their expansionism. In 1772 he created a new western county that encompassed Kentucky. Later that year, one of Washington's fellow officers, anticipating imminent grants, advised his friends to survey lands preemptively. When Bullitt publicly advertised his plans, Dunmore made no effort to stop him. Washington, Connolly, and many other holders of officers' certificates eagerly commissioned Bullitt to reserve choice tracts for themselves.[6]

Among Ohio Indians, Bullitt's visit to Chillicothe raised fears of renewed hostilities. His surveys confirmed the Hardman's suspicions that Europeans sought only "to deceive the Indians, to take their land and possessions." Several hundred Shawnees, convinced that "they wou'd soon be Hemmed in on all Sides by the White People," left the Scioto towns and moved west, possibly to the Little Miami and Mad River valleys in western Ohio. Then a group of Ohio Haudenosaunees set upon one of the surveyors' supply parties, killing one man, capturing another, and taking their loaded packhorses. The attack placed Shawnee leaders in a difficult position, as they had invited the culprits to Ohio just two years before. They persuaded the attackers to hand over their prisoner and sent British traders home for their protection. In September, Cornstalk sent a speech to Croghan laying out the Shawnees' grievances while reaffirming their commitment to peace. The Hardman then led a Shawnee delegation to Pittsburgh, where Croghan had invited them and six other western nations for a council. He likely hoped that the veteran diplomat would put the wayward Virginians in their place.[7]

Unfortunately for the Shawnees, nothing at the council went according to plan. Croghan intended to introduce the governor of the new Vandalia colony, but unbeknownst to him that scheme had collapsed. With no guidance or support from his patrons, he could only apologize and scramble to buy food for his four hundred guests. Meanwhile, British traders presented Cornstalk's speech, which accused the Ohio Haudenosaunee of planning "Mi[s] chief" and called on Guyasuta, as "a Headman of these People," to rein them in. Guyasuta—a longtime proponent of Kentucky's colonization—countered that the Shawnees had "hatched" the recent troubles "amongst themselves at Scioto." When the Hardman finally arrived, he found the council united against his nation. Croghan, no doubt relieved to divert attention from his own embarrassment, publicly accused the Shawnees of speaking "with a double tongue." They declared their people's innocence, but Guyasuta had successfully turned the tables, equating their objections to Bullitt's surveys with militant resistance. In September, Superintendent William Johnson called the Shawnees "the most attentive to the Six Nations Councils of any [Indians] to the Southward," but Guyasuta soon convinced him that they had "been always a disaffected people." Where they had hoped to win imperial support, the Shawnees instead found themselves on the defensive.[8]

Perhaps hoping to repair the damage, the Hardman and his companions stayed for the winter across the river from Pittsburgh, where they met regularly with colonial leaders. In late January, they watched with alarm as eighty white men marched into the town waving "red Flaggs" and firing guns into the air. In front of the empty fort, abandoned by the British army over a year before, the crowd rolled out a keg of rum, leading to much "drunkenness and confusion." Pennsylvania officials ordered the men to disperse, with little effect. When the raucous gathering finally broke up, some of the men fired shots at the Shawnee camp. The Pennsylvanians assured the Shawnees that the colonists' "constant assembling" and "warlike appearance" involved "Business intirely relative to themselves," but the Hardman understandably concluded that war was "still uppermost in their minds."[9]

Much like the dispute over Kentucky, the mayhem at Pittsburgh resulted from the machinations of Lord Dunmore. During the previous summer, while Bullitt stirred controversy at Chillicothe, the governor had visited the upper Ohio country and met the ambitious John Connolly. Together, the two men concocted a plan to seize the entire Ohio Valley for Virginia. In the first week of 1774, posted advertisements declared that Dunmore had appointed Connolly "Commandant of the Militia of Pittsburgh and its Dependencies" and announced a general muster at Fort Pitt. Pennsylvanian officials arrested and jailed Connolly, but dozens of men showed up anyway, leading to the raucous scene that so alarmed the Shawnees. Connolly soon escaped from jail; his supporters increasingly "insulted" Pennsylvania officials "in the most indecent and violent manner." On 30 March, he and his growing militia reoccupied Fort Pitt—dubbing it "Fort Dunmore"—and claimed civil and military authority under Virginia law. Though he initially promised to cooperate with Pennsylvania magistrates, his "parties of armed men" continually harassed them and their friends. On 6 April, as the Westmoreland court convened in Hannastown, he appeared at the head of 150 armed men, "with Colours flying" and "Swords drawn," and shut down their proceedings. Three days later, his men dragged three Pennsylvania judges from their homes and marched them to prison in Staunton, Virginia, more than two hundred miles away.[10]

Connolly achieved this coup by building a coalition of mutually antagonistic allies. During his 1773 visit, Dunmore had quietly assured George Croghan that Virginia, unlike Pennsylvania, would respect his land claims. The governor similarly reached out to Washington's partner William Crawford, a Pennsylvania official and Croghan foe, promising him land and a lucrative post as an official surveyor. Connolly, meanwhile, cultivated allies among anti-Pennsylvania colonists, who had bedeviled Crawford for years. The secrecy of these dealings won them a disparate collection of friends without having to address the animosities among them. In November, Dunmore began issuing Kentucky land grants to Virginia officers, just as Washington had hoped, and insisted that officials approve Connolly's claim around the Falls. When Connolly returned to Pittsburgh in January, he brought a stack of blank commissions, empowering him to handpick the militia officers and magistrates of the newly created "District of West Augusta." He doled these out strategically to Pittsburgh traders like John Gibson and to the friends and family of Croghan and Crawford. With similar encouragement, Dorsey Pentecost, an erstwhile Pennsylvania magistrate, and Abraham Teagarden, a longtime anti-Pennsylvania agitator, joined forces, rallying Monongahela colonists for Dunmore. This distribution of patronage, together with the hope that Dunmore would reward loyalty with land, transformed a set of longtime adversaries into a skeletal local government. Crawford, who had repeatedly butted heads with Teagarden, suspected that such men "would be equally averse to the regular administration of justice" under Virginia. But he and others set aside such misgivings in hopes of winning Dunmore's favor.[11]

Meanwhile, at his camp outside Pittsburgh, the Hardman grappled with the news that Shawnees had killed "several White people." The previous fall, a group of Delawares, Cherokees, and Shawnees had stumbled upon a Virginian camp near Cumberland Gap. Noting that the strangers had brought extra horses, cattle, and other supplies, they correctly identified them as prospective colonists bound for Kentucky, part of a land-grabbing venture inspired by Bullitt's surveys. The Indians attacked before dawn, killing an enslaved African-American and four white men, including the sons of the speculator William Russell and the hunter Daniel Boone. In the eyes of the attackers, the Russell party had trespassed on lands that the king had reserved for Indians, but the story that reached Pittsburgh omitted such details. The Indian agent Alexander McKee urged the Shawnee delegation to go home and "put a Stop to such flagrant Outrages" or face "the Resentment of the numerous White people settled now upon this River." The Hardman and his companions responded with the familiar rituals and rhetoric of frontier diplomacy: public condolence ceremonies and speeches blaming the attack on a few miscreants. But they also drew colonists' attention to "the very great Numbers of your people going down this River beyond the bounds fixed for them." This problem, the Shawnees noted, had brought about "all our Disturbances," including the attack on the Russell party.[12]

These events might suggest frontier mayhem, but all involved stressed their adherence to British policies. Both Shawnees and Cherokees faulted colonists for flouting imperial restrictions on colonization. A Shawnee party warned Virginian surveyors, in English, that George Croghan had encouraged them "to kill all the Virginians they could find on the River & rob & whip the Pennsylvanians." The Shawnees perhaps exaggerated Croghan's words, but he and other Indian agents had repeatedly told them that the king had barred colonists from Kentucky. Most colonists, though, believed that the Russell venture was legal. Pointing to Dunmore's recent land grants, they insisted that the government "much encouraged" the colonization of Kentucky. News of the killings was soon "in every ones mouth." From Williamsburg, Dunmore himself demanded that the nations involved hand over the perpetrators or face "the certain Vengeance of the Virginians."[13] Both colonists who coveted Kentucky and Indians who aimed to stop them found support in the words of Britain's appointed officials.

Militant opponents of colonization tried to exploit these growing tensions to build support for war, but they faced strong opposition. Embassies to the Cherokees and other nations urged them to "unite and oppose the Progress of the White People." To overcome widespread aversion to war, they claimed that a mysterious French trader called Sang Blanc ("white blood") had promised that a massive French and Spanish army would soon free Indians "from the Tyranny of the English." Militants hoped to use a spring conference at the Scioto towns to build support, using moderate leaders' "good speeches" as a cover while they promoted war behind the scenes. But they failed to win over the Six Nations or the Cherokees, without whose support they had little hope of success. Guyasuta spent the winter and spring visiting western nations to denounce the Shawnees and declare that the Six Nations wanted nothing to do with war. Cherokee leaders condemned the attack on the Russell party and eventually executed one of the perpetrators. Even those who favored killing "those people gone down the River" balked at a general conflict with the British colonies.[14] Notwithstanding the killings at Cumberland Gap, the united front necessary for war remained elusive.

In mid-April, the Hardman and his Shawnee delegation left Pittsburgh, no doubt glad to put distance between themselves and Connolly's rowdy militia. They paddled down the Ohio at a leisurely pace, stopping for a time at a Seneca town at the mouth of Beaver River. Perhaps alarmed by news of events upriver, the Senecas decided to follow the Shawnees to the Scioto. Neither the Shawnees nor the Senecas showed any apprehension of danger: the Senecas camped for several days at the mouth of Yellow Creek, across the Ohio from a colonist's improvised tavern. Farther downstream, the fourteen Shawnees stopped to buy food from a colonial homestead. To their surprise, the colonists there refused to sell them anything, telling them that white people had killed two Indians on the river the day before. Now more wary, the Hardman and his companions paddled to the mouth of Grave Creek, camped in the bushes, and prepared to defend themselves. Late in the day, shots rang out and Othawakeesquo, a Shawnee leader the British knew as Ben, fell dead. The Shawnees fired back, killing one of the attackers, then fled into the woods, abandoning the farewell gifts their Pittsburgh hosts had given them just days before.[15]

To the Shawnees, the attack seemed to come out of nowhere, but it, too, resulted from Dunmore's intrigues. That winter, a Virginia official, William Preston, had publicly announced a new surveying expedition, led by John Floyd, to begin in mid-April at the mouth of the Kanawha. Many hurried to join Floyd or raced ahead to claim their own tracts first. "No time should be lost in having [the land] surveyed," Washington warned, "lest some new revolution should again happen in our political System." Thomas Cresap's son Michael assembled eighty or ninety men at the mouth of the Little Kanawha, planning to join Floyd downriver. All involved understood that many Shawnees, Cherokees, and others opposed their surveys. Preston insisted that at least fifty men accompany Floyd to guard against Indian assault. Pittsburghers assumed Shawnees would attack the surveyors because colonial expansion was "a thorn in their eye." Shawnees did drive off some trespassers, as they had done for years, but without killing anyone. In early April, one party captured seven surveyors and held them for three days, then released them. A few weeks later, another Indian party similarly "Orderd" three of the surveyors "off the River." By the end of April, most land jobbers were "almost daily Retreating," but Floyd continued surveying, going well beyond even the limits that Preston had prescribed.[16]

Meanwhile, events near Pittsburgh raised new fears of war. Four Cherokees attacked two white traders on the upper Ohio, about forty miles downstream from Pittsburgh, killing one man, wounding the other, and making off with the canoe and its contents. By all accounts, the motive was greed: Richard Butler, who owned the canoe and employed the two victims, described the event as an isolated crime. Both in Pittsburgh and the Scioto towns, Indian leaders quickly began the familiar rituals of containment: expressing regret, condemning the culprits, and offering to help find them. But on the same day, a Shawnee man warned McKee that militant Indians planned to "strik[e] the English" that spring. McKee shared the report with Croghan, who in turn passed it on to Connolly, who had just seized power in Pittsburgh. Such reports of imminent attack, like occasional robberies of traders, were a familiar part of Ohio Valley diplomacy, and British officers had long since learned to treat them with skepticism. But Connolly, a political novice, instead penned a general alert warning colonists to "Guard against" Shawnee hostility. Panic ensued. In a separate notice, he urged friendliness "towards such Natives as may appear peaceable," but this message got far less attention than the threat of imminent attack.[17]

Connolly's warning traveled downstream from Pittsburgh just as rumors of Shawnee resistance spread upriver from Kentucky, growing more alarming with each telling. The stories met at the mouth of Wheeling Creek, where over one hundred land jobbers were assembling their own surveying parties. Fearing "an Indian War," many fled, but a large group, led by Michael Cresap, resolved to "fall on and kill every Indian they met on the river." They brushed aside warnings that randomly killing Indians "might involve the country in a war": these aspiring speculators cared less about preserving frontier peace than ensuring access to Kentucky lands. Cresap's party promptly ambushed a trader's canoe on the Ohio, killing two Indians on board. The next day they attacked the Hardman's party. A day or two later, thirty miles upriver, another band of colonists followed Cresap's example. Like Wheeling, Yellow Creek lay far upstream from the Kanawha boundary. No Indians had objected when Joshua Baker and other colonists built homesteads there. Baker and his neighbors sometimes "insulted and abused" passing Indian diplomats, but the Beaver River Senecas nonetheless camped for a week or so on the opposite shore, living "peaceably and neighbourly" and sometimes visiting Baker's tavern. But on receiving word of Cresap's attacks, Daniel Greathouse organized a gang to ambush them. Most hid in Baker's back room while others invited the Senecas across to drink. Four men and three women came over. After they got drunk, Greathouse's men leapt out and killed them, sparing only the infant daughter of John Gibson, a colonial trader. On hearing the gunshots, the victims' companions tried to canoe across the river to save them. The murderers lined up on the riverbank and shot the would-be rescuers as they paddled. All told, the murderers killed nine Senecas and wounded two more. They then gathered their families, fled eastward, and sent the baby girl to her white father.[18]

Dunmore did not intentionally provoke these atrocities—Cresap, Greathouse, and their followers acted on their own initiative—but his decisions nonetheless brought them about. By authorizing surveys and issuing land grants beyond the Kanawha, he defied imperial policy and triggered a land rush. Shawnees, determined to enforce the recognized boundary, seized small groups of surveyors, took their equipment, and released them with warnings of more severe punishment in the future. The land jobbers, convinced the governor would support them, responded with a killing spree. Both the Shawnees and Cresap's gang could argue that they were abiding by imperial policy. To be sure, neither group gave much credence to government dictates they disliked, but both eagerly exploited interpretations that favored their interests. Dunmore's and Croghan's contradictory promises gave both groups reason to think they could use force—even deadly force—without losing the favor of the imperial state.

Within days of the Yellow Creek massacre, thousands of upper Ohio colonists fled eastward, convinced of what one recent account calls the "inevitability of Indian reprisals." But for weeks afterward no such attacks took place. Immediately after the attacks, the Hardman and other survivors fled to his Muskingum Valley town of Wakatomica and began talking of vengeance. The most outspoken, Logan, was an unlikely militant: he was the son of a prominent Oneida diplomat, bore the name of a colonial official, spoke English well, and was known as "a friend to the white people." Now, after losing his family at Yellow Creek, he and other survivors resolved to avenge their losses. They threatened the dozens of white traders living in nearby towns, declaring "that wherever they might meet a white they would shoot him." Nonetheless, for over two weeks they harmed no one. The Hardman took charge of his fellow survivors, insisting that they "begin no war with the English." He privately told visiting Delawares that "His heart [could not] be good, untill he ha[d] Sent one party at least, against the Virginians," but made clear that he aimed to retaliate only against the killers and others who had occupied Indian land. Meanwhile, he and other Ohio Indians helped protect colonial traders, first by hiding them from Logan's band and then by sending them to Pittsburgh with an armed guard.[19]

Guyasuta, meanwhile, denounced the Shawnees and encouraged Virginians to blame the murders on the victims. When Connolly and McKee called Ohio Indian leaders to Pittsburgh to condole for their losses, Guyasuta showed up first. He had spent the winter persuading William Johnson and the Six Nations of the Shawnees' ill will, and now he repeated the performance. Rather than criticize the Kentucky land rush, he blamed the violence on the Hardman's people, claiming that "all other nations [we]re displeased with" them. If the Shawnees "would not listen to reason," he argued, "they ought to be chastised." This interpretation delighted Connolly, as it exonerated him and Dunmore while affirming Virginia's claim to Kentucky. After their meeting, Connolly issued a new proclamation warning of "immediate Danger from the Indians and particularly the Shawanese." Guyasuta then took his campaign on the road, with a guard of fifty men, to press the Wyandots and other nations to ignore Shawnee pleas for help. In Williamsburg, Dunmore, too, seized on Guyasuta's argument, insisting that "the Indians have been the aggressors" and bore responsibility for "the fatal consequences." The more experienced Croghan assured the governor that only "some few" Shawnees and Senecas had interfered with Virginia's surveys, but he tactfully avoided mentioning the boundary that Dunmore had brushed aside. In a 5 May condolence speech, Connolly stressed that people had been "killed on both Sides," implying that Indians shared the blame for the killings. He then offhandedly mentioned Dunmore's plans for Kentucky, noting that Virginia's governing council would soon meet to discuss "their settling in this Country."[20]

Connolly's self-serving performance defeated all peacemaking efforts. At the time, his Delaware and Seneca audience knew little about what had happened and had no desire to argue. But a few days later, when the Delaware diplomat White Eyes repeated the speech in the Muskingum towns, the survivors and the victims' friends and relatives could not help but take offense. Soon thereafter, Logan's followers killed and scalped their first victim, a Pennsylvania trader named Campbell, near Gekelemukpechünk. The Hardman, meanwhile, issued a blistering reply. He called Croghan and McKee liars, presumably referring to their previous assurances about the Kanawha boundary, and he insisted that the conflict stemmed from Virginians "passing up and down the Ohio, and making settlements upon it." Most dramatically, he rejected Connolly's plea to forgive and forget. Just as Connolly had asked Shawnees to overlook "what your people have done to us," he asked the Virginians to disregard "what our young men may now be doing." In late May, two Shawnee warriors visited Grave Creek, the site of the attack on the Hardman's party, and killed a colonist named Proctor. They brought his scalp back to Wakatomica, where ten Shawnee and Haudenosaunee warriors, led by Logan and the nephew of the dead Othawakeesquo, soon set out to attack whatever Virginians they could find on the Ohio.[21] By mid-June, Logan's band had killed and scalped thirteen men, women, and children.

But even after this belated vengeance, hope for peace remained. On 10 June, McKee noted "a cessation" of hostilities, with only a few "refractory" individuals still hostile. With "some wise interposition of government," he argued, peace could be restored. A week later, thirty British traders returned to Pittsburgh from the Scioto towns, leading 120 horses laden with goods, guarded by an armed Shawnee escort. They brought a much more conciliatory speech from the war leader Cornstalk, who had, "with great Trouble and pains," persuaded "the foolish People amongst us" to keep the peace until they found out whether "the white people in general" desired war. Rather than threatening violence, he asked Connolly to similarly restrain his own "foolish People" in the future. In mid-June, Logan's band returned to Wakatomica and promised to "sit Still" until they heard from the Virginians. The Hardman admitted that the April attacks "made us like a Crazy people," but nonetheless he pledged to "keep . . . the Roads open for the English." For over two weeks, Indians attacked no colonists. As tensions cooled, White Eyes tirelessly carried messages back and forth between Pittsburgh and the Shawnee towns. On 29 June he assured Connolly that leaders of all western nations—including the Shawnees—eagerly sought peace. Rather than allowing "rash inconsiderate men" to match violence with unending violence, he urged the Virginians to "take pity of them, That our young People as they grow up may hereafter enjoy the Blessings of that peace and Friendship established betwen us."[22]

Connolly and Dunmore, though, had already taken steps to escalate hostilities. In May, Dunmore called for 1,200 men to defend the province's western claims, while Connolly ordered his militia to treat any Indians east of the Ohio "as enemies." In early June, Dunmore urged militia commanders to prepare for war and to pursue Indians even "into their own Country and beyond the limits prescribed" by law. Echoing Guyasuta, he suggested building a fort on Point Pleasant, at the mouth of the Kanawha. Connolly's militia, meanwhile, largely ignored his distinctions between allied and enemy Indians. Indian envoys to Pittsburgh repeatedly complained of militia harassment. After Shawnee escorts brought thirty British traders safely to Pittsburgh, Connolly sent forty men to seize them. They escaped, but during their flight a militia patrol wounded one of them. In mid-June, one of Connolly's men shot at a Delaware who was helping McKee; in early July on Beaver River, another patrol briefly arrested and threatened a passing trader and his Delaware escorts; in late August, several militia attacked three Delawares who had come to Pittsburgh to trade, killing two. Connolly made little effort to stop such violence. He prohibited trade with Shawnees and refused to prosecute the Delawares' killers. Adding insult to injury, Connolly appointed Michael Cresap a militia captain while insisting that Indian leaders hand over "your imprudent young Men" to face Virginian justice. If they failed to do so, he warned, they would have to answer to "a very large Body of Virginians" already marching toward Ohio.[23]

But for all this bluster, Dunmore's political and financial problems seemed to make war unlikely. On 7 June, Connolly found his militia garrison debating a recent report that Virginia's House of Burgesses had dissolved without appropriating any money to pay them. Connolly set out to squash the rumor, only to learn that it was true: the governor had dismissed his legislature for criticizing imperial policies. His pro-Pennsylvania rival, Aeneas Mackay, gleefully spread the news around Pittsburgh. Connolly hurried to Mackay's home and "abuse[d] him in a most blasphemous and outrageous manner," but rage did not change his problem: he and Dunmore had set out to fight a war with no means of paying for it. As one observer noted, Dunmore had "no store either of provisions, amunition, or, what is worse, money," and no means of obtaining any without the Burgesses. Connolly paid his Pittsburgh garrison in goods bought on credit, but he had to promise the traders 300 percent interest. He tried to bully the upper Ohio population into obedience, only to earn, according to William Crawford, "the Displeashure of the People." Meanwhile, the need to harvest crops and guard families deterred potential recruits. Those who did volunteer often proved unwilling to stay on duty. One officer claimed his garrison would surely desert "unless I kill part and tye the Other." Without reinforcements, he warned, "we will have a war amongst our Selves without that of the Indians."[24]

Nonetheless, by exploiting hopes for land and official patronage, Connolly and Dunmore patched together a diverse coalition of supporters. To raise troops and laborers, Connolly handed out militia commissions to men like Crawford whose wealth, influence, and patronage ties "cou'd bring in Volunteers . . . to enter into Pay of Government." Such brokers tolerated Connolly's incompetence in hopes of winning the governor's favor and, with it, the prospects of land grants and official appointments. Crawford had little use for Connolly, but he nonetheless raised a large company at his order. Some of Crawford's men were indentured servants, temporarily released for militia service. All involved, including the servants' owners, gambled that Virginia would eventually fulfill Dunmore's promises of payment. With the backing of Crawford and other local leaders, Connolly called out local militia units, drafted townspeople to rebuild Fort Pitt, and sent out armed patrols. Dunmore similarly won Croghan's allegiance. When he learned that Dunmore planned to wage war, Croghan initially denounced him and reached out to pro-Pennsylvania adversaries. But Croghan's best hope of confirming his land claims still lay in winning Dunmore's support. After intermediaries brokered a rapprochement, he regretted having "too incautiously" cast aspersions on the governor's character and policies. Dunmore, who needed Croghan's diplomatic expertise, promised in exchange "a proclamation to forbid people to incroach upon his property."[25]

Similar pursuits of Dunmore's favor enabled the governor to raise an army in backcountry Virginia. Militia officers liked Dunmore's proposals because they coveted Kentucky land. William Preston, for example, served as both militia commander and head surveyor for Fincastle County, which at the time included Kentucky. The surveyors who clashed with Shawnees in April worked for Preston; he and his friends were eager to see those surveys completed. But rather than ordering out an unlawful and unfunded expedition, William Christian, a militia officer and speculator, suggested that they "encourage men to rise and go out without expresly ordering them to do so." Such an approach, he thought, could attract one hundred men in a few days "who would find their own provisions (& Each man a horse)" and "take their chance of pay." Christian also urged his colleagues to deceive recruits about their plans. He warned against saying "any thing publickly of attacking the [Scioto] Towns," guessing that they could more easily persuade men to join a longer campaign after getting them on the march. They issued officer commissions to popular local leaders like Daniel Boone, whose charisma brought at least one recalcitrant company back on duty. They also appealed to greed.

Preston stressed the Shawnees' "great Stock of Horses" and other opportunities for plunder, and he assured skeptics that the House of Burgesses would eventually "reward every Vollunteer in a handsome manner, over and above his pay." Lacking the legal authority and funds to draft, feed, or pay militia, Dunmore offered hope of future compensation. A successful campaign, he reasoned, would "oblige the Assembly to indemnify" militia expenses after the fact.[26] Left to their own devices, most backcountry Virginians had little reason, and no means, to band together to wage war against Shawnees. But the incentives that Dunmore and his deputies promised, or hinted at, eventually mobilized more than two thousand men: the largest fighting force the Ohio Valley had seen since the Seven Years' War.

By contrast, many Indians remained anxious to avoid conflict. In the spring of 1774, three Cherokees—a woman, her husband, Ketigeestie, and a man named Will—found a white man half drowned in the Tennessee River, the lone survivor of a capsized canoe. They revived the man and brought him home to the Watauga Valley of western North Carolina. The three rescuers stayed there for several days and attended a horse race along with colonists from the neighboring Holston Valley. One of these, Isaac Crabtree, had survived the attack on the Russell party, and he now persuaded some of the Holston crowd to take revenge. Two shot Will in the back, killing him. Ketigeestie and his wife found refuge in one of the houses, where the Wataugans defended them against Crabtree's vengeful gang until nightfall, when they escaped. At the first Cherokee town they reached, one of Will's relatives immediately called for a war party to take revenge, but Ketigeestie dissuaded them, arguing that without the Wataugans' aid, he and his wife would have died as well. Will's murder and scalping seemed to confirm that Virginians could not be trusted, but Cherokee leaders nonetheless acted quickly and decisively to avoid war with the British, their only source of gunpowder and shot. Oconostota, their "Great Warrior," voiced the widespread belief that the "White People means bad" but nonetheless assured British agents that he would wait to resolve the matter through familiar condolence rituals. At an early September council, he raged against militant Cherokees "till he foam'd at the Mouth," while his civil counterpart, Little Carpenter, angrily asked whether they had found a way to live without colonial trade. Such pragmatic considerations helped persuade most Cherokees to remain at peace.[27]

In Ohio, Logan's initial band of about a dozen warriors remained quiet for weeks after their early June raids. On 22 June, two full months after Yellow Creek, Christian averred that Connolly had exaggerated Indian hostility. But as Dunmore's forces mobilized, a growing coalition of militant Ohio Indians launched a wider assault on western Virginia. Logan's own motives remained personal. In a letter dictated to one of his captives, Logan explained that he had forgiven previous colonial atrocities, but that after Yellow Creek he "thought [he] must kill too." He stressed that other Indians were "not angry," perhaps still hoping to contain the conflict. Most of his new allies, though, fought to oppose Virginian expansion. As hostilities escalated, Shawnee militants reportedly brought a black wampum belt calling for war to the Cherokees' Overhill Towns, arguing that colonists had "surrounded" them and would eventually destroy them if they did not resist. Between late June and mid-July eight war parties, totaling perhaps one hundred men, carried out six separate attacks ranging from the Monongahela to Kentucky, killing at least ten colonists. Though the attackers remained few in number, the geographic breadth of their targets spread terror throughout the region. Just a few weeks after suggesting that the threat of war was overblown, Christian reported that homesteaders had fled in terror. In early August, the wave of attacks culminated when three warriors killed five western Virginia children.[28]

Even so, the attackers remained on the political margins. Key Ohio Indian leaders chose to overlook the Virginians' violence, largely because peace served their respective political agendas. Throughout 1774, Guyasuta threatened western nations with Six Nations retaliation if they supported the Shawnees. His efforts bore fruit: when Shawnees sought help against Dunmore's army, their neighbors rebuffed them. White Eyes, having failed to make peace, now aimed to contain the conflict and establish himself as Dunmore's most trusted Indian ally. He and other Delaware leaders had repeatedly tried to win British recognition of their nation's sovereignty, with little success. Dunmore's need for Indian allies offered a new opportunity to pursue this long-standing goal. He also sought to ensure that any Virginian invasion of Ohio stayed well away from the Delawares' Muskingum Valley towns. Over the months that followed, White Eyes worked diligently to restore peace, but he simultaneously assured Dunmore that he could depend on Delaware neutrality in case of an expanded war.[29] He carefully avoided questioning the governor's plans for Kentucky or his belligerence toward the Shawnees. Rather than halting escalation, his courtship of Dunmore isolated the

Shawnees still further, leaving them all the more vulnerable to Virginian aggression.

In late July, a man set out from Wakatomica to trade a horseload of goods for bear grease. On the road, he met a small group of Virginians, one of whom shot at him. The man raced home, leaving his horse and goods behind. The Hardman and his neighbors prepared for battle: most fled west to the Scioto towns, while the young men prepared to ambush the approaching militia. An advance party detected the ploy and the four hundred Virginians quickly overwhelmed the town's defenders. That night, three Delawares and an On-ondaga appeared and offered to mediate, but negotiations broke down when the Virginians demanded Shawnee hostages. The militia rampaged through the towns, torched everything they saw, and cut down seventy acres of grow-ing corn. They also burned hundreds of bushels of dry corn, only to find themselves short of food. The increasingly hungry Virginians soon turned for home, leaving Wakatomica a heap of ashes.[30]

In the wake of the attack, the Hardman's political authority evaporated. At the Scioto Valley Shawnee towns, the refugees from Wakatomica no doubt taxed the resources of their kin, some of whom blamed the growing war at least in part on the Hardman's militancy. While Wakatomica smoldered, the Scioto Shawnees announced that they had "dismissed" him "and chosen an-other in his place"—Cornstalk—whom they instructed to make peace. Corn-stalk in turn asked the Delawares to mediate with the Virginians. By mid-August, Indian attacks on Virginia had once again come to a halt.[31]

But the Virginians had little interest in talking. In Pittsburgh, Connolly once again insisted that the Shawnees hand over "all those who have Com-mitted Murders upon our Defenceless Women & Children." He failed to mention the crimes of Greathouse and Cresap, who now numbered among his officers. Dunmore's army continued to mobilize and the governor himself headed west to take command. In early September, he and his retinue pad-dled down the Monongahela to Pittsburgh, where he promptly closeted him-self with Connolly for an evening of heavy drinking. Dunmore wholeheartedly endorsed Connolly's "measures & ways of thinking" regarding the Shawnees, averring that Cornstalk's people had for "a long time . . . maltreated the Vir-ginians." When Delaware and Haudenosaunee spokesmen offered, once again, to mediate a peace, Dunmore failed to respond for five days, then pre-sented a long list of alleged Shawnee crimes: some exaggerated, some misat-tributed, and others fictitious. He agreed to hear Shawnee peace proposals, but rather than doing so at the traditional council fire of Pittsburgh, he invited the Shawnees to meet him as he led his army down the Ohio. In response, the militant coalition went back to war. On 1 September, thirty intrepid warriors ambushed four hundred Virginians as they moved downriver from Pittsburgh. Three or four men died on each side. The Virginians pursued the attackers to an abandoned village, where they found the scalps of their fallen comrades "hung up like Colours." Over the following days, Indians carried out a series of attacks against the mobilizing militia. By mid-September, small bands, including Logan's, had resumed attacking homesteads, but most militants now shifted their attention to Dunmore's invasion.[32]

As the Virginians approached, the Scioto Shawnees abandoned negotiation. On 6 October, they sent two separate messages to their Delaware neighbors, both accompanied by wampum strings. In one, Cornstalk pledged to keep the Shawnees' long-standing peace with Pennsylvania. In another, Shawnee war captains declared they would confront Dunmore's army "with all their warriors." The apparent contradiction reflected an emerging consensus. Anxious to avoid alienating their British trading partners entirely, Shawnees made clear that they planned to fight only the Virginians, because they were "gathering in great numbers" almost on their doorstep. After debating for months about how to respond to Bullitt's surveys and Cresap's murders, Shawnees found unity in the face of imminent invasion. When White Eyes urged the messengers to resume peace talks, they mockingly assured him that seven hundred warriors would soon "speak with the [Virginian] army" at the Kanawha. They expected to finish talking "by Breakfast time" and would then "speak with his Lordship" directly.[33]

Before dawn on 10 October, two men left the Virginian camp at Point Pleasant and set out to hunt. About half of Dunmore's army had assembled there, at the mouth of the Kanawha River, to prepare for their invasion of Ohio. The hunters stumbled upon a group of Shawnees, fled back to camp, and raised the alarm. Their commander, Andrew Lewis, dispatched two companies to investigate. Several hundred Shawnee warriors quickly repulsed them. The Shawnees had planned to descend before dawn and drive the army into the river, but the early warning gave the more wakeful of the Virginians time to rally. They mounted a vigorous defense, leading to a fierce, chaotic, and inconclusive battle. Having lost the advantage of surprise, the Shawnees soon retreated, leaving over two hundred Virginians dead or wounded and losing a few dozen of their own.[34]

Dunmore, accompanied by White Eyes, led the other half of his army down the Ohio from Pittsburgh to the mouth of the Hocking River. Together, he and Lewis commanded perhaps 2,200 men, far more than the Shawnees, but the scarcity of supplies left them little time to strike. Anxious to act before hunger and desertion weakened their forces, Dunmore and Lewis marched their armies into Ohio, with Dunmore following the Hocking and Lewis crossing overland. Dunmore, moving more quickly, installed his forces across the river from Chillicothe in a field he dubbed "Camp Charlotte." Lewis's men hurried to catch up. White Eyes, determined to avert more bloodshed, arranged a hasty peace council. Addressing the Shawnees as his "deluded brethren," Dunmore insisted that they return all captives, escaped slaves, and stolen horses; compensate Virginia for all goods taken since 1765; and hand over six hostages. When Cornstalk noted that his people had not begun the war, the governor recited his litany of alleged Shawnee crimes and swore he would not leave until they met his demands. Facing the imminent destruction of his people's towns, Cornstalk had no choice but to agree.[35]

Both Indians and colonists resented the peace agreement. Some Ohio Haudenosaunee neighbors refused to attend Dunmore's council and instead planned to flee northward toward Lake Erie. Happy to make an example of them, the governor dispatched William Crawford with 240 men to attack their towns, forty miles farther up the Scioto. The townspeople heard their predawn approach and most fled in the dark, leaving most of their horses, guns, and other possessions behind. Crawford's men killed six of the town's defenders and captured fourteen women and children, whom Dunmore later freed at White Eyes's request. For their part, Crawford's men auctioned off their plunder for £400 sterling and divided the proceeds among themselves. But other members of Dunmore's army were disappointed: Lewis's men in particular had looked forward to avenging their losses and plundering the Scioto towns. During their march they repeatedly ignored the governor's orders to stop. Rather than marching directly to Camp Charlotte, Lewis took a road that ran closer to the towns—he subsequently claimed that "the Guide mistook the path"—and sparked widespread panic. As Shawnee warriors prepared for battle, Dunmore raced to Lewis's camp and personally commanded him to halt. Lewis later reported he had to double the guard around his tent to prevent his men from killing the governor and White Eyes. But Lewis's men ultimately complied with their orders and returned home without the plunder they coveted.[36]

The war's anticlimactic ending calls into question the notion that Ohio

Valley colonists disdained political authority. However much they hated Dunmore, White Eyes, or the Shawnees, the militia had reason to comply with the governor's commands. Lewis and his officers hoped that Dunmore's favor would secure them rich Kentucky estates. Their men similarly expected payment for their services in either cash or land. Despite widespread resentment at being denied plunder and vengeance, the militia hesitated to jeopardize future opportunities by defying the governor's orders. So long as violence enjoyed at least tacit official support, hostilities had escalated. Once Dunmore personally demanded peace, attacks on Indians ceased, for a time.

On his return to Williamsburg, Dunmore found a packet of London correspondence excoriating him for his land grants, Connolly's abuses, and the Cresap and Greathouse murders. He defended his conduct in a long letter that was, in the words of the historian Richard White, "riddled with lies." In particular, Dunmore professed himself powerless to rein in what he called "the emigrating Spirit of the Americans." Lacking any "attachment to Place," he argued, the colonists wandered about the landscape, convinced that "the Lands further off, are Still better than those upon which they are already Settled." No authority could halt their meandering, as "they do not conceive that Government has any right to forbid" them. When they set out to seize Indian land, or slaughter the Indians who lived there, "the efforts of Magistrates and Government could not in the least restrain" them.[37]

These excuses resonate widely in both popular and scholarly interpretations of Anglo-American colonialism. But the picture he painted bore little resemblance to the causes of the war that would bear his name. Between 1765 and 1773, relative peace had prevailed. Many Indians chafed at the rush of colonists into the Monongahela country, but the prohibition of colonization west of the Kanawha promised a workable compromise. Contrary to Dunmore's mendacious screed, British colonists largely abided by the Kanawha boundary. Daniel Boone and other "long hunters" visited Kentucky in search of game, and aspiring speculators pined for land there, but Shawnee and Cherokee policing deterred them from establishing homesteads. Rather than an organic tide of independent-minded backwoodsmen, the colonization of Kentucky began with elite Virginians' demands for land and with their new governor's readiness to comply. The subsequent descent into war reflected Indians' and colonists' common desire for the favor of an internally contradictory imperial state. The lure of Dunmore's patronage enabled him to mobilize an army and secure the loyalty of key Indian leaders. The empire's imminent collapse, meanwhile, offered the region its best remaining hope for peace.

Dunmore's triumph soon faded. Within eight months of the Shawnee surrender, he fled Williamsburg as Virginia rose in revolution. But the governor's western adventures had reshaped Ohio Valley politics and accelerated colonization. White Eyes and Cornstalk emerged as preeminent peacemakers, eager to secure their peoples' remaining territory and to avert another war. The western alliance that Shawnees and others had so long envisioned had collapsed, thanks largely to Guyasuta's anti-Shawnee lobbying. In the upper Ohio Valley, Connolly's diverse anti-Pennsylvania coalition would endure well beyond Dunmore's departure. And the violence of 1774 left many Indians and colonists nursing injuries, mourning loved ones, and pondering vengeance. Above all, Dunmore's War encouraged hundreds of colonists to move west into the formerly forbidden ground of Kentucky.

CHAPTER 3

Opportunity, 1775–76

In early 1775, Cornstalk led a young girl on a chilly midwinter journey to Point Pleasant, where hundreds of his fellow Shawnees had fought invading Virginians the previous fall. This time he found about one hundred militia huddled in a hastily built stockade. Speaking for his own nation and their Haudenosaunee neighbors, Cornstalk expressed regret for the recent war, pledged to honor Dunmore's terms, and pleaded that the governor return his hostages. He also handed over the girl, whom his people had adopted at some time in the past, as well as some horses. In reply, the Virginian commander, William Russell, promised that if the Shawnees complied with Dunmore's demands, they had nothing to fear. But both Indians and colonists had reason to doubt these promises. Even Dunmore's native allies feared renewed Virginian aggression, and other Indians still bristled at colonial expansion. A few weeks after the meeting at Point Pleasant, a team led by Daniel Boone began widening a chain of ancient bison trails to the Kentucky River, clearing the way for others to follow. Before dawn on 25 March, a small group of Pekowi Shawnees and Cherokees attacked Boone's camp, killing two men and wounding another. Two days later they fell on another party nearby, killing two more. The roadbuilders pressed on to the Kentucky, where they built an outpost they called Boonesborough. Hundreds of colonists soon followed, enraging Ohio Indians and Cherokees. As antagonism mounted, Dunmore evacuated Virginia's Ohio River forts, including Russell's stockade. Beset by revolution, the governor soon escaped Williamsburg to the safety of a British warship.[1] No vestige of government authority remained between embittered Indians and land-hungry colonists. Prospects for peace seemed dim.

In the months that followed, however, fears of imminent war repeatedly proved groundless. When Dunmore fled, one of his Shawnee hostages escaped to warn his people that the colonists "were all determined upon War with the Indians." Fifty-two days later, after walking nearly five hundred miles, the Shawnee reached home and found Virginian goodwill messengers rather than soldiers. Similar warnings reached Cornstalk on his way to a Pittsburgh peace council, but when he arrived his hosts welcomed him with open arms. Several hundred miles downstream, an English traveler named Nicholas Cresswell and a band of colonists, paddling around a bend in the Ohio, found themselves surrounded by ten canoes "full of Indians." Assuming the worst, they jettisoned their cargo, loaded their guns, and paddled desperately for shore. But just before they opened fire, the Indians called out that "they were friends." On closer examination, their rifles proved to be "poles or paddles" and several of the imagined warriors proved to be "very handsome" Delaware women. Relieved, the colonists gave their new acquaintances some salt and tobacco and took no offense when they "laughed at us for our feares."[2]

This relative peace in the west stemmed from war and upheaval to the east. In April 1775, Massachusetts militia rebelled against royal troops. In the months that followed, most of the colonies' royal and proprietary governments collapsed, giving way to improvised committees, conventions, and an increasingly radical Continental Congress. In the Ohio Valley, motives for bloodshed—racial antipathy and competition for land—remained as strong as ever, while frequent intercultural interactions afforded many opportunities to kill. But without functional governments to support them, militants struggled to bridge internecine divisions, mobilize fighting men, or supply them with food and weaponry. Through mid-1776, Indians and colonists periodically harassed, threatened, or stole from one another, but they hardly ever resorted to deadly violence.[3] Rather than unleashing bloody chaos, the collapse of imperial authority sparked political innovation, as both Indians and colonists sought to build new relationships with one another and with colonial governments. As Crown and Congress competed for the loyalties of western allies, Ohio Valley inhabitants readily exploited the crisis for their own ends. When killing resumed, sporadically in mid-1776 and ferociously in mid-1777, British and revolutionary resources played a decisive role.

Late in the summer of 1776, hundreds of upper Ohio colonists assembled at Pittsburgh to fight Indians. Recent reports from Shawnee country warned that "an Indian War [wa]s inevitable" and that 1,500 Ojibwe and Odawa warriors would soon attack Fort Pitt. On the order of Congress's treaty commissioners, men hurriedly assembled for battle. One militia battalion, asked for 100 men, turned out 350. It was the largest mobilization of Ohio Valley

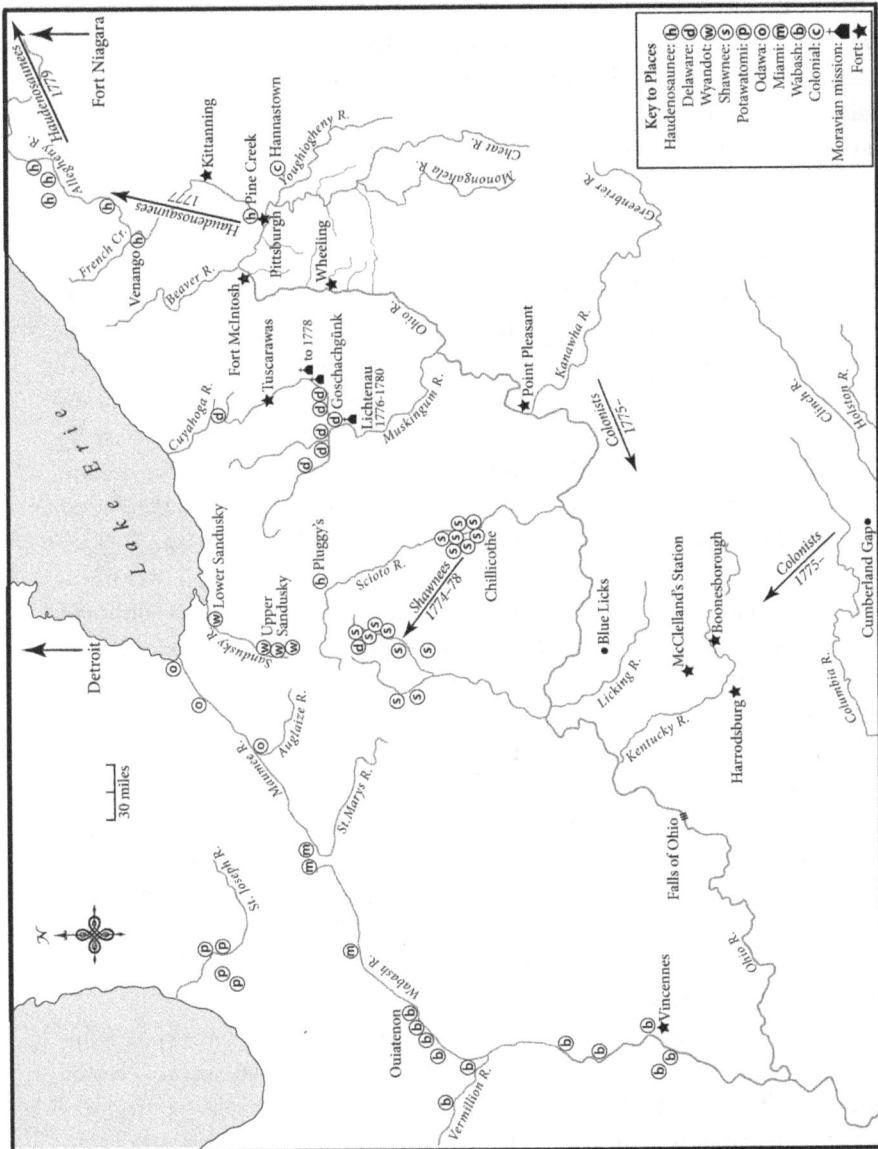

Figure 2. The Ohio Valley, 1775-79.

militia, by far, in the early years of the Revolutionary War. The congressional agents praised the colonists' "spirited conduct" and described them as "a race of hardy, experienced woods-men, whom it will be no easy task to overcome." But their mettle remained untested: rather than a fearsome horde, the approaching Ojibwes proved to be a handful of diplomats. When the surprisingly large militia army showed up, the agents thanked them for their trouble and sent them home. The men meekly complied. A month later, over six hundred Delaware, Shawnee, and Haudenosaunee men, women, and children made their way to Pittsburgh for a treaty council. The colonists who had so recently mobilized for war harmed none of them.[4]

Given previous and subsequent history, this reticence seems odd. Ohio Valley colonists frequently and notoriously voiced an eagerness to kill Indians. According to one congressional agent, many harbored "great Hopes of an Indian War & express[ed] great Joy at a prospect thereof." In 1774, and again starting in 1777, bands of colonists repeatedly murdered defenseless Indian men, women, and children. But in 1775 and 1776 such attacks became surprisingly rare. Small groups of colonists occasionally threatened, chased, and even shot at Indians around Pittsburgh, but did little damage. They attacked no Indian communities across the Ohio. The restraining power of the state—any state—posed no real obstacle: the congressional agents' authority rested on a few pieces of paper from Philadelphia. But without government backing, isolated homesteaders could do no more than threaten the Indians they hated. Far from self-reliant pioneers, Ohio Valley colonists looked to embryonic revolutionary governments for both material support and regional coordination. The march against the phantom Ojibwe army was an exception that proved the rule. Alone, fear or hatred of Indians did not spur colonists to action. But they did mobilize when faced with a specific and imminent threat, in response to orders from recognized political authorities, and under the aegis of formal county militias.[5] Political conflicts and the lack of key resources—both worsened by the revolutionary crisis—deterred Indian haters from going to war on their own.

In early 1775, county surveyor William Preston alerted Governor Dunmore to a dire new threat. Without deploying "an armed force," Preston warned, a "valuable & extensive territory will be forever lost to Virginia." Rather than fear of Indians, Preston's dread sprang from the intrigues of Carolina lawyers. Williamsburg newspapers had recently printed advertisements for land in a new colony called "Transylvania." Its founders, a coterie of attorneys led by one Richard Henderson, had gotten rich prosecuting debt-ridden backcountry farmers. Now they drew on that wealth to offer the Cherokee nation a large supply of goods for about half of present-day Kentucky. Many Cherokee men, who stood to lose some of their best hunting territory, denounced the offer, but older leaders eventually accepted the goods. Together with Dunmore's success in Ohio, Henderson's advertisements sparked widespread fervor for the "new found Paradise" in the west. They also reconciled the lawyers with many of the poor farmers they had persecuted. A few years before, Henderson had tried to arrest Daniel Boone for an unpaid debt; now Boone agreed to cut a road to the Kentucky River in exchange for a piece of the new colony. The March attacks on Boone's crew drove dozens back across the mountains, but a peaceful summer and fall attracted many more. Even well-connected Virginia speculators sought land from Transylvania, gambling that the scheme might eventually prove legitimate. Echoing Preston's alarm, the governor of North Carolina warned that "such Adventurers will possess themselves soon of all the Indian country."[6]

The Transylvania project flew in the face of imperial policy; the governments of Virginia and North Carolina quickly condemned it. But rather than rebelling against formal authority, the schemers hoped that legal loopholes, influence peddling, and well-directed offers of land would ultimately win them state approval. Everyone involved took pains to lend the project a semblance of legality. Henderson justified his purchase with a creative interpretation of legal precedents. He and his partners adopted the title "proprietors" in imitation of those who ruled colonies granted by the Crown. When royal authority collapsed they changed tack, pledging to support "the general cause of America" while urging Congress to acknowledge their claims. Congress rebuffed them, but the ambiguities of both British and revolutionary land policies offered hope for future state recognition. The Boonesborough colonists, well aware that their land rights stood on shaky legal ground, divided up land into small parcels and distributed them by lottery: a quasi-legal approximation of official procedure that they hoped would stand up in court. Henderson privately called them "a set of scoundrels," but he shared their desire for legitimation from some version of the Anglo-American state.[7]

The new Kentucky colonists found themselves in a precarious situation. Their very presence angered western Indians, who maintained they "[had] never sold these Lands." They could expect scant help from Dunmore, huddling aboard ship in Chesapeake Bay: through 1775 and 1776, the unfolding eastern revolution left aspiring westerners on their own. Material insecurity worsened their plight. In the spring of 1775, even the more established

Monongahela colonists faced food shortages—Dunmore's army had ex-hausted their grain supplies the year before—and the newcomers to Ken-tucky had even less. Within weeks of Boonesborough's founding, Henderson complained that his colonists had killed or driven off all the nearby game. By June, new arrivals could find no flour at Harrodsburg; Boonesborough re-portedly had "no bread at all." They keenly remembered the March attacks on Boone's roadbuilders, and subsequent rumors of Indians sent many flying eastward in panic, but they built only rudimentary defenses. Instead, colo-nists scattered across the landscape—hunting, farming, raising livestock, and, above all, claiming land—leaving them with little means of defending themselves. Nonetheless, throughout the spring, summer, and fall of 1775, Kentucky colonists reported no new attacks. By the spring of 1776, one colo-nist voiced "not . . . the least Dread or apprehention" of an Indian war.[8] As fears abated, westward migration swelled.

Henderson's scheme soon foundered, but Virginia's budding revolution-ary government continued what he had started. In the winter of 1775–76, the Transylvania partners doubled the price of land and reserved many of the best tracts for themselves. The bait-and-switch outraged many colonists, who petitioned Virginia to protect them against "the gentlemen stiling themselves proprietors." Rather than loyalty to the Old Dominion, this change of heart reflected the colonists' decision that Virginia was more likely to grant them legal title at a low price. Eager to reclaim Dunmore's western empire, the state's revolutionary convention took steps to secure its claim to the region. Starting in mid-1777, Virginia raised and paid militia companies to help de-fend Boonesborough and similar outposts, encouraging colonists to remain on the land rather than fleeing east for safety. In 1779, Virginia enacted a new land law that, at least in theory, honored the preemptive claims of early Ken-tucky colonists. Many would be disappointed—by the mid-1780s, byzantine procedures and a whirl of litigation left most of them landless—but in the interim, thousands of hopeful migrants moved west.[9]

Meanwhile, hundreds of miles upriver, a Haudenosaunee delegation met John Connolly to talk peace. Dunmore, falling from power, had instructed Connolly to disband his Pittsburgh garrison and court the friendship of western Indians. After symbolically wiping away their tears and "removing every uneasiness from the heart," Connolly agreed to meet his guests the next day at Fort Pitt. But it was not to be. That night, a band of armed colonists appeared out of the darkness to interrupt the council. But rather than attack-ing the Indians, they kidnapped Connolly. The next morning, when the

Haudenosaunees showed up to resume their talks, they found "nothing but his bed."[10]

Connolly's abduction had less to do with either Indians or the imperial crisis than with feuds among the region's nascent colonial elite. In 1774, Connolly and his pro-Virginia allies had seized control of Pittsburgh. Over the year that followed, they repeatedly persecuted their pro-Pennsylvania rivals. In the spring of 1775, they jailed two opponents for months; seized others' cattle, hogs, and land; and brought exorbitant lawsuits against all who opposed them. But news of revolution muddied the waters. In May, the two factions separately formed county committees and called for local militias to resist Parliamentary tyranny. As many suspected, Connolly remained loyal to his patron Dunmore, but most of his erstwhile allies resolved to "oppos[e] the invaders of American rights and privileges to the utmost extreme." When Dunmore fell from power, Connolly's opponents saw their chance for payback. They seized him in the middle of the night, dragged him over fifty miles to territory they controlled, and called for Continental troops to "prevent the Virginians from taking Possession" of Fort Pitt. But the captors underestimated their adversaries' fervor. The pro-Virginia faction seized three pro-Pennsylvania leaders and shipped them ninety miles down the Ohio "in an old Leaky Boat." A negotiated prisoner exchange ensued. On 29 June, Connolly returned to Pittsburgh and rejoined his Haudenosaunee guests, who had spent the intervening week camped quietly nearby, enjoying food and gifts from colonists anxious to befriend them.[11] With war raging in the east, and partisan animosity still heated in the west, neither faction dared alienate Ohio Indians or let their adversaries gain their favor.

The boundary dispute flared again in the fall, with deadly consequences. In September the Virginia Convention sent one hundred men to reoccupy Fort Pitt. Cresswell, returning from an amicable tour of Ohio Indian towns, found "nothing but quarreling and fighting" in Pittsburgh. Tensions cooled briefly in October, when large delegations of Delawares, Shawnees, and Senecas visited for a peace council, but violence broke out soon after the Indians left.[12] On a Pittsburgh street in late October, Connolly's wife, Susanna, came to blows with a woman who lived with Richard Butler, a prominent fur trader and pro-Pennsylvania partisan whom John Connolly had jailed the previous year.[13] Butler's friend reportedly "beat and abused [Susanna Connolly] in an outragious manner." She and Butler fled the scene, but a Virginian militia party, led by Susanna's alleged lover, Simon Girty,[14] quickly overtook and arrested them. Butler's allies hurried to his aid. A Connolly lieutenant, George

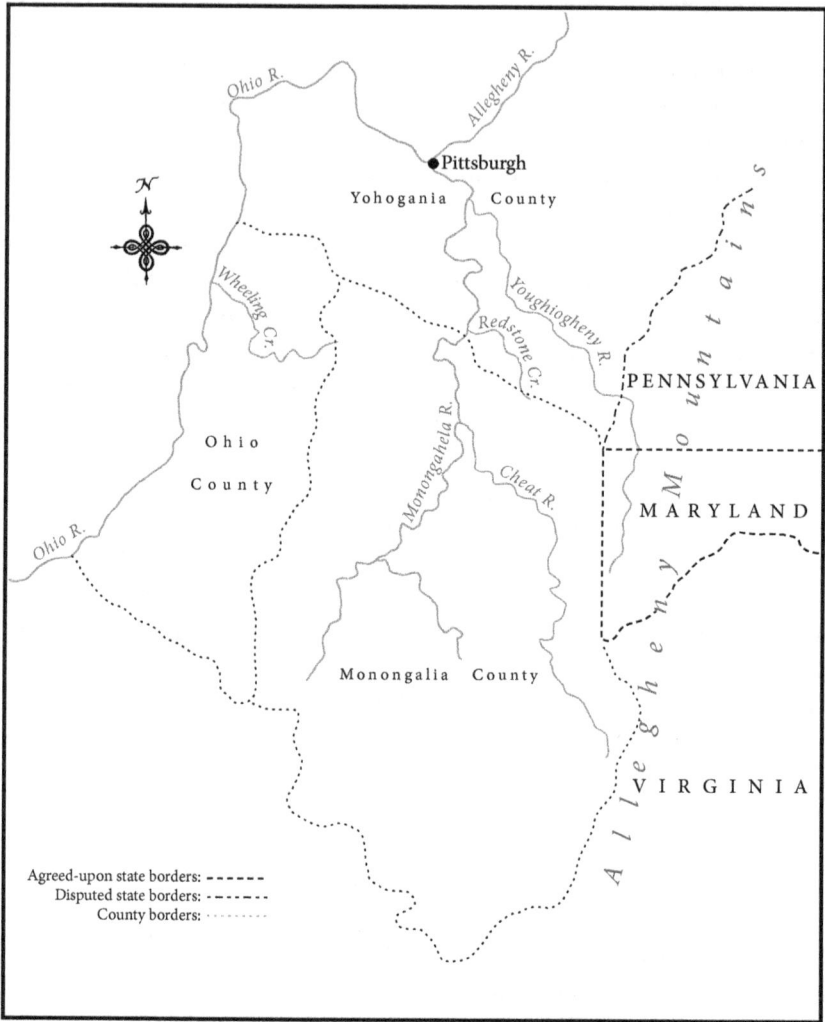

Figure 3. The Forks of the Ohio region, 1775–79 (Virginia claim).

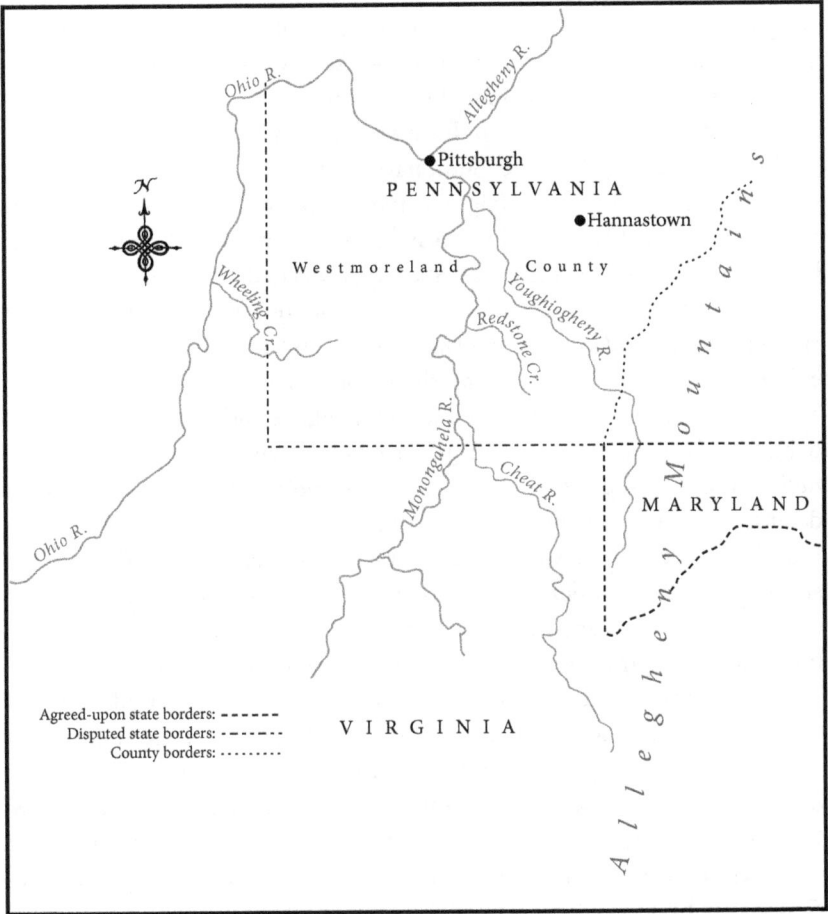

Figure 4. The Forks of the Ohio region, 1775–79 (Pennsylvania claim).

Aston, knocked Devereux Smith into a clay pit; when Aston charged a second time, Smith buried a knife in his chest. Aston died on the spot. His men
shot a musket ball through Smith's leg and beat him close to death as he lay
crippled on the ground. Only the intervention of a Virginian militia officer,
and the amputation of his wounded leg, saved Smith's life. Butler survived the
riot and soon went east to join the Continental Army; surviving evidence
reveals nothing about the fate of his mob-ridden friend.[15]

Both intercultural and revolutionary tensions, it seems, could fade next
to the fury of local partisanship. For the emerging upper Ohio elite, aspirations in land speculation and political advancement hinged on the favor of a
broadly recognized government. Such men needed effectual courts, led by
magistrates friendly to their interests, to extract rent from tenants, evict rival
land claimants, and control the labor of servants and slaves. The success of
either Virginia's or Pennsylvania's claim could mean the difference between
becoming a prominent landlord and public figure and being imprisoned for
debt.[16] By the time of the riot Virginia's revolutionary committee knew Connolly was conniving with Dunmore, but they nonetheless leaped to his wife's
defense. For her part, Butler's friend may have been associated with Ohio
Indians; Butler himself was a veteran trader and frontier diplomat.[17] But the
surviving evidence offers no sign that revolutionary tensions or attitudes
toward Indians had any bearing on the riot. Aston died and Smith endured
life-changing injuries for the sake of a factional dispute among colonists.

At the other end of the social ladder, the misery of servitude overshadowed both partisan and intercultural tensions. In one Kentucky-bound party,
two servants slipped away from their masters, paddled across the Ohio, and
disappeared into Indian country. One of their cotravelers puzzled over why
they ran away "in this wilderness Country" but they presumably dreaded Indians less than continued servitude. Hundreds of miles to the east, five of
George Washington's servants fled their upper Ohio worksite and sought refuge in "the Indens towns," but their hosts handed them over at the demand of
a white trader. So many enslaved African Americans did the same that Virginians insisted Shawnees hand over "our Negroes" as a condition of making
peace.[18] Intercultural animosity remained but could be dwarfed by antagonism within a divisive and unequal colonial population.

When upper Ohio colonists overcame such divisions and mobilized for
war, they relied on government initiatives. In the spring of 1775, nascent
county committees resolved to form "a military body" but failed to follow
through. After Dunmore evacuated his Ohio River forts, they remained

vacant for months until Virginia's revolutionary convention paid armed companies to garrison them. The convention also revived Virginia's lapsed militia law, establishing formal procedures for organizing, arming, and paying fighting-age men, as well as making "Just Returns of the Delinquent" so they "may be fined." Colonists often shirked militia duty despite such penalties, but the law established a structure that enabled officers to mobilize their neighbors at least sporadically. Even with these measures in place, county militias did little until late 1776. In November, some reportedly plotted to ambush passing Indian peace delegations, but the plan fell through. Widespread food shortages raised yet another obstacle to mobilization. When Virginia militia officers finally raised some men, they did so to guard nearby farmers as they harvested precious grain.[19] Militant colonists raged against Indians, but even defensive measures required government authorization and payment.

Virginia's promise to pay militia carried weight. As its last official act, the prerevolutionary House of Burgesses appointed a commission to pay Dunmore's 1774 army, those who had supplied it, and the "poor Widows and Orphans" of the fallen. That fall, the commissioners issued certificates to hundreds of claimants. By late 1776, the revolutionary Convention had paid out over £100,000 in Virginia currency to settle the expenses of the governor it had overthrown. For serving about two months, each man received a certificate worth £4–5 in Virginia currency, roughly equivalent to the assessed value of each steer bought to feed Dunmore's men. Some served five months or longer, for earnings that approximated the value of a good horse. In years to come, wartime inflation made such payments worthless, but for the moment they offered a tangible reward for military service, especially in cash-poor western Virginia.[20]

In some cases, communities persuaded militia to serve unofficially in hopes of future compensation, much as Dunmore's army had done. In January 1777, as the militia garrison at Grave Creek neared the end of its term, nearby colonists petitioned them to stay longer. Neither the governor nor the county militia commander had authorized a longer tour, or drafted more men to relieve them, but the colonists assured the garrison that the Dunmore's War commissioners would "in no ways refuse to pay you . . . for this Service done the Country." About twenty of the men signed a pledge to stay on "as Militia Soldiers" for an additional fifteen days. The terminology mattered: "militia soldiers" were entitled to wages, though only when authorized by Virginia officials. Noting that they acted "without proper orders," they agreed "to run the risk of the Colony's paying us," trusting that their commander would advocate for payment. David Shepherd, a local merchant, promised to feed the men, similarly gambling that the state would compensate him. He had experience in this area, having earned about £4 in certificates for supplying Dunmore's army.[21] The arrangement reflected the murky yet potent manifestation of state influence. Rather than simply complying with or ignoring official directives, the colonists and the garrison sought to manipulate the nascent revolutionary government into paying for extra protection. The plan emerged through local negotiations, with no input from officials other than the garrison's commander, but it hinged on expectations of state support.

The formal militia structure also helped resolve questions about leadership and organization. In mid-1776, thirty-seven Clinch Valley inhabitants petitioned Fincastle County's revolutionary committee to appoint a local militia commander. Living over one hundred miles and across a mountain ridge from the county seat, the petitioners explained they could not feasibly attend Fincastle's regular musters. To organize local defenses, they required "Some principal Officer here in this Valley" to lead them. Their favored candidate, Richard Lyman, seemingly lacked the necessary authority to "keep the men in Order Together." His friends might obey him out of personal respect and confidence, but the community in general would not. If their valley were attacked, Lyman would have to persuade men he hardly knew to leave their homes and march to meet the enemy. Whatever his qualities as a leader, personal influence alone might not overcome colonists' inclination to defend their own homesteads. To rally their neighbors, he and his officers wanted official appointments and the backing of Virginia law. With the county committee's support, the petitioners claimed, Lyman and his officers "Could Train our Militia with Much Ease" and prepare the valley to resist Indian aggression. Notwithstanding the upheaval of revolution, these colonists believed that the trappings of legal authority could strengthen frontier defenses.[22]

Internecine squabbles could impede even government-backed mobilization. In the summer of 1776, Congress authorized Pennsylvania's Westmoreland County committee to create a new battalion for frontier defense. To command the new unit, Congress appointed Aeneas Mackay, a Pittsburgh merchant with connections in Philadelphia but few friends among Westmoreland farmers. The county committee, under pressure from Mackay's opponents, saddled him with several antagonistic subordinates. For months, "Artfull Insinuations" and a "factious Disposition" plagued the officer corps.

Some complained that their station, an Allegheny River trading post forty-five miles from Fort Pitt, was too "remote" to protect "the defenceless frontiers." Meanwhile, the exorbitant price of provisions, and quarrels over how to pay for them, left the battalion poorly supplied. In November, several officers threatened to march their companies "where they Pleased" and to "shoot Down the first that would oppose them." Mackay regained control only by agreeing to distribute the men among frontier homesteads, where they could be more readily clothed and fed. Then, in December, Congress ordered the battalion to join Washington's army hundreds of miles to the east. The men set out on a long midwinter journey across Pennsylvania, with few blankets and little food or clothing. By the time they arrived, Mackay and many more had died.[23]

However much upper Ohio colonists may have wanted to fight Indians, they repeatedly failed to mobilize in large numbers. The scarcity of guns, ammunition, and provisions, as well as political fractiousness, geographic dispersal, and general poverty, posed serious obstacles. Households could ill afford to spare men who left home for war, and few colonists wielded the personal authority necessary to enlist others' cooperation. "The Militia on this side of the Hills is not to be depended on in case of emergency," Mackay noted. When threatened, "they fly with their respective families" rather than joining their neighbors to fight. Reports of Indian attacks—some imagined, some real—repeatedly failed to spur a coordinated response. When colonists did mobilize, they relied on the structure of formal county militias.[24] The nascent revolutionary state commanded scant resources or authority, but without its support frontier war seemed impossible.

Much as colonial disputes muted anti-Indian hostility, so, too, the politics of Indian communities discouraged new attacks on colonists. The traumas of recent wars had convinced many that they could not fight colonization militarily without powerful allies and reliable supplies of gunpowder. In addition, the upheavals of 1774 left many Ohio Indians short of food.[25] At the same time, the imperial crisis promised alternative ways to secure sovereignty. In 1775 and 1776 both the British at Detroit and the Americans at Pittsburgh sought western Indians' friendship without openly encouraging them to go to war. Some militants called for war to defend Kentucky, but without state support they won few converts. Meanwhile, as colonists warred over independence, Indians reshaped their own politics to suit native needs.

The most pressing needs revolved around the challenge of renewed colonial expansion. Delawares, Shawnees, and Mohicans all recognized a familiar pattern. First in New Netherland, and later in New York, New Jersey, and Pennsylvania, colonial governments had encouraged colonists to occupy ever more land, then used the resulting tensions as a pretext to demand additional territory. In reoccupying Ohio, these nations had aimed to distance themselves from the seaboard colonies. Now the rush of colonists to Kentucky signaled a new cycle of dispossession. To confront this growing threat, Ohio Indians proposed a wide range of strategies, nearly all of which involved building relationships with some manifestation of the Anglo-American state.

For years, Delaware leaders had sought British recognition of their nation's sovereignty, offering in exchange to accept the British king, embrace Christianity, and remake their society and economy along colonial lines. As White Eyes told a Virginian emissary, he wanted his people to live "as the White People do and under their Laws and Protection." But rather than blending into colonial society, Delaware leaders sought recognition as a distinct people, living in a defined territory, within the composite British empire. They persistently insisted on their right to their lands in eastern Ohio, citing a gift from their Wyandot neighbors, and labored to unify their scattered nation both politically and geographically. They also developed a more formal governing council to centralize decision making. As they adopted aspects of European culture, the Delaware integrated them with familiar traditions. In 1775, when they built a new capital, Goschachgünk, they laid out a European street grid and adapted it to their traditional kinship system, assigning a separate street to each clan. Above all, Delaware leaders angled to send a diplomatic mission to England in order to win formal recognition from the king.[26]

In 1775, as their Shawnee neighbors recovered from Dunmore's War, Delaware leaders had good reason to expect the formal recognition they coveted. As a reward for White Eyes's services, Dunmore had pledged to back their nation's territorial claims "with all his Interest" and to send a Delaware delegation to London to win royal approval. Accordingly, White Eyes appeared at a June 1775 council bearing a new belt of friendship for "King George our Mutual Father," pledging to make the Delawares and English "one people," with "one King . . . to govern us." He soon learned, no doubt to his chagrin, that he had embraced King George just as hundreds of thousands of colonists were disowning him. On 9 July, a Virginian messenger issued demands but failed to mention either the king or Dunmore's promises. In a private meeting, with his own interpreter, White Eyes carefully explained his arrangements with the recently deposed governor. In reply, the messenger explained Dunmore's fall from power but assured him that Virginia would "Amply reward him for his Services and damages."[27]

Recognizing in crisis an opportunity, White Eyes cultivated the rebels' friendship just as he had pursued the king's. In the months that followed, he helped persuade wary Indians to meet with congressional emissaries and tried to squash British warnings of treachery. At an October council, he vocally supported Virginian demands and praised the "Commands of our Saviour whose hands were Nailed to the Cross and sides Peirced for our Sins." At the same time, he reminded the council that when the English first arrived in America, his people had "made room for you to set down by Us," suggesting that colonists' right to their land originated not with the king they now spurned, but with the generosity of their Indian neighbors. He reiterated that the Wyandots had similarly given land to the Delaware and specified the boundaries in detail. He also explained Delaware government, identifying the leaders of the Turtle, Turkey, and Wolf phratries and noting the influence of Delaware women, whom he credited with keeping their people out of war. He delivered a separate speech and wampum belt from the mothers of his nation, who expressed joy at the prospect of continued peace, and urged the Virginians to share this message with "your Mothers our Elder Sisters the White Women," perhaps hoping they would perform a similar role among their own people.[28] Throughout, he balanced concessions and plans for change with reminders that Delaware women and men remained in charge of their own people and land.

In the months that followed, White Eyes continued promoting his agenda, with mixed results. He spent the winter in Philadelphia lobbying the rebels to honor Dunmore's promises. In April Congress voted to provide the Delaware with a minister, schoolmaster, and blacksmith, a steady supply of trade goods, and a formal arbitration system to resolve disputes, but the United States failed to fulfill these commitments. Congress also balked at recognizing Delaware territorial claims, chiefly for fear of antagonizing the Six Nations. White Eyes would spend the next three years trying to overcome this setback. But he personally received two horses, saddles, and $300 in cash, and a promise to resolve a dispute with two Philadelphia merchants. In addition, Virginia awarded him £57—about ten times the wages of a common militiaman—for his services during Dunmore's War. His goals remained elusive, but within a few months he had transformed himself from the trusted ally of a royal governor into a favored friend of the rebel Congress.[29]

Other Ohio Indian leaders balked at White Eyes's program of cultural transformation, but they similarly sought the rebels' friendship. The Six Nations council "scolded" Ojibwes and Odawas for spreading British warnings of colonial aggression and "reproved" members of their own league who considered going to war. Guyasuta, another onetime Dunmore ally, now accompanied congressional emissary Richard Butler on a tour to invite Ohio Indians to a peace council. At Delaware, Wyandot, Haudenosaunee, and Shawnee towns, Guyasuta repeatedly berated his hosts for not trusting the colonists. Such doubts remained legion, but many male and female leaders seemed eager to befriend the rebel Congress. They repeatedly equated Butler's invitations with the restoration of old alliances. A group of Haudenosaunee leaders addressed Butler as "Onas," their old name for the governors of Pennsylvania, and urged that "the Old love & Friendship that was made in Old times" be made "new and bright as Ever." Mekoche Shawnee spokesmen told Butler that they still held the old wampum "that made us Relations," asking that "As it was of Old let it be Again." These calls for restoring old ways contrasted sharply with White Eyes's vision of radical change, but they also reflected a similar desire to foster a personal and political kinship that balanced interdependence and autonomy.[30]

These efforts to befriend colonists cost some communities dearly. In the winter of 1775–76, a band of Shawnee men seized twenty prisoners, including two small children, and marched them over 150 miles, guarding them carefully to prevent escape. The story echoes many other tales of early American captivity, except that the captors raided Shawnee homes, and tore apart Shawnee families, on behalf of Virginia. Not for the first time, colonial emissaries had demanded that Ohio Indians hand over wartime captives, since adopted, as a condition of peace. Many adoptees came only after the warriors threatened to "take their Scalps" instead. Several later escaped Virginia and returned to their adoptive families. The two children, though, had been born and raised as Shawnees. Their mother had escaped from Virginian slavery and found refuge in the Scioto towns, where she met their Shawnee father. In 1774, the Shawnees handed her over to Dunmore, and they did so again after she escaped back to her family. But at the October treaty conference, Virginia's commissioners "insisted upon having the two Children" as well. The otherwise conciliatory Cornstalk balked, arguing that "as the Children were Bagat by our People we thought it very hard they shou'd be made Slaves of." But other leaders gave in. Many opposed their choice—hence the warriors' use of force—but enough accepted it to overcome the families' opposition.[31] Much like White

Eyes's services to Congress, Shawnees undertook this awful task to secure peace and friendship with their troublesome colonial neighbors. Virginia's demands challenged Shawnee leaders to exercise sovereignty in European terms: by controlling people and territory. For a time, such concessions carried the day, with the proponents of violent resistance pressed to the margins.

Even so, Indian leaders' submission to revolutionary demands sparked resentment and hostility. Early in 1775, Shawnees killed two Delaware hunters, probably in retaliation for that nation's support for Dunmore. Cornstalk later performed condolence rituals to restore the two nations' friendship, but even he privately berated Guyasuta and the Delawares for acting like "dogs or servants" to the British. In August 1776, a colonist "accidentally" shot a Delaware woman near Pittsburgh, but the Delaware council quickly brushed the incident aside, faulting the victim for going to the town "for Rum." The council's readiness to forgive and forget helped convince their newly appointed secretary that they were the Americans' "sensear friends," but the injured woman, and any number of other Delawares, no doubt saw the episode differently.[32] With each new American imposition or broken promise, not to mention outright assault, the value of White Eyes's and Cornstalk's hard-won friendships with the United States, and their own credibility as leaders and spokesmen, came further into question.

Some Indians rejected the pro-peace platform entirely. In August 1775 a Wyandot named Snip, whose friend had died at Virginian hands the year before, decided to go to war. On his way toward Kentucky, some Haudenosaunees persuaded him to turn back, but then he met two men, one British and one Wyandot, bringing a load of trade goods up the Scioto. According to Snip, the white man, John Edwards, admitted he had served in Dunmore's army. When they camped, Snip killed him in his sleep. The Wyandot trader fled and Snip made off with their goods. Word of the killing reached the Sandusky Wyandot towns during a visit from Butler. Dunquat, the Sandusky Wyandots' preeminent civil leader, announced the news "with tears in his eyes" and immediately performed a full condolence ceremony. Wyandot women confronted Snip with a large wampum belt, signifying their community's condemnation, and demanded that he return the stolen goods "& Not bring Evil on them." He bowed to the pressure and handed over his plunder. This outcome hardly measured up to European standards of justice, but it accorded well with Wyandot ones, and the events had transpired in Wyandot territory. Above all, both Butler and the Wyandots needed to put the incident behind them to move on with the pressing work of diplomacy.[33]

Snip was not alone. In the summer and fall of 1775 a Mohawk called Pluggy began cobbling together a motley coalition of Haudenosaunees, Shawnees, and Wyandots who staunchly opposed the colonization of Kentucky. Many, like Snip, had lost loved ones in Dunmore's War. Pluggy himself had attended the governor's peace council, only to return home and find "his blood relations lieing dead": victims of a Virginian surprise attack. Believing he "Could not depend on the faith of a treaty at all," Pluggy repeatedly taunted and threatened congressional emissaries and warned Indians to distrust colonial promises. Colonists themselves sometimes corroborated his warnings. In a meeting with Indians along the Ohio, Virginians boasted that they would soon cross the river to seize Indian land. In another encounter a former captive, after asking after his adoptive Shawnee mother, similarly warned of an imminent invasion. When such threats proved unpersuasive, Pluggy and his allies turned to exaggeration, deception, and subterfuge. After the Edwards murder, messengers hurried to tell the Pekowi and Chillicothe Shawnees that "the Windots had struck" the colonists, recasting an isolated murder as a national declaration of war. But they urged the Pekowis and Chillicothes to keep Cornstalk's Mekoche Shawnees in the dark. A few weeks later, militant Mohawks, Wyandots, and Odawas warned the Shawnees—again circumventing the Mekoche—of another impending invasion. But the Virginians remained south of the Ohio, and Pluggy's warnings won him few supporters. The militants' activities alarmed their neighbors: Mekoche Shawnee women repeatedly warned American emissaries that the Pekowis and Chillicothes wanted war. But until the end of 1775, none followed Snip's deadly example.[34]

To make a more compelling case for war, Pluggy and his allies looked to the British to endorse their cause, but they found little encouragement. British officials had suggested recruiting Indian allies since the outbreak of hostilities, but Guy Carleton, the governor of Quebec, instructed his subordinates merely to befriend the Great Lakes nations, so that the Crown could count on their aid in the future. At Detroit, Lieutenant Governor Henry Hamilton lavished gifts on visiting Indians and avidly warned them against Virginian perfidy but stopped short of an open call to arms. He did urge Indians to spy on the rebels' movements, and he persuaded Wyandot allies to seize and hand over John Dodge, a Sandusky trader and congressional spy. Pluggy and his allies twisted such statements to bolster their cause. In one telling, Hamilton had promised "to suply them with Amunition & much More" if they went to war. But rather than encouraging open hostilities, Hamilton advised Indian nations to fight only if the Virginians sent an army across the Ohio.[35] Without more explicit British support, few in Ohio cared to undertake a war with their colonial neighbors.

In late December, Pluggy and his allies seized an opportunity to more forcefully press their case. While scouting around Boonesborough, a small party of militants found two colonists out hunting. They killed and scalped one, a man named McQuinney, and captured his companion. It was the first attack on the infant colony in months. They brought McQuinney's scalp back to Ohio, where they proudly presented it as a symbol of the war they wished to wage. But most Ohio Indians still responded coolly. At Sandusky, Wyandot leaders declared they would "have no hand in such proceedings." One revolutionary official dismissed the killers as "a few Insignificant Rascals." Hoping for a better response from the British, Pluggy and his allies hurried to Detroit. When Hamilton greeted them, they presented him with McQuinney's scalp, calling it "a little meat to make you some broth": an invitation to endorse their calls for war. Caught off guard, Hamilton fumbled the transaction. First he declined the scalp, explaining that he wished to avoid suggesting that "he had authorised them to take it." Then, second-guessing himself, he took the scalp, only to "return it instantly untill such time as all the other Nations met." If the nations went to war, Hamilton promised, he would accept the scalp then. Having confused everyone, he offered his guests "something to refresh themselves" and promised to see them again in a few days. He soon resumed his familiar refrain, advising Indians to spy on the colonists' movements but not to attack them.[36] Rather than either endorsing or censuring the militants' call for war, Hamilton hedged, hoping to keep their allegiance while dodging responsibility for their actions.

Thanks in part to Hamilton's waffling, the first half of 1776 brought almost no deadly intercultural violence. Early in spring, a group of Wyandots attacked three colonists near the Falls of the Ohio, killing a man named Willis Lee, wounding one of his companions, and plundering their camp. But the event apparently stemmed from a peaceful encounter gone bad: the Wyandots had met with Lee's employer, speculator Richard Henderson, just a few days before. According to two colonists, the killers were "justly irritated" by Henderson's behavior. They also declined to scalp the dead man, suggesting that they viewed the incident as a private quarrel rather than an act of war. The episode could have triggered further violence, but did not. Lee's friends reportedly swore "Vengence against all Indians they should meet with," but they met with none and did not pursue the killers. Resulting rumors of war drove many Kentucky colonists eastward, but most returned after learning that "the greatest part of the news [was] false." For over two months after Lee's death, colonists reported no new attacks. Meanwhile, at Sandusky, diplomats from several Ohio nations resolved again to remain at peace "even though one or two foolish young men may do what is wrong."[37] The incident amplified intercultural resentment, and heightened fears of bloodshed, but led to no further hostilities.

Finding little support around Ohio and the Great Lakes, Pluggy and his allies looked in another direction. In early 1776, militant Haudenosaunee, Shawnee, and Odawa women designed massive wampum belts—one measured nine feet long—to call other nations to war. That spring, fourteen men carried the belts south, taking a long detour to avoid Kentucky colonists. After seventy days they reached the Cherokee town of Chota, where they called the entire nation to council. When all had gathered, the northerners appeared, their faces painted black, and recited a litany of colonial offenses. A Mohawk speaker declared that the Virginians "had without any provocation come into one of their Towns and murdered their people" and added that they had dunked British agent Guy Johnson "into a Hogshead of Boiling Tar." An Odawa called on all Indian nations to unite against "their common Enemies." Finally, a Shawnee complained that Virginia had "unjustly brought war upon their Nation" and filled Kentucky "with Forts and Armed Men." Declaring they would rather "die like Men than to dwindle away by inches," the speakers urged war, noting that with victory the Cherokees "might Hope to Enlarge their Bounds." The speeches were full of falsehoods and exaggerations—Guy Johnson, for example, had spent the previous six months safely in London—but they resonated with the Cherokees' own frustrations and fears. The young Cherokee commander Dragging Canoe took up the massive Shawnee war belt, accepting their call to arms. "[A]lmost all the young Warriors" from across the Cherokee nation followed suit. Older leaders who had previously urged peace now kept silent, perhaps acquiescing to a war that seemed inevitable. Soon thereafter, Cherokee warriors attacked a party of revolutionary militia. By mid-July as many as two thousand Cherokees had set out for war.[38] Nonetheless, within a few months Virginians and Carolinians had repulsed their attacks and destroyed Cherokee towns in retaliation.

The delegation from Ohio, meanwhile, turned for home, this time traveling directly through Kentucky. Inspired by the Cherokees, they split up to attack nearby colonists. Some of the group killed two men in separate attacks near Licking River. They brought their victims' scalps back to Ohio, just as they had done with McQuinney's six months before, hoping this time for a better reaction. Meanwhile, five of their companions staked out Boonesborough, where they found three teenaged girls paddling a canoe down the river. The warriors seized the girls and headed for the Ohio, dragging them through the woods for two days. Then, as they rested near salt springs called Blue Licks, a band of colonists led by Daniel Boone slipped up to their camp and opened fire. Two of the captors fell, mortally wounded. The other three fled, leaving the girls unharmed. But despite this dramatic rescue, the raids sparked widespread terror. In May, the Boonesborough colonist John Floyd had seen little reason to fear Indians; by late July he worried that "the greater part of the people may fall a prey to them." But Pluggy and his allies still struggled to find support. On learning that two Shawnee warriors had died at Blue Licks, Cornstalk quickly blamed the bloodshed on Pluggy's militants, rather than Boone's rescue party. Near Pittsburgh, Indians killed and scalped a man named Crawford, prompting "much uneasiness" and "frequent quarrels," but no further violence resulted, and the killers left Crawford's wife and children unharmed. Most Wyandot men spent the summer out hunting; a congressional messenger reported that they seemed "not to have aney notion of war."[39]

The contrast between the Cherokees and Ohio Indians reflected dissimilar access to British resources. As one British agent noted, the Cherokees were "so hemmed in" by colonists that they could not go to war "with any Safety untill they [we]re well supplied." Well aware of this problem, the northern militants assured Cherokees that Canada had "supplied them plentifully with Ammunition Arms & provisions." But the view from Ohio was murkier. British officers gave them gunpowder at Niagara and Detroit, but the revolutionary crisis weakened imperial credibility. Traders who had formerly mediated between Ohio Indians and the Crown either embraced the rebel cause or faded from view. Hamilton harassed rebel sympathizers but wielded scant influence south of Lake Erie. Meanwhile, Ohio Indians hosted Virginian and congressional representatives throughout 1775 and 1776. By contrast, the British agent Alexander Cameron remained in Cherokee country throughout; many nearby traders supported the royal cause as well. To obtain gifts of gunpowder, Ohio Indians had to make their way to Detroit, but Cameron kept the Cherokees supplied in their own towns. In April, British agents brought the Cherokees "21 Horse load of Ammunition" and assured them that an additional "100 Horse load" would soon follow. These shipments lent credibility to the northerners' promises of material support.

Like Hamilton, Cameron urged his Indian allies to remain at peace, but they felt confident that he and his British sponsors would continue to "furnish their whole nation with goods and ammunition." Not surprisingly, when Cherokees accepted the northerners' war belt, they insisted they went to fight "the Kings Enemies."[40]

In early September, Hamilton—perhaps inadvertently—bolstered the militants' calls for war. The flamboyant lieutenant governor likely chafed against his orders not to encourage attacks. In July, he had warned a congressional agent that his Indian allies were "ready at a Word to fall on the Frontier Settlements." The Indian agent Jehu Hay, a former army officer who had married into a Detroit merchant family, mediated and likely moderated Hamilton's dealings with western nations. But in early August, Hay left Detroit for several months, leaving his impulsive superior to his own devices. A few weeks later, White Eyes and a congressional envoy, William Wilson, came to Detroit to invite the Great Lakes nations to an upcoming Pittsburgh treaty. At the Wyandot town just upstream from the British fort, assembled leaders accepted Wilson's wampum belt and promised to "use all their influence . . . to preserve peace." The next day, Wilson repeated his speech in front of Hamilton and large Odawa, Ojibwe, Shawnee, and Haudenosaunee delegations. After an array of interpreters finished translating his words, Wilson presented the wampum belt to a Wyandot leader, who handed it to Hamilton. The British commander then denounced Wilson's superiors as "enemies and traitors to my King" and declared that "before I would take one of them by the hand, I would suffer my right hand to be cut off." He "tore the speech and cut the belt to pieces, and contemptuously strewed it about," and ordered White Eyes and Wilson to leave town immediately.[41]

Hamilton's performance made an impression. In the symbolic language of Great Lakes diplomacy, his destruction of Wilson's wampum signaled contempt for both his message and the Congress that sent it. As they made their way back to their towns, Pluggy and his allies recounted his speeches in ever more inflammatory terms. Even before the confrontation with Wilson, militants claimed that Hamilton advised them to "Stick their tomohawk" into the heads of any colonists they met, then "Cut of[f] Sum of the hair and Bring it to him." Hamilton may have said such things, or not, but he offered ample reason to think he approved. Above all, Hamilton gave each of his visitors from Pluggy's Town—militants who had been promoting war for months— ten pieces of lead shot and half a pint of gunpowder. In his presence, Dunquat, who had formerly condemned the attacks on Edwards and McQuinney, now sang a "War Song intimating that he would strike the White People." Three of his companions did the same. Hamilton's counterparts at Niagara offered similar gifts, prompting several Seneca leaders to echo Dunquat's song. Hamilton still discouraged Indians from attacking "defenceless Women & Children," insisting that they should fight only rebels who came "armed into the Indian Country," but like Cameron's distribution of gunpowder, his actions spoke louder than his words.[42]

In the weeks that followed, an emboldened militant coalition carried out a wave of attacks on Ohio Valley colonists. In September, a Delaware and Haudenosaunee reportedly killed two colonists near the mouth of the Tennessee River; other militants captured Ohio traders with rebel sympathies. By mid-October five different Wyandot and Haudenosaunee war parties had crossed the Ohio. On 9 October they killed two women and captured a boy near the mouth of Fish Creek. Eighty miles downriver, another band killed two men and wounded three more. A few weeks later, raiders killed two more men at the mouth of Grave Creek. Back in Ohio, militants increasingly harassed the Moravian missionaries. Hamilton, meanwhile, acknowledged that "several small parties" were attacking colonists but did nothing to discourage them, reasoning that the Virginians' "arrogance, disloyalty, and imprudence" had "justly drawn" this fate upon them. Thanks to his tacit encouragement, the sporadic killings of previous months now escalated into something like a coordinated campaign.[43]

Even so, Indian support for war remained limited. News of the Cherokee towns' destruction reinforced the belief that a war for Kentucky could succeed only with active British allies. Leaders like Guyasuta, White Eyes, and Cornstalk continued to speak out for peace. Wyandot leaders declared that of their nation, only Dunquat's clan favored war. Dunquat himself, despite his performance at Hamilton's council, continued to equivocate. In November, he sent ten men "to scout against the Virginians" but insisted that they would "go on slow & hunt by the way." He applauded the Delaware for their neutrality and insisted that he undertook his scouting expedition "only to oblige" the militants. In mid-November, Dunquat and other militant sympathizers put Hamilton's promises to the test, warning that a Virginian army had invaded Ohio, but the lieutenant governor still balked at endorsing war. He and the recently returned Hay repeated the familiar refrain—watch and wait—and handed out ammunition. Hamilton was rightly skeptical: once again, no invading army appeared. But this time Hamilton's dance earned him jeers and protests. Dunquat's Sandusky Wyandots insisted that he had previously endorsed war by desecrating Congress's wampum belt. When Hamilton simultaneously called for restraint, they had concluded that he was merely "joking with them." Frustrated with his apparent duplicity, they now berated him for "always inciting them to go to war against the White people, while he sat quietly and did not do anything." If he continued his double talk, they warned, "they would trample all of his Speeches under their feet" and "declare friendship with the Colonies."[44]

The Wyandots' friends and neighbors, the Muskingum Valley Delaware, were well ahead of them. In the summer of 1776, the Delaware council strengthened their friendship with the rebels, who had recently declared their colonies "free and independent states." The council pledged to help "preserv[e] the peace of this Conterey" and asked Congress to send them a secretary to handle their correspondence. White Eyes also requested help to build "a strong Place where we may be protected," including "Houses & a Fort." When Detroit traders bought large herds of Ohio Indians' cattle to feed the British garrison, the council seized the animals and sent them to Pittsburgh instead. When congressional envoy William Wilson set out to invite western nations to a new treaty council, White Eyes—together with other Delawares, Shawnees, and Wyandots—personally accompanied him all the way to Detroit. There, Hamilton's diatribe offended the Delaware diplomat, who insisted he had done nothing to warrant such abuse. Both he and Cornstalk, who witnessed the same performance, soon recommitted to their friendship with the rebels Hamilton despised.[45]

In October 1776, at a major council at Pittsburgh, congressional and Ohio Indian emissaries set about redefining their peoples' relations with one another. Revolutionary spokesmen announced that by declaring independence, the king's erstwhile subjects had become Americans and thus kin to their native neighbors. "[T]ho' you are Red, & we White," the commissioners reasoned, "yet we are all Children of the same Big Island. . . . We are the same people tho' of different Complexions, & our Enemies are the Same." They urged their Shawnee, Delaware, Mohican, and Haudenosaunee guests to remain neutral in the ongoing war for independence but promised to help if the British attacked them. Above all, they repeatedly denied that the states harbored "ill designs against you" or "covet[ed] your Lands." Indians' remaining territory "shall not be touched or intruded on," they pledged, "while the Sun shines, or the Rivers run." These assurances carefully addressed many Ohio Indians' leading concerns: physical security, respect for territory, and the promise of kinship between colonial and indigenous nations. But with the message of goodwill came a threat: if frontier violence escalated, they warned, America's "young Men . . . [would] seek for revenge for their slaughtered Kinsmen."[46]

White Eyes responded with an ambitious vision of his own, laying a new foundation for Ohio Indian sovereignty. Just like the United States, he announced, Delawares, Shawnees, and Mohicans had formed a new union. Speaking for this collective entity, he embraced the Americans' friendship as one confederation to another. He also challenged familiar depictions of his own nation's gender identity. For most of the preceding century, Six Nations spokesmen—and sometimes Delawares themselves—had called the Delaware a "nation of women." This term was not pejorative in origin: White Eyes suggested that his people's figurative womanhood had once made them "Head Counsellors in all Treaties." But by the second half of the eighteenth century Haudenosaunee speakers maintained that they had "cut off [the] legs" of the rhetorically female Delaware, leaving them with no political identity or territory of their own: an image that closely mirrored the English law of coverture. The Delaware's familiar claim to their land—that the Wyandot had recently gifted it to them—reflected this presumption of historic Delaware landlessness. White Eyes now jettisoned this argument, declaring instead that the Delaware and Shawnee had won their lands by conquering "the Nation Dallagai" perhaps a century before. This new narrative of Delaware sovereignty, rooted in a tale of ancient conquest, echoed the Six Nations' own claims to supremacy. It suggested a more aggressive, even militaristic identity, probably to impress the patriarchal colonists. But while asserting this new national virility, White Eyes also claimed his nation's traditionally female authority over decision making. "Brothers," he declared, "I am no Woman, neither are my Legs cut off: but as a Woman I stand firm ready to support our Friendship."[47]

With this dramatic announcement, White Eyes responded creatively to the opportunities of revolutionary crisis. Generations of Delawares had endured repeated displacement, thanks to Six Nations land sales and colonial disregard for their rights. For years, Ohio Indians had struggled to build a new western confederacy to counterbalance the league in colonial diplomacy. Now the split between colonists and Britain raised the possibility of a new political settlement that might address these long-standing grievances. White Eyes's story of ancient conquest, his description of the new confederacy, and his ambiguous redefinition of Delaware womanhood all aimed to make that vision a reality. To the Six Nations, he declared political and territorial independence (some Haudenosaunees later threatened to "punish and humiliate" his nation for his impertinence).[48] To the Americans, whose friendship he had cultivated for years, he more forcefully reiterated the Delawares' long-standing territorial claims, while also stressing their desirability as allies. And for his fellow Delawares, he envisioned a future that both honored their heritage as womanly counselors and embraced a new identity as a politically sovereign nation, fully recognized by their Anglo-American neighbors.

Many Indians at the treaty had little use for these proposals. As on previous occasions, the Allegheny Seneca Guyasuta defended the supremacy of the Six Nations league and the boundaries it had negotiated with the British empire. But despite their differences, both White Eyes and Guyasuta used the revolutionary crisis to defend national sovereignty. Above all, they aimed to secure their remaining territory from colonization. Round Face, another Seneca who spoke on behalf of warriors and women, berated the commissioners for allowing surveys on a nearby island. "You know the Boundary," he scolded.[49] Delaware and Shawnee speakers, while disputing Six Nations supremacy, echoed this emphasis on enforcing established borders. Familiar chains of patronage had collapsed, but Congress's need for allies offered the chance to cultivate new ones. Guyasuta aimed to restore the old covenant chain partnership, while White Eyes and Cornstalk sought a new union of confederations, but all sought some means of cementing sovereignty within the coming postrevolutionary order.

This desire to exploit the imperial crisis also transcended divisions between moderates and militants. White Eyes and Cornstalk may have championed diplomacy in part for spiritual reasons—both men had ties to the pacifist Moravians—but their strategy reflected above all a pragmatic assessment of political opportunity. Similarly, Pluggy and his allies sought to exploit Britain's war effort to halt colonial expansion. Militants drew on a tradition of nativist spirituality, but their case hinged on the expectation of a British alliance.[50] Both moderates and militants sought first and foremost to secure their nations' territories against the colonial invasion already sweeping over Kentucky. They recognized that they could do so only by forging a lasting relationship with an Anglo-American state, even as that state shattered and reassembled itself in the throes of revolution. In the bloody years to come, these parallel strategies facilitated mutual support and peacemaking among Ohio Indians, while undercutting British and congressional attempts to control their nominal allies.

By late 1776, the peoples of the Ohio Valley had ample reason to fear war. Though still sporadic, Indian attacks on colonists were becoming more frequent. The organization of militia in frontier counties raised the possibility of large-scale retaliation. In Ohio, rumors of Virginian invasion grew ever more alarming, thanks to the heated rhetoric of congressional envoys and the rebuilding of forts along the Ohio River. Indian diplomats had promised to punish those who broke the peace, but they worried that colonial strikes against Pluggy and his supporters would threaten their own communities as well.

Even so, as 1776 came to a close Ohio Indian militancy appeared to be waning. Just a few months after Dunquat sang his war song at Detroit, his wife spent Christmas at a newly established Moravian mission, where she showed a keen interest in the differences between the German pietists and the French priests who taught her own people at Detroit. She brought along trader Alexander McCormick, a rebel sympathizer whom Wyandot militants had captured a few months before. Rather than handing McCormick to Hamilton, she had adopted him as her brother and now returned him to his Delaware wife at Assünnünk, where he soon became one of Congress's more useful western informants. The visit convinced even the missionary David Zeisberger—who seldom gave non-Moravian Indians the benefit of any doubt—that the Wyandot and Odawa were now "almost inclin'd to lay down the Hatchet & to live in friendship with the Americans." The following spring, two Moravian Indian leaders visited Sandusky to promote an upcoming treaty council with the United States. They reported back that the Wyandots "received them well, were willing to listen to them, and [we]re inclined to accept peace."[51]

As Wyandots and Moravians celebrated Christmas, several midwinter war parties crossed the Ohio to attack Kentucky colonists. Pluggy and his allies had no qualms about Hamilton's contradictory messages, taking instruction instead from his gifts of gunpowder. On the Kanawha, a Shawnee band killed three colonists and took one prisoner; they carried out more such attacks in the weeks that followed. By March, their numbers reportedly exceeded sixty. Paying no heed to formal leaders like Cornstalk, they declared themselves "free men that had no King nor Chief," confident that "Detroit would provide them with Ammunition." But such freedom came at a price. Pluggy's party killed four men on Licking River, then moved on to a walled outpost called McClelland's Station. With too few men to storm the fort, and no heavy guns to topple its wooden walls, they soon retreated. Pluggy himself fell during the assault, having fatally overestimated his men's military capability.[52] However much terror they caused, and however much gunpowder Hamilton gave them, the militants still lacked the numbers and resources to overcome even a makeshift stockade.

Meanwhile, Cornstalk and a younger Shawnee man visited Point Pleasant with messages for the Virginian garrison of a newly built fort. The Shawnees camped across the Ohio; on 29 November a Wyandot man joined them. The next day, they conferred as best they could with the Virginian commander Matthew Arbuckle, despite knowing little of one another's languages. Soon afterward Haudenosaunee warriors seized one of Arbuckle's men and escaped into the woods. In retaliation, the Virginians set out to seize the Wyandot stranger. Cornstalk, afraid for his guest's life, tried to hide the man, but the Virginians found him and imprisoned him in the chilly fort. Three weeks later, a group of Indians appeared with the captured militiaman in tow. Somehow, Cornstalk and the prisoner's Wyandot kin had found the young Virginian and persuaded his captors to hand him over. Placated, Arbuckle released his own hostage in exchange. No one died.[53]

These dissimilar encounters, characterized by misunderstanding, distrust, and the near-constant threat of violence, exemplified the early years of revolution in the Ohio Valley. For a year and a half after Dunmore's War, intercultural violence largely ceased. It resumed with Pluggy's raids in 1776, but on a much smaller scale. The collapse of state authority deterred Indians and colonists from waging war. Arbuckle's small garrison was short on food, gunpowder, and blankets; Cornstalk's Shawnees keenly remembered the invasion of 1774; and Pluggy's raiders struggled against even rudimentary colonial defenses. Meanwhile, imperial crisis fostered political and diplomatic creativity. Both Indians and colonists labored to shape a new political order, often by cultivating new coalition partners. Virginians and Pennsylvanians, loyalists and rebels, all sought Indians' friendship. Both the militant Pluggy and the more moderate Dunquat pressed Hamilton for support, recognizing that their political and military prospects hinged on British backing. White Eyes and Cornstalk, meanwhile, sought new patrons in the emerging revolutionary regime. Distrust and hatred remained, but political expediency prevailed. Instead of fostering chaos, state failure had brought relative peace.

CHAPTER 4

Reluctance, 1777–79

In early August 1777, Dunquat, the Half-King of the Sandusky Wyandots, took a detour off the road to war. He had set out with two hundred warriors to attack Virginian forts on the Ohio, but he stopped en route to visit the resolutely neutral Muskingum Valley Delaware. Dunquat, while proudly calling himself "a man of war," praised their neutrality as well as the pacifism of the neighboring Moravian mission of Lichtenau. More remarkably, the Wyandot embraced the missionary David Zeisberger as a "father," pledged to treat him "as my own body," and promised to protect the Moravians against other Indians. For the following two weeks, the Delawares listened to Dunquat's doubts about the war he had set out to fight. Just a few months before he had been "inclined to accept peace." He now went to fight only "as a favor" to Henry Hamilton, the British commander at Detroit. He repeatedly postponed his army's departure, declared he did not plan "to do much harm," and hoped the troublesome conflict would end soon. He berated impatient allies for wanting "to go kill innocent women and children," and he refused to let them leave without him. The constant arguing convinced Zeisberger that "they had not yet decided for sure what they would do." Then Delaware messengers reported the approach of a large army from Fort Pitt. The news proved false, but the specter of invasion brought debate to a halt. Dunquat attacked Wheeling and killed fifteen men but, to his surprise, found the garrison well prepared. He retreated to Goschachgünk with his wounded, where he declared he was "happy to see" Zeisberger again. At the time, he did not know that his new "father" had almost certainly warned the Virginians of his plans.[1]

This half-hearted campaign began the Revolutionary War in the Ohio Valley. In his landmark history of the region, Richard White dubs this struggle "a contest of villagers": independent Indians and colonists with only loose ties to British and revolutionary armies.[2] This interpretation contains some truth: time and again fighting men chose to kill, or not, with scant regard for the orders of government-appointed commanders. Like Dunquat at Lichtenau, Ohio Valley inhabitants mobilized haltingly, foiling attempts to launch major campaigns. In consequence, those who went to war usually targeted noncombatants. British-allied Indians assailed colonial homesteads and stockades, while revolutionary expeditions torched Indian towns and murdered Indian prisoners and allies. But however much gentlemen officers wrung their hands, their allies' brutality hinged on the gunpowder, provisions, and coordination that their governments provided. Indian-hating militiamen ignored orders routinely, but, when deprived of government support, their companies collapsed and colonists fled in droves. Indian war parties acted more independently, but their coalition's strength nonetheless hinged on British backing.

Rather than a determined struggle of Indians and colonists eager to shed each other's blood, the war of the late 1770s exuded uncertainty, hesitation, and failure. Its intermittent ferocity resulted less from intercultural hatred than from British and revolutionary governments' determination to control the Ohio Valley. In 1775, imperial collapse had left the region's peoples to fend for themselves, yielding relative peace. Shortages of food and ammunition, as well as the memories of Dunmore's War, deterred all but the most militant from renewing hostilities. Then, beginning in 1777, British and revolutionary officials funneled resources into the region, each hoping to build a western bulwark against the other. This material support only partially and erratically addressed local needs, but it helped win over pragmatists and undercut peacemakers, tipping the political balance toward militancy.

Yet even as bloodshed escalated, opportunities remained to slow or even halt the killing. The Wyandot, central players in the British Great Lakes alliance, repeatedly offered to make peace with the United States. The Delaware of Goschachgünk and Lichtenau acted as intermediaries, even as both the British and Americans pressured them to go to war. This Wyandot-Delaware collaboration reflected shared goals: protection for people and crops, state recognition of territorial sovereignty, and peace with their Indian neighbors. The two nations cultivated warring state patrons, but they simultaneously held to an older and deeper friendship with one another. By 1780, their bids for peace had failed, in large part because of the arrogance and ineptitude of American commanders.

*   *   *

On 18 June 1777, about six weeks before Dunquat's visit to Lichtenau, Henry Hamilton shed his usual garments and donned something resembling the garb of a Great Lakes Indian warrior. He painted his face and torso and picked up a large belt of wampum beads, colored red to represent blood. Thus adorned, he and his officers walked to the council house, stood before a large assembly of western Indians, and gave their best impression of a traditional "War Song." This singular performance had dramatic implications. For the first time since the beginning of the Revolutionary War, a British commander had openly asked Great Lakes Indians to wage war against the American rebels. The audience joined in the singing, accepting the call to arms, though some, like Dunquat, did so half-heartedly. After the council, Hamilton rewarded his new allies with weaponry, laying a strong foundation for the new military alliance.[3]

Some in the audience were fighting already, with Hamilton's tacit encouragement. For the past year and a half, Hamilton's orders had barred him from calling Indians to war, but he had regularly offered militants gunpowder while publicly deriding his king's enemies. By late 1776 small bands of Ohio Indians had begun attacking colonial outposts in Kentucky, reasoning correctly that Hamilton would continue to supply them with gunpowder. By March 1777, sixty-four Shawnees had reportedly gone to war, together with perhaps a few dozen Haudenosaunees and Wyandots. Through the spring they repeatedly attacked Ohio Valley colonists from Grave Creek to Harrodsburg, killing about fifteen, capturing a woman and seven children, burning houses, and slaughtering livestock. A Shawnee community condemned one captive militiaman to death by ritual burning. But even as these horrors mounted, they remained limited in scale. Warriors attacked in parties of a few dozen at most; by contrast, perhaps eight hundred Shawnees had fought at the 1774 Battle of Point Pleasant. Some Ohio Indian towns supported the attacks, but others opposed them. Equally important, the Anishinaabeg to the north, and the Miami and other Wabash nations to the west, stayed out of the fighting.[4]

Then British Secretary of State George Germain ordered Hamilton to raise parties of western Indians to "excit[e] an alarm upon the frontiers of Virginia and Pennsylvania." With these orders, and the resulting "War Song," the shape and scale of fighting changed dramatically. The call to arms won over moderates like Dunquat and expanded the militant coalition to include the Anishinaabeg and Wabash nations as well. In the months that followed, hundreds went to war and returned carrying scalps and captives. In just two summer days, warriors killed and scalped a woman and her child on the upper Monongahela, captured a family of seven near Raccoon Creek, and killed a militia sergeant and captured two young men on the Ohio River. At Kittanning, on the Allegheny, an Ojibwe war party ambushed a group of militia, killing three. Nearly three hundred miles to the south, on the Greenbrier River in southwest Virginia, another group killed three men, wounded another, and captured one woman. Dunquat failed to capture Wheeling, but a few weeks later his Wyandots ambushed forty-six militia downstream from the fort. Fewer than half the Virginians escaped alive. By early 1778, warriors supplied at Detroit had captured 73 prisoners and taken 129 scalps. In the fall of 1778, more than four hundred Shawnee warriors set out against Kentucky; one report estimated that eight hundred to one thousand warriors were attacking frontier Virginia and Pennsylvania.[5]

But if those warriors took up arms at Hamilton's urging, they fought on their own terms and for their own reasons. In many respects, they held to long-standing patterns of Great Lakes warfare, favoring ambushes that minimized their own casualties and enabled them to take captives, especially women and children, to be adopted into their communities. They wreaked havoc on isolated homesteads and unwary militia patrols, but usually failed to overcome stockade defenses. Resentment of colonial expansion motivated many, especially those who had gone to war before Hamilton's song, but political and economic calculations contributed as well. Great Lakes Indians depended heavily on access to trade that the British controlled. Hamilton's offer of food, blankets, gunpowder, and other supplies served important needs that could not be met otherwise. The call to arms also brought diplomatic opportunities. Dunquat's Wyandots in particular aimed to secure British recognition of their boundaries, including territory they hoped to decolonize, insisting that "what Lands they should drive the Rebels from should be vested in them as by right of conquest."[6]

In early 1778, Daniel Boone led twenty-eight men to a salt spring called Blue Licks. The people of Boonesborough desperately needed salt to preserve meat, their primary food source until the following year's harvest. As the men boiled down the brine at their kettles, Boone went out to check his beaver traps. He ran into about one hundred Shawnee warriors, marching on the town that bore his name. Eighteen months before, near the same spot, he had recaptured his daughter and two other girls from a handful of Shawnees and

Cherokees. Now the tables had turned, thanks to British support. The colonization of Kentucky offended Shawnees no less in 1776 than in 1778, but imperial backing persuaded a critical mass to endorse a war to defend their land—including the land on which Boonesborough now stood. Boone saved his town by persuading his woefully outnumbered saltmakers to surrender and pledging that the rest of the community would follow suit in the spring. When the prisoners reached Chillicothe, Shawnee families adopted many of the men. At least one, Joseph Jackson, lived with them for over twenty years, seemingly content. Others, including Boone, later escaped and returned to Kentucky, where the people of Boonesborough flatly refused the Shawnees' terms.[7] This failed attempt at compromise gave Shawnees all the more reason to embrace the British alliance.

British support and encouragement had spurred this escalation of violence, but British officers largely failed to dictate its nature and scope. Germain asked Hamilton to protect loyalists from attack, but he placed a greater priority on "crushing the Rebellion," using "every means . . . that Providence has put into His Majesty's Hands." Accordingly, although Hamilton promised safe passage and sanctuary to the King's "faithfull & loyal Subjects," his allies' indiscriminate attacks gave colonists little reason to trust him. On one occasion, British-allied warriors left his proclamation alongside the charred remains of a burnt homestead, whose occupants they had taken as captives. Indians complied with British calls for restraint only as far as they coincided with their own priorities. Rather than handing over prisoners as Hamilton asked, his allies preferred to adopt them. Of seventy-three taken in 1777, only twenty reached British hands. Of the nearly thirty saltmakers captured with Boone, Shawnees delivered only four to Detroit. To Indian families, ransoming an adopted captive amounted to selling a blood relative. In 1778, Indians captured an upper Ohio colonist named Peggy West and her two daughters. A year later, one of the daughters reached Detroit, where the British commandant and his wife took her in. They attempted to track down her mother and sister, whom Delaware families had adopted, but their fate is unclear.[8]

Hamilton's war dance formed a coalition uniting British patrons who wanted Indians to wage war, and Indians who wanted to gain supplies and reclaim lost territory. The British got the war they wanted, spreading terror across the Ohio Valley, but driving colonists from Kentucky proved more difficult. As the fighting dragged on, British-allied Indians began to question their choice of patron. Fortunately for the British, colonists' atrocities against Indians seemed to leave little room for doubt.

A few weeks after Boone's men set out to make salt, the Delaware elder Micheykapeecci and her family left home to make sugar. They traveled to an old town site about fifty miles north of Pittsburgh, where they planned to collect maple sap, boil it down, and pack the sweet residue for the year ahead. Days of heavy rain slowed their progress. Then, without warning, they heard a burst of gunfire and saw several hundred white men descending on their camp. Micheykapeecci's son, the only man in the group, fired his gun once, wounding an attacker, before he himself was shot. As he fell, one of the white men ran up and "sunk [a] tomahawk in his head." An old woman met the same fate. The dying man's wife and children escaped into the woods. As Micheykapeecci tried to follow, a gunshot tore off the end of her little finger. Then one of the white men grabbed her. Later, she told the interpreter Simon Girty that a Munsee Delaware group was camped at a nearby salt spring. Girty and a group of the white men found them, killed three more women and a boy, and took a fourth woman captive. Micheykapeecci and the Munsee woman traveled to Pittsburgh as prisoners but were soon released. The American commander expressed regret for his men's "Savage Conduct," but kept the precious kettles and other plunder.[9]

Much like the capture of Boone's saltmakers, the attack on Micheykapeecci's family displayed a scale of mobilization the Ohio Valley had not seen since Dunmore's War. It also heralded a wave of similar attacks on neutral and allied Indians. Most accounts attribute these atrocities to "Indian haters" whom "American officials could not control." The categorical bloodlust of Ohio Valley colonists, in this view, overwhelmed the pragmatic diplomacy of Congress and the Continental Army.[10] Many colonists, to be sure, wanted Indians dead, but the distinction between enlightened officialdom and hateful killers obscures the real roots of escalation. However much congressional agents and army officers opposed such atrocities in principle, they themselves had made them possible. Emerging revolutionary governments procured the money, food, and ammunition necessary to mobilize colonists to fight Indians. Like their British counterparts, revolutionary officials repeatedly failed to direct or control the violence they enabled. Militia recalcitrance stymied both basic defensive measures and grandiose plans to capture Detroit and Niagara. Nonetheless, by organizing, arming, and deploying hundreds of colonial militia, revolutionary governments enabled Indian haters to kill.

A year before the assault on Micheykapeecci's camp, the congressional Indian agent George Morgan reported that upper Ohio colonists were eager to wage war on Indians. They had plotted "to massacre our known Friends at their hunting Camps" and threatened visiting Indian diplomats, whom Morgan lodged "in my own Chamber for their Security." Some, he alleged, longed to fight Indians "on account of the[ir] fine Lands." This hostility, he warned, could lead to a large-scale conflict that the embattled revolutionary movement could not win. The United States could have abandoned Indian haters to kill, or be killed, on their own. But ignoring the Ohio Valley jarred with the ambitions of American land speculators, Morgan included. Congress could tighten its grasp on the region only with the help of colonists on the ground, and the prospect of war threatened to send them packing. "If the Inhabitants once get alarmed," one official warned, "there will be no Stopping of their Flight, & the Country will be soon depopulated." To avoid that calamity, congressional agents recommended stationing Continental troops in forts along the Ohio and giving the region's colonists gunpowder and shot. Of course, encouraging colonists to stay risked antagonizing Ohio Indians, many of whom still hoped to reverse the loss of Kentucky, but the agents believed they could appease native nations by "buying . . . their friendship" with gifts. Morgan similarly urged Congress to appoint "an Officer of Abilities," someone "cool & experienced" with "a liberal mind," to supervise frontier defense and diplomacy.[11] He trusted that rational and enlightened authority figures, backed with the requisite military force, could bring unruly westerners to heel.

The state-appointed commanders of the new county militias sympathized with Morgan's desire for order. Pennsylvania entrusted Westmoreland County's defenses first to William Lochry, a longtime magistrate and prominent pro-Pennsylvania partisan, and then to his brother Archibald. Dorsey Pentecost, a prominent landowner and erstwhile Pennsylvania official, now acquired an array of appointments under Virginia, including command of Yohogania County's militia. Ohio County's David Shepherd, another veteran of the local courts, belonged to a family of Virginia merchants who supplied the militia garrisons he commanded. These men varied considerably in background and education, and backed opposing factions in the still rancorous boundary dispute, but they shared a desire to cement their positions in the upper Ohio Valley's emerging political and economic elite. They could do so only with the friendship and patronage of eastern officials.[12]

State authority also proved critical to militia effectiveness. In the first half of 1777, revolutionary governments established the legal framework for county militias, stipulating that on-duty militia receive the same wages as regular troops and empowering officers to fine delinquents. Across the upper Ohio Valley, commanders used this system to garrison a string of small forts at key river crossings. Even in remote Kentucky, Virginia officials organized a formal county militia. Virginia governor Patrick Henry dispatched ammunition, authorized powder magazines, and ordered local militia officers to keep their men's "arms and accoutrements . . . in the best possible order." In April, General Edward Hand of the Continental Army arrived at Fort Pitt with a small force of regulars. In a series of meetings, Hand and local militia officers implemented defensive measures and began planning a campaign across the Ohio against British-allied Indians.[13]

Morgan and others hoped these measures would preserve order, but instead they fueled more violence. Sending large bodies of armed and untrained men to distant corners of the region made attacks on neutral and allied Indians all the more likely. Actual violence corresponded with the scale of mobilization. When militia companies merely occupied small forts and maintained defensive patrols, attacks on Indians remained sporadic and opportunistic. In June, a band of white people—likely a Westmoreland militia patrol—killed several Senecas returning home from a Pittsburgh council. Another group of Indians quickly retaliated, killing two or three of the attackers. In late July, when Indians killed a militia sergeant on the Ohio, the victim's companions threatened two Delaware messengers who happened to pass nearby. John Gibson, a veteran trader and interpreter turned army officer, saved the messengers' lives only "with the utmost Difficulty." But other Delaware messengers continued to pass back and forth without interference. Militia patrols occasionally found and skirmished with British-allied raiders, but they were too few, too scattered, and too disorganized even to defend their communities effectively, let alone carry out large-scale attacks.[14]

That changed in August, when General Hand called for two thousand men to march on British-allied Wyandot and Haudenosaunee towns. He asked each of the four upper Ohio counties to raise two hundred men to rendezvous at Fort Pitt. From there they would embark downriver to Point Pleasant, where hundreds of western Virginians would join them. The plan foundered almost immediately. Congress had recently ordered the county militias to send one third of their available men to the Continental Army, leaving commanders hard-pressed to raise more. In addition, they insisted on leaving some at home for local defense. Of the few men available, many objected to Hand's demand that they serve a six-month tour of duty. Others complained about delayed payments for prior militia service. With western counties so "considerably drain'd of men," officers had scant hope of recruiting the number that Hand required. Feeding the army proved another obstacle. The general argued that the state governments should bear the cost of provisions, but Virginia commissary William Aylett countered that Congress ought to pay. Caught in between, militia commanders raised supplies on their personal credit. Finding and paying for horses, oxen, and wagons presented still more difficulties. At least one militia company could not even supply its men with guns. By early November, only a few hundred militia had assembled at Fort Pitt. Hand abandoned his plans and assigned the men to defensive duty. He then headed downriver to make similar arrangements for the two-hundred-odd Virginians who had assembled at Point Pleasant, where food supplies were already running low.[15]

Meanwhile, Mekoche Shawnee leaders, anxious to keep Hand's army away from their towns, sent two messengers to Point Pleasant themselves. For more than two years, the fort there had repeatedly welcomed Shawnee diplomats. A recent attack, though, made the Virginian commander Matthew Arbuckle wary of the Shawnees' goodwill. Rather than reassuring the messengers of his friendship, Arbuckle "thought proper to detain" them. Perplexed, the veteran diplomat Cornstalk sent his son Elinipsico for an explanation. Arbuckle offered none, but he insisted on seeing Cornstalk and other Shawnee leaders as soon as possible. Cornstalk came alone. Arbuckle confined him with the others, explaining that he was "well satisfied the Shawanese are all our enemies." When the militia arrived for Hand's expedition, Cornstalk and the messengers remained as hostages. Shortly thereafter Elinipsico returned, concerned for his father's well-being, and joined him in captivity. The next day, the Shawnees heard a loud commotion outside the fort. The wife of the fort's interpreter, herself an adopted Shawnee, warned them that Indians had killed a militiaman named Gilmore, who had gone out hunting to feed the increasingly famished garrison. Gilmore's friends, who had arrived with him only a few days before, demanded vengeance. Arbuckle briefly defended his prisoners but backed down when the militia "cocked their guns [and] threatened [him] with instant death." Cornstalk met them at the door and took "seven or eight bullets" through his body. Elinipsico fell behind him. A third hostage attempted to escape through the chimney "but was shot down." The fourth "was shamefully mangled" and tortured before he died. Rather than taking action against the murderers, Arbuckle found witnesses to testify that "it was not in his power" to stop the slaughter. When Hand arrived a week later, he, too, concluded that "it would be vain for me to bring the perpetrators of this horrid act to justice." Instead he dismissed the assembled militia. The killers and their companions "returned home Shortly before Christmass."[16]

A few months later, a similar string of events led to the attack on Micheykapeecci's sugar camp. After returning to Fort Pitt, Hand learned that the British had stockpiled supplies on the Cuyahoga River. Eager for some kind of victory, he raised several hundred militia to seize the goods. They set out on the one-hundred-mile overland journey in the middle of February, a season when, Hand reasoned, Indians "might Suppose us to be inactive." The flaw in his plan became apparent when "heavy Rains . . . together with the Melting of the snow" rendered the rivers impassable. After turning back, the damp militiamen stumbled upon the tracks of Micheykapeecci's family. Scouts followed the tracks to a town large enough to house fifty to sixty people, but they failed to notice that only a handful were there at the time. Hand "conjectured they were Warriors coming into Our Settlements & proceeded to Attack them." On storming the town, they killed a man and a woman and captured Micheykapeecci. Hand then sent a detachment to the nearby Munsee camp, where they killed three more women and a boy.[17]

In attributing these murders to state weakness, historians echo Hand himself, who insisted he "could not prevent" his men's "Impetuous" brutality. Like Hamilton, his British counterpart, Hand sought to distance himself from the actions of men he had mobilized for war. Such excuses ring hollow. Hand's expedition fell through, in part, because too few colonists answered his call to arms. However readily some militia would "Murder a defenceless unsuspecting Indian," many refused to join his army at all. Hand himself ordered Cornstalk's murderers to Point Pleasant without enough food to support them, necessitating Gilmore's ill-fated hunt. He also ordered the attack on Micheykapeecci's camp. The general's abortive attempts to wage a more orderly war brought about the very kinds of atrocities he was supposed to prevent. And he accepted that outcome. His distaste for murder and his desire for Indian allies were overshadowed by the imperative to win the Ohio Valley for the United States. Hand tolerated the militia's "Savage Conduct" as a necessary evil, a price he willingly paid for their future services in battle.

These killers of defenseless women and children, he mused, "would Behave well if they had men to contend with."[18]

On that point, Hand was wrong. To be sure, Ohio Valley colonists were a hardy lot. Since arriving in the mid-1760s, those in the Monongahela country had fended off British soldiers, Pennsylvania magistrates, and Virginian speculators. They now enjoyed government support: local militia officers raised over one hundred men to guard small forts, and Hand supplied them with ample food and ammunition. Until late March 1778, the area seemed reasonably secure. But then Dunquat's Wyandots attacked three separate homesteads on Dunkard Creek, killing five colonists and capturing four. Panicked inhabitants fled, leaving their forts unguarded. Within days, they had "entirely evacuated" the surrounding area. In mid-April, on the upper Monongahela, a Haudenosaunee party killed three more and captured seven, then burned an abandoned fort just a few miles from the county magazine. The attackers met so little resistance that they took time to kill and skin the colonists' sheep. John Evans, the local militia commander, complained that "the forts [we]re all a Breaking" as families fled for safety. Evans soon followed, leaving the militia's precious provisions unguarded. The raiders promptly torched his stockade, destroying nine thousand pounds of salted pork. Elsewhere, news of the raids eviscerated local defenses and emptied hundreds of square miles of recently colonized territory. By mid-May, no one remained in northern Westmoreland County and its militia commander, Archibald Lochry, feared "a General Evacuation" of all frontier forts. In southwest Virginia, his counterpart William Preston reported that "the People below me are quite Cleared off," pulling back the frontier by at least thirty miles. Terrified colonists upstream begged Preston for protection, but they refused to help defend the homes of others. At Fort Pitt, a beleaguered General Hand warned that, without reinforcements, "this whole country will be abandoned or over-run by the enemy in a short time."[19]

Army officers blamed cowardice, faulting colonists for "constantly calling for reinforcements whilst [they] themselves run away." But the weakness of frontier defenses had more to do with social and material circumstances. A household's ability to defend itself hinged on the presence and resolve of a wider community acting together for the greater good. In a newly created landscape of scattered small farms, with churches, courts, and militias in their infancy, such collaboration proved a tall order. The militias' effectiveness depended on the widespread cooperation of men with minimal military training, most of whom had known one another for a few years at most. Neighbors huddled for safety in makeshift stockades, but doing so enabled attackers to strike their fields and livestock. In Kentucky, fear of attack prevented colonists from sowing crops. Hundreds of miles upriver, Indians burned Westmorelanders' "Houses, Barns and Grain." At Point Pleasant, Dunquat's forces killed nearly all of the garrison's 150 cattle, depriving the militia of their only nearby food source. Chronic lack of salt prevented colonists from preserving meat, and livestock that were left unslaughtered sometimes starved for lack of winter forage. Where cattle remained for sale, eastern merchants paid a premium to drive them across the mountains to the war-torn seaboard colonies.[20]

To solve these problems, colonists turned to the nascent revolutionary governments. At Fort Pitt, Hand fielded endless pleas for troops to protect stockades, mills, and fields. A southwest Virginia militia officer warned that his county could avoid ruin only with help from either "Congress or our own State." Alarmed by the retreating frontier, government officials tried to oblige. Virginia dispatched a militia company to guard far-off Boonesborough and bought food and ammunition "for the general use of the So. Western Frontier." A local militia commander sold colonists gunpowder from the county arsenal, explaining that they "could not be supplied elsewhere." On another occasion, the Fort Pitt garrison sent 1,500 pounds of army flour to deter colonists at Ligonier from fleeing. In a span of a few months, Pennsylvania's executive council sent Lochry a large supply of ammunition, as well as £3,500 to buy rifles, salt, and horses. Lochry in turn promised his neighbors militia pay and rations simply for remaining in place. Their refusal to flee, he reasoned, itself amounted to military service.[21]

Even with state support, mobilizing and supplying Ohio Valley colonists proved an immense challenge. East of the mountains, Congress and the states repeatedly failed to equip the Continental Army with necessary food, clothing, and blankets. Delivering them to scattered outposts across the Alleghenies posed more problems. Robbery, corruption, and the lack of boats or horses repeatedly kept shipments from their destinations. In southwest Virginia, forted-up colonists fed militia out of their own meager supplies, gambling that the official commissary would someday repay them. But payment proved a problem as well. By the late 1770s, wartime inflation rendered paper currency all but worthless. Congress and the states bought supplies and paid militia with certificates, but recipients had no way to redeem them for hard money.[22]

These challenges crippled the militia. Men volunteered readily to garrison stockades near their homes, but they resisted orders to defend other areas, let alone march across the Ohio. Some exploited the ongoing boundary dispute to avoid militia drafts, and many who did show up subsequently deserted. Officers struggled to collect fines from cash-poor farmers, leaving them no money for supplies. An uncertain chain of command made matters worse. Virginia governor Patrick Henry, deeming Hand's defensive plans "too complex," told county commanders to ignore them and act on their own initiative. South of Wheeling, colonists refused to send men to guard a distant fort and threatened to "move off with our families and stock" if Hand did not back down. Upriver, another community seized "all the Ammonition and Guns" intended for the local militia, promising to "stay & Difend themselves" and "Acct. wt. the publick" for the cost.[23] Such resources could bolster local defenses, but quickly escaped the control of the governments that provided them.

Finding little help from the official militia, some communities tried to organize their own defenses. In Pennsylvania's Bedford County, east of the Alleghenies, inhabitants "voluntarily formed ranging Parties" to patrol the surrounding countryside. These select rangers could do far more, the organizers argued, than militia drafted from the general population, most of whom "would only be a dead weight & unnecessary expence." But the volunteers remained on duty only after community leaders petitioned Hand to pay them "as Militia in actual service." Even the scheme's promoters stressed that the rangers needed "officers to Command them . . . & persons appointed to furnish them with Provisions." When colonists downstream from Pittsburgh proposed raising a similar company, they similarly turned to Hand for supplies. In the fall of 1778, Westmoreland County leaders raised 150 volunteers to attack the Allegheny Valley Senecas, but they, too, relied on the Continental Army for provisions and ammunition. After marching ninety miles those supplies ran out, thanks to "much waste and destruction," and the Westmorelanders turned back without seeing a single Seneca.[24]

These military failures had little to do with lack of courage or fighting ability: as individuals, many colonists possessed both. But personal virtues alone could not mobilize, supply, or command collective military operations. In contrast to eastern colonies like Massachusetts, whose inhabitants had shared militia service for generations,[25] Ohio Valley colonists lived in a newborn, scattered, and fractious society with tenuous interpersonal ties, weak social institutions, and chronic shortages of food and other vital supplies. The resources and coordination necessary for large-scale mobilization proved hard to come by, even with the aid of Congress, state governments, and the Continental Army. Upper Ohio colonists outnumbered their Indian neighbors and repeatedly demonstrated a readiness to kill them, but without state aid they lacked the means to wage war.

Even after British and revolutionary regimes mobilized the region for war, opportunities for peace remained, thanks to both military failures and Indian diplomacy. Ongoing violence undermined these efforts, but the greatest impediments proved to be the ineptitude and prejudices of Continental Army officers. Ohio Indians repeatedly proposed peace talks, and each time revolutionary leaders bungled their end of the negotiations.

These bids for peace revolved around the neighboring towns of Goschachgünk and Lichtenau. The Delaware built Goschachgünk in 1775 as part of their program of cultural adaptation. They laid it out in a grid pattern, following the model of Moravian mission towns, assigning different clans to different streets. White Eyes and Netawatwees initially suggested the Moravians settle there as well, but many of their people refused to accept resident missionaries. For his part, Zeisberger preferred to run his own mission, where he could closely regulate his converts' education, family structure, and sexuality. So the Moravians founded Lichtenau a short distance downriver, within walking distance yet physically separate. Despite Zeisberger's supervision, the mission remained a Delaware and Mohican place, where Isaac Glikhican and other "Indian helpers" governed day-to-day affairs. A onetime war leader and councilor, Glikhican personally converted many other Delawares, including Israel Welapachtschiechen, a widely respected elder whose fused elbow earned him the title "Straight-Armed Man." Both men remained active in Delaware politics and diplomacy. The mission's proximity to Goschachgünk strengthened ties between Christian and non-Christian Delawares while also respecting the differences between them. It enabled Delaware leaders to employ the missionaries as scribes and kept the Moravians well informed of events in the surrounding world.[26]

These twin towns became centers for diplomacy, thanks to their close ties to the generally pro-British Wyandot to the northwest. The two nations had enjoyed a close relationship for years. The Delaware had settled in the Muskingum Valley at the Wyandots' invitation. The arrangement gave the Delaware a new homeland, while the Wyandot gained friendly neighbors to help protect their own territory. Like the Delawares of Lichtenau, many

Wyandots considered themselves Christian, though they followed the Catholicism of French Jesuits rather than the Protestantism of German Moravians. In both cases, they had accepted new beliefs and rituals while maintaining substantial control over their communities. In 1777, Dunquat's people answered Hamilton's call to arms, while White Eyes, Gelelemend, and Glikhican persuaded most Delawares to remain neutral. White Eyes became the United States' closest Ohio Indian ally. But these contrasting positions did not lessen Wyandot-Delaware goodwill. Dunquat's embrace of the Moravian missionaries as kin, even as he went to war against the United States, reflected this deep-seated amity.[27]

In the months after Hamilton's war song, White Eyes, Glikhican, and Welapachtschiechen resolved a series of crises that threatened to poison Delaware-American relations. In September 1777, messengers from Fort Pitt warned that General Hand planned to "eradicate" all Indians. Soon afterward, rumors of Virginian attack sparked a panic, but White Eyes investigated personally and found only a herd of wild horses. About a week later new letters from Hand and Morgan assured them of U.S. goodwill and offered to build a fort to protect the Delaware for the duration of the war. Morgan also sent a precious supply of salt. Reassured, Delaware leaders renewed their commitment to neutrality, openly deriding Hamilton's plan to "restore Peace by making War." In the spring of 1778, Micheykapeecci returned home and reported the attack on her family. Then a group of defecting interpreters and Indian agents visited on their way from Fort Pitt to Detroit. Their warnings split the Goschachgünk council. One Delaware community, led by Wandochale and his son Buckongahelas, had already joined the British alliance. Many others argued that the Americans "were offering [them] peace with one hand and were using the hatchets against [them] with the other." Moravian Delawares intervened. Welapachtschiechen lobbied wavering council members, while Glikhican joined White Eyes on a new peace delegation to Fort Pitt. There, they persuaded Hand to define a territory where Delawares could hunt without fear of American attacks.[28] These concessions helped preserve Goschachgünk's neutrality.

The Wyandots, meanwhile, began to doubt the value of their British alliance. In May 1778, Dunquat and one hundred warriors returned to Lichtenau on their way to attack Point Pleasant. As usual, Zeisberger noted that the Wyandots were "all orderly and polite." Many attended Moravian religious services, where some prayed with their rosaries as their Jesuit teachers had taught them. In the weeks that followed, similarly well-behaved warriors passed through, always respecting the missionary's dislike of native ceremonies. Their kinship seemed firm, but Dunquat's campaign went badly. On 16 May the Point Pleasant garrison repulsed his attack; two weeks later, ten of his men died attacking a small Virginian stockade. A war that Dunquat had joined reluctantly had become far more costly than expected. At a June council, Hamilton congratulated his allies for driving the colonists "a great distance from your hunting grounds," and his superiors later agreed that the Wyandots could keep any land they "conquer[ed] from the Rebels." But the disastrous Point Pleasant campaign revived old divisions between more and less militant factions, convincing White Eyes that his friends were becoming "more disposed" toward peace. A delighted General Hand promised that if the Wyandot called in their warriors and attended an upcoming treaty at Fort Pitt, the United States would "enter into friendship with them."29

Militant bravado and Moravian panic together foiled this bid for peace. From Detroit, Hamilton rallied his allies to squash the Delaware proposals. War captains from various Great Lakes nations threw their weight behind him. Odinghquanooron, a Detroit Wyandot leader, publicly scolded the Delaware for "turn[ing] [their] heads towards the Rebels." Rumors reached Goschachgünk that the other nations "wanted to force [the Delaware] to join in the war," and White Eyes concluded that the Wyandot would not heed his proposals. In mid-July Odinghquanooron came to Lichtenau with eighty Wyandot warriors and a few British agents. As usual, they "behaved very quietly and politely," but accused Zeisberger of reporting their movements to the Americans. The missionary had done just that, and he did so again as soon as messengers could get away with his letters, but now he feared for his life. Terrified, he told Morgan that White Eyes wanted the United States "to send an army against the Wyandotts &c," and he insisted that negotiations would be fruitless. These warnings made a strong impression: the congressional commissioners charged with making peace concluded they could not do so unless "the War be carryed in to [Indian] Country."30

Zeisberger underestimated Wyandot interest in peace. Less than a month later, Odinghquanooron returned to Lichtenau and told Glikhican that his men had suffered "much danger, hunger, and trouble," while accomplishing little. With Glikhican's encouragement, he agreed to offer the United States terms, asking only respect for Wyandot territory. If the Americans marched on Detroit, he promised his people would "shake hands ... & make Peace," provided that the army leave their "Towns along the Road unmolested." But Zeisberger had given up on the Wyandot. A week after sending Odinghqua-

nooron's message, the erstwhile pacifist renewed his call for an army, predict-
ing that "there [would] be no Peace" without military conquest. A few days
later, translating letters from Fort Pitt, his fellow missionary John Heckewelder
told the Delaware that the congressional treaty commissioners "tore up and
rejected the Wyandot Chief's message . . . as soon as they had read it." General Lachlan McIntosh, who had recently replaced Hand at Fort Pitt, later
boasted that several Indian nations had "earnestly applyed to [him] for
Peace," but that he would give them "no Encouragement" until he marched
an army into their territory.[31] Zeisberger's pleas for an American invasion
were about to be answered.

The rejection of Odinghquanooron's proposal reflected shifting American debates over Indian relations. Revolutionary officials and Ohio Valley
colonists broadly agreed on the need for an offensive campaign, and they all
coveted Indian land, but they disagreed over the best means to that end.
Some, including Morgan, blamed hostilities on British trade networks and
thus called for a naval campaign on Lake Erie to cut off the forts at Detroit
and Niagara. But many favored instead "an immediate attack" on enemy
towns, taking Indian leaders as hostages, and seizing "all the Lands of the
ofending Tribes or nations." By the summer of 1778, the debate had turned
against Morgan. In appointing treaty commissioners, Congress rejected him
in favor of Andrew Lewis, who had helped lead Dunmore's 1774 invasion. In
July, Virginia's revolutionary council authorized McIntosh to draft as many
militia as needed "to carry on an expedition against the hostile Indians, &
chastise them as they deserve." Congress promptly agreed. McIntosh himself
clung to the dream of capturing Detroit, but he favored an overland campaign through Delaware and Wyandot country. To cow Indians into submission, he planned "to keep possession" as he went by building and maintaining
forts.[32]

As McIntosh planned for war, a small group of Delaware leaders arrived
to make a treaty. Hundreds of Indians had attended prior councils, but now,
mindful of Cornstalk's fate, few dared risk American hospitality. The delegation's leaders—Gelelemend, Pipe, and White Eyes—represented the Turtle,
Wolf, and Turkey phratries of the Delaware nation. Where previous councils
had dragged on for weeks, these negotiations lasted only a few days, leaving
little time for customary speechmaking. But in these brief meetings, the Delaware forged an agreement that addressed nearly all their chief concerns. In
their opening speech, the commissioners invited the Delaware into a confederation, suggesting that Congress would treat them "as their own people."

The eventual treaty guaranteed to the Delaware "all their territorial rights in the fullest and most ample manner." The United States also promised to build a fort to protect Delaware old men, women, and children and to establish "a well-regulated trade, under the conduct of an intelligent, candid agent." Above all, the treaty laid out a path for integrating an autonomous Delaware nation into the emerging American polity. The final article declared that allied Indian nations might "form a state whereof the Delaware nation shall be the head, and have a representation in Congress." As White Eyes signed the document he likely considered it a promising roadmap for a new political order. But the concessions came at the price of military alliance. After years of championing neutrality, White Eyes now pledged to fight the United States' enemies. McIntosh promptly appointed him "Lieutenant Colonel of all the Indian Nations" between the Ohio and the Mississippi.[33]

The hard-won alliance soon soured. In late September, White Eyes returned to Goschachgünk, where Zeisberger read and translated the treaty to a host of visiting Indians. British-allied Munsees pleaded to the Delaware Council for "Pardon and peace," but McIntosh spurned their offer just as he had rejected the Wyandots'. Meanwhile, most Delawares balked at sending warriors to join the American army. Pipe, who had signed the treaty, now moved his town closer to Sandusky, where he declared he would take "all his Men to one Side" and stay out of the war altogether. The third signer, Gelelemend, later claimed they had agreed to provide only guides, not warriors, and alleged that the interpreter John Gibson had misrepresented the treaty's contents.[34]

His achievements in jeopardy, White Eyes hurried back to Pittsburgh. The contents of his saddlebags evoked the cultural fluidity of his career: garments made of buckskin, linen, and silk; a European felt hat and an American fur cap; breech clouts and breeches; a bag of body paint and a pair of spectacles; a rifle and a peace pipe; and a large wampum belt and "Sundry Papers." He joined McIntosh's army as it built a new fort, named after the general himself, at the mouth of the Beaver River. On 4 November they marched into Ohio; two Moravian Indian messengers marched with him and the army for two days and reported that all was well. On reaching home, one announced that "there is real peace." But by then, White Eyes was dead, "treacherously put to death" by one of his new allies.[35]

At the time, writing from Philadelphia, Morgan warned that White Eyes's loss could cause the United States "very great difficulties." But his fears proved ill-founded. Other Delaware leaders, most notably Gelelemend and the

Moravian Welapachtschiechen, continued the murdered diplomat's work. Pipe and Wingenund, despite misgivings, ultimately joined them. Thanks to their efforts, the Delaware-American alliance endured for over two more years, as did attempts to make peace between Americans and Wyandots. These efforts failed less because of White Eyes's death than because of the failings of the Continental officers to whom he had pledged his service.[36]

On 22 November, Isaac Glikhican and a Delaware delegation met McIntosh's army at an old village site called Tuscarawas, about fifty miles upstream from Goschachgünk. As the army arrived, the Delawares lined up "with great regularity," gave "Three Indian Cheirs," and fired off an orderly salute with their guns. McIntosh's less disciplined militia replied with a "hasty Running Fire round [their] whole lines." Despite the news of White Eyes's death, Glikhican reported that he "heard and enjoyed nothing but kindness" from the general and his men. The Delawares in turn gave McIntosh venison and deerskins and invited his army downriver to Goschachgünk "to Build a fort for their Defence and Safety."[37] One of White Eyes's chief goals—physical protection for his people—seemed close to fruition.

All such hopes died when McIntosh spoke. Addressing the crowd through the interpreter John Gibson, the general first declared he had come to Ohio to defend his Delaware allies. But rather than building a fort at Goschachgünk, he would build one at Tuscarawas "as it is in my path to Detroit." Next he announced he would make peace with any British-allied Indians who surrendered within the next two weeks, and he pledged to hunt down those who refused. But then he pleaded with his hosts to bring him corn, "and also all the Horses, Cattle, Hogs, deer skins, Venison or anything else you can spare," promising to pay either in certificates or in worthless paper currency. The Delawares, unimpressed, politely "Signifyed their approbation and thanks." Having shown his desperation for supplies, the general concluded by warning that any warriors who failed to join his army "Should be looked upon as Enemys to the United States of America." Unable to contain themselves, the Delawares broke into "a General Laugh."[38]

Not for the last time, a United States commander had overestimated his leverage over Ohio Indians. McIntosh dreamed of dispatching armies on long campaigns, securing supply lines with a chain of forts, and cowing the enemy into submission. But by the time he addressed the Delawares, that vision had proven a mirage. Eager to take the field, he began his campaign in late fall, when the landscape offered scant forage for his army's livestock. Because of salt shortages, the army could preserve no meat, so once-fat cattle slowly wasted away or strayed past inattentive sentries into the woods. Famished packhorses crumpled under their loads, forcing the army to abandon its food reserves. McIntosh had drafted most of them as militia for three-month terms ending 1 January. When he called for replacements, their commanders howled in protest and Virginia's government countermanded him. With no hope of reaching Detroit, he resolved to leave a small garrison of regulars in a new fort at Tuscarawas and wage another campaign in the spring. As the militia built Fort Laurens, a structure they nicknamed "fort Noncence," each man subsisted on about a cup of flour per day. When they finished, the general sent them home with nothing to eat but raw cowhide: all that remained of his army's meat supply.[39]

The remaining Tuscarawas garrison faced a grueling winter. Dunquat had told the Americans he could come to terms only if their army stayed "at some distance from my Towns." By building "fort Noncence," McIntosh directly threatened those towns, so the Wyandots resolved to oppose him with "all [their] might." While reiterating goodwill for their Moravian friends, Dunquat's men quickly attacked the fort. Its commander, the onetime Delaware captive John Gibson, turned to his adoptive nation for food. In early December, Glikhican brought several horseloads of corn from Lichtenau, and Gibson repeatedly sent men for more. But by building the fort fifty miles upriver, McIntosh had made it difficult for his Delaware allies to supply it. Zeisberger, who had urged the army to invade, quickly grew disillusioned. "They made many promises about how they would protect us," he complained, "but we did not receive any protection from them. On the contrary, they bring the war into our Town and we then have to protect them." The aged Israel Welapachtschiechen talked one war party out of ambushing two of Gibson's men. Grateful for their help, Gibson urged his superiors "to doe something for the poor Moravians and the friendly Delawares." But Zeisberger now reasoned that bringing soldiers any nearer to Lichtenau would only invite attack. Gibson had enough trouble defending his own fort. In late February, when eighteen men ventured out to gather firewood, Dunquat's warriors ambushed them, capturing two and killing the rest, all within sight of the walls. A weeks-long siege ensued. By the time fresh supplies arrived, Gibson and his men had eaten the boiled remains of their shoes.[40]

But just as McIntosh's plans collapsed, the opposing alliance began to splinter. Dunquat and other Great Lakes Indians depended on the aid of increasingly unreliable British allies. During the winter, Hamilton led an army into the Wabash Valley, leaving Detroit short of troops and food. His Ohio allies protested angrily, noting that McIntosh's army "threatened their Lands." The British, one Wyandot observed, were becoming "as smooth Tongued as the Virginians." News of the American alliance with France, their onetime ally, deepened Wyandot doubts. Then, in late March, news arrived that Hamilton had surrendered to the Virginians. Wyandot leaders rushed to Detroit to demand food, troops, and cannon. Without such support, they warned, they would have to make peace, "being not able to fight the enemy alone." Disappointed with the response, Dunquat welcomed Delaware diplomats he had scorned just weeks before, called his erstwhile British allies "good for nothing," and pledged to help end hostilities. In doing so, he adhered to a long-standing vision of Delaware and Wyandot nations jointly protecting their lands and people. For over a year he had pursued that goal through an alliance with Britain; now he embraced an alternative route to the same end.[41]

In April, at Upper Sandusky, ten British soldiers chopped down "thick timber," arranged the logs into a makeshift wall, rolled out four small cannon, then blew the wall to pieces. Their commander, Henry Bird, boasted to his Wyandot audience that he would do the same to Fort Laurens. His men repeated their laborious presentation several times but failed to impress the Wyandots: it was too little, too late. They flatly refused to help, perhaps doubting that Bird could haul the guns across miles of swampy terrain. In early May, both the Detroit and Sandusky Wyandots resolved to make peace; Ojibwes and Odawas soon joined them. McIntosh's replacement, Daniel Brodhead, reported that most Ohio Indians were "not hostile at present"; in July, William Crawford noted that Indians had "don very Litle mischef this Summer." When Bird tried once more to rally his allies, Dunquat publicly denounced the venture. Bird fumed, calling Wyandot leaders "either Rascals or Cowards." Other British officers branded them "Rebbels" for becoming "friends to the States." But their change of heart reflected a pragmatic reassessment of their options. Hamilton's defeat, the new Franco-American alliance, and shortages at Detroit all raised serious doubts about their British allies, while the Delaware-American alliance suggested another way to achieve their goals.[42]

But they could forge a lasting peace only with American cooperation. Wyandot leaders reached out once more to the United States, with the Goschachgünk Delawares again acting as go-betweens. They suggested holding a council at Beaver Creek, rather than Pittsburgh, to keep away from the unruly colonial population. No doubt remembering Cornstalk, one spokesman asked Brodhead not to bring "too many of Your Young Men" to their council, noting, "I should not be able to speak my Mind so free if so many People were present." Dunquat urged Brodhead to avoid Sandusky when he attacked Detroit, suggesting that he sail across Lake Erie instead. But apart from evacuating the untenable "fort Noncence," Brodhead largely ignored the Wyandots' demands. He insisted on holding the council at Pittsburgh with all his soldiers present. He had proved a steady friend to the Delaware, but he had little interest in negotiating with erstwhile British allies, whom he described as "the wolves of the forest." Even as he exchanged goodwill messages with the Wyandots, he resolved to avoid making peace "until they are sufficiently drubbed for their past iniquities." In late August, in coordination with a Continental Army campaign to the east, he carried out such a drubbing against the Allegheny Valley Senecas and Munsees. The Westmoreland volunteers had tried and failed to attack these towns the year before. Now Brodhead's larger and better-organized campaign caught them off guard. The inhabitants fled just hours ahead of his army's arrival, enabling the troops to burn 130 houses and cut down over 500 acres of corn. In his report, Brodhead gleefully described leaving the Senecas "quite destitute of food."[43]

Brodhead's belligerence left little chance of a successful treaty. When Wyandot, Delaware, and Mekoche Shawnee delegations assembled for the long-planned council, they found Brodhead still absent. He returned a few days later, showing off plundered horses, deerskins, and other goods. The visitors watched him auction off his booty and distribute the proceeds among his six hundred soldiers and militia. Preening with triumph, Brodhead opened the council by declaring that "the wicked every where must be punished." Hoping to foment a Haudenosaunee-Wyandot war, he demanded that his guests help him "destroy" the British and Senecas. Appalled, the Wyandots turned to the familiar protocols of Great Lakes diplomacy. Chiding Brodhead for his militancy, principal chief Duyenty tried to clear a metaphorical "stoppage from [his] ears" so he could hear "the friendly speeches of your brothers." He pledged to return all American captives "safe and well" and to never again aid the British. But rather than joining Brodhead in war, Duyenty declared his people "love[d] all the Nations and hate[d] none." He urged the Americans not to attack the Shawnees until they heard the Wyandots' calls for peace. Echoing Dunquat, Duyenty asked that American troops avoid Wyandot towns and insisted that the United States respect Wyandot territory, the boundaries of which he described in detail.[44]

Brodhead, still reveling in his destruction of Seneca crops, conceded nothing. He mocked his guests for assuming "that a few flattering words would, with giving up our prisoners, secure to them their lives, the lives of their women & children, & their lands." To make peace, he insisted, any Indian nation must leave "some of their great men" as hostages until they had "killed & taken as many from the English & their allies as they have killed & taken from the Americans." In marching on Detroit, he declared he would "take [his] choice of roads," and he flatly refused to stop any attacks on "the wicked Shawnese." Like McIntosh, the predecessor he despised, Brodhead badly overestimated his strategic position, in large part because of his contempt for the Indians with whom he negotiated. By refusing to recognize Wyandot territory, keep their armies away from Wyandot towns, or respect the Wyandots' wish for peace, both McIntosh and Brodhead left Ohio Indians little reason to negotiate. Even the unreliable British offered them more than the stubborn and hostile Americans. At the close of the council Brodhead congratulated himself for his unbending performance, but he had actually set the stage for further bloodshed. When the snows melted the next spring, the peoples he thought he had conquered went back to war.[45]

Despite their mutual antipathy, Ohio Valley Indians and colonists had many reasons to avoid war. Political disunity, logistical problems, and the vulnerability of noncombatants all discouraged large-scale conflict. They mobilized in 1777 because both the British empire and the nascent United States used their resources to overcome these obstacles. British and American initiatives led directly to a devastating wave of violence, mostly against noncombatants. Imperial and Continental officers denounced their allies' brutality in writing but nonetheless accepted it as a cost of mobilization. For years, Delaware leaders tried to mediate a peace between their Indian and colonial neighbors. Wyandots and others periodically welcomed these overtures. Though they chose different means, the Delaware and Wyandot pursued similar ends: physical security, territorial sovereignty, and preserving their long-standing friendship with one another. Continental army commanders repeatedly spurned their proposals, confident they could force an unconditional surrender with brute force. Their obstinacy, together with an inability to carry out their threats, doomed the region to several more years of horror.

Meanwhile, the Moravian experiment at Lichtenau came to an end. With Delaware neutrality a dead letter, and the promise of army protection a mirage, Zeisberger and his followers put distance between themselves and their unconverted neighbors. By drawing lots, the Moravians determined that God wanted them to reestablish two older mission towns upstream, at a seemingly safe distance from both "fort Noncence" and Goschachgünk. In June 1779, Dunquat declared he could no longer protect them against Britain's remaining Indian allies, further hardening their resolve. Over the spring and summer most of the congregation rebuilt and moved to Schönbrunn and Gnadenhütten. The following winter, as the Wyandots rejoined the British alliance, the last residents abandoned Lichtenau to establish a new mission, called Salem. As all their neighbors resolved on war, they sought security in isolation. Their days as peacemakers were over.[46]

CHAPTER 5

Horrors, 1780–82

In mid-April of 1782, a man calling himself John Bull asked Congress for information about a rumored "Massacre of a Number of Christian Indians" at the Muskingum Valley mission of Gnadenhütten. Bull, an assistant Moravian missionary, had heard that his son Joseph "fell [as] the first Sacrifice" of nearly one hundred murdered men, women, and children. Born to an English Quaker family in Pennsylvania, Bull had joined the Moravians as a young man and soon met and married another recent convert, a Mohican woman baptized Christiana. Much as she had taken a European name, he adopted the Mohican name Schebosh, meaning "running water," in place of his English one. Through thirty-five years of marriage, Schebosh and Christiana raised three children while enduring the mission community's repeated displacements. In the early 1770s, they helped build new mission towns in the Muskingum Valley, at the invitation of the Delaware nation. They inhabited a multicultural and multilingual world, living in a Mohican family, serving a German church, and periodically contending with English officials, all while living in Delaware country. But now, the news of his son's murder convinced Schebosh there was no place for his family in the land of their birth. In his grief, he told Congress he would soon "set out [from Philadelphia] for Pittsburg and from thence . . . go as far as God will permit him."[1]

The mass murder at Gnadenhütten both resulted from and epitomized a war of attrition that tore apart the Ohio Valley in the early 1780s. This conflict featured few conventional clashes between opposing armies. Instead, British governor Frederick Haldimand and Continental commander-in-chief George Washington sought to burden one another with droves of hungry refugees. Both sides eschewed large-scale campaigning in favor of short forays against noncombatants. Rather than embracing colonists who, in their view, had moved west "to shun the oppression of Congress," British commanders aimed to drive the migrants "back upon their Brethren" in the seaboard colonies, where they would drain rebel supplies. For their part, revolutionary forces emulated the 1779 Brodhead and Sullivan campaigns, which "laid waste the whole of the Senecca Towns their Crops & their Country" and forced thousands of Haudenosaunees "to flee to Niagara for refuge."[2]

These mirroring strategies caused great suffering on all sides, but they yielded different long-term outcomes. As British-allied Indians pushed colonists eastward, Virginian land policies pulled them back. Early in the war, Dunmore's land grants and the Transylvania scheme had drawn hundreds of colonists to Kentucky. Expansion-minded Virginia signaled it would honor their claims, spurring thousands more to follow suit. Even when hostilities escalated, the lure of legal title to fertile land persuaded many to move west. Then, in 1779, Virginia enacted a land law that explicitly rewarded colonists who had seized land preemptively. In practice, convoluted procedures and overlapping claims left many landless, but the legal incentive only accelerated migration to Kentucky. Some moved north of the Ohio River, hoping a similar policy would someday apply there. By contrast, colonial attacks repeatedly and permanently displaced many Ohio Indian communities. By war's end, the Delawares and Shawnees of southern and eastern Ohio—including Schebosh's Moravians—had abandoned their old homes and created new polyglot communities closer to Lake Erie. There, they increasingly relied on British support, which they could maintain only by bringing in colonial prisoners and scalps. And so the horrors continued, until the old empire made peace with the new one.[3]

Schebosh's mentor, David Zeisberger, liked to depict his missions as remote islands of Godliness, caught between Christian-hating Indians and Indian-hating colonists. Revolutionary officials, meanwhile, depicted the Gnadenhütten murderers as an independent band of thugs with no regard for their authority. Both were wrong. Like Schebosh, Moravian Indians had lived for years in a multicultural world, in which they bridged ethnic, cultural, and religious divides. Though church doctrine aimed to shield mission communities from outside influence, both missionaries and converts participated actively in regional politics and diplomacy. British-allied Delawares and Wyandots regarded them as kin, while the Continental Army valued them as allies. Moravian Indian leaders like Isaac Glikhican and Israel Welapachtschiechen commanded widespread respect and had often served as go-betweens and peacemakers. Their close ties to both sides of the conflict played a pivotal role in the events leading to the catastrophe.

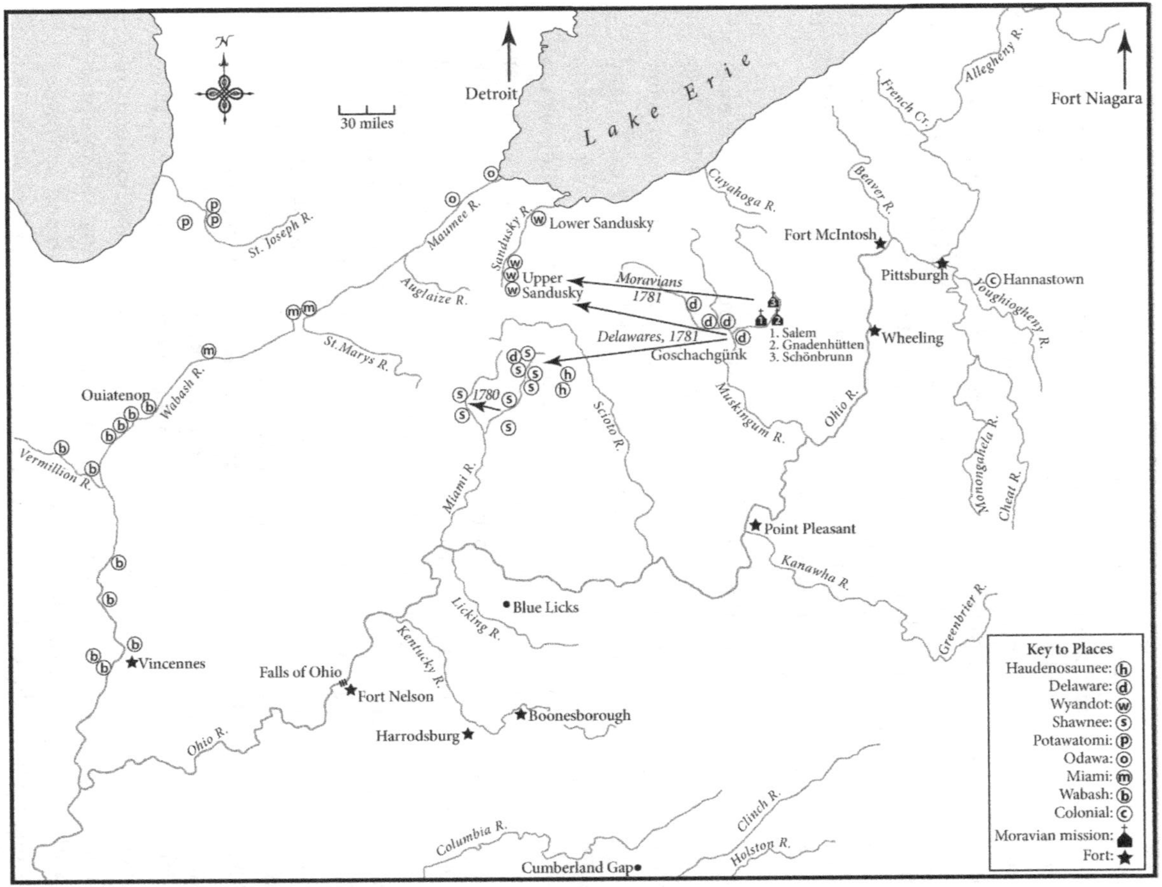

Figure 5. The Ohio Valley, 1780–82.

The actions of the murderers similarly reflected their ties to the wider world. Rather than acting independently, or in rebellion against more humane American officials, the murderers set out for the mission towns on the orders of a state-appointed militia commander. Moreover, they mobilized under Pennsylvania militia law, a tool that the nascent revolutionary state had placed at their disposal. They modeled their "campaign" on previous expeditions led by Continental Army officers. In the massacre's aftermath, Continental commanders collaborated with the murderers to plan similar forays against the Wyandots and Delawares of Sandusky. In this light, the familiar story of remote frontier barbarity proves closely intertwined with the structures and policies of the emerging Anglo-American state. Rather than an exceptional tale of hatred-fueled cruelty, the Gnadenhütten massacre reflected the systematic brutality of state-sponsored frontier war.

In September 1779, Fort Pitt commandant Daniel Brodhead failed to make peace with British-allied Wyandots. His blunder revived the crumbling British alliance, with dire consequences for Ohio Valley colonists. After a summer of relative peace, Sandusky Wyandots resumed attacking camps and homesteads, along with Haudenosaunee and Shawnee allies. The ensuing winter, Ohio Indians gathered at Wakatomika to renew their commitment to the war. The Piqua Shawnee Wryneck, a proponent of neutrality just a year before, now rallied the allies to fight. From the northwest, the St. Joseph Potawatomis, who had previously ignored the British call to arms, now sent dozens of warriors to join them. In March and April five or six parties of British-allied Indians carried out attacks from the outskirts of Pittsburgh to the stockades of Kentucky. Within eight weeks, the Wyandots and their allies killed or captured forty-three men, women, and children in the upper Ohio counties alone. Dunquat himself ambushed a sugar camp a few miles from Fort Pitt, killing five men and capturing six children and teenagers, one of whom he later adopted into his family. In Kentucky, raiders carried out thirteen attacks in different locations, killing about a dozen men and capturing several more. On the Ohio, a multiethnic party attacked two boatloads of Kentucky-bound migrants, killing two men and capturing twenty-three, mostly children. The captives included an enslaved woman and her owner. By one account, the captors dressed the slave in her owner's clothing and forced the owner to "act as her waiter." From Detroit, the British commandant Arent De Peyster declared he had armed about two thousand Indians for war, and he boasted that his Delaware and Shawnee allies were "daily bringing in Scalps & Prisoners." In mid-1779, Brodhead had boasted that the Wyandots had "bid farewell to the English forever"; a year later, all Wyandot men from both Detroit and Sandusky, "except the aged, and part of them," had reportedly taken up arms for the Crown.[4]

This resurgent militancy stemmed from Ohio Indians' recent dealings with both contending armies. Throughout the war, different Indian communities had allied with one side or the other, or neither, or both, but their diverse strategies reflected common underlying concerns. They sought first and foremost the physical security of their people, towns, and crops, as well as official recognition of their territorial boundaries. Equally important, they strove to maintain peace and friendship with their Indian neighbors, even when they adhered to opposing alliances. Finally, they required access to European trade for tools, weapons, blankets, and sometimes food. Brodhead's rejection of the Wyandots' proposals, and insistence that they wage war on neighboring nations, made clear that they could expect no peace or trade from Pittsburgh. So they turned again to Britain, hoping the king's men might start fulfilling their promises. Unlike Brodhead, British officers in the Great Lakes and Canada increasingly sympathized with their native allies' needs. Questioned about his expenses, De Peyster insisted on furnishing food, clothing, and canoes to "the familys of all the Indians" who visited his post. From Quebec, General Haldimand called for driving colonists out of Kentucky in order to "secure to the Indians their natural right to that Country, confirmed to them by Treaty."[5] If nothing else, De Peyster and Haldimand understood what their allies wanted to hear.

But British understanding often failed to yield effective material support. Time and again, Ohio Indians heard promises of troops "to protect [their] Women & Children," but they only rarely received substantial aid. In the fall of 1779, Indians representing all the Ohio nations repeatedly asked for British troops to defend against Brodhead's threatened assault. De Peyster had no men to spare. Meanwhile, Haldimand continually pressed his subordinates to minimize "the vast treasure lavished upon these People," noting that "however they may threaten to forsake us . . . it is impossible they can exist without our aid." But Indians who did not receive desired supplies often refused to fight. One party returned home when De Peyster refused them a keg of rum. Morgan, a talented young Shawnee, did the same when the British failed to replace his stolen saddle. Indians also took exception to the European practice of releasing prisoners on parole, which sometimes forced them to "fight twice against the same Person." Such grievances amplified doubts about other British promises. During a Virginian assault on their towns, Shawnees refused to let a British artilleryman borrow two horses to haul away the king's cannon. To punish such behavior, Haldimand ordered that gifts be reserved to those Indians who were "most attentive" to British direction, a policy that did little to reconcile his independent-minded allies.[6]

These tensions reflected schisms within the broad British alliance. Despite a shared antipathy for Ohio Valley colonists and a common interest in British trade and patronage, differences among allied Indians hindered their collective efforts. In the spring of 1780, De Peyster grudgingly sent fifty soldiers with two small cannon to help attack the Virginian outpost at the Falls of the Ohio. Hundreds of warriors from the Wabash and Great Lakes nations joined them, creating an unusually impressive combined army. But Ohio Indians' need to defend their towns jarred with their northern and western allies' desire to take horses, captives, and scalps. The Wyandots refused to participate and instead attacked the upper Ohio Valley, which posed a greater threat to Sandusky. The Shawnees similarly insisted on first attacking small communities in the Licking Valley, arguing that bypassing them would leave their own towns "naked & defenceless." The Licking Valley colonists surrendered quickly and Great Lakes warriors promptly seized children to take home for adoption, ignoring a British promise to leave colonial families intact. The warriors eventually returned their captives, but then slaughtered the colonists' cattle, leaving the meat to rot. They then decamped to raid colonial horse herds, leaving the Ohio Indians and the British with hundreds of captive mouths to feed, many miles to traverse, and too few men and supplies to attack the Falls. The British commander reluctantly led his men and his prisoners back to Detroit, grumbling that he could have "gone through the whole country without any opposition, had the Indians preserved the cattle."[7]

At Fort Pitt, Brodhead's 1779 triumph faded quickly. Instead of peace, his intransigence had brought mounting terror and bloodshed. He dreamed of retaliating against Sandusky but logistical barriers repeatedly stymied his plans. Long-standing obstacles—factional divides, lack of provisions, the dubious value of government credit, and colonists' reluctance to undertake long campaigns—only worsened as the war dragged on. In 1780, parasites killed nearly all the upper Ohio Valley's swine, and the army lacked salt to preserve what little meat remained. Farmers increasingly refused to sell their produce for congressional paper, prompting Brodhead to commandeer food by force. In retaliation, colonists hid their cattle in the hills and "threaten[ed] to rise in arms" against the troops. One provisioning party failed to find enough food to feed itself. Local militia commanders faced similar problems. Many men refused to undertake militia service at all, often citing uncertainty about state and county boundaries. Virginia and Pennsylvania nominally resolved their boundary dispute in 1779, but failed to survey the actual line for several more years, fueling ongoing hostility between their local partisans.[8]

A dispute between Brodhead and Westmoreland County militia officers exemplified both the importance of government support and the divisiveness that plagued revolutionary defenses. The Westmorelanders, led by county commander Archibald Lochry and his father-in-law, Joseph Erwin, maintained government-supported ranging companies, recruited for six- to twelve-month terms. A long list of accusers reported that they chronically misused government-issued money and weaponry. Guns meant to arm frontier communities never reached their intended recipients; men paid to patrol the frontier allegedly worked on their commanders' farms or "loiter[ed] away their Time at the Taverns, or straggling about the Country." In late 1779, as the terms of two Westmoreland companies neared completion, Brodhead sought to recruit their members as regular troops, hoping to keep them under closer supervision. But when he ordered the companies to Fort Pitt, the Lochry faction refused to comply, demanding that Brodhead feed and pay their men, but not command them. Brodhead tried to arrest the recalcitrant officers, including Erwin; when they eluded him, he stopped supplying their men with food. The dispute simmered down by spring—Brodhead got his men and helped supply a new ranging company—but animosity between army and militia officers would plague the region until war's end.[9]

With no means of attacking Britain's Great Lakes ports, revolutionary commanders instead set out to burn Indian towns and crops. Such expeditions required only weeks of militia service rather than months, and revolutionary governments typically supported them with ammunition, officers, and sometimes regular troops. Virginian officer George Rogers Clark, who had famously captured Henry Hamilton at Vincennes, took charge of operations in Kentucky. There, militia officers ordered homesteads to provide one or two men along with fifteen or twenty days' supply of food, while Virginia provided ammunition. British officers reported that the Kentucky militia could raise "three or four thousand in a few days" to raid across the Ohio. In an August 1780 raid, Clark and one thousand men destroyed four Shawnee towns and their crops, leaving the inhabitants to face starvation. The Virginians killed one captive "by ripping up her Belly & otherwise mangling her" and dug up graves in hopes of receiving a government-issued bounty for the corpses' scalps. In retaliation, the Shawnees captured and burned to death one of Clark's men. They then rebuilt their towns to the northwest, asking their neighbors to help feed them through the winter.[10]

But while short forays spread horror, longer campaigns yielded frustration and defeat. Clark's designs on Detroit fell prey to the fractiousness and recalcitrance of Ohio Valley colonists. He needed hundreds of men from both Kentucky and the upper Ohio Valley, along with provisions for many weeks of campaigning. Virginia gave him ample money, and Pennsylvania openly encouraged its citizens to join him. But despite this formal state support, many in the Ohio Valley still opposed him. Brodhead and western Pennsylvania officials accused Virginia of seeking only "to acquire more extensive territory" and warned that Clark's long campaign would leave Pittsburgh and its environs all but defenseless. Others feared that if Clark got the flour and beef he demanded, the upper Ohio Valley would face shortages. Many simply refused to participate. Militia officers warned that men would "suffer any punishment" rather than march with Clark. Meanwhile, wartime inflation prevented Clark and his allies from hiring volunteers or even from clothing the recruits they could find.[11]

When persuasion and payment failed, Clark turned to coercion. Virginia had empowered him to draft men for his campaign. Pennsylvania had not, but in Westmoreland County Lochry and his allies resolved to do so anyway. In the disputed region, longtime Virginia partisans, led by Dorsey Pentecost, decreed that they could draft any men living in territory that Virginia had previously claimed. Lochry's and Pentecost's rivals accused them of using "armed force . . . to dragoon the Inhabitants" into a "hyghly oppressive and abuseive" draft. But ordering a draft was one thing; implementing it quite another. In Monongalia County, rioting colonists at least temporarily halted Clark's draft. Elsewhere, continued doubts about the Pennsylvania-Virginia boundary convinced many colonists to refuse militia duty "under any government whatever." Clark and his allies assailed their critics' homesteads, destroying their crops and livestock, breaking a mill, and threatening to kill them and their families.[12]

Despite this brief reign of terror, far fewer men mobilized than Clark had hoped, and many of those who did soon deserted. Determined to press on regardless, Clark set off downriver; Lochry followed a few days later with about one hundred men, hoping to catch up. They never did. A party of British-allied Indians, led by Mohawk Joseph Brant, captured one of Lochry's messengers and learned his location, direction, and numbers. Brant's men descended on their camp, killing dozens, including Lochry, and capturing the rest. In Kentucky, colonists demanded that Clark abandon his campaign and build defensive stockades. With too few men to march into Ohio, he bowed to the pressure. Meanwhile, divisions within Brant's party prevented them from pursuing Clark downriver or attacking his fort at the Falls. As the abortive campaign came to a close, both Clark and Brant griped about what they might have done with more compliant followers. Both colonists and Indians continued to depend on government resources to go to war, but they paid little heed to official directives that contradicted their own needs.[13]

These abortive campaigns underscored both the flimsiness of government authority and the potency of government influence. Mobilizing either Indians or colonists proved a tall order. Britain's Indian allies depended on gifts of food, blankets, weaponry, and other supplies, and the periodic support of imperial troops. But once in the field they acted according to their own divergent interests and priorities, with little regard for British officers or other Indians. Even with government support, colonists' recalcitrance and internal divisions left revolutionary defenses haphazard, permitting only short forays to burn Indian crops. Much like the escalation of 1777–78, the renewed warfare of 1780 resulted directly from state sponsorship of violence. And, once again, the scale and direction of that violence quickly escaped official control.

By 1780, the Goschachgünk Delawares were the only Ohio Indians who remained at peace with the United States, and that friendship seemed tenuous. They had no wish to go to war with their Shawnee and Wyandot neighbors, let alone other Delawares. Dunquat decried their support for "Virginian Devils" and urged them to maintain their old friendship. Congress perennially failed to provide promised food, trade goods, and military protection. Brodhead repeatedly postponed sending troops to fortify Goschachgünk and refused to share army flour with his allies unless they paid in venison. Many Pennsylvanians and Virginians, meanwhile, openly threatened their lives. The following spring, Delaware misgivings mounted on hearing that Pennsylvania had "offered a high reward for Prisoners & Indian scalps."[14]

Delawares adhered to this dubious alliance for both economic and political reasons. During the war, Ohio Valley trade had collapsed. By the spring of 1779, the nation's leaders complained that women and children were suffering for lack of blankets, clothing, and other necessities. They also worried that British-allied Indians might attack their towns in retaliation for their neutrality. Gelelemend and Welapachtschiechen likely concluded that they could obtain physical and economic security only through a military alliance. But their decision also reflected an older strategy that predated the current conflict: the pursuit of formal diplomatic recognition within the composite polity of the Anglo-American state. Delaware leaders aimed to secure a place for their nation in the future postrevolutionary order, either as an additional state of the union, as their 1778 treaty had promised, or as a distinct nation bound to the American confederation through ties of trade, kinship, and diplomacy. They also clung to the hope that they could help mediate a peace between the United States and British-allied Indians.[15]

The alliance endured thanks in large part to the work of a Moravian Indian. A widely respected leader of the Delaware Turkey phratry, Israel Welapachtschiechen had accepted baptism at the urging of his wife, an adopted captive from Pennsylvania, but he remained active in politics and diplomacy. In late 1778 he returned to the Delaware council, replacing the murdered White Eyes as an advisor to Gelelemend and a champion of the nation's fragile friendship with the United States. The following spring, Gelelemend and Welapachtschiechen led a Delaware delegation to Philadelphia, where they pleaded for their nation's sovereignty, territory, and neutrality. When Welapachtschiechen and the others returned from Philadelphia, they had to take a long detour to avoid "several Parties made up to destroy them." Meanwhile, Brodhead recruited a few young Delawares to fight, nullifying the delegation's case for neutrality. When Gelelemend and Welapachtschiechen returned to Fort Pitt, a young Delaware man proudly presented them the scalp of a British-allied Delaware war captain. After years of campaigning for peace, Gelelemend now accepted the scalp, a symbolic declaration of war. During the months that followed, Delaware warriors increasingly joined Brodhead's men as scouts and in battle.[16]

In October 1780, Gelelemend and Pipe led more than thirty warriors to Pittsburgh to join Brodhead for a planned campaign. Pipe, the Delaware leader who had clung longest to neutrality, now threw in his lot with the United States. On reaching Fort Pitt, they presented Brodhead with deerskins, which he had promised to accept as payment for food and other goods. But the commandant had nothing to offer in return. He had failed to raise militia and struggled even to feed his garrison. More Delawares, including women and children, soon arrived with more deerskins to trade, but Brodhead had "neither Bread nor Meat" to sell them. Instead he pleaded for patience and assigned a few soldiers to guard them. After two weeks, the

Delawares awoke one night to find their camp surrounded by armed men. Joseph Erwin, a Westmoreland militia officer and Brodhead antagonist, and forty colonists had marched thirty miles to Pittsburgh, determined to "destroy" the United States' only Ohio Indian allies. According to Brodhead, they aimed to kill men, women, and children, perhaps to claim Pennsylvania's new scalp bounty. But when they reached the camp, Brodhead's sentries stood their ground. Erwin's gang had no compunction about slaughtering Indians, but they balked at attacking their white guards. Instead, they returned home, likely grumbling at the lost opportunity. The Delawares hurried away as well. Back at Fort Pitt, Brodhead worried that "it may not be an easy matter to call them out again."[17]

Erwin's gang failed to kill any Delaware people, but they did kill the United States–Delaware alliance. A few leaders, fearing both the British and Americans, again asked Brodhead to build a fort for their protection. But the pro-American camp had dwindled to a handful. Gelelemend and Welapachtschiechen renounced politics, left Goschachgünk, and settled near the Moravian mission of Salem. British sympathizers found an increasingly warm welcome in Delaware country, where they publicly threatened to kill all those who remained "Friends to the states." During February, the Moravians received repeated reports that the Goschachgünk Delawares were "arming themselves and preparing for war." On the 26th, word reached Gelelemend that the nation's council had resolved to join the British alliance. He and John Heckewelder, a missionary, sent urgent messages to Brodhead warning that the Delawares were "getting ready to go to fight you."[18]

Gelelemend's warnings freed Brodhead from the perennial challenge of distinguishing friendly Indians from enemies, offering instead the simpler prospect of a "general Indian war." He promptly mobilized about three hundred regulars and Virginia militia—Lochry and Erwin offered scant help from Westmoreland—and marched into Ohio. Brodhead's men surrounded Goschachgünk without warning, trapping its inhabitants between their guns and the swollen Muskingum River. About forty men, women, and children fell into their hands, offering little resistance. The attackers killed forty cattle, plundered all they could carry, and burned the rest. Brodhead wanted to march onward, but his men refused. Soon after they set out for home, militiamen killed and scalped their fifteen adult male prisoners. Brodhead released the surviving women and children, after assuring them that he had not sanctioned the killings. His little army soon ran out of food, only to be brought meat and corn by Moravian Indians. As they sated their hunger, some of the men plotted to slaughter their Moravian benefactors, but Brodhead and an Ohio County militia commander, David Shepherd, quashed the scheme. Meanwhile, over 160 Delaware refugees fled to Sandusky, begging for food. At Detroit, De Peyster mused that he need no longer doubt their nation's loyalty.[19]

Despite their differences, both Erwin's abortive raid and Brodhead's destruction of Goschachgünk exemplified how government influence spurred frontier violence. Current or former militia officers, as well as a recently elected sheriff, led the Erwin gang. Their experience mobilizing men for state-sanctioned duty undoubtedly helped them organize this unsanctioned foray. Equally important, Pennsylvania entrusted Westmoreland militia officers with money, weapons, and other supplies. The would-be murderers probably loaded their guns with state-issued powder, redirecting government resources to serve their own ends. And though Brodhead distanced himself from both the Erwin gang and his prisoner-killing militia, he had scant love for Indians himself, insisting that "much confidence ought never to be placed in any of the colour." Though he insisted the militia had killed the prisoners against his orders, he simultaneously threatened to "Beat all the Indians out of this Country" within seven months. Equally important, he and his subordinates had raised and supplied the men he could not control. Tellingly, Brodhead's official report mentioned only that his men had "killed fifteen Warriors," not that they were prisoners. Like his predecessors, Hand and McIntosh, he disclaimed responsibility for the atrocities of the men he nominally led, but nonetheless tolerated them as a necessary cost of frontier warfare.[20]

In mid-August 1781, a large force rode into Gnadenhütten under an English flag. Dunquat and Abraham Kuhn, a German-born Wyandot adoptee, led parties from Upper and Lower Sandusky, with Detroit Wyandots behind them. Shawnee and Haudenosaunee warriors followed, along with Pipe and Wingenund, Brodhead's erstwhile Delaware allies. Other Delawares, Mohicans, and Ojibwes rounded out the army. British agent Matthew Elliott, Sandusky trader Alexander McCormick, and several other white men accompanied them. Over several years of war, such visits had become commonplace. As usual, the Moravians offered their guests food and the warriors "behaved in a friendly way," though McCormick, an old friend to the missionaries, warned them to expect trouble. And, as usual, missionary David Zeisberger dispatched a messenger to Fort Pitt to warn of the warriors' approach. He begged Brodhead to keep his message secret, "for it wou'd prove dangerous" if the British and their allies learned of his warning.[21]

In a formal council at Gnadenhütten, Dunquat urged his "Cousins the Christian Indians" to move to Upper Sandusky, warning that they lived "in a dangerous place." His words reflected sharp disagreements among his allies. Dunquat and Pipe considered the Moravians beloved kin, with whom they might disagree without losing affection. Other British-allied Indians, as well as Elliott, thought the missionaries and their followers at best suspect, and at worst adversaries deserving capture or death. By inviting them to Sandusky, Dunquat hoped to both guard the Moravians from his allies and sever their ties to his enemies. Some Moravians welcomed the proposal, but many objected, citing rumors that the Delawares at Sandusky were now "tired of the war and [were] starving." Zeisberger, meanwhile, distrusted Dunquat's promises, dreading physical violence less than the spiritual danger of associating with non-Moravian Indians. For guidance, he looked to his church's daily "watchword," from Isaiah 8:10: "Take counsel together, and it shall come to nought; speak the word, and it shall not stand: for God is with us." Rather than heeding mortals like Dunquat, Zeisberger argued, they should trust in God's presence "and hope that all would go well."[22]

Tactful enough not to refuse outright, the Moravians promised to answer the following spring, noting that leaving their crops midsummer would expose them to "extreme need and misery." This answer appeased Dunquat, who was well aware of the region's precarious food supplies, but it frustrated his allies, including Elliott. Some called for slaughtering the missionaries and their Indian assistants, until "a leading chief"—likely Dunquat himself— threatened to kill anyone who harmed them. The dispute further frayed Anglo-Wyandot relations; at one point, Wyandots tore down and burned Elliott's British flag. Some of the warriors began "to dance, to play, and to carry out their own devices" in defiance of the Moravians' long-respected prohibitions. The Moravian Indians, still divided over Dunquat's invitation, busied themselves feeding their troublesome guests. The very pregnant missionary Anna Sensemann moved upriver to Schönbrunn to give birth in comparative peace. Meanwhile, small war parties scouted upper Ohio forts, captured some colonists, and brought them back to Gnadenhütten.[23]

When they returned, a young prisoner, taken near Wheeling, admitted that Zeisberger's letters had put "the Country in General . . . on their Guard." The Moravians' critics now called for blood. Dunquat gave them one more chance to move voluntarily. When Zeisberger continued to stall, the

Wyandots seized, stripped, and bound him and his fellow ministers. Others pillaged their houses, then sent parties to Salem and Schönbrunn to bring in the remaining missionaries, including Anna Sensemann and her three-day-old son. They slaughtered the Moravians' livestock, leaving the meat to spoil in the summer sun, and burned crops and fences. Some converts wanted to fight back, but cooler heads prevailed. Together with friends among the warriors, Moravian Indian leaders persuaded the captors to untie the missionaries and give them back some of their clothing. The obstinate Zeisberger covered his nakedness with one of Sensemann's old nightgowns. Meanwhile, a recently converted woman stole Pipe's horse, "the best in the whole company," and hurried off to report the missionaries' plight to Fort Pitt. In retaliation, Delaware warriors seized and threatened to kill her kinsman Isaac Glikhican. Dunquat stepped in to interrogate him. As they met, the two men no doubt recalled their meeting four years before at Lichtenau, where Glikhican had championed his Moravian teachers and Dunquat accepted them as figurative fathers. In the intervening years, Dunquat, Glikhican, and other Ohio Indian leaders had strived to balance the demands of their various alliances with the metaphorical kinship that bound them together, insisting that they could remain friends, and kin, with their enemies' friends and with their friends' enemies. That hope had now faded, but some sense of kinship remained: Dunquat quickly pronounced Glikhican innocent and set him free.[24]

As the Moravians endured a forced march to Sandusky, the British and their allies continued to debate their fate. The Delaware war captain Buckongahelas, who had joined the British alliance early in the war, warned that even at Sandusky, the Moravians could send messages to Fort Pitt. He urged De Peyster to move them north to Detroit, where the British could keep a closer eye on them. British agents Alexander McKee and Matthew Elliott agreed. By contrast, Pipe agreed that the Moravians had "always apprized the Enemy of our Manouvers," but pointed out that he himself, as a onetime member of the U.S.-allied Goschachgünk council, had compelled the missionaries to write letters on their behalf. If he could shift allegiances to the British, he implied, so could the Moravians. He added that he wanted to keep the missionaries nearby "to instruct our people." Dunquat similarly welcomed the Moravians and urged them to help defend the Sandusky towns from rebel attack. De Peyster acceded to their demands: he released the missionaries after a brief interrogation and agreed that they should stay at Sandusky.[25]

Unfortunately, because the Moravians left their crops unharvested, they further drained an already overtaxed local food supply. Ohio Indian women planted corn, beans, and squash for local subsistence, but they did not traditionally grow surplus crops for market. Their fields could not easily accommodate large numbers of refugees. Clark's August 1780 attack had left Shawnees "destitute of shelter . . . or Food." The following spring, Brodhead similarly displaced the Goschachgünk Delawares, heightening the crisis. In previous years Ohio Indians in need had turned to the Moravians, who often sold surplus grain and livestock. Their forced migration eliminated that emergency food supply and added hundreds more hungry refugees. Those with food to spare demanded ever higher prices. As winter neared, Shawnees, Delawares, and Wyandots faced dire shortages. The cost-cutting De Peyster recognized that the Ohio Indians' plight enabled Britain to purchase their allegiance more cheaply. He aimed to send just enough food, clothing, and ammunition to keep his allies south of Lake Erie, both to maintain a buffer against rebel attack and to avoid feeding thousands of refugees at Detroit.[26]

De Peyster was similarly unwilling to feed the 350 Moravians who were now, he knew, "starving in the woods." Some had predicted they could prosper at Sandusky by selling milk and butter, but in swampy northern Ohio their remaining cows starved for lack of forage. White traders periodically offered the missionaries food but could not feed hundreds of converts. Those who sought help from the Shawnee towns found even higher prices there. Already disenchanted with the British, some Moravians privately hoped that friends at Fort Pitt might somehow come to their aid. Welapachtschiechen, whom Shawnees had captured months earlier, now rejoined the congregation at Sandusky, bringing the wampum belts and medals he had received from the United States. Others visited friends and kin among a small band of U.S.-allied Delawares who had settled on an island near Fort Pitt, where the garrison grudgingly fed them. As the Moravians faced famine, some wondered whether they might find more security with the United States.[27]

Soon after reaching Sandusky, the Moravians asked Dunquat for permission to return to the Muskingum towns to salvage their abandoned crops. Unable to feed them himself, the Wyandot could hardly refuse. Those who left included Welapachtschiechen's son Jacob; his daughter-in-law Christina; and her father, assistant missionary John Schebosh. In the weeks that followed, those at Sandusky heard contradictory reports of their fortunes. First a returning war party reported that the area was "perfectly quiet . . . and no danger to be feared." A week later, messengers declared that some of the corn gatherers "had been taken prisoners by white people, and also some of them put to death," and that a rebel army was marching on Sandusky. A week later, new reports dismissed the rumored invasion and maintained that Schebosh and five others were captured, not killed. Schebosh's son Joseph immediately set out for Fort Pitt to check on his father and sister. Meanwhile, more Moravians set out for the Muskingum, along with some Goschachgünk Delawares who faced the same plight. Then, in early February, Christina and Joseph Schebosh returned to Sandusky with several others. Those who had been captured were all well and their father had traveled eastward to report the missionaries' fate to Moravian elders. Most important, "the Americans had behaved in every Respect to them as Friends" and promised "they would not be molested in their Returning to save their Corn." With this news, dozens more Moravians hurried back to their old homes, including Joseph Schebosh; his brother-in-law, Jacob; and the veteran diplomats Glikhican and Welapachtschiechen. With no help to be had from the Wyandots and Shawnees, the unharvested corn on the Muskingum offered "their only hope of getting the means of life."[28]

Upper Ohio Valley farms, by contrast, had enjoyed a rare bumper harvest, yielding over fifteen tons of surplus flour. Nonetheless, controversy still hindered military and civilian authorities. At Fort Pitt, a weeks' long dispute erupted between Brodhead and John Gibson, a Delaware adoptee and veteran trader turned Continental officer, with each denying the other's right to command. The resulting confusion may have allowed news of Zeisberger's warning to spread across the region, despite his request for secrecy. Among the nascent regional elite, "Commission Hunters" angled for official appointments that promised both personal wealth and public influence. Those who won such posts continually struggled with colonists who rejected their authority. Some former Virginia partisans now called for a new trans-Appalachian state. In late 1781, General William Irvine took charge of Fort Pitt, where he struggled to raise militia, deemed the fort "a heap of ruins," and found his troops "deplorable, and at the same time despicable." Seemingly everyone wished to attack British-allied Indians, but Irvine noted that "Burning their empty Towns has not the desired effect. They can soon build others." The United States could secure its frontier, he argued, only by defeating Indians in battle and driving their British sponsors "out of their Country." He saw little likelihood of that happening without a large and expensive campaign. "As matters now stand," he warned Washington, "this country must be given up."[29]

The region's chronic factionalism flared most heatedly in newly created Washington County, in the far southwestern corner of Pennsylvania. The state government initially awarded many local appointments—including that of militia commander—to Irish-born James Marshel, whose family controlled large tracts of land on upper Cross Creek. Anti-Pennsylvania partisans, led by Pentecost, repeatedly stymied his efforts, but they, too, sought recognition as legitimate political authorities. A wealthy mill and landowner on Chartier's Creek, Pentecost had once served as a Pennsylvania magistrate, but he defected to the Virginia camp in 1774. Now his faction swept the new county's first elections, and Pentecost himself won a seat on Pennsylvania's executive council. He subsequently presented himself as a trustworthy councilor in Philadelphia, but he continued to foment antigovernment resistance at home. Other erstwhile Virginians proved more cooperative, including David Williamson, one of the largest landowners in the western part of the county. A Pennsylvanian by birth, Williamson had served for several years in the Virginian militia, but he now quietly accepted a commission under Marshel. In October 1781, he led an expedition to investigate the abandoned Muskingum mission towns. On that occasion, he brought back and released Schebosh and the others, alive and well.[30]

With the support of Williamson and other ex-Virginians, Marshel's efforts began to bear fruit. During the fall of 1781, he mobilized men through "volunteer plans," in which individuals accepted militia assignments, and received militia pay, by choice rather than by draft. This method presumably made possible Williamson's visit to the mission towns. To establish a draft for future needs, he divided the adult male population geographically into five battalions, which he subdivided into companies of fifty to seventy men. Each company consisted of eight "classes," to be called on tours of duty in rotation. The battalions began electing officers and submitting class rolls in September and October. In November Marshel declared the militia were almost "in full form." Later that month, he successfully drafted men to garrison the fort at Wheeling, and in January he drafted another detachment to relieve them. His work went smoothly in the western part of the county, where inhabitants most needed militia protection, but faced more opposition in the Monongahela Valley, long a hotbed of anti-Pennsylvania sentiment. Early in 1782, "a Large Mob" interfered with the election of militia officers at Tenmile Creek, probably doubting that Marshel would count the ballots honestly. Instead, the crowd insisted on a voice vote, which its favored candidates won "by a great Majority." Marshel, seeing little alternative, complied. By giving

Pennsylvanian commissions to longtime Pennsylvania opponents, he and his government gained a semblance of legitimacy.[31]

Meanwhile, the United States' few remaining Indian allies made new homes around Pittsburgh, hoping for security and fearing further violence. Nonhelema, one of the only Shawnee leaders to have supported the Americans throughout the war, lived with her daughter in a house in the Fort Pitt orchard, making and selling moccasins and other "beautiful articles." Betsey, a Delaware woman, lived in the fort itself with her children and husband, John Gibson. Meanwhile, Gelelemend and perhaps a few dozen Delaware men, women, and children huddled through the winter on Smoky Island, a twenty-acre woodland a few hundred yards downstream. Even more than their famished counterparts at Sandusky, they now depended wholly on their military allies for food, supplies, and physical protection. The fort's commanders supported them, but nearby colonists and soldiers grew increasingly hostile. In January, two corporals from the garrison allegedly tried to murder Moses, a former Moravian convert who had joined Gelelemend's band. Irvine sharply censured the men, but a court-martial found insufficient evidence to convict them. Like Brodhead and Gibson before him, Irvine stationed regular soldiers to guard the Delawares' camp. Then he left Fort Pitt to visit his family and to lobby for a more welcome assignment. In his absence, Gibson barely kept his poorly clothed and seldom paid men from mutiny.[32]

Thanks to a mild winter, Wyandot and Delaware warriors attacked upper Ohio colonists early in 1782. In mid-February, Robert Wallace returned to his Raccoon Creek homestead to find "his wife and children gone, his house broke up, the furniture destroyed, and his cattle shot and laying dead about the yard." He raised a party of his neighbors to pursue the attackers, but a heavy snowfall that night, and the dozens of warrior footprints nearby, deterred them. The captors soon killed Jane Wallace and her smallest child, probably because they could not keep up, but her husband did not learn of their deaths, or of the survival of his remaining son among the Wyandots, for nearly three years. Elsewhere, six warriors captured John Carpenter and his two horses on the road from Buffalo Creek to Pittsburgh. The cruelest of his captors, Carpenter later reported, "called themselves Moravians" and spoke German. After swimming the frigid Ohio, captors and captive found refuge at the Muskingum mission towns, where both Carpenter and the warriors reportedly warned the corn-gathering Moravians "to be off," as "the whites . . . would follow up the warriors, and fall upon them." They then headed on toward Sandusky. Soon Carpenter got hold of his horses and escaped, riding all the way to Fort Pitt.[33]

Carpenter's report of the Moravians' return revived long-standing suspicions that they were aiding warriors, if not participating in raids themselves. In the past, colonists had called for attacks on the mission towns but failed to launch actual expeditions: acting on their own, the plotters had no means of raising the necessary men and supplies. This time, James Marshel answered their call. On 1 March he drafted the first and second classes of six companies, over one hundred men in total, "to go to Muskingum" and investigate the Moravian towns. These were men from his own and nearby townships, on the west side of the county, including the friends and neighbors of Carpenter and the Wallaces. This requisition dwarfed his previous drafts to patrol the frontier or occupy small stockades. On 4 and 5 March he called up several more classes, this time from the eastern battalions. No doubt some of those drafted failed to appear, while others joined voluntarily. But Marshel's initiative had turned a nebulous and inconclusive series of musings into a real expedition. The formal structure he had devised, the ammunition he supplied, and his position as Pennsylvania's appointed militia commander together overcame the obstacles that had foiled prior attempts. Within days, over 160 men gathered at the Ohio and elected David Williamson to command. They swam across the river, then rode westward to Gnadenhütten.[34]

In some respects, Marshel rebelled against army authority.[35] He pointedly failed to consult with the acting commander of Fort Pitt, John Gibson, a well-known supporter of the Moravians. A year before, David Shepherd, Marshel's Virginian counterpart, had helped Brodhead squash an anti-Moravian plot; now, Marshel threw his authority behind one. Nonetheless, his defiance of the army hinged on his position as Pennsylvania's appointed militia commander. If Marshel thumbed his nose at the army, he did so by exploiting his position within the emerging revolutionary state.

On the Muskingum, the Moravians stayed to salvage more corn, trusting in "the good treatment" reported by Williamson's former captives. As they neared the end of their harvest, Joseph Schebosh went to fetch stray horses in the woods to the north. As he worked, a rifle shot tore through his arm. Falling to the ground, he saw three white men running toward him with tomahawks. He identified himself as the son of "Minister Schebosh" and asked why they had shot him. He got no answer. The men hacked him to death, cut off his scalp, and moved on toward the town. Across the river, Joseph's brother-in-law, Jacob, busied himself bagging corn while another man loaded bags into a nearby canoe. Suddenly a large group of white men appeared riding toward Gnadenhütten. Jacob recognized some of them from his capture the previous fall, but before he could greet them one raised his rifle and shot the man by the canoe. The wounded man managed to paddle across the river but then fell down and did not rise. Swallowing his greeting, Jacob ran into the woods in panic. The white men recognized his horses, just as he had recognized them, and later asked where he was, but he stayed out of sight, too terrified to return.[36]

Back at Gnadenhütten, twelve-year-old Thomas watched more than one hundred militia surround the town, on both sides of the river. Thomas, a third-generation Christian, was born and raised in Gnadenhütten. His Wampanoag father and grandfather were baptized in the 1740s; his Munsee Delaware mother, in 1767. Together with his parents; his older brother, Petrus; and four-year-old sister, Sara, he had endured the forced march to Sandusky, the long hungry winter, and the desperate return to the Muskingum. The militia found them and dozens more scattered through the fields, gathering and bagging corn. To their relief, Williamson offered to take them to Fort Pitt, promising to "Show them every Mark of Friendship," just as he had treated those he had taken in October. Unaware of Joseph Schebosh's fate, the group readily agreed. At the militia's urging, they retrieved tools and other possessions they had buried in the woods for safekeeping, and even extracted honey from a nearby beehive. They handed over everything to their new friends, including "all Rifles, Hatchets, Axes &c."[37]

At the time, Johann Martin, one of the missionaries' Mohican assistants, and his son were working in the woods west of the river. On their return, they were alarmed to find the fields empty of people and full of hoofprints. They climbed a nearby bluff for a better view of the town, where they saw the Moravians walking "up and down the Streets together with the white People," seemingly "quite merry together." Reassured, he sent his son to join them and set off to share the news with the Moravians of Salem, a few miles downriver. There he met with several of his fellow assistants, including Isaac Glikhican and Jacob's father, Israel Welapachtschiechen. On hearing of the militia's arrival, Welapachtschiechen brought out the wampum belts and strings that documented his long friendship with the United States. Hoping "that God had prepared a Way & place for them," he and the others sent messengers to the Americans asking for refuge. The next day, the Salemites welcomed the white men as guests, offered them food, and pledged to go "wherever they intend[ed] to take them." Two unconverted Delaware men, kin to one of the missionaries' assistants, insisted on coming with them out of a desire to become Christians. A former convert, Catharina, who had been expelled from the congregation for committing adultery, also begged to be taken along. A few, anxious about their starving families, set off instead for Sandusky. The rest departed together for Gnadenhütten. Before they left, the militia burned the town to the ground.[38]

As they made their way up the river, the militiamen seemed friendly. Some discussed scripture with the missionaries' assistants, several of whom spoke English. Others grilled Welapachtschiechen and Glikhican about frontier politics. The younger men "were playing all the Way" with their Moravian contemporaries, including Israel's son David and twelve-year-old Tobias, who later reported they had "no Apprehension of any Danger." Then, as they neared Gnadenhütten, someone spotted a canoe on the riverbank stained with blood, and the "bloddy Tracks of a wounded Person": the man Jacob had watched die. When they reached the town and joined the rest of Williamson's party, games and conversation gave way to threats and rough handling. The white men bound their hands and herded men into one house and women and children into another, together with the people of Gnadenhütten. Some accused the Moravians of going "to war against them" or harboring those who had. They argued that the Christian Indians had stolen their horses, tools, even cups and saucers, reasoning that only "White People" used such things. Isaac and the others protested that they had fed visiting warriors only under duress, and had tried to help their captives. They detailed how they had fed Brodhead's men the year before and warned colonists of enemy attacks. Welapachtschiechen even "[held] up the Speech wampum" he had received during his embassy to Congress. The militia were unimpressed.[39]

The captors' erratic behavior reflected the expedition's size, lack of discipline, and internal divisions. Some of the men were trigger-happy while others were more inclined to talk scripture. The men who approached Gnadenhütten from the north, on both sides of the river, had chosen to shoot first. Williamson's main party, by contrast, had surrounded the town and brought the scattered Moravians together for questioning. Both the conduct of the militia at Salem and the Moravians' willingness to surrender their possessions suggest that many in the party at least feigned goodwill toward their captives. According to one report, based on militia accounts, they had "liv[ed] with them apparently in a friendly manner for three days." Nonetheless, a vocal minority of the expedition—perhaps one in four—insisted that the Moravians "must Dye." Williamson, who endured sharp criticism for failing to kill his captives four months before, now proved more sympathetic to the "Bigotted notions" of Indian haters. Withholding his own opinion, he told his men to choose "either to carry the Indians as Prisoners to Fort Pitt, or to kill them." Some spoke against the slaughter, calling the captives "good and true Christians," but no one dared to protect them from the murderers' wrath. Instead, by one account, they "wrung their Hands, and called God to witness that they were not guilty of the Blood of these innocent creatures." But most remained silent, perhaps contemplating their share of the plunder.[40]

On learning their fate, the captives begged a day's respite for "praying and preparing for Death." The militia gave them a few hours. In the women's house, Christina, a Mohican widow baptized over thirty years before, begged Williamson in English to save them. He replied that "he could not help her." Johann Martin's two sons, Anton and Paulus, somehow freed themselves and ran for safety; militiamen shot them down before they reached the river. In the men's house, Abraham, another aged Mohican, openly confessed his sins, trusting that God would "forgive us all." The women began singing hymns and psalms and the men joined in, filling the ears of the "condemning Party" as they debated methods of execution. The next morning, as the Moravians sang, Thomas watched a white man push into the men's house, throw a rope around Abraham's neck, and drag him outside. The others kept singing. The man almost immediately came back, carrying a bloodstained mallet that a Moravian cooper had once used to pound barrel staves. One by one, he brought the mallet down against each man's skull. After fourteen lay dead, he handed the tool to another, who continued the slaughter. Those who remained sang on. One by one they crumpled to the floor: Israel Welapachtschiechen; Isaac Glikhican; Johann Martin; Samuel Moor; Adam Wulalowechen; the recently widowed Abel and his infant son, Jonas; Thomas's father, Philippus; his older brother, Petrus. Thomas himself, one of the youngest in the house, likely watched the others die before receiving a similar blow himself. As their fathers, brothers, husbands, and sons fell silent, the women in the other house still sang. There, the murderers first struck down Judith, "a very loving old Widow." Then the others: Glikhican's wife, Anna Benigna; her sister, niece, three daughters, and baby grandson; the missionaries' assistant, Amalia, and her three young daughters; and dozens more. They "kept on singing as long as there were three alive."[41]

Only two escaped the slaughter. As the women died, Tobias and another boy hid in a cellar underneath the house. As blood poured through the floorboards, Tobias squeezed out through a small hole and fled into the woods. The other boy could not fit and stayed behind to die. In the men's house, Thomas came to his senses, feeling sharp pain where someone had cut off his scalp. Nearby Abel struggled to get to his feet until a white man gave him "several severe blows" to the head. He did not rise again. Thomas lay still. After the white man disappeared, he slipped out and found Tobias in the woods. From their hiding place, the two twelve-year-olds watched the militia pillage and burn the houses and bodies. The boys, as well as Jacob, eventually joined the people of the third mission, Schönbrunn, who had fled shortly before the militia reached their town. Refugees again, the survivors made their way toward Sandusky to share the awful news.[42]

Word of the massacre spread quickly. On Smoky Island, Gelelemend's small band mourned their Moravian kin and worried about their own safety. Then, in the wee hours of 24 March, the Delawares woke to sounds of armed struggle. A band of armed men had quietly canoed across the river, overwhelmed or conspired with the army's posted guards, and attacked the sleeping camp. Several young men fought off the attackers long enough for Gelelemend to escape to Fort Pitt with the women and children. Two other survivors made their way to Sandusky. But four Delawares paid with their lives, including two who held officers' commissions in the Continental Army. The murderers declared they would next attack Fort Pitt and kill the acting commander John Gibson, along with his Delaware wife and children. For months to come, the Delawares kept to the fort and Irvine restricted colonists' access, wondering how well his underpaid and underfed garrison would fight against Indian-hating white men.[43]

The massacre surely illustrated militiamen's meager regard for Indian lives: even those who opposed the slaughter declined to interfere with it. But focusing on the attitudes of either murderers or bystanders obscures how government-sponsored warfare brought it about. As war dragged on, the region's inhabitants increasingly looked to state support for both subsistence and physical protection. For years, upper Ohio colonists had begged for aid, and the Continental Congress, together with Pennsylvania and Virginia, had answered by providing money, supplies, and an institutional structure for new county militias. The resulting monster now escaped the control of the governments that created it. At Fort Pitt, Gibson wanted to help the Moravians, but he lacked either the material resources or the political support to do so. His predicament reflected how little armies and governments could control the consequences of their own initiatives. Instead of a tool for enforcing official policy, the militia became a mechanism through which colonists redirected state resources for their own ends.

News of the slaughter prompted wide-ranging responses. At Detroit, De Peyster invited the remaining Moravians to settle on his own land along Lake Erie. The missionaries and many converts accepted the offer, but others renounced the mission and sought to avenge their lost loved ones, as did the victims' non-Christian kin. In Philadelphia, newspapers initially noted that the militia had killed over fifty old men, women, and children, but nonetheless they characterized the action as a successful attack on the enemy. The murderers' critics soon spread more accurate accounts. Upper Ohio colonists characteristically split, with "some condemning, others applauding" the slaughter. In early May, Pennsylvania's executive council asked Irvine and Pentecost to investigate. Gibson, a longtime ally of the Moravians, hoped to find witnesses to testify against the murderers. But neither Irvine nor Pentecost wished to risk antagonizing the murderers and their supporters. Instead, they quickly squashed the inquiry, explaining that it might "produce a Confusion, and Ilwill amongst the people." William Moore, the president of Pennsylvania's Executive Council, got the message. He asked Irvine to pass on any new information but tacitly accepted that no real investigation, let alone prosecution, would take place. Over two months later, the state's General Assembly called for further inquiry, but no one complied.[44]

This pointed inaction reflected the heterogeneity of emerging state institutions. Both Irvine and Pentecost enjoyed considerable influence, thanks largely to government affiliations. As commander of Fort Pitt, Irvine struggled to manage a rarely paid and occasionally mutinous garrison, but he nonetheless controlled the region's largest supply of gunpowder, flints, and other military necessities. Pentecost, ironically, used his place on Pennsylvania's Executive Council to rally resistance to its policies. While both Irvine and Pentecost represented state institutions, and derived political influence from them, their own interests deviated considerably from those of legislators in Philadelphia. Both sought to extend state influence, and cultivate state patrons, but only to the extent that doing so aligned with their own ends. They had little to gain, and much to lose, by demanding justice for the massacre victims.[45]

Instead, Irvine sought to bank political capital by enabling further militia violence. Weeks before the abortive investigation, he pledged to help Marshel and Williamson organize another expedition, this time "to destroy with fire and sword . . . the Indian town and settlements at Sandusky." Marshel again drafted Washington County militia and recruited volunteers who earned exemption from future drafts. Like the Gnadenhütten murderers, all no doubt hoped for plunder. Irvine supplied ammunition, helped purchase provisions, and sent his aide-de-camp as military advisor. Tellingly, he neglected to mention these plans to George Washington until late May, when the expedition was already under way, ensuring he received no orders that might interfere with the militia's plans. Marshel and his allies ultimately mobilized and equipped several hundred men. To command, the men elected William Crawford, Washington's old partner in land speculation. Irvine instructed Crawford to exchange any prisoners they could not carry away, a token effort to exonerate himself for any new massacre. But the men themselves scoffed at such restrictions. As they marched, they left messages and "Effegies" in every camp, openly threatening "to extermenate the whole Wiandott Tribe."[46]

Buoyed by their purported success at Gnadenhütten, Crawford's men overestimated their abilities. They moved slowly and noisily. The Sandusky Wyandots and Delawares learned their plans before they set out, and for once the British alliance did not disappoint them. Two hundred Shawnees and a company of mounted British rangers arrived at Sandusky just as the expedition approached. Together with Delawares, Wyandots, and other British-allied Indians, they quickly routed the undisciplined militia. While Williamson led the flight back to the Ohio, warriors captured Crawford and a number of others and handed them over to the Sandusky Delawares. Many of these refugees, including Pipe, had struggled for years to stay out of the war, moving repeatedly to evade British and American demands. In the months since Gnadenhütten, they and other British-allied Indians had handed over many prisoners to the British alive, taking pains to contrast their conduct with Williamson's. But they knew that many of Crawford's men had been at Gnadenhütten and that they had aimed to commit similar atrocities at Sandusky. In retaliation, the community burned Crawford and two other officers to death.[47]

Through the ensuing summer, British-allied Indians battered colonial defenses, deepening colonists' dependence on Irvine and the United States. A large force burned Hannastown, home to Westmoreland County's makeshift courthouse. In Kentucky, Indians ambushed and destroyed a substantial militia detachment at Blue Licks. Elsewhere, smaller war parties resumed attacking colonial homesteads and stockades. Some colonists fled eastward. Those who remained demanded the aid of regular troops. Noting that they could not simultaneously harvest grain and guard the fields, communities

begged Irvine for soldiers. Meanwhile, Marshel and other militia commanders urged Irvine to personally command a new, larger, and more disciplined
campaign into Ohio. The influence of regular army officers and troops, they
reasoned, would enable them to avoid repeating Crawford's debacle. Irvine,
eager to strengthen his own authority and that of the United States, complied.
Together with Clark in Kentucky, he planned a multipronged campaign to
destroy "all the Indian settlements within two hundred miles." With the
promise of payment, plunder, and Irvine's leadership, hundreds of men volunteered themselves, their horses, and their crops to support his campaign.[48]

Much like British-allied Indians, the trauma of state-sponsored warfare
left colonists dependent on government support, which in turn fueled more
warfare. But then it ended. In August and September, De Peyster and Irvine
received orders to halt all offensive operations. For a few months, violence
persisted: many combatants wanted to fight on. Irvine called off his own
preparations, but he tacitly supported Clark's November attack on Chillicothe. For their part, a few British-allied warriors continued raiding for
months after De Peyster called them in. They, like Clark, claimed that news of
peace reached them late. But such excuses lost their purchase within a few
months. More importantly, guns, ammunition, and money stopped flowing
into militants' hands. De Peyster fretted about demands for food from "the
approaching bands of Indians, who will come to represent the nakedness of
their families." His superiors, however, insisted that he prioritize conserving
"the Public money." Upper Ohio colonists similarly pleaded for food, clothing, and tax relief. They hated Indians as much as ever. Irvine, once a critic of
anti-Indian brutality, now called for the "total extirpation" of the western nations. But without the imperative of military conflict, both Britain and the
United States sought to curb expenditures. Without their support, even the
most militant Indians and colonists lacked the means to wage war.[49]

CHAPTER 6

───────────

Failures, 1783–95

In the summer of 1783, just south of the Ohio River, several Shawnee hunters met three Kentucky colonists. A year before, these people had been at war, but now their thoughts turned to trade. The Shawnees needed "licker and sault"; two of the white men promised to bring some to sell them, leaving their companion behind to hunt. Some days later, Cherokees—reportedly horse thieves—killed this man in the woods. On learning of his death, Shawnee leaders reported it to the nearest militia outpost and added that another group of Shawnees had killed two colonists they found stealing horses north of the Ohio. The militia commander did not fault them for killing the thieves and hoped they would drive the Cherokees from their land. He added that traders would soon visit the Shawnee towns to sell them the salt they needed.[1] Animosity and horse thievery endured, and periodically brought bloodshed, but open warfare had given way to tentative diplomacy.

This de-escalation of violence jarred with the widespread opinion, popular among land speculators and American officials, that "an immortal hatred" between Ohio Valley Indians and colonists drove them to "kill or be killed." Many insisted that racial antipathy led inexorably to racial violence, a theory that neatly deflected blame from the United States' demands for Indian land. If Congress took "proper measures" to "conciliate the affection of the Indians," they insisted, dispossession and colonization could proceed without bloodshed. One overeager land jobber insisted that he could cross the Ohio to "spy out the choicest and best spots" without giving offense, because he had "Soothed" Indians with "presents and otherwise" beforehand. When violence erupted, such speculators invariably pleaded innocence and pointed to the savagery of "back woods men."[2]

Such views permeate the documentary record, but a closer look reveals a more nuanced story. In 1783, Anglo-American peace deprived combatants of the resources they had used to wage war. Hostilities diminished accordingly, enabling the region's peoples to reshape relationships with a still complex array of governments. British agents nurtured ties to Ohio Indians and refused to surrender the forts of Detroit, Niagara, and Michilimackinac. Pennsylvania officials had settled their decades-long border dispute with Virginia, but they struggled to govern or even survey the state's boundaries. Virginia faced similar challenges in Kentucky. Across the region, army officers, Indian agents, and county administrators twisted official policies to serve their own ends. But governments nonetheless cast a long shadow. Though Indians and colonists often disregarded official demands, they also recognized that they could not achieve their own goals—above all, securing land—without the backing of an effective state. Ohio Indians, no longer united by war, vied with one another for the friendship of British and American officials. Colonists, feuding among themselves, jockeyed for the support of legislators and magistrates. All might embrace the government representatives or attack them, depending on the matters at stake. Amid this uncertainty, diplomacy among erstwhile enemies brought new hopes of peace.

Those hopes soon collapsed, thanks to the United States' implacable demands for Indian land. Congress and the states had amassed a daunting war debt, while widespread postwar inflation and bankruptcy left scant means of raising revenue. These woes gave ample reason to avoid frontier conflict, which Secretary of War Henry Knox warned "would exceedingly embarrass the United States." But neither could Congress afford to leave the west in peace. The land business—obtaining territory cheaply from Indians, and selling it to colonists and speculators—offered the new nation its best hope for financial solvency. Many American officials hoped to profit personally as well. But these profits could be won only if the United States directly managed the process of dispossession and colonization. Left to their own devices, Indians and colonists might turn for protection to British Canada or Spanish Louisiana, shattering nationalists' dreams of a continental American empire. By insisting on colonizing Ohio, Congress antagonized Ohio Indians and disregarded Kentuckians' chief grievances.[3] The failures of United States diplomacy drove both groups to seek alternative solutions, with deadly results.

A few months after the Treaty of Paris, congressional emissary Ephraim Douglass made his way to Upper Sandusky, home of the Delaware leader known as Pipe. He followed in the footsteps of the Crawford expedition, which Pipe and his allies had routed less than a year before. Well aware that

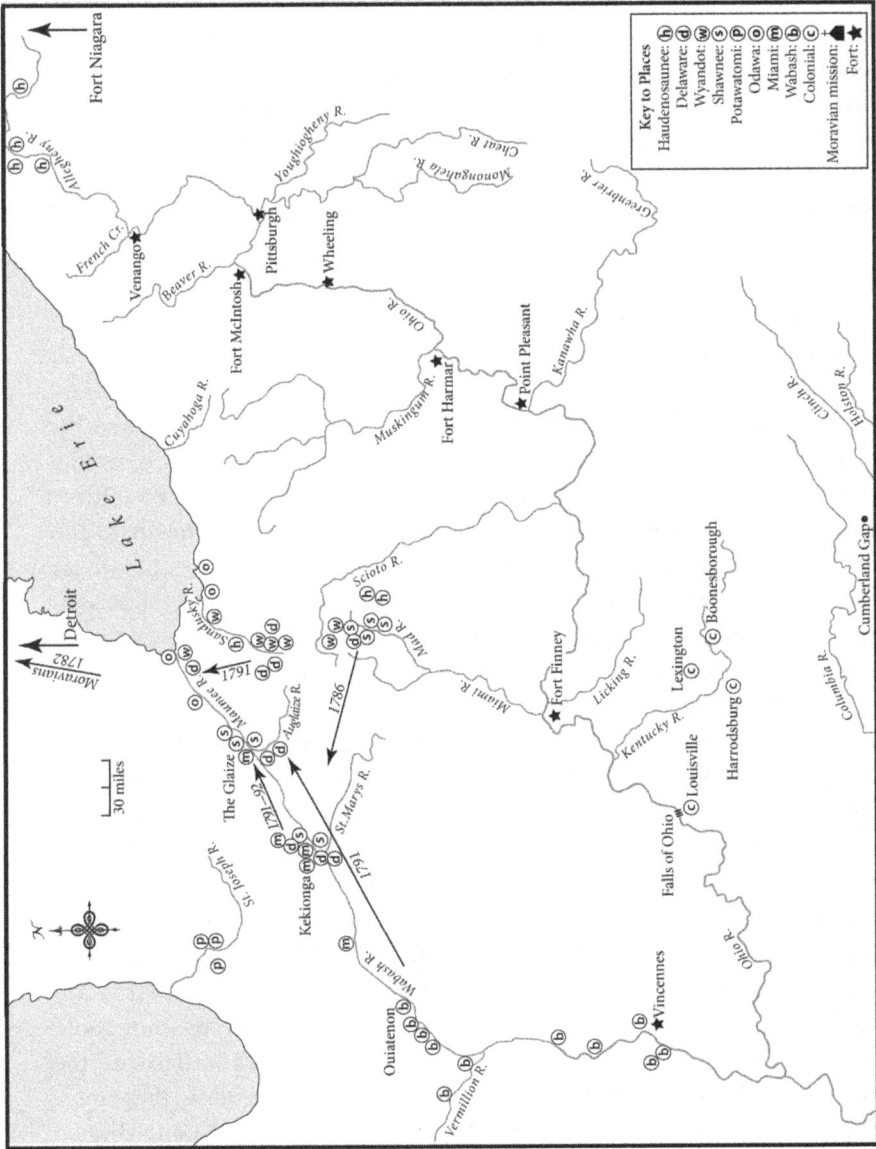

Figure 6. The Ohio Valley, 1783–95.

Pipe's people had burned Crawford to death, Douglass and his two companions no doubt wondered whether they would face a similar fate. But Pipe greeted them "with every demonstration of joy," showing "greater Civility than is usual with them in time of profound Peace." Crawford's tormentor aided Douglass with gusto, sending messengers to other nations, advising him on Indian diplomacy, and personally escorting him to a council at Detroit. Pipe made no apologies: he proudly showed his guests the battlefield and boasted that he could have killed Crawford's entire army if not for the rashness of his Shawnee allies. But his hospitality nonetheless impressed Douglass, who concluded that western Indians were "heartily tired of the war and sincerely disposed to Peace."[4]

Douglass was visiting a social landscape transformed by war. Pipe's own town had relocated several times within a few years, first to remain neutral, then to support the U.S.-Delaware alliance, and finally to join the British-allied Wyandots at Upper Sandusky. Others, displaced by American attacks, gravitated toward different town clusters. The people of Buckongahelas, the most consistently pro-British Delawares, made their home on the Mad River among the repeatedly displaced Shawnees. Others built new towns to the northwest, among Miamis on the upper Maumee River. Still more Shawnees and Delawares moved farther west to the Wabash Valley or across the Mississippi. The dispersal of old town clusters and the emergence of new ones reflected the political diversity of Ohio Indian nations. The Upper Sandusky cluster, led by Pipe and the Wyandot Dunquat, welcomed and accommodated the Americans, while the Maumee towns were more attentive to British messages from Detroit. The Mad River towns stood somewhere in between, with the relatively militant Buckongahelas living just upriver from the Mekoche Shawnees, who echoed Pipe's eagerness for peace. Such divisions were not new. Although Pipe and Buckongahelas both belonged to the Delaware Wolf phratry, Pipe had long lived near Lake Erie and the Wyandots, while Buckongahelas had closer ties to the Scioto Valley Shawnees. For decades, Dunquat's Sandusky Wyandots had alternately deferred to their Detroit kin and defied them. Now, recognizing that a future American invasion could reach and destroy their towns, Pipe and Dunquat resolved to befriend the United States.[5] With ethnic and national ties increasingly tenuous, these multiethnic town clusters became the fundamental units of Ohio Indian politics.

When Douglass reached Niagara, the last stop on his tour, he found less welcoming hosts. His messages bolstered rumors that the British had surrendered western lands to the United States, making their Indian allies "the dupes of the war." The Mohawk leader Joseph Brant, Pipe's wartime ally, pressed the congressional emissary to recognize native sovereignty. Douglass claimed that the Treaty of Paris gave the United States an exclusive right to all lands south of the Great Lakes; Brant countered that Britain could not give up lands it did not own. Later that summer, during a council at Lower Sandusky, Brant and British agent Alexander McKee insisted that the treaty left intact the Ohio River boundary of 1768. Brant further called on all western nations to deal with the United States collectively and sell no land without consulting "the voice of the whole." Where former generations of Six Nations leaders had demanded deference to their league's authority, Brant now envisioned an interethnic pact in which Shawnees, Delawares, and other nations enjoyed an equal voice. Those attending the Sandusky council, including Dunquat, quickly agreed to Brant's proposals.[6] But the new coalition sat on an ambiguous foundation: while everyone agreed that the Americans should respect the Ohio River boundary, they differed considerably on how to respond if they did not.

In the summer of 1784, the United States invited Six Nations leaders to meet at Fort Stanwix, where British and Haudenosaunee negotiators had drawn the 1768 boundary. In accord with diplomatic protocols, Brant and the league's civil leadership stayed at home and sent a delegation of military commanders, who offered to help make peace between the United States and all of the "free and independent" Indian peoples east of the Mississippi. Instead, the U.S. commissioners invited them to propose a new boundary between their own nations and the United States. After several days' discussion, the Allegheny Seneca Cornplanter suggested a large cession in present-day Pennsylvania, offering the Americans ample new land while preserving the Haudenosaunee homeland south and east of Lake Ontario. The Americans countered by demanding that the Six Nations also surrender lands to the west, including a corridor along the Niagara River. Together, the territory in question encompassed one Seneca community entirely, split another in half, and cut off the Six Nations from allies in Canada and Ohio. The delegation protested but had few options. The commissioners branded the Haudenosaunee "a subdued people" and warned that "*you* now stand out *alone* against our *whole force*." To underscore their words, armed militia surrounded the fort, trapping the delegation inside. Cornplanter haggled, winning a higher purchase price and the right to hunt in ceded territory, but the Americans refused to accept any less land. Rather than paving the way for peace, the delegation left Fort Stanwix having signed a treaty they had no authority to make.[7]

A few months later, a similar scene unfolded on the upper Ohio. Initially, the United States invited the Delaware and Wyandot to a council on the Cuyahoga River, relatively close to the Upper Sandusky towns. Hundreds of Delawares and Wyandots awaited them there in the December cold. But ice-choked rivers convinced the commissioners to change the venue to Fort McIntosh, about thirty miles downstream from Pittsburgh. A shorter and easier trip for the commissioners meant a much more arduous one for their guests, ensuring that far fewer Indians, and only those most committed to befriending the United States, made the journey. Pipe and Dunquat both attended, as did Abraham Kuhn, a German-born Wyandot leader from Lower Sandusky. Buckongahelas was absent, as were the Detroit Wyandots, without whose consent Dunquat and Kuhn's authority was at best suspect. As at Fort Stanwix, the congressional and Pennsylvanian commissioners paraded their soldiers, demanded an immense territory, and offered only token concessions. And as at Fort Stanwix, the Delaware and Wyandot delegations finally signed the treaty, leaving hostages to show their good intentions.[8]

As news of the treaties spread, protests mounted. Following Brant's lead, many Ohio Indian leaders insisted that no legitimate treaty could take place unless their nations first reached consensus among themselves. Some lectured American messengers that they could not expect to make a lasting peace by "tak[ing] our Chiefs prisoners, and com[ing] with Soldiers at your backs." Buckongahelas traveled south to recruit southern Indians to join the united front. Brant pressed the British for military aid and told all who would listen that Britain had not, and could not, give away Indian lands. He and other critics of the treaties repeatedly made clear that they wanted peace but insisted that the Americans "must not think to take what Land they pleased." Some claimed that by signing the treaty, Pipe and Dunquat had "broke faith" with their people. The following summer, Cornplanter tried to give back his copy of the Fort Stanwix treaty, insisting that the commissioners had lied about its contents. But he, Pipe, and Dunquat all ultimately defended the treaties. When Pipe learned that a Delaware hostage had escaped, he brought his own son and nephew to replace him. They may have gambled that befriending the Americans would better serve themselves, and their communities, than the alternative.[9] Their towns stood closer to the American stronghold of Fort Pitt, and farther from the British outposts on the lakes, than other Seneca, Wyandot, and Delaware communities, leaving them more vulnerable to attack. The imperative of physical security, after several years of war, may have carried the greatest weight.

In mid-1783, Douglass had found Ohio Indians eager for peace and friendship with the United States. Two years later, relative peace endured, but goodwill had eroded. Congress's demands, and its denial of native sovereignty, fueled resentment and hostility. Some veterans of the British alliance now sought to build an enduring confederation that transcended ethnic divisions. Anticipating American hostility, they looked to Canada for aid. Even so, fear of American attack, and desire for American patronage, prompted some to accept the United States' terms and to urge others to do the same. On all sides, Ohio Indians aimed to build enduring and mutually advantageous relationships with either the United States, Britain, or both, but they did so in myriad ways.

Less than a year after his meetings with Pipe and Brant, Douglass faced defiance from a different quarter. While waiting for Congress to pay him, he won several government appointments in Pennsylvania's newly created Fayette County, where he set about trying to establish "the authority of the court" and instill a "habitude of obedience" among his new neighbors. He made little progress, thanks to those he termed "the rabble of this country." One warm summer night, as Fayette tax collector Philip Jenkins sat at home with friends and family, three men charged through the door brandishing pistols and clubs, their faces "streak'd with Black." In thick German accents, the invaders threatened to kill anyone who moved, then began beating Jenkins on the head. In between blows, they demanded his commission, assessment lists, and all the money he had collected. When Jenkins protested, they pummeled him again, then ransacked the house by candlelight. They warned that if Jenkins or anyone else tried to collect taxes in the area again, he would "be a Dead man and we will burn all you have." Then they made off with all his money, papers, and valuables, including "a pocket Bottle, [a] Razor and some soap."[10]

The people whom Douglass aspired to govern had a long history of resisting government authority, often by exploiting the boundary dispute between Virginia and Pennsylvania. Virginia had abandoned its claim in 1779, but Pennsylvania's attempts to levy taxes nonetheless prompted "a general outcry." Dorsey Pentecost, a former Virginia partisan who now served on Pennsylvania's Executive Council, urged his constituents to pay no taxes, calling instead for the formation of a new western state. Following Pentecost's lead,

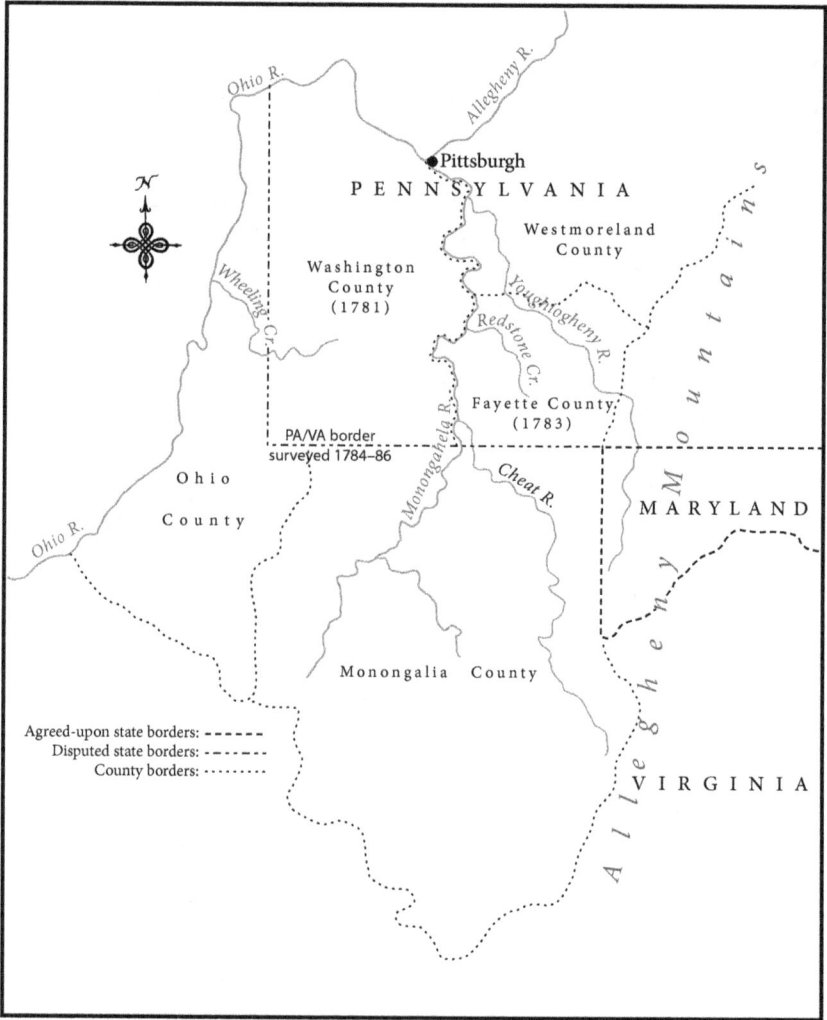

Figure 7. The Forks of the Ohio region, post-1779 borders.

men drafted for militia duty ignored their assignments and instead ob-
structed government officials, especially those involved in seizing the property of bankrupt families. They demanded that their officers resign
Pennsylvania commissions and threatened to tar and feather those who did
not. Others intimidated constables, shot at tax assessors, and declared themselves independent of Pennsylvania. In June 1782, when an official surveying
party set out to mark the new state line, armed men refused to let them pass,
correctly deeming the boundary "a prelude to the taxes." Army officers feared
the separatists might try to seize Fort Pitt and its arsenal. After the war, Loyalist refugees joined the tax resisters, who grew more aggressive. Jenkins's
assailants assaulted and robbed at least two other Fayette County tax collectors. The state offered a £50 reward, but Douglass had little hope of appre-
hending the culprits: they enjoyed too much support. When officials jailed
one suspected bandit, twenty-eight friends broke him out, then descended
on his captor's home, stole his horse, and "cautioned him against meddling
with any of them thereafter." Not surprisingly, tax collection ground to a
halt.[11] The government of Pennsylvania had won independence from Britain,
but it struggled to police its own citizens.

In both the upper Ohio Valley and Kentucky, intracultural diversity and
competition heightened tensions further. Ethnic, economic, and factional divisions had existed since the first colonists' arrival. Now a postwar financial
crisis heightened conflict between debtors and creditors. Colonists along the
Ohio, who had borne the brunt of wartime attacks, resented less vulnerable
inhabitants who had spurned calls for collective defense. Meanwhile, tangled
land claims fueled years of litigation. In Kentucky, tensions emerged between
the ubiquitous Scots-Irish, known as "cohees," and tidewater Virginians
called "tuckyahoes." The latter included scions of the Chesapeake gentry who
aspired to both landed wealth and political power, threatening the hard-
earned smallholdings of their humbler neighbors. The relatively irreligious
elite also grated against backcountry Baptists, whose egalitarian beliefs
threatened planters' control over slaves and servants. The gentry considered
the Baptists "a very superstitious, hypocritical set" prone to "ranting." For
their own part, Baptists thought the gentry had "no religion at all." Such conflicts hindered both governing and military recruiting. Left to their own devices, as one observer noted, Kentucky leaders could not assemble enough
men "to carry on any kind of expedition—such is the division amongst
them."[12]

Other colonists crossed the Ohio. Soon after the Gnadenhütten massacre, more than five hundred colonists reportedly backed a plan "to go Settle on the Indians' land." Some aimed to create "a new state on the Muskingum": the territory of the United States' Delaware allies. They knew from long experience that the official system of land sales would favor the wealthy and well connected. As one group told their new Shawnee neighbors, they had to take land "before their great People engross'd it, which they expected would soon be the case." Like earlier colonists in the upper Ohio Valley and Kentucky, this new wave gambled that preemptive occupation would secure them legal title sometime in the future. Some insisted that cutting down trees and planting crops entitled them to four hundred acres. Such claims directly threatened Congress's plans to pay war debts through land sales. One army officer warned that, without intervention, "the whole Federal territory will not raise One thousand Pounds." In the summer of 1783, dozens of emigrant-laden boats passed Fort Pitt "to encroach on the Indian Country." The Fort Pitt garrison seized some of the boats, fired on others, and periodically crossed the Ohio to drive off homesteaders, with little long-term effect. By 1786, five to ten heavily laden boats passed each day.[13]

But even as Ohio Valley colonists ignored specific government policies, they used emerging state institutions for their own ends. Rival factions among the nascent colonial elite battled with one another to secure the perquisites of local office, such as fees for government services and influence over contracts. The benefits of government appointments raised the stakes of local elections. In Pennsylvania, disappointed candidates often petitioned the Executive Council to overturn results, alleging that their rivals had ignored minimum property requirements or accepted voters who had not sworn allegiance. Not surprisingly, the council tended to favor those known as loyal civil servants. Longtime Pennsylvania partisans howled in protest when their pro-Virginia rivals won local elections; to secure their positions, the erstwhile Virginians assured Pennsylvanian officials of their newfound loyalties. Whatever they might think of Pennsylvania, those on all sides needed the council's goodwill to triumph over their rivals. In denouncing one another, the petitioners rhetorically embraced state law and state institutions as authoritative arbitrators in local disputes.[14]

The pursuit of government contracts tied some members of the colonial elite still more closely to revolutionary governments. To assert their authority in the region, Congress, Pennsylvania, and Virginia needed local contractors to secure supplies, build roads, and survey lands. Competition for contracts fostered patronage networks linking merchants, surveyors, army officers, and government officials. Veteran Pittsburgh trader David Duncan had provisioned the wartime garrison at Fort Pitt; with the coming of peace, he promptly resumed trading with Ohio Indians. By the mid-1780s, his agents ranged from the upper Allegheny River to the Shawnee towns of western Ohio. Duncan himself traveled repeatedly to British-occupied Detroit to cultivate business partners and sell upper Ohio grain. He also pursued government contracts to supply the western army and treaty commissioners, and he angled to acquire choice tracts of land. Although trading with erstwhile enemies attracted criticism, Duncan won over civil and military authorities by making himself useful. Army commander Josiah Harmar relied on him for detailed accounts of British and Indian activities, and Duncan and his partners, most notably William Finley, helped prominent officials buy choice western lands. They kept particularly close ties to former Fort Pitt commandant William Irvine, whom Duncan had served during the war. In 1786, Irvine entered Congress, and Duncan quickly sought help in both securing the title to a lucrative salt spring and winning a contract to provision the western army. In exchange, he offered the new congressman a share in the spring and kept an eye on Irvine's own land claims. After many false starts, Duncan won a contract to supply thirty thousand rations for the 1788 Treaty of Fort Harmar.[15]

Duncan's relationships with Irvine and Harmar were part of a web of patronage stretching from Congress through the military and commercial hub of Pittsburgh to army garrisons and Indian communities throughout the Ohio Valley and around Lake Erie. Cumulatively, such networks gave upper Ohio merchants and traders an ever greater stake in the effectiveness of state authority, even as they profited from state weakness. Congress spent so much money in the region because of its tenuous military and political position. But to secure the profits they envisioned, Duncan and his allies needed the nascent Anglo-American state to pay its bills, uphold land titles, and keep the peace. The flow of patronage and profits fused public endeavors with private ones, and formal partnerships with the extralegal exchange of favors. In the process, representatives of state authority gained a personal interest in acquiring Indian land, even at the cost of political and military stability. Harmar and his officers, charged with maintaining frontier peace, simultaneously angled for a share of the lands that Indians were determined to defend. Harmar himself asked Congressman Irvine to use his "influence" to help him get a slice of the Muskingum Valley. Duncan, by contrast, railed against Congress's haste to colonize Ohio, reasoning that war would ruin his trading business, but his eagerness for Harmar's and Irvine's patronage deterred him from protesting too loudly.[16]

Other colonists used emerging institutions for local and personal purposes. In early 1782, the magistrate Abner Howell conducted a double marriage uniting Sabitha Colt with Cornelius Miller, and Jeniah Colt with an unnamed woman. Both couples paid for Howell's services in silver coin—a scarce commodity. The two couples set up housekeeping nearby, in the same neighborhood where everyone involved had lived for years. But two other neighbors denounced the double wedding, pointing out that three of the four newlyweds were already legally married, two of them—the Colts—to one another. By law, both marriages were bigamous and therefore invalid; Howell's ceremony was legally meaningless. When questioned on the matter, Howell gloated that, legal or not, "he had Got the hard money for what he had done." The exchange of silver reflected the ritual's importance to the participants: cash-poor western Pennsylvanians typically did without official marriage licenses, but the Colts and Millers paid for them despite their dubious legality. And they were not alone: in the weeks after the double wedding, Howell reportedly planned to conduct three more marriages "of the same kind."[17] Paying for the local magistrate's stamp of approval helped overcome doubts about the legality and perhaps morality of the marital rearrangement. When the state took the form of Philip Jenkins, tax collector, many upper Ohio colonists considered it a scourge. But when it manifested as Abner Howell, a magistrate willing to bend the law to his neighbors' interests, it found a much warmer welcome.

The usefulness of pliable officials spurred western Pennsylvanians to petition their government to subdivide townships, shrinking the bailiwicks of local magistrates like Howell. In smaller townships, constituents were more likely to know their magistrates personally, and they did not travel as far to plead their cases. In theory, at least, colonists could have managed without such officially commissioned magistrates. They could have either resolved their disputes privately or created local courts independent of state authority. But in practice, the fractiousness of colonial society hindered independent conflict resolution. Moreover, the courtroom provided a useful site for the public performance of reconciliation, goodwill, and mutual respect. For many Ohio Valley colonists, then, the localization of judicial authority made the courts more useful, more accountable, and more convenient to their purposes.[18] Tax collectors faced persecution. Violent resistance went unpunished. But colonists still looked to governments to help them achieve their goals, less because of respect for state authority than the bitter divisions between them and their neighbors. Amid countless local conflicts over marriages, property disputes, and local elections, contending factions sought advantage by enlisting the support of public officials. Out of such internecine quarrels, the flimsy frontier state began to gain traction.

On a fine evening in October 1785, in the pine forests that have since become greater Cincinnati, fifteen cattle declared their independence from the United States. For two weeks, the animals had floated down the Ohio on a leaky flatboat, unsheltered from repeated downpours and chilly autumn nights. Congressional Indian commissioner Richard Butler had brought them to feed his soldiers while they built a new fort and hosted an upcoming treaty with the Shawnees. On reaching their destination, near the mouth of the Miami River, Butler brought the beasts ashore but "they seemed wild and not inclined to settle." That night, the cattle slipped away and headed back upriver. The soldiers' attempts to round them up made them only "more wild and ungovernable." After two nights and a day of searching the woods, their pursuers gave up the chase.[19]

Butler had hoped to awe Indians and colonists alike with the power of the United States, but he could not manage even his ambulatory meat locker. Hungry soldiers would likely follow the cattle's example. Those who remained would hardly intimidate anyone. But where Congress's resources fell short, the peoples of the Ohio Valley stepped into the breach. Four visiting Wyandots helped recover some of the cattle and carried speeches from Butler to Indian towns. Kentucky colonists hunted deer to replace Butler's lost beef. A few days later, a Kentucky woman paddled across the Ohio with a day's supply of bear meat. Another nearby community sold him eighty pounds of salted bison. Some colonists even sold Butler meat on credit, tactfully overlooking Congress's financial woes. Meanwhile, Nonhelema, a leader of the Mekoche Shawnees, promoted Butler's mission among her people. Her son and daughter carried messages constantly between the new outpost—Fort Finney—and the Shawnee towns, assuring all who listened of Butler's good intentions. Together, this eclectic mix of allies enabled Butler to welcome a large Shawnee delegation for the treaty.[20]

Butler received so much help because Ohio Valley inhabitants hoped that he might negotiate a treaty that addressed their disparate concerns. A few months earlier, an Ohio Haudenosaunee leader called Captain Wolf had mapped out such an agreement. A Virginian delegation, led by James

Sherlock, had come to the Shawnee town of Wakatomica to retrieve wartime captives. Wolf instead handed over a tightly bound land hunter, recently found with several others north of the Ohio River. Wolf noted that at previous meetings, Sherlock and others had announced that the United States would not object if Indians harmed "the People who were encroaching upon us," reasoning that such intruders brought it "upon themselves." Acting on this suggestion, a Cherokee band had recently killed and scalped seven trespassers near the mouth of the Scioto. But most Ohio Indians preferred to handle the problem diplomatically. Captain Wolf had sent most of his captives home with a stern warning; now he brought the last of them to the council to make a point. He demanded that colonists respect the boundary "settled by our forefathers": the Ohio River. If they did so, the assembled Indian leaders pledged to return the captives that Sherlock sought and to continue peaceful trade and diplomacy.[21]

Wolf's proposal addressed leading concerns of both Indians and colonists. After a decade of war and colonization, many Indians were resigned to the loss of Kentucky but were loath to surrender land north of the Ohio. Many insisted that no nation could cede more territory until all western nations reached consensus. As Wolf made clear to Sherlock, securing peace hinged on maintaining the Ohio River boundary. For their part, many Kentucky colonists cared less about Ohio land than protecting the families and property they already had. During the war, British-allied Indians had adopted countless captives into their own families, spiritually replacing lost loved ones. In 1783, colonists and Shawnees began negotiating an exchange of prisoners, but the adoptees' families of origin struggled to get them back. Wa-ba-kah-kah-to, a prominent Pekowi Shawnee leader, refused several offers to ransom his adopted daughter, insisting that she "was not a slave to be sold" but rather "one of his family." When congressional commissioners arrived in Kentucky to hold a treaty with the Shawnees and their neighbors, colonists traveled long distances to beg for the return of lost children. Others complained that they had lost nearly all their horses, the region's most mobile and lucrative commodity, to Indian raiders.[22] A new peace agreement could have satisfied both Shawnees' and Kentuckians' demands. Affirming the Ohio River boundary would have bolstered the influence of moderate Indian leaders, enabling them to more effectively deter horse stealing and return adopted captives. With no prospect of obtaining legal title, the rush of land hunters across the Ohio would likely have slowed, and those who persisted would have had to confront their Indian neighbors without military protection. To be sure, some Indians and colonists would have continued stealing one another's horses and sometimes killing each other, but with meaningful concessions moderate leaders could have more easily contained such outbreaks of violence.

However, Congress's appointed treaty commissioners insisted on Ohio's colonization, making any such agreement impossible. Their obstinacy reflected speculative ambitions as much as official instructions. Butler, a veteran trader and diplomat, had been noting desirable locations for over a decade. His letters seamlessly moved from discussing politics to describing valuable tracts. Samuel Parsons, a Connecticut jurist and Continental general, had lost his personal fortune in the war and now sought to regain it in Ohio. During his trip west, he scouted out promising lands for family and friends. Neither had any love for the colonists of Kentucky. Butler called for more army outposts to keep Kentuckians under control, while Parsons reportedly dismissed them as "a Banditty of Refugees not worthy of Congress's Notice." The third commissioner, George Rogers Clark, sought to create a new colony across the river from Louisville.[23] Congress had chosen agents who cared far more about acquiring Ohio than befriending Indians, protecting Kentucky horse herds, or recovering adopted captives.

Because of these personal ambitions, as well as their orders from Congress, the commissioners flatly refused to negotiate. During the Fort Finney meeting, the Shawnee war leader Kekewepellethe promised that he and his fellow warriors would return "every one" of their nation's adopted captives: an important step toward addressing Kentuckians' chief grievance. The commissioners, however, demanded that the Shawnees join the Delawares and Wyandots in surrendering all of southern and eastern Ohio to the United States. When Delawares and Wyandots questioned that cession's legitimacy, the commissioners held firm, dashing any hope of recovering the captives. In reply, Kekewepellethe challenged the Americans' claim to sovereignty. "God gave us this country," he declared: "it is all ours." Laying on the council table a string of black and white wampum beads, a sacred symbol of his people's voice, he insisted that the Americans retract their demands. Clark lifted his cane, swept Kekewepellethe's wampum onto the floor, and crushed the beads under his boot. Then, threatening "the destruction of your women and children," the commissioners stormed out, leaving the Shawnees six days to change their minds.[24]

This dramatic display won the commissioners their treaty but dashed any hope of peace. After a short but heated debate, Molunthy, the Shawnees' head civil chief; Kekewepellethe; and several other Shawnee leaders signed and left hostages as security for their compliance. Over the months that followed, Shawnee hunters regularly visited the fort to trade. Enforcing the treaty, though, proved impossible. Molunthy delivered only a handful of captives, some of whom soon ran away to rejoin their adoptive families. With Congress demanding all or nothing, most Shawnees preferred to yield nothing. Desperate for other options, Molunthy and other treaty signers appealed to Britain for help, complaining that the Americans were "striving to work our destruction." Meanwhile, Wyandots, Delawares, and Shawnees warned American traders that they would resist any surveyors north of the Ohio. Even the accommodating Pipe and Dunquat urged Congress to postpone surveying until they made "a firm Peace first with all the Nations." Fear of attack delayed the surveys for months. At the same time, raids against Kentucky homesteads escalated. Though one army officer dismissed the raiders as "a few Banditi of the Cherokees," Shawnees, Ohio Haudenosaunees, and Anishinaabeg now joined them. Increasingly, the raiders killed and captured colonists in addition to taking horses. And unlike the war years, when British-allied Indians had adopted or ransomed most of their prisoners, now those they captured were less likely to survive. In September 1786, a Cherokee war party brought thirteen scalps and four female prisoners to Wakatomica. Eighteen months before, Wolf had released his captured Virginian land hunter at the same town. Now, the townspeople ritually tortured and killed two of the captives, a mother and daughter.[25] To many Kentuckians, reports of their fate vindicated calls for war.

In June 1786, Kentucky militia officers, led by Fort Finney commissioner George Rogers Clark, proposed an expedition "to chastise" Wabash Valley towns. They hoped to march in early August with 1,500 volunteers, "determined not to return without distroying their country or Reducing them to terms of our own." The organizers faced large hurdles. Persuading so many men to join a long campaign, and raising the necessary supplies, would prove difficult. Even if they could raise the men, the organizers doubted their reliability. During the Revolutionary War, lack of experience and discipline had plagued Kentucky's defenses. In a 1782 battle at Blue Licks, Hugh McGary had led 170 militia into a deadly ambush, losing over a third of his men. The officers hoped for regular army support, but Knox insisted that U.S. forces be used only to defend against "unprovoked aggression." Virginia governor Patrick Henry, whose brother-in-law had recently died in battle with Indians north of the Ohio, called for "attacking the Enemy in their Towns," but

Congress refused to endorse a plan that would likely lead to a long and expensive war.[26] Nonetheless, Clark and his allies managed to mount not one but two expeditions, totaling near two thousand men. They defied Congress by exploiting their standing as government officials. They creatively misconstrued official directives, connived with sympathetic army officers, and used their formal authority to dragoon men. Their campaigns violated U.S. policy but depended nonetheless on the local manifestations of state power.

Both military and civil authorities abetted the expedition planners. Army officer Walter Finney, who commanded a garrison near Louisville, privately scoffed at Congress's peace policy, arguing that money spent on treaties would be better invested in war. In June, Finney proposed lending his garrison's cannon to the expedition, citing his "Conviction that arms must be used against the Indians." General Harmar balked at this scheme, but he ambiguously advised Finney to "co-operate with the militia of Kentucky," suggesting acquiescence to militia leadership. Knox, sitting one thousand miles away, howled in protest, with little effect. Like Finney and Harmar, Governor Henry hesitated to countermand Congress, but he noted that the Articles of Confederation permitted militia to attack preemptively if they "received certain advice" of imminent invasion and lacked time to consult Congress. The Kentuckians lacked such "certain advice," and Congress had already rebuffed them, but the governor implied that they could exploit the loophole to justify their campaign. The expedition promoters needed little prodding. In a hastily penned legal opinion, three Kentucky magistrates announced that the governor's message empowered militia officers to draft men and impress supplies. Citing this document, the officers ordered up their companies and commandeered salt and livestock, threatening to kill any who resisted their demands.[27] This interpretation of the governor's message was dubious at best, but claiming government sanction was essential to the expedition's prospects. Without the authority of the militia law, and the power to fine delinquents and impress supplies, the organizers could not have raised the men, grain, and livestock they needed.

Many colonists opposed these demands, especially in eastern Kentucky; the expedition organizers countered with force. Eli Cleveland, an aged Fayette County magistrate, publicly denied the plan's legality, ridiculed its promoters, and threatened to kill anyone who tried to impress his property. Others, citing Cleveland's opinion, forcibly reclaimed requisitioned cattle. In retaliation, militia commander Levi Todd ordered half a dozen men to seize Cleveland's "Beef, Bacon, and pack horses" and to kill the old man if he resisted. When the militia reached the plantation, Mary Cleveland, Eli's wife, blocked the farm gate, only to see the militia tear down the fence and drive off her livestock, while one of Todd's men "presented a gun at her brest." Soon thereafter, Todd and his allies arrested Eli, stripped him of his officer's commission, and petitioned the governor to annul his appointment as magistrate. Todd responded similarly even to minor interference, insisting that he "intended to rule by an Arbitrary power" until the expedition was over. When a storeowner refused to hand over a third bushel of salt—having already surrendered two—their militia smashed his store and seized both the salt and the merchant himself, insisting that he join the expedition. A band of militia broke into the home of Phillip Eastin, a Revolutionary War veteran, tied him by the wrists to a horse's tail, and forced him to run after them until his shoes were worn through. Militia officers thus used the pretense of legal sanction, together with a cohort of armed supporters, to assume dictatorial power. They voiced deference to higher authorities but made clear they would ignore any attempt to restrain them.[28] State influence and state resources thus launched an expedition that openly defied congressional policy.

But if eastern policymakers could not control frontier officers, neither could the officers control the men they nominally commanded. Contrary to their reputation as dogged Indian fighters, most Kentuckians preferred not to march hundreds of miles from home, leaving their families unguarded, to attack towns that might or might not be home to troublesome raiders. Moreover, Clark's vaunted leadership proved less inspiring than advertised. He expected 1,500 to 2,000 men; only 1,100 showed up. After marching several hundred miles in September heat, their bodies wore down and their food spoiled. Rumors swirled that a large army awaited them. As they camped a few miles from the Indian town at the mouth of the Vermillion River, someone reportedly cried out, "Who's for home?" Needing no more encouragement, most of the men "turn'd back in Full Disorder." Attempting to save face, Clark occupied the French town of Vincennes and offered to negotiate with the Wabash nations. Neither the Indians nor the French were impressed. Clark's rivals, meanwhile, eagerly denounced him to eastern officials. Within months, he had lost both his military command and his post as congressional Indian commissioner.[29]

Meanwhile, militia officer Benjamin Logan mounted a second expedition against the Mad River Shawnee towns, a less distant and more familiar foe. In strategic terms, they were an odd target. Some of their inhabitants, particularly the Mekoche division, had labored persistently to keep the peace. But their towns were closer to Kentucky than any other Indian communities, making them easier to attack. Organizers expected Clark's men to serve nearly two months; Logan's campaign lasted about fifteen days. As Clark's undersized force headed for the Wabash, Logan set about rounding up "all the Delinquents and Deserters" as well as one-half of the militia not yet called for duty. Nearly eight hundred men signed on, many of them aiming to escape the fines they faced for refusing to join Clark. They faced little resistance. Many Shawnee warriors had gone to the Wabash country to fight Clark, and a deserter from Logan's army warned the town's inhabitants to flee before the attack. Those who remained were mostly pro-treaty Mekoches who considered themselves at peace with the United States. The Kentuckians pounced, killing ten men, including several elders, capturing thirty-two women and children, and torching the towns. The stragglers included Clark and Butler's ally Nonhelema as well as the aged Molunthy, who flew the United States flag outside his cabin. In the middle of their now-smoldering village, a crowd of Kentuckians surrounded the captives. One of the onlookers, Hugh McGary, had led his men into the disastrous Blue Licks ambush four years before. Now, he pressed to the front and demanded to know whether Molunthy had been in that battle. Perhaps misunderstanding the question, Molunthy nodded. McGary seized a nearby axe, knocked the old man to the ground, split open his head, and removed his scalp. Some of McGary's companions were outraged, but enough men supported him that Logan did nothing about it until after their return to Kentucky.[30]

Logan's triumph over a few dozen women, children, and old men did little to discourage raids against Kentucky. Within months, warriors from the Wabash towns resumed "plundering the inhabitants of their horses & occasionally murdering them." The attack on America's closest Shawnee allies only intensified hostilities. As one army officer noted, "Partial strokes on the Defenceless part of a Nation serves only to Irritate the Wariors, and unite them more generally for War." More Shawnees raided Kentucky after Logan's attack, he reported, than before. Ohio Haudenosaunees and Cherokees soon captured nine Kentucky women and ritually burned eight of them to death. Such scenes were becoming more common: one trader reported that "they Dont mean to Keep many Prisoners now but Kill all before them." In April 1788, one Kentucky leader reported that Indians had killed nearly thirty colonists in the previous four months. Even so, many western Indians still hoped for peace. At the time of Logan's attack, leaders from an array of western nations were preparing to meet at the Shawnee towns to discuss Congress's demands. With the intended council site reduced to ash, the council relocated to the Wyandot towns near Detroit, where the assembled leaders demanded that Congress "keep back your people." But they still focused primarily on Congress's own hunger for land. They announced they would "form a strict connection with the U.S." only if the Americans halted all surveys and respected the old Ohio River boundary. As a veteran trader explained, if the United States insisted on taking Ohio, "war must be the End of it."[31] Congress's unwavering territorial demands scuttled all efforts to halt the bloodshed.

As congressional intransigence paved the way to war, Logan and his allies began trying to make peace. Logan hoped to succeed where the treaty commissioners had failed, by offering his own prisoners in exchange for Indians' adopted captives. From the charred remains of the Mad River towns, Logan wrote to Shawnee leaders proposing to trade the thirty-two women and children he had captured for "a proportionable number of our people." He did so with no guidance from Congress, Virginia, or the nearby army garrison, earning sharp condemnation from its commander. Logan's strategy calls into question the assumption that Ohio Valley militiamen sought primarily to shed Indian blood. To be sure, Kentucky colonists placed little value on Indian lives: while a court-martial ultimately convicted McGary of killing Molunthy, it punished him with only a year's suspension from duty. But Logan's proposal signaled that he and his followers would just as readily negotiate with their Indian neighbors as fight them. Shawnee leaders accepted his offer. In May and again in August, Shawnee delegations came to Kentucky and exchanged their adopted children for Logan's prisoners. The meetings featured considerable ceremony, including messages of goodwill, haggling over exactly how many captives would be handed over, and assurances on both sides that remaining captives would be returned at future meetings. Once again, the adoptees' reluctance to leave their Shawnee families complicated matters. One teenaged girl who spoke no English was "a good deal surprised" on being introduced to her biological father and "much more dejected when she found she was to be taken from the Indians, perhaps forever." Despite these difficulties, within two years nearly all of the Shawnee captives had been redeemed.[32]

One of those captives, Nonhelema, had sacrificed her own wealth to serve the United States during the Revolutionary War. After the war, when congressional commissioners demanded her people's land, she and her children had aided them. She subsequently petitioned Congress to compensate her for her service and losses by granting her part of her homeland. Instead she found herself a prisoner, though she was likely released in one of Logan's exchanges. Her petition to Congress, meanwhile, lay neglected for three years. In 1788, a committee recommended granting her request, but there is no indication that she ever took advantage of the United States' belated gratitude. It seems more likely that Logan's raid, Molunthy's murder, and her own subsequent captivity crushed her hopes of peaceful coexistence in her old homeland. She and her family may have migrated north or west with their fellow Shawnees. Many resettled in the Maumee Valley of northwest Ohio, an area that would soon become the hub of resistance to congressional policy.[33]

The failure of Nonhelema's hopes for a peaceful postwar settlement reflected both the flimsiness and potency of the emerging Anglo-American state. In 1786, the United States could neither restrain nor punish either its nominal citizens in Kentucky or its nominal allies in the Shawnee towns. By insisting on seizing and selling Indian lands, Congress effectively guaranteed that attacks would continue. Not surprisingly, the growing violence on the frontier, and the growing indifference of both Indians and Kentuckians to congressional dictates, sparked fears that the new nation might lose its already tenuous grip on the Ohio Valley. Nonetheless, as violence escalated, state resources continued to play a central role. Clark and Logan could mount their expeditions only by using formal militia authority to coerce recalcitrant colonists. Similarly, Ohio Indian leaders continued to appeal to Congress and Britain to respect and enforce their boundaries and help protect them from rampaging Kentuckians. Even with congressional influence at its nadir, few influential leaders on either side of the frontier could imagine a peaceful future without state patronage.

In the spring of 1787, thirty-four years after they first met, Guyasuta and George Washington embarked on new projects. The old warriors had been allies, then enemies, then allies, and yet again enemies. Now Washington sat in Philadelphia, presiding over a convention assembled to amend the Articles of Confederation. The meetings brought forth a new federal republic, laying the foundation for future relations between the United States and Indian nations. Meanwhile, Guyasuta repeated their 1753 journey up the Allegheny, this time escorting a detachment of American soldiers to Venango, an abandoned Seneca town at the mouth of French Creek. On that spot in 1763, Guyasuta's warriors had destroyed a British fort and slaughtered its garrison. In 1779, revolutionary forces, on Washington's orders, had burned the

Senecas' homes and crops, driving them to the swelling refugee camp at Niagara. Despite this bloody history, both sides now overcame their lingering animosities. The Americans delivered the Senecas fifty bushels of corn. In return, some young Senecas hunted and scouted for them. As they did so, the soldiers built a new fort near whatever remained of the one that Guyasuta had burned. The American commander, Jonathan Heart, assured his superiors that the Senecas showed "the strongest Marks of friendship."[34]

Like Pipe and Dunquat, Guyasuta and his nephew and successor, Cornplanter, had adjusted to the peace of 1783 by cultivating American patronage. The peace enabled Haudenosaunee refugees to return home from overcrowded camps around Niagara, but their dispersal revived old geographic and political divisions. While other Senecas founded a major new community at Buffalo Creek, and kept close ties to the British, the people of Cornplanter and Guyasuta returned to the upper Allegheny and cultivated American patrons at Pittsburgh. Cornplanter quickly gained credibility among army officers and prominent colonists. When he visited Fort Pitt, leading citizens fed his delegation at their own expense, signaling eagerness to befriend their erstwhile enemies. In 1786, when the Senecas faced dire food shortages, Fort Pitt's commander readily supplied them, deeming "it for the interest of the United States not to send them away empty." When Heart received orders to build a new fort at Venango, 150 miles upstream, he initially planned to travel secretly, but wiser men persuaded him he could succeed only with Seneca aid.[35]

The soldiers' arrival at French Creek deepened this mutual reliance. The Senecas provided the garrison with guides, venison, and information, and in turn they looked to their new neighbors for grain and medical care. When smallpox struck the Senecas and other Ohio Indian towns, the uninfected fled for safety and the sick turned to Heart, who deemed that "Humanity compells me to give them some assistance," even at the risk of infecting his own men. The following winter, when a six-foot snowfall kept the Senecas from their usual hunting territory, they instead hunted near Heart's fort, where they knew they could find support. Heart also recommended—likely at Cornplanter's urging—that Connecticut grant Indians large tracts for hunting and town building in the state's new western reserve. He also sharply condemned the likes of Benjamin Logan for "continually killing & plundering" their Indian neighbors. Heart's tact and benevolence won him praise. His superior, Josiah Harmar, boasted that "no officer . . . manages the Indians better." In 1789, when Heart was reassigned elsewhere, some Senecas worried that his departure heralded war.[36]

But however much Heart despised Virginian thuggery and promoted intercultural cooperation, his own ambitions—like those of Butler, Clark, Harmar, and countless others—hinged on Indian dispossession. He privately hoped to become a "proprietor in Lands," but his poverty forced him to do so through patronage: cultivating well-placed sponsors, aiding them with his knowledge and services, and exploiting their favor to gain legal title. Heart drew exceptionally accurate maps, and during his military service he had learned a great deal about the region's resources. In 1786, for example, he and his men escorted the first official surveyors west of the Ohio. He promptly offered to share the knowledge he had gained with his "Friends." Soon after arriving at French Creek, he boasted that he had "sufficient Influence with the Indians here to procure some very trusty young Men" to help such friends locate desirable tracts. If they lobbied for favorable land policies, he hinted, his expertise and connections could make them rich. He relied in particular on congressional treaty commissioner Samuel Parsons, a fellow Connecticut native and Continental Army veteran, who eagerly accepted Heart's suggestions. Late in 1789, the two undertook a canoe journey from Pittsburgh toward Lake Erie, aiming to find desirable land, identify the best water routes, and negotiate with nearby Indians. On the return trip Parsons capsized and drowned in the Beaver River. Bereft of his patron, Heart spent the following months hawking the information they had gleaned, while completing surveys for several other well-placed New Englanders.[37]

In guiding Heart and his men to Venango, and supporting the fort they built there, Guyasuta and Cornplanter inserted themselves into this patronage network, with ties to army officers, Pittsburgh merchants, members of Congress, and an array of eastern speculators. These coalition partners shared a common preoccupation: getting a step ahead in the coming Ohio land rush. Here the Senecas saw an opportunity, just as Guyasuta had in 1770 when he re-befriended the land-hungry Washington. Speculators like Heart and Parsons eagerly sought native allies to share their expertise and bolster their claims. By collaborating with such patrons, the Senecas pursued decades-long objectives: physical security, beneficial terms of trade, and recognition of their nation's sovereignty. After watching their homes and crops burn in 1779, and enduring years of deprivation at Niagara, such goals seemed worth the sacrifice of land.

Having gambled their future on the patronage of the United States, Cornplanter and his people could ill afford to retaliate for American abuses. Their patrons in Congress and the army offered them little protection against nearby colonists, who repeatedly insulted, robbed, and even killed them. Nor were they protected against deceitful intermediaries. In negotiations with veteran diplomats John Gibson and Richard Butler, Cornplanter agreed to sell Pennsylvania a triangle of land along Lake Erie. In exchange, the Senecas reserved half the Lake Chautauqua fishery, as well as hunting and fishing rights throughout the ceded territory, and were promised "one thousand dollars in fine prime goods," to be distributed in Pittsburgh. The Senecas undertook a grueling midwinter journey, enduring colonial attacks and thievery as well as the cold, only to receive one hundred blankets that "were all moth eaton and good fornot'g." Cornplanter accused Gibson of fraud and demanded compensation. Some Pittsburghers supported their claim, but Pennsylvania ignored it. In late 1790, Cornplanter led a Seneca delegation to Philadelphia and won limited concessions. Though both federal and state governments refused to reconsider their legally dubious land grabs, Pennsylvania now compensated the Senecas for earlier stolen payments and reserved a tract of land on the Allegheny to Cornplanter personally. Cornplanter also won a generous annual pension, as well as federal promises to protect remaining Haudenosaunee lands against state governments and speculators. These terms fell far short of satisfying his nation's demands, but they seemed more promising than renewed hostilities. Soon after, Senecas sent eighty young men to support U.S. forces, supplied intelligence to American commanders, and urged other western nations to avoid war.[38]

As Cornplanter haggled, Congress rushed to survey and sell land north of the Ohio. It delegated the task to the geographer Thomas Hutchins, who pressed ahead despite threats of Indian attack and spotty military support. Like Heart, Hutchins lacked personal wealth but sought to leverage his knowledge to win the friendship and assistance of more prosperous investors. As his men drew a rectangular grid over eastern Ohio, Congress hurriedly sold large tracts to private land companies, which established new colonies at the mouths of the Muskingum and Miami rivers. In January 1789, Arthur St. Clair, the territory's newly appointed governor, held a council with nearly six hundred western Indians, hoping to reconcile them to a colonial project already well under way. Like his predecessors, St. Clair flatly refused to negotiate. Pipe and others signed the treaty, but many others refused or declined to attend at all.[39]

Meanwhile, the Philadelphia convention drafted a new constitution, creating a stronger federal government with authority to levy taxes, maintain an army, and manage relations with "the Indian tribes." A few months after St. Clair's inconclusive treaty, Washington became the first president of the United States. He and other American officials hoped that the new system would enable them to more efficiently sell lands, negotiate with Spain, and strengthen federal authority over colonists and Indians. Pennsylvania soon adopted a new constitution of its own, similarly centralizing power in the hands of a governor, strengthening state courts, and weakening the legislature. In 1792, the Kentucky gentry effected an amicable separation from Virginia, consolidating their control over the region's rapidly growing population. At the same time, a wave of bankruptcies deepened economic inequality, driving many into tenancy or wage labor. Neighbors sometimes banded together to defend property from confiscation, but policy changes, and the new state and federal constitutions, systematically undercut local independence. These changes weakened western colonists' ability to resist state demands, but they did not submit quietly. In 1791, Congress enacted an excise tax on whiskey that fell disproportionately on the Ohio Valley's small-scale distillers, threatening the livelihood of countless farmers. Not surprisingly, when federal tax collectors appeared, colonists greeted them with harassment, defiance, and sometimes tar and feathers.[40]

As Americans surveyed and colonized, a multiethnic town cluster known as "the Glaize" became a center of anticolonial organizing. As in the past, militants drew on both widespread resentment of colonization and a long tradition of nativist spirituality, but their appeal still hinged on hopes for British support. Veteran intermediaries like Joseph Brant and Alexander McKee—both of whom now received British salaries—urged Indians to defy Congress's territorial demands and called on imperial officials to support them. The officials waffled but repeatedly handed out weapons and supplies at the Great Lakes forts of Niagara, Detroit, and Michilimackinac. In 1790, the growing militant alliance turned back an American expedition sent to level their towns. The following year, St. Clair led a still larger army into Ohio. His superiors, anxious to expedite land sales, forced him to take the field late in the season, poorly supplied, with a force largely comprising untrained militia. The Americans' slow progress enabled the western alliance—led by Little Turtle (Miami), Blue Jacket (Shawnee), Buckongahelas (Delaware), and others—to gather a large multiethnic army and plan a daring and well-organized attack. In the wee hours of 4 November, the warriors routed the militia, overwhelmed and disabled the American artillery, and descended on the army's main camp. After a short fight, St. Clair and his men fled in disarray, echoing the 1755 rout of Braddock's army on the Monongahela. More than six hundred soldiers and camp followers died, including Butler and Heart. The allies wounded or captured hundreds more. American Indian peoples have never inflicted a bloodier defeat upon the forces of the United States.[41]

The overwhelming victory gave nonalliance members such as Cornplanter new leverage to win diplomatic concessions. Anxious to avoid making new enemies, federal officials now hastened to address Haudenosaunee grievances. In the spring of 1792, 160 Senecas sheltered at the Venango fort, receiving daily allowances of "bread & meat" while awaiting a shipment of federal goods. The commandant fed them without authorization, reasoning that doing so was good "policy." Army officers just as eagerly acceded to Cornplanter's requests for European-style agricultural equipment, and men to teach the Senecas how to use it, as well as instruction in how to read and write English. Then, in 1794, Cornplanter and other Haudenosaunee leaders won unprecedented concessions at the Treaty of Canandaigua. The United States' chief negotiator, Timothy Pickering, refused to return the Erie triangle, but he recognized Seneca claims to several major tracts along the Niagara River and the eastern end of Lake Erie, which the United States had bought in the disputed 1784 Treaty of Fort Stanwix. This concession ensured the survival of Seneca communities at Cattaraugus and Buffalo Creek.[42]

Meanwhile, the Washington administration seized the west. A new commander, Anthony Wayne, led a larger, better-trained, and more regularly supplied army into Ohio, building a series of forts from the Miami to the Maumee. The Americans won no decisive victories, but they fended off the allies' attacks. As they occupied ever more territory, and destroyed Maumee Valley towns and crops, the alliance began to splinter. Blue Jacket, with a diminished force, tried to halt the American advance at a place called Fallen Timbers, near the mouth of the Maumee River, but Wayne's disciplined troops repelled the assault. Then, critically, a British outpost on the Maumee refused to aid or open its doors to the retreating warriors. Facing no more large-scale resistance, the Americans torched the Glaize. A new treaty with Britain soon transferred the Great Lakes forts to the United States, just as a treaty with Spain promised the opening of the Mississippi to American commerce. Meanwhile, Washington dispatched a large army into western Pennsylvania to crush the movement that his supporters derisively dubbed the "whiskey rebellion." The following year, Wayne concluded the Treaty of Greenville with representatives of the western nations, including Buckongahelas, Blue Jacket, Little Turtle, and other erstwhile alliance leaders. With no more hope of British support, they "acknowledge[d] themselves to be under the protection of the said United States."[43]

Together, the events of 1794–95 cemented the sovereignty claims of the United States and, with them, systems of local government that fit federal specifications. Colonists southeast of the Ohio reconciled themselves to the limited sovereignty of Pennsylvania, Virginia, and Kentucky within the new union. Those northwest of the river became subject to a federally appointed territorial government, with the promise of eventual statehood. For Indians, the treaties of Canandaigua and Greenville, among others, affirmed Indian self-rule and promised to protect what remained of Indian lands, just as Ohio Indians had demanded for decades. But the United States recognized that sovereignty only in the form of ethnic nations—rejecting both long-standing traditions of local autonomy and more recent pursuits of multiethnic confederation—and acknowledged only Indian leaders who acceded to federal supremacy. This new political framework, in which a federal union presided over limited sovereignties called "states," "territories," and "tribes," paved the way for future waves of dispossession and colonization. In 1797, federal and state officials connived with New York speculators to seize the bulk of the territory guaranteed to the Six Nations just three years before. On the Allegheny River, Senecas retained less than 27,000 acres in New York, as well as Cornplanter's tract in Pennsylvania. In the twentieth century, when the U.S. Army Corps of Engineers built Kinzua Dam, one-third of that land sank beneath the rising waters.[44]

At first glance, the forceful imposition of federal authority stabilized the region. Where Indians and colonists had once slaughtered one another, United States officials could now preside over a process they called "settlement": a reassuring term that seemed to promise peace, order, and stability. To be sure, "settlement" entailed dispossessing native peoples, but the new treaty system aimed to do so with less bloodshed, and thus more cheaply. To twenty-first-century eyes, the unruly frontier began to look more like part of a modern state. But the narrative of ungoverned mayhem yielding to state-managed order turns historical causation on its head. Rather than lawless impulse, colonization and bloodshed sprang from government initiatives, often depending directly on government-supplied resources. A tenuous postwar peace collapsed largely because of Congress's unwavering territorial demands. Even after the bloody raids of 1786, Ohio Indians and Kentuckians continued to pursue informal diplomacy to restore lost captives, an imperative that congressional emissaries had brushed aside in their quest for land.

Meanwhile, Indians and colonists continued to seek more advantageous relationships with colonial governments. Pipe, Dunquat, and Cornplanter befriended American officials, while Brant, Buckongahelas, Blue Jacket, and Little Turtle solicited and periodically received aid from the British. Government patronage bolstered leaders' personal influence and—erratically— brought needed resources to native communities. Colonists similarly strived to maintain local autonomy but found themselves increasingly reliant on governing institutions. They resisted tax collection and debt enforcement, and they also pressed for the subdivision of townships in order to make local courts more accountable (and useful) to their communities. As rival factions contended for control of local government, they sought vindication from eastern officials. As with Indians, internecine divisions magnified the value of official patronage, binding leaders more closely to the emerging federal state.[45] Just as the region's violence stemmed from government interventions, so the eventual consolidation of state power reflected Ohio Valley inhabitants' long-standing attempts to make governments work for them.

Conclusion

In March 1785 colonist John Amberson called for a convention to form a new government for colonists living north of the Ohio River. Brazenly defying the Confederation Congress, he posted an advertisement declaring that "all mankind . . . have an undoubted right to pass into every vacant country, and there to form their own constitution." The United States, he claimed, had no authority either to restrain colonization or to sell uninhabited lands. To some nineteenth- and twentieth-century historians, this daring proposal exemplified the mentality of early Ohio Valley colonists. Frederick Jackson Turner may have had Amberson in mind when he celebrated those who "turned their backs upon the Atlantic Ocean, and with a grim energy and self-reliance began to build up a society free from the dominance of ancient forms."[1]

This book, by contrast, argues that Amberson was an anomaly. Instead of spreading indiscriminately across the land, colonists migrated in large numbers only where shifting government policies offered hope of military protection, links to markets, and a chance at a legitimate land title. Migrants often violated such policies, but government initiatives nonetheless shaped their behavior. While some, like Amberson, directly challenged state power or advocated political separation, they most often attached themselves to another established government, rather than echoing Amberson's call for self-rule. Many others acquiesced to state authority while trying to manipulate it to serve their own ends. If colonists shared Amberson's dogged independence, they seldom allowed it to govern their actions. Perhaps for these reasons, his call for a new constitution fell stillborn: one meeting endorsed the plan, but it proceeded no further.[2]

As Amberson's bid for self-government fizzled, western Indians pursued a political revolution of their own. Abandoned by British allies, and confronted with Congress's intractable demands for Ohio, representatives of a host of western nations declared themselves a confederation and insisted that no members could cede territory without the consent of all. Their project echoed both the wartime unity of the British alliance and an older movement rooted in nativist spirituality. Like Amberson, the confederationists envisioned an independent polity able to defend its peoples from Congress's demands. Unlike Amberson, they made considerable progress: resolving disputes, conducting diplomacy, and defeating American troops in battle. But even the confederationists fell short of the unity they sought. Some western Indians sought separate accommodations with the United States. Others left the region entirely, moving west across the Mississippi. And even the confederation's most ardent leaders recognized that they could preserve political independence only with the commercial and military backing of British Canada. When that support fizzled, their movement collapsed.[3]

Much as the myth of self-reliant colonists has obscured their dependence on colonial governments, so, too, the drama of warfare has overshadowed the politics of Ohio Indians. Hindsight—the knowledge of subsequent dispossession—tempts us to discount natives' legal and diplomatic strategies and instead celebrate military resistance. But examined more closely, and without retrospective blinders, the political maneuverings of White Eyes, Cornstalk, Dunquat, Pipe, Nonhelema, and Guyasuta, among others, show a subtlety and sophistication that belie easy distinctions between accommodation and militancy. Rather than either submitting to Anglo-American power or waging war against it, such leaders aimed to protect native territory and sovereignty by forging new relationships with colonial neighbors. They pursued varied and often conflicting strategies, both diplomatic and military, while also rebuilding their own political systems to contend with colonial demands. In the near term, they failed; Cornstalk and White Eyes were murdered. By the mid-1800s, the federal government recognized only one Indian nation in the entire Ohio Valley: the small Seneca territory on the upper Allegheny. Nonetheless, these efforts to build a new political order shaped the emerging United States, most notably by establishing precedents for the modern government-to-government relationship between the federal republic and tribal nations. Rather than discounting White Eyes as a tragic victim of colonial violence, we might better salute his vision of self-governing Indian peoples within a composite Anglo-American state. He and his allies were about two hundred years ahead of their time.

The image of independent and defiant Indians and colonists arose in large part from the self-serving complaints of government officials. However much Ohio Valley inhabitants depended on state aid, they rarely submitted meekly to official dictates. Colonists drove off tax collectors, seized land preemptively, and flouted the orders of military superiors. Indians ignored trade regulations, demanded goods, and largely ignored British commands. Both groups readily appropriated government-supplied weaponry for their own purposes, sometimes to kill people their patrons did not want them to kill. Moreover, the specter of unstoppably land-hungry and war-mongering colonists rationalized a profitable policy of aggressive dispossession. If governments displaced Indians too slowly, aspiring speculators argued, colonists' relentless westering could cost the United States its budding western empire, leaving the region "an Assylum for a Banditti without Principle or Law attached to no Government."[4] By depicting Ohio Valley inhabitants as rebellious and bloodthirsty, British and American officials justified policies that further empowered—and often enriched—themselves and their friends.

Ironically, the interventions that officials promoted brought about much of the bloodshed they decried. To be sure, colonists and Indians often killed each other on their own initiative, but most large-scale violence took place as part of, or because of, government-funded or government-led operations. Small groups of colonists built local stockades and fended off attacks, but they failed to orchestrate substantial campaigns without the money, supplies, and organizational structure of formal institutions. The culture of Ohio Indians was better suited to small-scale campaigning, but past traumas made them loath to renew hostilities without the support of a competing empire. Rather than springing directly from hatred, vengeance, and competition, major atrocities hinged on access to weapons and other supplies, as well as the political capital necessary to mobilize potential killers. British and revolutionary officers commonly bemoaned and denied responsibility for the savagery of their allies, but such protests were disingenuous or at best naive. Equally important, by encouraging colonization and violence, governments further destabilized the region, deepening Indians' and colonists' dependence on official patronage.

The politics of the revolutionary Ohio Valley thus involved a many-sided process of statecraft, understood literally as ongoing attempts to shape a new political order. From the 1760s through the 1780s, a wide range of Indians, colonists, and government officials sought to revise the structures that had prevailed in previous decades. Delaware and Shawnee leaders labored to balance traditions of local autonomy with new structures for centralized decision making. Some western Haudenosaunee sought independence from the Six Nations, while others hoped to restore the league's supremacy. In both Pennsylvania and Virginia, provincial and later revolutionary officials claimed jurisdiction over large swaths of the Ohio Valley, while coteries of investors angled to win royal and later congressional approval of their schemes. As colonists moved into the region, they—like Ohio Indians—assessed how well these disparate claims to authority might serve their own needs and then built coalitions accordingly. One government after another failed to subdue the Ohio Valley's peoples, but their attempts both spurred and drew strength from the ensuing intrigues and bloodshed. This unsettling helped constitute, in fits and starts, an emerging federal state.

This western revolution was less a dramatic break than a staggered and nonlinear process. In the 1760s, the region's inhabitants had contended with a composite British empire, which comprised a messy array of provincial and proprietary governments as well as more or less formal alliances with native polities. In the 1770s, that system collapsed, triggering war, uncertainty, and opportunities to shape a new political order. In the 1780s and 1790s, a new composite polity emerged: an imperial republic independent of the old metropole, comprising member states, territories, and Indian nations. Each of these possessed some measure of self-government, subordinated to varying degrees to the oversight and protection of the union. Over thirty years of upheaval, a rough-hewn order, marked by significant local autonomy, diverse government forms, and a transoceanic imperial center, gave way to a more precisely defined system, characterized by reduced local autonomy, more standardized government forms, and a less distant, but still transmontane imperial center. The new system proved adept at dispossessing Indian nations, redistributing land to colonists, and integrating the resulting territories into the union, but Indian nations themselves remained, both culturally and constitutionally, within the new composite order. This new Anglo-American colonialism accelerated in the nineteenth and twentieth centuries, with government initiatives, resources, and incentives playing an ever more central role.[5]

In September 2014, Mexican police opened fire on several busloads of student protesters in the city of Iguala, killing six. Another forty-three students were taken away and never heard from again. Their disappearance sparked nationwide protests. Four months later, the nation's attorney general announced that local police, acting on the orders of Iguala's mayor, handed the students over to drug traffickers, who murdered them, incinerated their bodies, and threw the remains in a river. The atrocity, officials maintained, stemmed from local corruption and had nothing to do with the ruling regime. But many Mexicans rejected (and still reject) this theory. In the months that followed, thousands filled the streets with the slogan *"fue el estado"* (it was the state).[6]

In conventional usage, "the state" is understood to exist alongside, but separate from, civil society. It theoretically monopolizes the legitimate use of force and thus stands against those who, like drug cartels, use force illegitimately. Where criminals wield extensive power, the state is considered to be weak. The Mexican protesters have little use for these theoretical distinctions. Instead, they call attention to close ties between government, police, and military officials and the criminals they nominally oppose. The ubiquity of such connections, at many levels of government, explains why state initiatives against drug cartels, as well as popular challenges to federal policies, make so little headway. As one arm of the state pursues drug traffickers, others abet their crimes. Both licit and illicit resources enable government forces to suppress opposition. The mass murder at Iguala exemplified this wider trend, creating a flashpoint for popular outcry. Whether the lost students died at the hands of the police, the army, or government-protected drug traffickers, protesters insist on calling to account the multifaceted Mexican state.

Like the Mexican protesters, the peoples of the revolutionary Ohio Valley recognized that the state took many shapes, and served many functions, well beyond the domain of formal government officials. In the sense of effective administration—enacting policies, enforcing laws, punishing crimes, even waging war—governments were notoriously weak and depended on local cooperation. Rather than top-down institutions imposing order, frontier governments comprised coalitions of individuals, many of them working at cross purposes. Nonetheless, by distributing and mobilizing resources, governments reshaped the region's history. Army roads and quasi-legal land grants, deliveries of gunpowder, and the organization of militias together made possible both mass colonization and horrific violence. These outcomes often flew in the face of official pronouncements, and thus appear to reflect state weakness, but they nonetheless hinged on the availability of—or hopes for—resources that only governments could provide. Ascribing these events to impulsiveness or hatred obscures how state institutions and government officials made them possible.

Histories of the United States devote considerable attention to conflicts between different governments, or between governments and their critics. These concerns predispose historians to define "government" in narrow terms, denoting certain public institutions and the people who run them. The case of the revolutionary Ohio Valley suggests that this narrow conception of

"government" often shortchanges historical reality. Much like the Iguala police, the murderers of Cornstalk, White Eyes, and the Gnadenhütten Moravians committed crimes their governments condemned. Like their present-day
Mexican counterparts, British and revolutionary officials wrung their hands
at their allies' and subordinates' wrongdoing. But unintended outcomes remain outcomes. Anglo-American colonialism took hold in the Ohio Valley
largely because governments offered both incentives to move and resources
to kill.

Governments wielded such influence because of Indians' and colonists'
ongoing attempts to build a new political order that might offer physical security, economic prosperity, and formal recognition of landownership. Few,
if any, imagined the federal republic that ultimately took shape. But as governments came and went, their collective efforts lent cohesion and ultimately
coercive power to the emerging regime. In contrast to the classic Weberian
state, this frontier polity comprised a nebulous, fragmented, and multifaceted array of individuals and communities, linked together by networks that
facilitated the distribution of resources and the escalation of violence. It appears powerless—one might even call it a "failed state"—but looks are deceiv-
ing. Government resources, and government-led mobilization, plunged the
Ohio Valley into horror.

NOTES

Note on Naming

1. Matthew Arbuckle to John Neville, 26 Dec. 1776, Morgan 1:32; Arbuckle to John Stuart, 2 Nov. 1776, RUO 211–12; [Jehu Hay], journal, 24 Dec. 1776 and 19 Jan. 1777, Henry Hamilton Papers, Burton Historical Collection, Detroit Public Library (this journal was formerly attributed to Hamilton, but internal evidence indicates it was written by Hay); James H. Merrell, *Into the American Woods: Negotiators on the Pennsylvania Frontier* (New York: W. W. Norton, 1999), 57–59.

2. Alyssa Mt. Pleasant, "Independence for Whom? Expansion and Conflict in the Northeast and Northwest," in *The World of the Revolutionary American Republic: Land, Labor, and the Conflict for a Continent*, ed. Andrew Shankman (New York: Routledge, 2014), 124 (Hanodagonyes); Thomas S. Abler, "Kayahsota," in *Dictionary of Canadian Biography*, vol. 4 (University of Toronto/Université Laval, 2003), http://www.biographi.ca/en/bio/kayahsota_4E.html ("the Cross"); exhibit labels, Seneca-Iroquois National Museum, Salamanca, NY ("Standing Paddles"); [George Morgan], note, 30 July 1776, frame 77, George Morgan Papers, 1775–1822, Library of Congress, microfilm, https://lccn.loc.gov/mm77033464 ("Coquai,tah,ghai,tah").

3. Answer of the Five Nations, 6 Sept. 1722, *History of the Dividing Line and Other Tracts*, 2 vols. (Richmond, VA, 1866), 2:251 ("Assaragoa"); Merrell, *Into the American Woods*, 122–23 ("Onas"); MMD 168n294 ("Schwonnaks"); Thomas McElwain, "'Then I Thought I Must Kill Too': Logan's Lament: A 'Mingo' Perspective," in *Native American Speakers of the Eastern Woodlands: Selected Speeches and Critical Analyses*, ed. Barbara Alice Mann (Westport, CT: Greenwood, 2001), 108 ("Mingos"). According to one story, White Eyes's people accepted the label "Delaware" as a courtesy to their European visitors, recognizing that their guests could not pronounce "Lenape" correctly: see the section entitled "Why did the Lenape people accept the name 'Delaware'?," official website of the Delaware Tribe of Indians, http://delawaretribe.org/blog/2013/06/26/faqs/ (accessed 30 Sept. 2016).

4. Harriet Maxwell Converse, *Myths and Legends of the New York State Iroquois*, Museum Bulletin no. 125, ed. Arthur Caswell Parker (Albany: State University of the State of New York, 1908), 33.

5. See James H. Merrell, "Second Thoughts on Colonial Historians and American Indians," *William and Mary Quarterly* 69, no. 3 (July 2012): 473–76. Contra Merrell, a burgeoning (and generally anticolonial) literature uses the term "settler colonialism," and therefore "settler," to distinguish colonialisms that displace or eliminate indigenous peoples from those who extract resources and control commerce and labor while leaving the local population in place: see, for example, Daiva Stasiulis and Nira Yuval-Davis, eds., *Unsettling Settler Societies: Articulations of*

Gender, Race, Ethnicity and Class (London: Sage, 1995); Lynette Russell, ed., *Colonial Frontiers: Indigenous-European Encounters in Settler Societies* (Manchester: Manchester University Press, 2001); A. Dirk Moses, ed., *Genocide and Settler Society: Frontier Violence and Stolen Indigenous Children in Australian History* (New York: Berghahn, 2004); James Belich, *Replenishing the Earth: The Settler Revolution and the Rise of the Angloworld, 1783–1939* (New York: Oxford University Press, 2009); Lisa Ford, *Settler Sovereignty: Jurisdiction and Indigenous People in America and Australia, 1788–1836* (Cambridge, MA: Harvard University Press, 2011); Patrick Wolfe, "Settler Colonialism and the Elimination of the Native," *Journal of Genocide Research* 8, no. 4 (2006): 387–409. I think the distinction is worth making, but the euphemistic history behind "settler" and "settlement" leaves me wary of these terms. "Territorial colonialism" and "genocidal colonialism" are possible alternatives. David Preston provocatively applies the term "settler" to both native and colonial populations in *The Texture of Contact: European and Indian Settler Communities on the Frontiers of Iroquoia, 1667–1783* (Lincoln: University of Nebraska Press, 2009).

Introduction

1. McClure 27, 40.

2. Walter L. Hixson, *American Settler Colonialism: A History* (New York: Palgrave Macmillan, 2013), 1 ("from the bottom up"); James H. Merrell, *Into the American Woods: Negotiators on the Pennsylvania Frontier* (New York: W. W. Norton, 1999), 295 ("land fever"); Patrick Griffin, *American Leviathan: Empire, Nation, and Revolutionary Frontier* (New York: Hill and Wang, 2007). Aquatic metaphors bubble up throughout Ohio Valley historiography, including my own work: John Robinson Harper, "Revolution and Conquest: Politics, Violence, and Social Change in the Ohio Valley, 1765–1795" (Ph.D. diss., University of Wisconsin–Madison, 2008), 30, 71, 136, 161. I thank David Preston for pointing out the similarly prominent analogies to madness and for identifying the crucial role of government in Monongahela Valley colonization: David L. Preston, *The Texture of Contact: European and Indian Settler Communities on the Frontiers of Iroquoia, 1667–1783* (Lincoln: University of Nebraska Press, 2009), 245–52. See also R. Brian Ferguson and Neil L. Whitehead, eds., *War in the Tribal Zone: Expanding States and Indigenous Warfare* (Santa Fe, NM: School of American Research Press, 2000), ACLS Humanities E-Book, http://hdl.handle.net/2027/heb.03246.

3. For detailed studies of these intergovernmental disputes, see James Patrick McClure, "The Ends of the American Earth: Pittsburgh and the Upper Ohio Valley to 1795" (Ph.D. diss., University of Michigan, 1983); Daniel P. Barr, "Contested Land: Competition and Conflict Along the Upper Ohio Frontier, 1744–1784" (Ph.D. diss., Kent State University, 2001); Paul B. Moyer, *Wild Yankees: The Struggle for Independence Along Pennsylvania's Revolutionary Frontier* (Ithaca, NY: Cornell University Press, 2007).

4. Bethel Saler, *The Settlers' Empire: Colonialism and State Formation in America's Old Northwest* (Philadelphia: University of Pennsylvania Press, 2014), 7 ("fluid networks"); Kathleen DuVal, *Independence Lost: Lives on the Edge of the American Revolution* (New York: Random House, 2015), xxi ("advantageous interdependence"); Jeremy Adelman and Stephen Aron, "From Borderlands to Borders: Empires, Nation-States, and the Peoples in Between in North American History," *American Historical Review* 104, no. 3 (1999): 841 ("car[ing] little"); Robert Michael Morrissey, *Empire by Collaboration: Indians, Colonists, and Governments in Colonial Illinois Country* (Philadelphia: University of Pennsylvania Press, 2015); Jack P. Greene, "Colonial History and National History: Reflections on a Continuing Problem," *William and Mary*

Quarterly 64, no. 2 (2007): 235–50. Here I draw heavily on the historiography of state formation, including G. M. Joseph and Daniel Nugent, eds., *Everyday Forms of State Formation: Revolution and the Negotiation of Rule in Modern Mexico* (Durham, NC: Duke University Press, 1994); Florencia E. Mallon, *Peasant and Nation: The Making of Postcolonial Mexico and Peru* (Berkeley: University of California Press, 1994); Michael J. Braddick, *State Formation in Early Modern England c. 1550–1700* (Cambridge: Cambridge University Press, 2000), 90; Steve Hindle, *The State and Social Change in Early Modern England, c. 1550–1640* (Basingstoke, UK: Palgrave, 2000); Lauren Benton, "Colonial Law and Cultural Difference: Jurisdictional Politics and the Formation of the Colonial State," *Comparative Studies in Society and History* 41, no. 3 (July 1999): 563–88; Wim Blockmans, André Holenstein, and Jon Mathieu, eds., *Empowering Interactions: Political Cultures and the Emergence of the State in Europe 1300–1900* (Farnham, UK: Ashgate, 2009); Mara Loveman, "The Modern State and the Primitive Accumulation of Symbolic Power," *American Journal of Sociology* 110, no. 6 (May 2005): 1651–83; Mats Hallenberg, Johan Holm, and Dan Johansson, "Organization, Legitimation, Participation: State Formation as a Dynamic Process—the Swedish Example, c. 1523–1680," *Scandinavian Journal of History* 33, no. 3 (Sept. 2008): 247–68. In refuting the Hobbesian assumption of stateless chaos, and in chronicling local attempts to shape new regulatory systems, I echo Elinor Ostrom, *Governing the Commons: The Evolution of Institutions for Collective Action* (Cambridge: Cambridge University Press, 1990).

5. Richard White argues that eighteenth-century Great Lakes diplomacy relied on creative responses to cultural misunderstandings. Europeans and Indians could build alliances because their mutual confusion fostered new ways of resolving differences: Richard White, *The Middle Ground: Indians, Empires, and Republics in the Great Lakes Region, 1650–1815* (New York: Cambridge University Press, 1991). In late eighteenth-century diplomacy, confusion remained central, but the most important misunderstandings were intentional. On social networks, coalition building, and brokers, see Jeremy Boissevain, *Friends of Friends: Networks, Manipulators and Coalitions* (Oxford: Basil Blackwell, 1974), 171; Rogers Brubaker and Frederick Cooper, "Beyond 'Identity,' " *Theory and Society* 29, no. 1 (2000): 14–16; Daniel K. Richter, "Cultural Brokers and Intercultural Politics: New York-Iroquois Relations, 1664–1701," *Journal of American History* 75, no. 1 (1988): 40–67; Clara Sue Kidwell, "Indian Women as Cultural Mediators," *Ethnohistory* 39, no. 2 (1992): 97–107; Susan Sleeper-Smith, *Indian Women and French Men: Rethinking Cultural Encounter in the Western Great Lakes* (Amherst: University of Massachusetts Press, 2001).

6. Boissevain, *Friends of Friends*, 147–48; André Holenstein, "Empowering Interactions: Looking at Statebuilding from Below," in *Empowering Interactions: Political Cultures and the Emergence of the State in Europe 1300–1900*, ed. Wim Blockmans, André Holenstein, and Jon Mathieu (Farnham, UK: Ashgate, 2009), 15–16; Roger V. Gould, "Patron-Client Ties, State Centralization, and the Whiskey Rebellion," *American Journal of Sociology* 102, no. 2 (Sept. 1996): 400–429; Roger V. Gould, "Political Networks and the Local/National Boundary in the Whiskey Rebellion," in *Challenging Authority: The Historical Study of Contentious Politics*, ed. Michael P. Hanagan, Leslie Page Moch, and Wayne T. Brake (Minneapolis: University of Minnesota Press, 1998), 36–53.

7. Gregory Evans Dowd, *A Spirited Resistance: The North American Indian Struggle for Unity, 1745–1815* (Baltimore: Johns Hopkins University Press, 1992), 13–15; White, *Middle Ground*, 75–93; Gregory Evans Dowd, *War Under Heaven: Pontiac, the Indian Nations and the British Empire* (Baltimore: Johns Hopkins University Press, 2002), 191–203. Cf. Richard Slotkin, *Regeneration Through Violence: The Mythology of the American Frontier, 1600–1860* (Middletown, CT: Wesleyan University Press, 1973); Richard Drinnon, *Facing West: The Metaphysics of*

Indian-Hating and Empire-Building (Minneapolis: University of Minnesota Press, 1980); Peter Silver, *Our Savage Neighbors: How Indian War Transformed Early America* (New York: W. W. Norton, 2008); Alden T. Vaughan, "Frontier Banditti and the Indians: The Paxton Boys' Legacy," *Pennsylvania History* 51, no. 1 (1984): 1–29.

8. Charles Tilly, *The Politics of Collective Violence* (Cambridge: Cambridge University Press, 2003), 8. See also Ian Kenneth Steele, *Betrayals: Fort William Henry and the Massacre* (New York: Oxford University Press, 1990); Christopher R. Browning, *Ordinary Men: Reserve Police Battalion 101 and the Final Solution in Poland*, 2nd ed. (New York: HarperCollins, 1998); Alison Palmer, *Colonial Genocide* (Adelaide, Australia: Crawford House, 2000); Ferguson and White-head, *War in the Tribal Zone*; Wayne E. Lee, *Crowds and Soldiers in Revolutionary North Carolina: The Culture of Violence in Riot and War* (Gainesville: University Press of Florida, 2001); Ned Blackhawk, "The Displacement of Violence: Ute Diplomacy and the Making of New Mexi-co's Eighteenth-Century Northern Borderlands," *Ethnohistory* 54, no. 4 (2007): 723–55; James D. Fearon and David D. Laitin, "Explaining Interethnic Cooperation," *American Political Science Review* 90 (1996): 715–35; Christian Gerlach, "Extremely Violent Societies: An Alternative to the Concept of Genocide," *Journal of Genocide Research* 8, no. 4 (2006): 455–71. By restricting this discussion to deadly intercultural violence, I consciously and regretfully omit countless other forms of violence. See, for example, Sharon Block, *Rape and Sexual Power in Early America* (Chapel Hill: University of North Carolina Press, 2006); Elliott J. Gorn, " 'Gouge and Bite, Pull Hair and Scratch': The Social Significance of Fighting in the Southern Backcountry," *American Historical Review* 90, no. 1 (Feb. 1985): 18–43.

9. Patricia Nelson Limerick, *The Legacy of Conquest: The Unbroken Past of the American West* (New York: W. W. Norton, 1987); Richard White, *"It's Your Misfortune and None of My Own": A History of the American West* (Norman: University of Oklahoma Press, 1991); William Cronon, George A. Miles, and Jay Gitlin, eds., *Under an Open Sky: Rethinking America's Western Past* (New York: W. W. Norton, 1992); María E. Montoya, *Translating Property: The Maxwell Land Grant and the Conflict over Land in the American West, 1840–1900* (Berkeley: University of California Press, 2002); Jeffrey Ostler, *The Plains Sioux and U.S. Colonialism from Lewis and Clark to Wounded Knee* (Cambridge: Cambridge University Press, 2004); Stacey L. Smith, *Freedom's Frontier: California and the Struggle over Unfree Labor, Emancipation, and Reconstruction* (Chapel Hill: University of North Carolina Press, 2013); Michel Hogue, *Metis and the Medicine Line: Creating a Border and Dividing a People* (Chapel Hill: University of North Carolina Press, 2015); Benjamin Madley, *An American Genocide: The United States and the California Indian Catastrophe, 1846–1873* (New Haven, CT: Yale University Press, 2016); William J. Novak, "The Myth of the 'Weak' American State," *American Historical Review* 113, no. 3 (June 2008): 752–72.

10. Here I draw heavily on the historiography of settler colonialism, which has only begun to inform early American historiography: Daiva Stasiulis and Nira Yuval-Davis, eds., *Unsettling Settler Societies: Articulations of Gender, Race, Ethnicity and Class* (London; Sage, 1995); Lynette Russell, ed., *Colonial Frontiers: Indigenous-European Encounters in Settler Societies* (Manchester: Manchester University Press, 2001); Alan Lester, *Imperial Networks: Creating Identities in Nine-teenth Century South Africa and Britain* (New York: Routledge, 2001); Lauren Benton, *Law and Colonial Cultures: Legal Regimes in World History, 1400–1900* (Cambridge: Cambridge University Press, 2001); John C. Weaver, *The Great Land Rush and the Making of the Modern World: 1650–1800* (Montreal: McGill-Queen's University Press, 2003); A. Dirk Moses, ed., *Genocide and Settler Society: Frontier Violence and Stolen Indigenous Children in Australian History* (New York: Berghahn, 2004); James Belich, *Replenishing the Earth: The Settler Revolution and the Rise*

of the Angloworld, 1783–1939 (New York: Oxford University Press, 2009); Lisa Ford, *Settler Sovereignty: Jurisdiction and Indigenous People in America and Australia, 1788–1836* (Cambridge, MA: Harvard University Press, 2011); Saler, *Settlers' Empire*; Elizabeth Elbourne, "The Sin of the Settler: The 1835–36 Select Committee on Aborigines and Debates over Virtue and Conquest in the Early Nineteenth-Century British White Settler Empire," *Journal of Colonialism and Colonial History* 4, no. 3 (2003): 1–49; Patrick Wolfe, "Settler Colonialism and the Elimination of the Native," *Journal of Genocide Research* 8, no. 4 (2006): 387–409; Greene, "Colonial History and National History."

11. Helen Hornbeck Tanner, ed., *Atlas of Great Lakes Indian History* (Norman: University of Oklahoma Press, 1987), 43–44; White, *Middle Ground*, 187–88; Michael N. McConnell, *A Country Between: The Upper Ohio Valley and Its Peoples, 1724–1774* (Lincoln: University of Nebraska Press, 1992), 208–9; Amy C. Schutt, *Peoples of the River Valleys: The Odyssey of the Delaware Indians* (Philadelphia: University of Pennsylvania Press, 2007), 103–14; Stephen Warren, *The Worlds the Shawnees Made: Migration and Violence in Early America* (Chapel Hill: University of North Carolina Press, 2014), 180–207.

12. McClure 27 ("tribes"), 42; report from Philadelphia, *Virginia Gazette* (Rind), no. 343, 3 Dec. 1772, [2].

13. DGW 1:143, 154; White, *Middle Ground*, 223–56; Fred Anderson, *The Crucible of War: The Seven Years' War and the Fate of Empire in British North America, 1754–1766* (New York: Alfred A. Knopf, 2000); Jane T. Merritt, *At the Crossroads: Indians and Empires on a Mid-Atlantic Frontier, 1700–1763* (Chapel Hill: University of North Carolina Press, 2003); David L. Preston, *Braddock's Defeat: The Battle of the Monongahela and the Road to Revolution* (New York: Oxford University Press, 2015); Thomas S. Abler, "Kayahsota," in *Dictionary of Canadian Biography*, vol. 4 (University of Toronto/Université Laval, 2003), http://www.biographi.ca/en/bio/kayahsota_4E.html.

14. Historians disagree about Guyasuta's importance in forging the 1763 alliance. Gregory Dowd, the author of the leading book-length study of the war, argues that his role has been overstated: Dowd, *War Under Heaven*, 105–6. See also Tanner, *Atlas*, 48; White, *Middle Ground*, 271–77; Thomas S. Abler, *Cornplanter: Chief Warrior of the Allegany Senecas* (Syracuse, NY: Syracuse University Press, 2007), 30.

15. DGW 2:304, 310; *Minutes of Conferences, Held at Fort Pitt, in April and May, 1768* (Philadelphia: William Goddard, 1769), 13–14, 22; proceedings of George Croghan with the Indians, 1 Aug. 1770, enclosed in Croghan to Thomas Gage, 8 Aug. 1770, AS 94, TGP.

16. Croghan, journal, 1 June 1771, box 8, folder 11, GCP; White, *Middle Ground*, 227–40; Anderson, *Crucible of War*, 24–32, 61.

17. DGW 2:304 ("head"); Isaac Hamilton to Gage, 16 Aug. 1772, AS 113, TGP ("Influence"); Gage to William Johnson, 7 Oct. 1772, PWJ 12:994 ("true situation"); Alexander McKee to Johnson, 31 Dec. 1772, PWJ 8:679; Johnson to Gage, 18 Nov. 1772, PWJ 8:638–41; CRBJ 7 Sept. 1775; McConnell, *A Country Between*, 79–80; McClure, "Ends of the American Earth," 41–42, 55.

18. McClure 49–50, 58–59, 84–86, 99 ("underbrush," 58; advantage," 59; "resentment," 85); Jones 89 ("game"), 101–2 (no meat"); *Minutes of Conferences*, 18; White Mingo, speech to commissioners, 21 Aug. 1776, Morgan 2:15–16; [Griffin Greene] to "Peter," n.d., Northwest Territory Collection, William L. Clements Library, University of Michigan, Ann Arbor; McConnell, *A Country Between*, 210; Stephen Aron, *How the West Was Lost: The Transformation of Kentucky from Daniel Boone to Henry Clay* (Baltimore: Johns Hopkins University Press, 1996), 6, 13–16, 18, 21–27; Nathaniel Scheidley, "Hunting and the Politics of Masculinity in Cherokee

Treaty-Making, 1763–75," in *Empire and Others: British Encounters with Indigenous Peoples, 1600–1850*, ed. Martin Daunton and Rick Halpern (Philadelphia: University of Pennsylvania Press, 1999), 167–85. For precolonial forest management, see R. W. Kimmerer and F. K. Lake, "The Role of Indigenous Burning in Land Management," *Journal of Forestry* 99, no. 11 (1 Nov. 2001): 36–41; Marc D. Abrams and Gregory J. Nowacki, "Native Americans as Active and Passive Promoters of Mast and Fruit Trees in the Eastern USA," *Holocene* 18, no. 7 (2008): 1123–37.

19. McClure 61 ("well built," "large corn field"), 67–68 ("regular & thrifty," 68), 107; Cresswell 74–75; Jones 52, 56, 57, 87; John Harvie, John Montgomery, and Jasper Yeates to William Wilson, 3 Aug. 1776, Commissioners of Indian Affairs to John Anderson, 5 Sept. 1776, and Anderson to commissioners, 24 Sept. 1776, Yeates; George Morgan, letterbook and journal, 14–16, 30–31, HSP; Charles Beatty, *The Journal of a Two Months Tour . . . to the Westward of the Alegh-Geny Mountains* (London: William Davenhill and George Pearch, 1768), 13–14n, 71–73n. For Anipassicowa's name, cf. Cornstalk, speech, 13 Oct. 1775, RUO 115–16; Tanner, *Atlas*, maps 13, 15, 16; McConnell, *A Country Between*, 209.

20. Cresswell 72, 73, 75–79, 82, 85, 129, 141; Beatty, *Journal of a Two Months Tour*, 62; proceedings of George Croghan, 2 Aug. 1770, enclosed in Croghan to Gage, 8 Aug. 1770, AS 94, TGP; Peter C. Mancall, *Deadly Medicine: Indians and Alcohol in Early America* (Ithaca, NY: Cornell University Press, 1995). The literature on Great Lakes Indian women and trade is large. See Sylvia Van Kirk, *Many Tender Ties: Women in Fur-Trade Society, 1670–1870* (Norman: University of Oklahoma Press, 1980); Lucy Eldersveld Murphy, *A Gathering of Rivers: Indians, Métis, and Mining in the Western Great Lakes, 1737–1832* (Lincoln: University of Nebraska Press, 2000); Sleeper-Smith, *Indian Women and French Men*; Karen Marrero, "On the Edge of the West: The Roots and Routes of Detroit's Urban Eighteenth Century," in *Frontier Cities: Encounters at the Crossroads of Empire*, ed. Jay Gitlin, Barbara Berglund, and Adam Arenson (Philadelphia: University of Pennsylvania Press), 67–86.

21. Cresswell 77–78; DDZ 1:25; McConnell, *A Country Between*; Schutt, *Peoples of the River Valleys*; Warren, *Worlds the Shawnees Made*; Sami Lakomäki, *Gathering Together: The Shawnee People Through Diaspora and Nationhood, 1600–1870* (New Haven, CT: Yale University Press, 2014), 76–77. For preceding centuries of dispersal, see Daniel K. Richter, *Before the Revolution: America's Ancient Pasts* (Cambridge, MA: Harvard University Press, 2011), ch. 1.

22. MMD 225 ("Wyandot language"), 148, 184, 345, 404, 469; McClure 86 ("indian acquaintance"); Jones 58, 60–61, 85–88. On captive adoption, see Christina Snyder, *Slavery in Indian Country: The Changing Face of Captivity in Early America* (Cambridge, MA: Harvard University Press, 2010); Daniel K. Richter, "War and Culture: The Iroquois Experience," *William and Mary Quarterly* 40, no. 4 (Oct. 1983): 528–59.

23. Colin G. Calloway, *The American Revolution in Indian Country: Crisis and Diversity in Native American Communities* (Cambridge: Cambridge University Press, 1995), 160; Schutt, *Peoples of the River Valleys*, 57, 112, 133–34, 156–58; Robert S. Grumet, *The Munsee Indians: A History* (Norman: University of Oklahoma Press, 2009), 3–7, 18–19, 301n30; Cary Miller, *Ogimaag: Anishinaabeg Leadership, 1760–1845* (Lincoln: University of Nebraska Press, 2010), 237n2; Erik R. Seeman, *The Huron-Wendat Feast of the Dead: Indian-European Encounters in Early North America* (Baltimore: Johns Hopkins University Press, 2011), 9–12; Tyler Boulware, *Deconstructing the Cherokee Nation: Town, Region, and Nation Among Eighteenth-Century Cherokees* (Gainesville: University Press of Florida, 2011); Warren, *Worlds the Shawnees Made*, 77–78; John L. Steckley, *The Eighteenth-Century Wyandot: A Clan-Based Study* (Waterloo,

Ontario: Wilfrid Laurier University Press, 2014), 5–6, 40–41; Lakomäki, *Gathering Together*, 14, 23–24.

24. MMD 18n42; Michael Witgen, *An Infinity of Nations: How the Native New World Shaped Early America* (Philadelphia: University of Pennsylvania Press, 2012); Steckley, *Eighteenth-Century Wyandot*, 27; Lakomäki, *Gathering Together*, 17–18; Michael A. McDonnell, *Masters of Empire: Great Lakes Indians and the Making of America* (New York: Hill and Wang, 2015), 9–13; Heidi Bohaker, "*Nindoodemag*: The Significance of Algonquian Kinship Networks in the Eastern Great Lakes Region, 1600–1701," *William and Mary Quarterly* 63, no. 1 (Jan. 2006): 23–52.

25. MMD 357 ("widespread"), 339, 391–92, 425, 436, 490; Beatty, *Journal of a Two Months Tour*, 42–43; McClure 76–77.

26. Lakomäki, *Gathering Together*, 18, 35–36, 39–40; White, *Middle Ground*, 325–26; Daniel K. Richter, *The Ordeal of the Longhouse: The Peoples of the Iroquois League in the Era of European Colonization* (Chapel Hill: University of North Carolina Press, 1992), 42–43; Gail D. MacLeitch, *Imperial Entanglements: Iroquois Change and Persistence on the Frontiers of Empire* (Philadelphia: University of Pennsylvania Press, 2011), 22–23.

27. Jones 73–74 ("strangers"); Cresswell 82 ("no more honor"), 75 ("poor house"); George Croghan, answers to a questionnaire regarding Indians, [1773?], box 7, folder 38, GCP ("Never Suffer"); Joseph Jackson, interview, Apr. 1844, Draper 11C:62.5–6; James Smith, *An Account of the Remarkable Occurrences in the Life and Travels of Col. James Smith* (Lexington, KY: John Bradford, 1799), 139–40, 147; McClure 61–84.

28. Kathleen DuVal, *The Native Ground: Indians and Colonists in the Heart of the Continent* (Philadelphia: University of Pennsylvania Press, 2007); Witgen, *Infinity of Nations*; McDonnell, *Masters of Empire*; Brett Rushforth, "Slavery, the Fox Wars, and the Limits of Alliance," *William and Mary Quarterly* 63, no. 1 (2006): 53–80; Juliana Barr, "Geographies of Power: Mapping Indian Borders in the 'Borderlands' of the Early Southwest," *William and Mary Quarterly* 68, no. 1 (Jan. 2011): 5–46.

29. McConnell, *A Country Between*, 225–29; Hermann Wellenreuther, "White Eyes and the Delawares' Vision of an Indian State," *Pennsylvania History* 68, no. 2 (Spring 2001): 139–61; Lakomäki, *Gathering Together*, 78–84.

30. In this respect, the Ohio Indians' dilemma mirrored that of the nascent United States, whose leaders labored to mold their new nation into a form that European nations would recognize as legitimate: Eliga H. Gould, *Among the Powers of the Earth: The American Revolution and the Making of a New World Empire* (Cambridge, MA: Harvard University Press, 2012).

31. McClure 104–5; Edward Hand to Katherine Hand, 4 and 10 June 1777, box 1, folder 2, EHP; William Irvine to Anne Irvine, 8 Jan. 1782, Draper 2AA:10.

32. McClure 105–6.

33. Henry Stuart, account of proceedings with Indians, 25 Aug. 1776, CO5/77 fol. 182 ("wherever a Fort"); Beatty, *Journal of a Two Months Tour*, 71–73n; Croghan to Thomas Wharton, 9 Dec. 1773, "Letters of Colonel George Croghan," *Pennsylvania Magazine of History and Biography* 15, no. 4 (1891): 437; Cresswell 38, 39; McClure 45–46, 130; J. McClure, "Ends of the American Earth," 61–75; Preston, *Texture of Contact*, ch. 6.

34. Cresswell 62 ("two Englishmen"), 38 ("acting"); McClure 105–6 ("drinking parties"), 47 ("illiterate preachers"), 43, 103; Charles Edmonstone to Gage, 17 May 1772, AS 111, TGP; Beatty, *Journal of a Two Months Tour*, 10–22; Albert H. Tillson, *Gentry and Common Folk: Political Culture on a Virginia Frontier, 1740–1789* (Lexington: University Press of Kentucky, 1991), 62, 66–68.

35. Cresswell 70; Thomas P. Slaughter, *The Whiskey Rebellion: Frontier Epilogue to the American Revolution* (New York: Oxford University Press, 1986), 66, 70–71; Aron, *How the West Was Lost*, 21–23; R. Eugene Harper, *The Transformation of Western Pennsylvania, 1770–1800* (Pittsburgh, PA: University of Pittsburgh Press, 1991).

36. Croghan to Gage, 2 Nov. 1771, box 5, folder 31, GCP ("Unruly Settlers"); McClure 53–54 ("from Justice"); Donna B. Munger, *Pennsylvania Land Records: A History and Guide for Research* (Wilmington, DE: Scholarly Resources, 1991), 79–82; J. McClure, "Ends of the American Earth," 195–96; D. Barr, "Contested Land," 235–38, 256–59.

37. Boyd Crumrine, ed., *Virginia Court Records in Southwestern Pennsylvania: Records of the District of West Augusta and Ohio and Yohogania Counties, Virginia, 1775–1780* (Baltimore: Genealogical Publishing Company, 1974), 32–33, 35, 38, 47, 60; Eric Hinderaker, *Elusive Empires: Constructing Colonialism in the Ohio Valley, 1673–1800* (New York: Cambridge University Press, 1997), 202; Francis S. Fox, "The Prothonotary: Linchpin of Provincial and State Government in Eighteenth-Century Pennsylvania," *Pennsylvania History* 59, no. 1 (Jan. 1992): 41–53; J. McClure, "Ends of the American Earth," 272–81; D. Barr, "Contested Land," 297–99.

38. Arthur J. Alexander, "Pennsylvania's Revolutionary Militia," *Pennsylvania Magazine of History and Biography* 69, no. 1 (1945): 15–25; Hannah Benner Roach, "The Pennsylvania Militia in 1777," *Pennsylvania Genealogical Magazine* 23, no. 3 (1964): 161–230; Francis S. Fox, "Pennsylvania's Revolutionary Militia Law: The Statute That Transformed the State," *Pennsylvania History* 80, no. 2 (Spring 2013): 204–14; Michael A. McDonnell, *The Politics of War: Race, Class, and Conflict in Revolutionary Virginia* (Chapel Hill: University of North Carolina Press, 2007), 92–93.

39. McClure 119, 41–42, 105; Warren R. Hofstra and Robert D. Mitchell, "Town and Country in Backcountry Virginia: Winchester and the Shenandoah Valley, 1730–1800," *Journal of Southern History* 59, no. 4 (1993): 621; Harper, *Transformation of Western Pennsylvania, 1770–1800*.

40. Proceedings of George Croghan with the Indians, 1 Aug. 1770, enclosed in Croghan to Gage, 8 Aug. 1770, AS 94, TGP ("no head Man"); Tillson, *Gentry and Common Folk*, 61–63; Richard R. Beeman, "Deference, Republicanism, and the Emergence of Popular Politics in Eighteenth-Century America," *William and Mary Quarterly* 49, no. 3 (1992): 401–30. For Swearingen's background, see J. McClure, "Ends of the American Earth," 277–78, 280–81; petition of the captains of MacKay's battalion, 16 Oct. 1776, Yeates; Daniel Brodhead to all concerned, 20 Feb. 1781, box 1, vol. 1, DBP; Tillson, *Gentry and Common Folk*.

Chapter 1

1. Francis Fauquier to William Murray, 12 Apr. 1767, *The Official Papers of Francis Fauquier, Lieutenant Governor of Virginia, 1758–1768*, 3 vols., ed. George Reese (Charlottesville: University Press of Virginia, 1981–83), 3:1437–38 ("meritorious act"); Fauquier to Earl of Shelburne, 24 May 1767, *Papers of Francis Fauquier*, 3:1480–81 ("wish[ed] for nothing"); Murray to Thomas Gage, 16 May 1767, AS 65, TGP; George Croghan, abstract from journal, 24 May 1766, enclosed in Croghan to Gage, 26 May 1766, AS 51, TGP; John Penn to the Earl of Shelburne, 21 Jan. 1767, CRP 9:352–53. Peter was likely identical to either "Cutfinger Peter" or "John Peters," both of whom were listed as Delaware war leaders at a 1765 peace council at Fort Pitt: Croghan, "Journal of Transactions," 8 May 1765, CRP 9:256.

2. Richard White, *The Middle Ground: Indians, Empires, and Republics in the Great Lakes Region, 1650–1815* (New York: Cambridge University Press, 1991), 340 ("ragtag refugees");

Michael N. McConnell, *A Country Between: The Upper Ohio Valley and Its Peoples, 1724–1774* (Lincoln: University of Nebraska Press, 1992), 240, 258 ("state of war"); Alden Vaughan, "Frontier Banditti and the Indians: The Paxton Boys' Legacy," *Pennsylvania History* 51, no. 1 (1984): 8, 6; Daniel P. Barr, "Contested Land: Competition and Conflict Along the Upper Ohio Frontier, 1744–1784" (Ph.D. diss., Kent State University, 2001), 208.

3. William Johnson to Gage, 18 Apr. 1767, *The Documentary History of the State of New York*, 4 vols., ed. E. B. O'Callaghan (Albany, NY: Weed, Parsons, & Co., 1850–51), 2:849 ("any Traders"); Fauquier to Murray, 12 Apr. 1767, *Papers of Francis Fauquier*, 3:1437–38; Gage to Johnson, 5 Apr. 1767, PWJ 12:295–96; Gage to Johnson, 28 June 1767, PWJ 5:574; David L. Preston, *The Texture of Contact: European and Indian Settler Communities on the Frontiers of Iroquoia, 1667–1783* (Lincoln: University of Nebraska Press, 2009), 220.

4. John Steel et al. to Penn, 2 Apr. 1768, CRP 9:507; John Holmes to Penn, 7 Feb. 1768, CRP 9:464; Penn to Steel et al., 24 Feb. 1768, CRP 9:483; minutes of the Provincial Council, 16 Apr. 1768, CRP 9:481–82; Preston, *Texture of Contact*, 256–58.

5. Nicholas B. Wainwright, ed., "George Croghan's Journal: April 3, 1759 to April [30], 1763," *Pennsylvania Magazine of History and Biography* 71, no. 4 (Oct. 1947): 376, 378, 405 ("plenty of Game," 405); DGW 2:295, 293n1; Croghan, abstract from journal, 23 May 1766, enclosed in Croghan to Gage, 26 May 1766, AS 51, TGP; [William Crawford], "A Map of the Land abt. Red Stone and Fort Pitt," [1770?], Library of Congress Geography and Map Division, http://hdl.loc .gov/loc.gmd/g3820.ct000360 (accessed 10 Sept. 2016); Thomas Hutchins, "A New Map of the Western Parts of Virginia, Pennsylvania, Maryland and North Carolina" (London, 1778); Charles Beatty, *The Journal of a Two Months Tour . . . to the Westward of the Alegh-Geny Mountains* (London: William Davenhill and George Pearch, 1768), 29–30, 34–35; Neville B. Craig, ed., "The Journal of George Croghan [1765]," *Olden Time* 1, no. 9 (Sept. 1846): 404; Murray to Gage, 16 May 1767, AS 65, TGP; McClure 49, 53, 56–58, 100; Helen Hornbeck Tanner, ed., *Atlas of Great Lakes Indian History* (Norman: University of Oklahoma Press, 1987), 44–48 and maps 9, 13, and 15; McConnell, *A Country Between*, 208–9.

6. Croghan, "Journal of Transactions with the Indians" [1765], CRP 9:252 ("expecting"), 258 ("our Brethren"), and 261 ("Open the trade"); Craig, "Journal of George Croghan [1765]," 405, 409; *Minutes of Conferences, Held at Fort Pitt, in April and May, 1768* (Philadelphia: William Goddard, 1769), 17–18; George Croghan, journal, 4 Sept. 1770, box 8, folder 11, GCP. For Shawnee and Delaware migrations, see McConnell, *A Country Between*, 208–9; Sami Lakomäki, *Gathering Together: The Shawnee People Through Diaspora and Nationhood, 1600–1870* (New Haven, CT: Yale University Press, 2014), 91–92.

7. Johnson to Gage, 24 Nov. 1767, *Documentary History of the State of New York*, 2:886; DGW 2:297–98.

8. Croghan to Johnson, [3 June 1767], PWJ 5:561 ("the King's orders"); Ohio Company documents, 1745–62, *George Mercer Papers: Relating to the Ohio Company of Virginia*, ed. Lois Mulkearn (Pittsburgh, PA: University of Pittsburgh Press, 1954), 249, 251, 69, facing 226; Thomas Woods, deposition, 19 Sept. 1771, PA 4:435; deed of Garret Pendergrass, Feb. 1770, Society Collection, HSP; Preston, *Texture of Contact*, 224–25, 245–52; Nicholas B. Wainwright, *George Croghan: Wilderness Diplomat* (Chapel Hill: University of North Carolina Press, 1959), 275–78; Albert H. Tillson, *Gentry and Common Folk: Political Culture on a Virginia Frontier, 1740–1789* (Lexington: University Press of Kentucky, 1991), 74–75; John Mack Faragher, *Daniel Boone: The Life and Legend of an American Pioneer* (New York: Holt, 1992), 89–90; James Patrick McClure, "The Ends of the American Earth: Pittsburgh and the Upper Ohio Valley to 1795" (Ph.D. diss.,

University of Michigan, 1983), 9–17, 31–35; D. Barr, "Contested Land," 23–56, 157, 171–72, 199–201.

9. [John] Baynton, [Samuel] Wharton, and [George] Morgan to Johnson, 28 Dec. 1766, *The New Régime, 1765–1767*, ed. Clarence Walworth Alvord, Collections of the Illinois State Historical Library, vol. 11 (Springfield, IL: Illinois State Historical Library, 1916), 465; Croghan, abstract from journal, 24 May 1766, enclosed in Croghan to Gage, 26 May 1766, AS 51, TGP; Alexander Mackay, notice, 22 June 1766, PA 4:251–52; Fauquier, proclamation, 31 July 1766, PA 4:255; Murray to Gage, 24 June 1767, AS 66, TGP; William Crawford to George Washington, 29 Sept. 1767, GWP; Croghan to Johnson, 18 Oct. 1767, PWJ 12:374; Alfred Proctor James, *The Ohio Company: Its Inner History* (Pittsburgh, PA: University of Pittsburgh Press, 1959), 6–7, 13, 30–32, 49, 76; McClure, "Ends of the American Earth," 202–3; D. Barr, "Contested Land," 29–30, 37–38, 199, 207–8.

10. Daniel J. Hulsebosch, *Constituting Empire: New York and the Transformation of Constitutionalism in the Atlantic World, 1664–1830* (Chapel Hill: University of North Carolina Press, 2005), 8; Peter Karsten, *Between Law and Custom: "High" and "Low" Legal Cultures in the Lands of the British Diaspora—the United States, Canada, Australia, and New Zealand, 1600–1900* (Cambridge: Cambridge University Press, 2002).

11. Petition of traders, 18 Dec. 1767, PWJ 6:19–20 ("one half"); Croghan to Gage, 8 Aug. 1770, AS 94, TGP ("every Farmer"); Crawford to Washington, 29 Sept. 1767, GWP ("more oblidging"); Thomas Smallman, "Names of the Traders gone into the Indian villages," 1 June 1767, misfiled with Murray to Gage, 16 May 1767, AS 65, TGP.

12. Crawford to Washington, 29 Sept. 1767, GWP; D. Barr, "Contested Land," 198–99.

13. John W. Jordan, ed., "James Kenny's 'Journal to Ye Westward,' 1758–59," *Pennsylvania Magazine of History and Biography* 37, no. 4 (1913): 419; John W. Jordan, ed., "Journal of James Kenny, 1761–63," *Pennsylvania Magazine of History and Biography* 37, no. 1–2 (1913): 199; Angus McDonald to Henry Bouquet, 8 Apr. 1762, *The Papers of Col. Henry Bouquet*, ed. Sylvester K. Stevens and Donald H. Kent, Northwestern Pennsylvania Historical Series (Harrisburg: Pennsylvania Historical Commission, 1940–43), ser. 21648, part 1, 66–67; "Indian Proceedings," 16 June 1765, PWJ 11:791; Alexander McKee to Johnson, 18 June 1765, PWJ 11:796; Steel et al. to Penn, 2 Apr. 1768, CRP 9:507; Boyd Crumrine, ed., *Virginia Court Records in Southwestern Pennsylvania: Records of the District of West Augusta and Ohio and Yohogania Counties, Virginia, 1775–1780* (Baltimore: Genealogical Publishing Company, 1974), 531; application #2844, 5 Apr. 1769, New Purchase Register, ser. #17.43, Records of the Land Office, Pennsylvania State Archives, http://www.phmc.state.pa.us/bah/dam/rg/sd/r17sda.htm#17.43 (accessed 10 Sept. 2016). Mohawk Peter may have been related or even identical to the Delaware Captain Peter, whom Ryan killed at Redstone, but the available evidence suggests they were probably two separate individuals: Preston, *Texture of Contact*, 218–20.

14. *Minutes of Conferences*, 4, 11, 14–15, 21 ("remove," 11; "disagreeable," 21); Preston, *Texture of Contact*, 258–61.

15. *Minutes of Conferences*, 22.

16. McKee, journal, n.d., PWJ 7:184 ("as much theirs"); Red Hawk, speech, n.d., PWJ 7:406–8; Earl of Hillsborough to Johnson, 4 Jan. and 13 May 1769, *Documents Relative to the Colonial History of the State of New-York*, 15 vols., ed. E. B. O'Callaghan (Albany, NY: Weed, Parsons, & Co., 1853–58), 8:144–45, 165–66; Gage to Johnson, 3 and 23 Apr. 1769, PWJ 12:709, 6:708–9; Isaac Hamilton to Gage, 10 Aug. 1769, AS 87, TGP; Wharton to Johnson, 16 Aug. 1769, PWJ 7:96–97; Croghan to Johnson, 22 Dec. 1769, PWJ 7:315–17; McClure, "Ends of the American Earth," 90;

Wainwright, *George Croghan*, 28, 257; William J. Campbell, *Speculators in Empire: Iroquoia and the 1768 Treaty of Fort Stanwix* (Norman: University of Oklahoma Press, 2012). Cf. Randolph C. Downes, *Council Fires on the Upper Ohio: A Narrative of Indian Affairs in the Upper Ohio Valley Until 1795* (Pittsburgh, PA: University of Pittsburgh Press, 1940), 143; Woody Holton, *Forced Founders: Indians, Debtors, Slaves, and the Making of the American Revolution in Virginia* (Chapel Hill: University of North Carolina Press, 1999), 27–30.

17. Murray to Gage, 16 May 1767, AS 65, TGP ("Lawless Raskals"); Henry Stuart, account of proceedings with Indians, 25 Aug. 1776, CO5/77 fol. 169v ("People Hunting or Settling"); Alexander Cameron, pass to Ogayoolah, 20 Sept. 1773, enclosed in John Stuart to Gage, 14 Sept. 1774, AS 123, TGP ("Deer Skins"); Gage to Croghan, 21 Mar. 1766, box 6, folder 8, GCP; Mackay, notice, 22 June 1766, PA 4:251–52; Croghan, journal, 21 Sept. 1770, GCP; Robert Callender to Penn, 21 Apr. 1771, PA 4:411–12; McKee, report, 14, 18, and 22 May 1771, enclosed in Charles Edmonstone to Gage, 24 Aug. 1771, AS 105, TGP; Stuart to Gage, 7 Sept. 1772, AS 114, TGP; Croghan to Michael Cresap, May 1774, "Turmoil at Pittsburgh: Diary of Augustine Prevost, 1774," ed. Nicholas B. Wainwright, *Pennsylvania Magazine of History and Biography* 85, no. 2 (1961): 153; Stephen Aron, *How the West Was Lost: The Transformation of Kentucky from Daniel Boone to Henry Clay* (Baltimore: Johns Hopkins University Press, 1996), 5, 18–19.

18. Cf. Gregory Evans Dowd, *A Spirited Resistance: The North American Indian Struggle for Unity, 1745–1815* (Baltimore: Johns Hopkins University Press, 1992), 42–45.

19. Shawnee chiefs, speeches, 25 Sept. 1769, enclosed in George Turnbull to Gage, 30 Sept. 1769, AS 87, TGP; Johnson to Gage, 21 Dec. 1768, PWJ 12:673; McConnell, *A Country Between*, 251–52; White, *Middle Ground*, 351–53; Dowd, *Spirited Resistance*, 42–45.

20. Croghan to Johnson, 10 May 1770, PWJ 7:652 ("Gineral Union"); McKee, journal, n.d., *Papers of Sir William Johnson*, 7:184 ("Defend themselves"); Stuart to Lord Botetourt, 13 Jan. 1770, enclosed in Stuart to Gage, 27 Jan. 1770, AS 89, TGP ("General Confederacy"); McKee to Johnson, 31 Dec. 1772, PWJ 8:679 ("[Co]ntempt and Neglect"); Croghan to Johnson, 18 Oct. 1767, PWJ 12:374; Croghan to Benjamin Franklin, 2 Oct. 1767, box 5, folder 28, GCP; Croghan to Johnson, 8 Aug. 1769, PWJ 7:78–79; McKee to Croghan, 20 Feb. 1770, PWJ 7:404–6; Gage to Johnson, 8 Oct. 1770, PWJ 12:872; Croghan, journal, 16 Sept. 1770; Stuart to Gage, 12 Dec. 1770, AS 98, TGP; John Wilkins, journal of transactions, 8 Aug.–1 Oct. 1770, 22 Apr. 1771, and 11–15 Nov. 1771, AS 138, folder 20, TGP; McConnell, *A Country Between*, 262–63; Dowd, *Spirited Resistance*, 40–43.

21. Red Hawk, speech, n.d., enclosed in McKee to Croghan, 20 Feb. 1770, PWJ 7:408 ("great trouble"); McKee to Croghan, 20 Feb. 1770, PWJ 7:404–6 ("own measures"); Holton, *Forced Founders*, 24–25. McKee's mother was an adoptive Shawnee, and Shawnees therefore considered him one of their own: Larry L. Nelson, *A Man of Distinction Among Them: Alexander McKee and the Ohio Country Frontier, 1754–1799* (Kent, OH: Kent State University Press, 1999).

22. "Information concerning an Indian conspiracy," 7 Mar. 1771, PWJ 8:6 ("Strike," "their Councils"); Edmonstone to Gage, 3 Apr. 1771, AS 101, TGP ("dread[ed]"); minutes of proceedings, 20 Dec. 1770, enclosed in Edmonstone to Gage, 27 Dec. 1770, AS 99, TGP ("Confirm"); McKee, report, 6 June 1771, enclosed in Edmonstone to Gage, 24 Aug. 1771, AS 105, TGP ("great confusion"); Intelligence Received from a Chief of the Shawanese, n.d., enclosed in Edmonstone to Gage, 9 Mar. 1771, AS 100, TGP; Callender to John Penn, 21 Apr. 1771, PA 4:411; McKee, remarks, [July 1771], PWJ 12:916; Tyler Boulware, *Deconstructing the Cherokee Nation: Town, Region, and Nation Among Eighteenth-Century Cherokees* (Gainesville: University Press of Florida, 2011), 147–51.

23. Croghan to Barnard Gratz, 11 May 1773, Draper 7J:136 ("small furrs"); Croghan to Michael Gratz, 29 July 1773, box 4, Indian Wars & Indians, case 4, Gratz ("small Cargo"); Jones 89; Gratzes to Croghan, 11 June and 13 Sept. 1773, folder 11, box 6, GCP; George Croghan to Gratzes, 18 July 1773, box 4, Indian Wars & Indians, case 4, Gratz; George Croghan, account with White Eyes, Sept.–Nov. 1773, box 2, folder 44, DAF; John Lacey, "Journal of a Mission to the Indians in Ohio, July–September, 1773," *Historical Magazine, and Notes and Queries Concerning the Antiquities, History, and Biography of America*, 2nd ser., 7, no. 2 (1870): 105; "Regulations for Indian Affairs in the Middle Department," 10 Apr. 1776, AA4 5:1663–64.

24. Croghan, journal of transactions, 29 Apr. 1765, CRP 9:254 ("all the people"); McKee, journal, [1769], PWJ 7:185 ("the Six Nations"); Callender to Shippen, 22 Apr. 1771, PA 4:413 ("Establish Schools," "annex"); Jones 89 ("be religious"), 98–99; MMD 97; Jordan, "Journal of James Kenny, 1761–63," 158–59; Beatty, *Journal of a Two Months Tour*, 52, 70; Earl P. Olmstead, *David Zeisberger: A Life Among the Indians* (Kent, OH: Kent State University Press, 1997), 182–200; McConnell, *A Country Between*, 226; McClure, "Ends of the American Earth," 56. On Neolin, cf. Dowd, *Spirited Resistance*, 36.

25. McClure 61, 74–76, 81–84, 94–96 ("to promote," 83); Jones 98–99 ("protect them"). Jones refers to his informant only as "Killbuck," a name applied to both Bemineo and Gelelemend, but Bemineo was more critical of the Moravians: MMD 135–36, 608. See also Dowd, *Spirited Resistance*, 68–72; "Extracts from the Journal of John Parrish, 1773," *Pennsylvania Magazine of History and Biography* 16, no. 4 (1893): 448; Hermann Wellenreuther, "White Eyes and the Delawares' Vision of an Indian State," *Pennsylvania History* 68, no. 2 (Spring 2001): 153–55.

26. "Speech sent from the Chiefs of the Delawares, Munsies, and Mohekins . . . to the Governors of Pennsylvania, Maryland and Virginia," [1771], box 6, folder 30, GCP ("the Great King"); Hugh Wallace to Johnson, 7 Oct. 1772, PWJ 8:609; Johnson to Gage, 1 Jan. 1773, PWJ 8:688–89; Lacey, "Journal of a Mission to the Indians," 7; "the Gov'rs Answer to New Comer's Message," 26 Nov. 1773, PA 4:469; MMD 97; Jones 98–99. The planned embassy to London had many precedents: Alden T. Vaughan, *Transatlantic Encounters: American Indians in Britain, 1500–1776* (Cambridge: Cambridge University Press, 2008); Coll Thrush, *Indigenous London: Native Travelers at the Heart of Empire* (New Haven, CT: Yale University Press, 2017).

27. Lakomäki, *Gathering Together*, 75.

28. Thomas Woods, deposition, 19 Sept. 1771, PA 4:435 (quotations); minutes of the Provincial Council, 16 Apr. 1768, CRP 9:508; McClure, "Ends of the American Earth," 142–43; D. Barr, "Contested Land," 235–36.

29. Crawford to James Tilghman, 9 Aug. 1771, PA 4:424 ("Keep off"); George Wilson to Arthur St. Clair, 14 Aug. 1771, SCP 1:258 ("to appose"); DGW 2:295; Robert Lettis Hooper Jr. to Johnson, 9 Feb. 1771, PWJ 7:1132–33; Crawford to Washington, 20 Apr. and 2 Aug. 1771, GWP; Croghan to St. Clair, 4 June 1772, PA 4:452–53; St. Clair to Joseph Shippen, 18 July 1772, SCP 1:265–67; Croghan to Wharton, 11 Nov. 1772, "Letters of Colonel George Croghan," *Pennsylvania Magazine of History and Biography* 15, no. 4 (1891): 431–32; Crawford to Washington, 12 Nov. 1773, GWP; Thomas Smith to Shippen, 7 Apr. 1774, PA 4:619; Francis Wade to Johnson, 20 Apr. 1774, PWJ 8:1125–26; D. Barr, "Contested Land," 235–42; Wainwright, *George Croghan*, 28, 257, 274–75, 277–78; McClure, "Ends of the American Earth," 90.

30. Washington to Crawford, 21 Sept. 1767, account book 2, GWP ("temporary expedient"); Crawford to Washington, 7 Jan. and 13 Oct. 1769 and 5 May 1770, ser. 4: general correspondence, GWP; applications 374 and 1304, 3 Apr. 1769, New Purchase Register (accessed 3 June 2014).

31. Application 2736, 3 Apr. 1769, and 3357, 13 June 1769, New Purchase Register (accessed 3

June 2014); McClure, "Ends of the American Earth," 276–79, 286. Where Pennsylvania's claims were uncertain, Crawford surveyed but did not buy, even as he worked as a magistrate to enforce the province's jurisdiction: Crawford to Washington, 7 Jan. 1769, ser. 4: general correspondence, GWP.

32. David L. Preston's catalog of Indian-colonist murders in Greater Pennsylvania and the Ohio country between 1760 and 1774 indicates a decline in bloodshed during the early 1770s: Preston, *Texture of Contact*, table 3.

33. John Armstrong to Penn, 29 Jan. 1768, CRP 9:448–49 ("carried off"); Vaughan, "Frontier Banditti," 3, 8–9; Gregory Evans Dowd, *War Under Heaven: Pontiac, the Indian Nations and the British Empire* (Baltimore: Johns Hopkins University Press, 2002), 191–203; Boulware, *Deconstructing the Cherokee Nation*, 138–39.

34. Preston, *Texture of Contact*, 232–33. Richard White argues that British officials in the 1760s largely failed to emulate the French alliance system of previous decades, but the French period had witnessed ample violence as well. Both before and after the midcentury wars, violence was prevalent but contained by energetic and creative diplomacy: see *Middle Ground*, 75–82, 315–16, and 339–51; Brett Rushforth, "Slavery, the Fox Wars, and the Limits of Alliance," *William and Mary Quarterly* 63, no. 1 (2006): 53–80.

35. Preston, *Texture of Contact*, 233–42 ("Ill treatment," 242), table 3; *Minutes of Conferences*, 8, 9 ("equally concerned," 9); Johnson to Gage, 20 July 1765, PWJ 11:862; Gage to Johnson, 19 May 1766, PWJ 12:91–92; Croghan, abstract from journal, 22–23 May 1766, enclosed in Croghan to Gage, 26 May 1766, AS 51, TGP; Thomas Smallman, "Names of the Traders gone into the Indian villages from F. Pitt," 1 June 1767, misfiled with Murray to Gage, 16 May 1767, AS 65, TGP; McKee to Croghan, 20 Sept. 1767, PWJ 5:686–87; Croghan to Gage, 10 Oct. 1767, AS 71, TGP; Penn to Johnson, 18 Feb. 1768, CRP 9:469–70; White, *Middle Ground*, 348.

36. On Paxton and the Susquehanna Valley, see Peter C. Mancall, *Valley of Opportunity: Economic Culture Along the Upper Susquehanna, 1700–1800* (Ithaca, NY: Cornell University Press, 1991); Jane T. Merritt, *At the Crossroads: Indians and Empires on a Mid-Atlantic Frontier, 1700–1763* (Chapel Hill: University of North Carolina Press, 2003). For Staunton and cismontane Virginia, see Warren R. Hofstra, *The Planting of New Virginia: Settlement and Landscape in the Shenandoah Valley* (Baltimore: Johns Hopkins University Press, 2005). For Bemineo and Gelelemend, see Callender to Shippen, 22 Apr. 1771, PA 4:413.

37. Edmonstone to Gage, 20 Sept. 1769, AS 87, TGP ("through the Negligence"); David Owens and John Williams, deposition, 10 Sept. 1769, enclosed in Edmonstone to Gage, 10 Sept. 1769, AS 87, TGP. David Owens was a veteran trader and Delaware interpreter: Jones 18, 26, 33–34; James H. Merrell, *Into the American Woods: Negotiators on the Pennsylvania Frontier* (New York: W. W. Norton, 1999), 93. Charles Martin may also have been a trader: DGW 2:301; Edmonstone, speech, 14 Mar. 1772, enclosed in Edmonstone to Gage, 23 Mar. 1772, AS 109, TGP.

38. Richard Brown, deposition, 7 Sept., Guyasuta and Edmonstone, speeches, 10 Sept., and Edmonstone to Penn, 11 Sept. 1771, PA 4:430–34 (quotations on 431, 433–34); Gerald H. Smith, ed., *Bedford County, Pennsylvania: Quarter Sessions, 1771–1801* (Westminster, MD: Heritage, 2010), 16 ("gaol fees"); St. Clair to Shippen, 24 Sept. 1771, SCP 1:261; Croghan, journal, 3 Sept. 1771. Similarly, in early 1770, William Crawford agreed to procure evidence against his servant John Ingman, the alleged murderer of "Indian Stephen," but there is no evidence that Ingman came to trial: Botetourt to Penn, 20 Mar. 1770, PA 4:365–66; Vaughan, "Frontier Banditti," 12–13.

39. Murray to Gage, 16 May 1767, AS 65, TGP ("Whole People"); *Minutes of Conferences*, 17 ("Rum").

40. Croghan, journal, Apr.–Sept. 1771 ("not a Village," 1 Sept. 1771); Edmonstone to Gage, 24 Sept. 1770, AS 96, TGP ("Unexperienced Lad"); Croghan to Gage, 13 July 1770, AS 93, TGP; Edmonstone to Gage, 16 July, 11 Aug., and 27 Dec. 1770, AS 93, 94, and 99 TGP; Croghan, proceedings, 8 and 17 July 1770, enclosed in Croghan to Gage, 8 Aug. 1770, AS 94, TGP; White, *Middle Ground*, 343; Peter C. Mancall, *Deadly Medicine: Indians and Alcohol in Early America* (Ithaca, NY: Cornell University Press, 1995).

41. Croghan, proceedings, 12, 21, and 24 July and 1 Aug. 1770, enclosed in Croghan to Gage, 8 Aug. 1770, AS 94, TGP; Croghan to Gage, 13 July 1770, AS 93, TGP; Croghan to Gage, 8 Aug. 1770, AS 94, TGP. Croghan initially confused the Cheat River and Redstone events, but a closer examination of his journal shows that they were separate incidents.

42. Croghan to Gage, 8 Aug. 1770, AS 94, TGP ("call'd in," "attacking"); Croghan, proceedings, 24–26 July and 1–2 Aug. 1770, enclosed in Croghan to Gage, 8 Aug. 1770, AS 94, TGP ("revenging," 1 Aug.)

43. For the Two Creeks migration, see Croghan, journal, 4 Sept. 1770; McKee, report, 6 May 1771, enclosed in Edmonstone to Gage, 24 Aug. 1771, AS 105, TGP; Morgan to Congress, 8 Nov. 1776, AA5 3:600; MMD 92. For militancy, see Stephen Forrester to [John Stuart], 7 Sept. 1772, enclosed in Stuart to Gage, 30 Sept. 1772, AS 114, TGP. For the evacuation of Fort Pitt, see McClure 40, 85; Downes, *Council Fires*, 132. For the killing of the woman and children, see McKee, report, 18 May 1771, enclosed in Edmonstone to Gage, 24 Aug. 1771, AS 105, TGP; Guyasuta and Edmonstone, speeches, 10 Sept. 1771, PA 4:434. McKee's informant blamed Haudenosaunees; Guyasuta blamed Delawares. Edmonstone placed the attack near the Greenbrier River in western Virginia; McKee placed it close to the Kanawha. The victims were likely part of the Stroud family, whose deaths were mentioned (and exaggerated) in Earl of Dunmore to Earl of Dartmouth, 24 Dec. 1774, DHDW 374; and in Alexander Scott Withers, *Chronicles of Border Warfare*, annotated ed., ed. Reuben Gold Thwaites (1895; Parsons, WV: McClain Printing Company, 1975), 136–37. Both Dunmore and Withers are highly unreliable. Thwaites, who edited both, asserts that Shawnees killed the Strouds on Elk River, a tributary of the Kanawha whose headwaters lie close to the Greenbrier. But the evidence is too fragmentary to support a firm conclusion.

Chapter 2

1. Journal of James McAfee, 13 June and 9–13 July 1773, in *The Woods-McAfee Memorial*, ed. Neander M. Woods (Louisville, KY: Courier-Journal, 1905), 429–34 ("first [came]," 430); Thomas Bullitt and Cornstalk, speeches, and Richard Butler, letter, 9–10 June 1773, *Woods-McAfee Memorial*, 439–40; Shawnees, speech, 28 June 1773, PWJ 8:834–35; *Minutes of Conferences, Held at Fort Pitt, in April and May, 1768* (Philadelphia: William Goddard, 1769), 12–13, 19–20; Jones 52–54; MMD 147–48; Thomas Perkins Abernethy, *Western Lands and the American Revolution* (New York: Russell and Russell, 1959), 84–87; Sami Lakomäki, *Gathering Together: The Shawnee People Through Diaspora and Nationhood, 1600–1870* (New Haven, CT: Yale University Press, 2014), 78–80.

2. Butler, letter, 10 June 1773, *Woods-McAfee Memorial*, 439.

3. For critical assessments, see Richard White, *The Middle Ground: Indians, Empires, and Republics in the Great Lakes Region, 1650–1815* (New York: Cambridge University Press, 1991), 364; Michael N. McConnell, *A Country Between: The Upper Ohio Valley and Its Peoples,*

1724–1774 (Lincoln: University of Nebraska Press, 1992), 274–75. For more positive interpretations, see Patrick Griffin, *American Leviathan: Empire, Nation, and Revolutionary Frontier* (New York: Hill and Wang, 2007), 99; James Corbett David, *Dunmore's New World: The Extraordinary Life of a Royal Governor in Revolutionary America* (Charlottesville: University of Virginia Press, 2013), 91–92. For a more nuanced account, see Eric Hinderaker, *Elusive Empires: Constructing Colonialism in the Ohio Valley, 1673–1800* (New York: Cambridge University Press, 1997), 189–93.

4. Advertisement, *Pennsylvania Journal*, no. 1565, 2 Dec. 1772, [3]; Nicholas B. Wainwright, *George Croghan: Wilderness Diplomat* (Chapel Hill: University of North Carolina Press, 1959), 287 ("intimately"); George Croghan to John Jennings, 1 June 1767, box 2, folder 36, DAF; George Morgan to John Baynton and Samuel Wharton, 5 Apr. 1768, in George Morgan, letterbook and journal, 131–33, HSP; Isaac Hamilton to Thomas Gage, 8 Aug. 1772, AS 113, TGP; McClure 47; George Croghan, return of employees, 15 Apr. 1767, *The New Régime, 1765–1767*, ed. Clarence Walworth Alvord, Collections of the Illinois State Historical Library, vol. 11 (Springfield, IL, 1916), 557; John Connolly, "A Narrative of the Transactions, Imprisonment, and Sufferings of John Connolly, an American Loyalist," *Pennsylvania Magazine of History and Biography* 12, no. 3, 4 (1888): 310–11; Margaret Pearson Bothwell, "Edward Ward: Trail Blazing Pioneer," *Western Pennsylvania Historical Magazine* 43, no. 2 (1960): 102, 111–12.

5. William Crawford to George Washington, 15 Mar. and 1 May 1772, ser. 4, general correspondence, GWP ("As soon as," 15 Mar.); John Connolly to Washington, 18 Sept. 1772, GWP; petitions, 1769–1772, VSP 1:260–66; DGW 2:293–94, 304, 310, 317–18, 322–23; Woody Holton, *Forced Founders: Indians, Debtors, Slaves, and the Making of the American Revolution in Virginia* (Chapel Hill: University of North Carolina Press, 1999), 7–9, 27; David L. Preston, *The Texture of Contact: European and Indian Settler Communities on the Frontiers of Iroquoia, 1667–1783* (Lincoln: University of Nebraska Press, 2009), ch. 6.

6. "A friend to the true interest of Britain in America," *Virginia Gazette* (Rind), no. 349, 14 Jan. 1773, [3] ("Chinese wall"); Washington to Lord Dunmore, 15 June 1771, 13 Apr. 1773, and 2 Nov. 1773, account book 2, pp. 142, 168, and 210, GWP; Connolly to Washington, 29 June 1773, GWP; Washington to William Crawford, 25 Sept. 1773, account book 2, p. 169, GWP; William Crawford to Washington, 12 Nov. 1773, GWP; Abernethy, *Western Lands*, 84, 87–88; David, *Dunmore's New World*, 63.

7. MMD 166 ("to deceive"); conference with Kayaghshota, [5 Jan. 1774], PWJ 12:1052 ("Hemmed"); extract of a letter from Pittsburgh, 17 Aug. 1773, *Virginia Gazette*, no. 387, 7 Oct. 1773, [2]; John Armstrong to Washington, 17 Aug. 1773, GWP.

8. Cornstalk, speech, 25 Sept. 1773, PWJ 12:1032–33; Indian conference, 9 Oct. 1773, PWJ 12:1034 ("hatched"); conference with Kayaghshota, [5 Jan. 1774], PWJ 12:1048 ("double tongue"); William Johnson to the Earl of Dartmouth, 22 Sept. 1773, PWJ 8:890 ("most attentive"); Johnson to Frederick Haldimand, 19 Mar. 1774, PWJ 8:1085 ("disaffected people"); Croghan to Barnard Gratz, 11 May 1773, Draper 7J:136; Croghan to Wharton, 15 Oct. and 9 Dec. 1773, "Letters of Colonel George Croghan," *Pennsylvania Magazine of History and Biography* 15, no. 4 (1891): 434–37; meeting with the Six Nations, Wyandots, Ottawas, and Delawares, 7 Oct. 1773, folder 30, box 6, GCP; Alexander McKee to Johnson, 16 Oct. 1773, PWJ 12:1038–39.

9. McKee, journal, 8 Mar. 1774, PWJ 12:1085 ("red Flaggs," "constant assembling"); Devereux Smith to [William] Smith, 10 June 1774, AA4 1:468 ("warlike appearance"); Arthur St. Clair to John Penn, 2 Feb. 1774, SCP 1:280 ("drunkenness"); "Remarks on the Proceedings of Dr. Connolly," 25 June 1774, SCP 1:282n1.

10. Advertisement, 1 Jan. 1774, SCP 1:272n2; William Crawford to Penn, 8 Apr. 1774, SCP 1:294 ("insulted"); Aeneas Mackay to Penn, 4 Apr. 1774, PA 4:485 ("armed men"); Thomas Smith to Joseph Shippen, 7 Apr. 1775 [1774], PA 4:618 ("Colours"); Connolly to Washington, 29 Aug. 1773, GWP; Mackay to St. Clair, 11 Jan. 1774, SCP 1:271–73; Joseph Spear to St. Clair, 23 Feb. 1774, SCP 1:284; St. Clair to Shippen, 25 Feb. 1774, SCP 1:284–85; Connolly, declaration, [6 Apr. 1774], SCP 1:293n1; Mackay to James Wilson, 9 Apr. 1774, box 4, folder 63, DAF; Andrew McFarlane to Penn, 9 Apr. 1774, PA 4:487–88; Thomas Smith to Shippen, 13 Apr. 1774, PA 4:488–89; George Wilson, deposition, 25 Apr. 1774, PA 4:492–93; Mackay to Penn, 5 May 1774, PA 4:494–95; Devereux Smith to [William] Smith, 10 June 1774, AA4 1:469–70; David, *Dunmore's New World*, 70.

11. William Crawford to Penn, 8 Apr. 1774, SCP 1:292 ("equally averse"); Washington to William Crawford, 25 Sept. 1773, account book 2, GWP; William Crawford to Washington, 12 Nov. 1773, 29 Dec. 1773, and 10 Jan. 1774, GWP; William Preston to Washington, 7 Mar. 1774, GWP; Mackay to Penn, 4 Apr. 1774, PA 4:484–86; Abernethy, *Western Lands*, 87–89; Wainwright, *George Croghan*, 286–87; James Patrick McClure, "The Ends of the American Earth: Pittsburgh and the Upper Ohio Valley to 1795" (Ph.D. diss., University of Michigan, 1983), 275–93.

12. McKee, journal, 27 Feb.–8 Mar. 1774, PWJ 12:1080–81 ("White people," "put a Stop") and 1084 ("great Numbers"); William Ogilvy to Haldimand, 8 June and 18 July 1774 and enclosures, AS 119 and 121, TGP; John Mack Faragher, *Daniel Boone: The Life and Legend of an American Pioneer* (New York: Holt, 1992), 92–96.

13. John Floyd to Preston, 26 Apr. 1774, DHDW 7 ("to kill all the Virginians"); Campbell to Alexander Cameron, 20 June 1774, enclosed in John Stuart to Gage, 14 Sept. 1774, AS 123, TGP ("much encouraged"); Campbell to Preston, n.d., DHDW 39 ("every ones mouth"); Dunmore to Stuart, 5 Apr. 1774, enclosed in Ogilvy to Haldimand, 8 June 1774, AS 119, TGP ("Vengeance"); Cameron, pass to Ogayoolah, 20 Sept. 1773, enclosed in Stuart to Gage, 14 Sept. 1774, AS 123, TGP.

14. Cameron to [Stuart], 18 June 1774, enclosed in Stuart to Gage, 3 July 1774, AS 120, TGP ("unite and oppose"); John Caldwell to [Gage], 29 Sept. 1774, AS 123, TGP ("Sang Blanc"); McKee, journal, [16 and 25 Apr. 1774], PWJ 12:1088 ("good speeches," "those people"), 1092–94; Johnson to Gage, 4 July 1774, PWJ 12:1114–15; Campbell to Preston, 16 Oct. 1774, DHDW 278; MMD 183.

15. McKee, journal, 17 and 24 Apr. and 1 May 1774, PWJ 12:1090, 1096; Shawnee speech, 20 May 1774, PA 4:497; "The Cosh" [Schebosch], letter, 24 May 1774, PA 4:499; Devereux Smith to [William] Smith, 10 June 1774, AA4 1:468; Ebenezer Zane to John Brown, 3 Feb. 1800, Thomas Jefferson Papers at the Library of Congress, Series 1: General Correspondence, 1651–1827, https://www.loc.gov/collections/thomas-jefferson-papers/; John Gibson, deposition, 4 Apr. 1800, Jefferson Papers; George Rogers Clark to Samuel Brown, 17 June 1798, GRC 8:5–7.

16. Washington to William Crawford, 25 Sept. 1773, account book 2, GWP ("No time"); William Preston, advertisement, *Virginia Gazette* (Purdie and Dixon), no. 1168, 24 Feb. 1774, [3] ("prevent insults"); MMD 189 ("would attack"); Floyd to Preston, 26 Apr. 1774, DHDW 7–8 ("Orderd," "almost Daily"); John Floyd, deposition, 28 Oct. 1778, VSP 1:310; John Gibson, deposition, n.d., Jefferson Papers; Abernethy, *Western Lands*, 102–5. A rumor reached the upper Ohio Valley that some of the surveyors attacked a party of Indians, killed several, and took thirty horseloads of deerskins: William Crawford to Washington, 8 May 1774, GWP. Such an attack could have happened, but the lack of any corroborating evidence, and its absence from Shawnees' subsequent lists of grievances, suggests that it did not. Michael Cresap or one of his

associates could have invented the story to deflect blame for the outbreak of hostilities. The preponderance of the evidence suggests that no one died in the confrontations in Kentucky and that Cresap and his gang started the killing on 26 Apr.

17. McKee, journal, [16–17 Apr. 1774], PWJ 12:1087–90 ("strik[e]"); Connolly 2 ("Guard against," "towards such"); "The Cosh" [Schebosch], letter, 24 May 1774, PA 4:499; Butler, "Account of the Rise of the Indian War," 23 Aug. 1774, PA 4:569.

18. Connolly 1–2; McKee, journal, 24 Apr. 1774, PWJ 12:1090; intelligence received at Pittsburgh, 3 May 1774, Prevost 148–49; James Chambers et al., declarations, 1798–1800, *Jefferson's Notes, on the State of Virginia; with the Appendixes—Complete*, Appendix 4 (Baltimore: W. Pechin, 1800), 39–53, Eighteenth Century Collections Online, Gale Group.

19. David, *Dunmore's New World*, 78 ("inevitability"); John Heckewelder, declaration, n.d., *Jefferson's Notes, Appendix 4*, 46 ("friend to the white people"); GD 8–14 May 1774 ("wherever they might"; "begin no war"); Connolly 3, 13 ("His heart," 13); Gilbert Simpson to Washington, May 4, 1774, GWP; "Indian intelligence," 5 June 1774, PA 4:508–9; McKee 7–16, 22; MMD 195–96; W. M. Beauchamp, "Shikellimy and His Son Logan," in *Twenty-First Annual Report of the American Scenic and Historic Preservation Society* (New York, 1916), 599–611.

20. Croghan to Connolly and McKee, 4 May 1774, and Croghan to Dunmore, [May 1774], Prevost 149 ("all other nations"), 151 ("some few"); Connolly, "Journal of My Proceedings," 3–4 ("immediate Danger"); Dunmore, answer to the Six Nations and Delawares, 29 May 1774, Prevost 155 ("aggressors"); McKee 5–6, 9–10 ("killed on both Sides," "their settling," 9–10); Johnson to Gage, 4 July 1774, PWJ 12:1114–15.

21. Shawnee answer to condolence speeches, n.d., AA4 1:479 (quotations). White Eyes heard Connolly's speech of 5 May in Pittsburgh and promised to deliver it personally to the Ohio Indian towns: McKee 9–10. On 9 May he reached the Moravian mission of Schönbrunn and likely presented the speech to the Delaware council soon thereafter. Campbell was killed around 15 May. See David Zeisberger and "The Cosh" [Schebosch], letters, 28 and 24 May 1774, PA 4:498–99; Devereux Smith to William Smith, 10 June 1774, AA4 1:468–69; extract of a letter from Fort Pitt, 12 June 1774, DHDW 36; William Crawford to Washington, 8 June 1774, GWP; Connolly 17; MMD 191–99.

22. McKee, extract of letter, 10 June 1774, PA 4:511; McKee 13, 16–17, 23, 27–29, 32–33, 35–36, 48–49 ("great Trouble," 28; "Crazy people," 32; "rash inconsiderate men," 35); John Montgomery to Penn, 30 June 1774, PA 4:533 ("sit Still"); "The Cosh" [Schebosch], letter, 24 May 1774, PA 4:500; "Indian intelligence," 5 June 1774, PA 4:508–9; MMD 191–92, 199–202, 204, 215.

23. Connolly 3, 4, 7–8, 11[a], 11[b], 13, 17 ("as enemies," 17); Dunmore to County Lieutenants, 10 June 1774, DHDW 34 ("own Country"); McKee 5, 27, 32, 36–37, 63–64 ("imprudent young Men," 36–37); St. Clair to Penn, 22 and 26 June 1774, PA 4:523–24, 530; letter from Carlisle, 4 July 1774, DHDW 66–67; MMD 210–11; Prevost 127; William Wilson, deposition, 13 July 1774, PA 4:543–44; Connolly, advertisement, 18 June 1774, PA 4:521; David, *Dunmore's New World*, 84. For Cresap, see an extract of a letter from Redstone, 18 Aug. 1774, AA4 1:723; Pittsburgh payrolls, 1775, Accession 41, RG #1, Virginia Colonial Government Records, Library of Virginia, fols. 5–10, miscellaneous reel 78, microfilm.

24. Devereux Smith to [William] Smith, 10 June 1774, AA4 1:470 ("abuse[d] him"); Prevost 132 ("no store"); William Crawford to Washington, 8 May 1774, GWP ("Displeashure"); James Robertson to Preston, 26 July and 1 Sept. 1774, DHDW 99, 174 ("unless I kill part," 99); Michael Woods to Preston, 3 Sept. 1774, DHDW 175; Connolly 6–8, 10, 11[b].

25. Connolly 6–8, 10, 11[b] ("cou'd bring," 6–7); Croghan to Dunmore, [May] and 15 Sept.

1774, Prevost 151–52, 160–61 ("too incautiously," 160); Prevost 118, 134–41 ("a proclamation," 139); Valentine Crawford to Washington, 13 May 1774, GWP; St. Clair to Penn, 22 June 1774, PA 4:523–25; Pittsburgh payrolls, 1775.

26. Dunmore to County Lieutenants, 10 June 1774, DHDW 34 ("oblige the Assembly"); Preston, circular letter, 20 July 1774, DHDW 92 ("every Vollunteer," "great Stock of Horses"); William Christian to Preston, 22 June and 12 June 1774, DHDW 44 ("encourage men") and 83 ("any thing publickly"); Floyd to Preston, 26 and 28 Aug. 1774, DHDW 163–64, 167–68; Campbell to Preston, 28 Aug. 1774, DHDW 170–72; Albert H. Tillson, *Gentry and Common Folk: Political Culture on a Virginia Frontier, 1740–1789* (Lexington: University Press of Kentucky, 1991), 48–55, 66–68, 73–75; Faragher, *Daniel Boone*, 102–6; Hinderaker, *Elusive Empires*, 193–94; Holton, *Forced Founders*, 117–19.

27. Oconastotah to Cameron, [June 1774], enclosed in Ogilvy to Haldimand, 18 July 1774, AS 121, TGP ("White People"); [Cameron] to [Stuart?], 10 Oct. 1774, Chalmers ("foam'd"); Cameron to [Stuart], 4 July 1774, enclosed in Ogilvy to Haldimand, 18 July 1774, AS 121, TGP; Campbell to Cameron, 20 June 1774, enclosed in Stuart to Gage, 14 Sept. 1774, AS 123, TGP; Campbell to Preston, n.d., DHDW 38–39.

28. Logan to Michael Cresap, 21 July 1774, DHDW 246–47 ("must kill"); Edward Wilkinson to Cameron, 26 June 1774, enclosed in Ogilvy to Haldimand, 18 July 1774, AS 121, TGP ("surrounded"); Christian to Preston, 22 June and 4 July 1774, DHDW 42–46, 63–66; Christian to Joseph Cloyd, 29 June 1774, DHDW 56–57; Charles Lewis to Preston, 9 July 1774, DHDW 73–74; John Pollock, &c., depositions, 15 July 1774, PA 4:544–45; Valentine Crawford to Washington, 27 July 1774, GWP; Robertson to Preston, 12 Aug. 1774, DHDW 140–42; Preston, letter, 13 Aug. 1774, AA4 1:707–8; Preston to Washington, 15 Aug. 1774, GWP; MMD 204, 212; Connolly 17; William Robinson, declaration, 28 Feb. 1800, Jefferson Papers; "Narrative by Captain John Stuart of General Andrew Lewis' Expedition," *Magazine of American History with Notes and Queries* 1, no. 11, 12 (1877): 674–75.

29. Speeches at Detroit, 19–23 Aug. 1774, enclosed in Richard Lernoult to Haldimand, 31 Aug. 1774, AS 122, TGP; Huron Indians, answer, 7 Sept. 1774, Chalmers; Caldwell to [Gage?], 29 Sept. 1774, AS 123, TGP; MMD 222; McKee 32–33, 48–49, 53–54, 58–59; MMD 218, 236–38, 250.

30. Angus McDonald to Connolly, n.d., DHDW 151–54; extract of a letter from Redstone, [Aug. 1774], AA4 1:722–24; MMD 221–22.

31. McKee 57–58; MMD 222–23. The editors of Zeisberger's diaries suggest that the Hardman, as head civil leader, had handed authority to the head military leader, as was customary at the beginning of a war. McKee's account indicates otherwise. Rather than reflecting traditional divisions of authority, the incident signaled the flexibility of such divisions: a civil leader had drawn the nation into war, while a military leader took on the role of peacemaker.

32. McKee 59–60 ("Committed Murders"); Prevost 131, 132, 135, 138–39 ("measures & ways," 131); Christian to Preston, 7 Sept. 1774, DHDW 186 ("hung up like Colours"); councils, [Sept. 1774], AA4 1:872–76; Campbell to Preston, 9 and 17 Sept. 1774, DHDW 192–95, 202–4; William Doack to Preston, 22 Sept. 1774, Draper 3QQ:101; Preston, letter, 28 Sept. 1774, AA4 1:808; William Fleming, journal, n.d., DHDW 281–82; MMD 223, 229.

33. MMD 231–32 ("all their warriors," "gathering"); Fleming to William Bowyer, n.d., DHDW 256 ("speak with the army").

34. Fleming to Bowyer, n.d., DHDW 254–57; Isaac Shelby to John Shelby, 16 Oct. 1774, DHDW 270–76.

35. Dunmore, speeches at Camp Charlotte, n.d., Chalmers ("deluded brethren"); MMD

236–38; Prevost 143; Christian to Preston, 8 Nov. 1774, DHDW 301–7; Valentine Crawford to Washington, 1 Oct. 1774, GWP; White, *Middle Ground*, 362–64.

36. Fleming, journal, n.d., DHDW 290 ("the Guide"); William Crawford to Washington, 14 Nov. 1774, GWP; MMD 236–38; Christian to Preston, 8 Nov. 1774, DHDW 301–7; Andrew Lewis to Samuel Campbell, n.d., *Virginia Historical Register, and Literary Adviser* 1, no. 1 (Jan. 1848): 32–33; Hinderaker, *Elusive Empires*, 193–94.

37. White, *Middle Ground*, 363n94; Dunmore to Dartmouth, 24 Dec. 1774, DHDW 371, 376. Dunmore's superiors ultimately approved his conduct: David, *Dunmore's New World*, 93.

Chapter 3

1. Cornstalk and William Russell, speeches, n.d., Chalmers; Thomas Cresap to Lord Dunmore, n.d., Chalmers; Daniel Boone to Richard Henderson, 1 Apr. 1775, in *Boonesborough: Its Founding, Pioneer Struggles, Indian Experiences, Transylvania Days, and Revolutionary Annals*, ed. George W. Ranck, Filson Club Publications No. 16 (Louisville, KY: Filson Club, 1901), 168–69; Dunmore, message to House of Burgesses, 5 June 1775, AA4 2:1189–90; Russell to William Fleming, 12 June 1775, RUO 15–16; Oconestoto to Virginia Convention, 24 June 1775, RVRI 3:219; Michael A. McDonnell, *The Politics of War: Race, Class, and Conflict in Revolutionary Virginia* (Chapel Hill: University of North Carolina Press, 2007), 49–74; James Corbett David, *Dunmore's New World: The Extraordinary Life of a Royal Governor in Revolutionary America* (Charlottesville: University of Virginia Press, 2013), 94–95.

2. James Wood, diary, 24 June, 9, 18, and 31 July 1775, RUO 34, 39, 42, 57–58 ("all determined," 57); Cresswell 64–65 ("full of Indians"); James Rogers, information, 24 Sept. 1775, RUO 70.

3. Patrick Griffin attributes such fluctuations in violence to the changing role of state authority in the region. Only effective state institutions, he suggests, could have restrained Indians and colonists from slaughtering one another: *American Leviathan: Empire, Nation, and Revolutionary Frontier* (New York: Hill and Wang, 2007). Griffin's argument jars with chronology. If state influence tended to restrain violence, and its absence encouraged it, then one would have expected violence to peak in 1775 and 1776, when provincial governments fell apart and revolutionary governments were in their infancy. Yet these years of political upheaval yielded relative peace in the west. By contrast, the years that brought large-scale warfare—1774 and 1777—also brought renewed government attention.

4. Matthew Elliot to commissioners, 31 Aug. 1776, Morgan 2:19–20 ("Indian War"); commissioners to Committee of Congress, 25 Sept. 1776, AA5 2:511–13 ("spirited conduct," 513); commissioners to county lieutenants, 31 Aug. 1776, RUO 190–91; MMD 332.

5. George Morgan to Dorsey Pentecost, 16 Feb. 1777, Morgan 1:35 ("great Hopes"); "Treaty with Western Indians," 15 Sept. 1775, RUO 27–32; speech to the Mingos, 27 Oct. 1776, Yeates.

6. William Preston to Dunmore, 10 Mar. 1775, RUO 3–4 ("valuable & extensive"); John Brown to Preston, 5 May 1775, RUO 10 ("new found"); Josiah Martin to Earl of Dartmouth, 12 Nov. 1775, *Colonial and State Records of North Carolina*, ed. William L. Saunders (Raleigh, NC: P. M. Hale, 1886–1907), 10:324, Documenting the American South, http://docsouth.unc.edu/csr/index.html ("such Adventurers"); advertisement, *Virginia Gazette* (Dixon and Hunter), no. 1265, 4 Nov. 1775, [4]; Henderson, journal, May 1775, *Boonesborough*, 177 ("set of scoundrels"), 174–75; George Rogers Clark to Jonathan Clark, 6 July 1775, GRC 8:9–10; Cresswell 59, 60; John Mack Faragher, *Daniel Boone: The Life and Legend of an American Pioneer* (New York: Holt, 1992), 106–9; Stephen Aron, *How the West Was Lost: The Transformation of Kentucky from Daniel Boone to*

Henry Clay (Baltimore: Johns Hopkins University Press, 1996), 59–62, 65–67; Eric Hinderaker, *Elusive Empires: Constructing Colonialism in the Ohio Valley, 1673–1800* (New York: Cambridge University Press, 1997), 198, 199, 205–6; Claudio Saunt, *West of the Revolution: An Uncommon History of 1776* (New York: W. W. Norton, 2014), 17–28.

7. Transylvania proprietors, petition, 25 Sept. 1775, *Boonesborough*, 216 ("general cause"); Henderson, journal, Apr.–May 1775, ibid., 172–77 ("set of scoundrels," 177); James Hogg to Henderson, Jan. 1776, ibid., 224–29; Thomas Perkins Abernethy, *Western Lands and the American Revolution* (New York: Russell and Russell, 1959).

8. Cresswell 38–40, 59, 60 ("never sold," 60); James Nourse, "Journey to Kentucky in 1775," *Journal of American History* 19, no. 2–4 (1925): 122, 256–58 ("no bread," 258); John Clark to Jonathan Clark, 12 Aug. 1776, GRC 8:17 ("the least Dread"); Henderson, journal, Mar.–July 1775, and Henderson to proprietors, 12 June 1775, *Boonesborough*, 169–80, 184–93; George Rogers Clark to Jonathan Clark, 6 July 1775, GRC 8:10; Hinderaker, *Elusive Empires*, 197–99. According to Cresswell, news of a nearby Indian attack reached him near the falls of the Ohio on 6 June: Cresswell 59. I have found no other evidence supporting this rumor. Nourse, Cresswell's companion at the time, mentioned no attack in his own journal. Richard Henderson, writing from Boonesborough on June 12, stated that no one had attacked the Kentucky colonists since March, and Henderson's journal mentions no attacks through July. The rumor that Cresswell recorded was likely a warmed-over account of the March attacks.

9. James Harrod et al., petition to the Virginia Convention, received May 1776, *Boonesborough*, 243 ("gentlemen stiling"); [Levi Todd], "Transactions in Ky. from 1774 to 1777," n.d., Draper 15CC:158; Kentucky inhabitants, petition, 15 June 1776, GRC 8:11–13; Committee of West Fincastle, petition, 20 June 1776, *Boonesborough*, 244–47; Executive Council of Virginia, journal, 12 Aug. 1778, FAUO 126; Aron, *How the West Was Lost*, 68–73; Hinderaker, *Elusive Empires*, 199–206; Honor Sachs, *Home Rule: Households, Manhood, and National Expansion on the Eighteenth-Century Kentucky Frontier* (New Haven, CT: Yale University Press, 2015), 27–40.

10. "Treaty Between Virginia and the Indians at Fort Dunmore (Pittsburg) June, 1775," *Virginia Magazine of History and Biography* 14, no. 1 (July 1906): 61.

11. West Augusta Committee, resolutions, 16 May 1775, RVRI 3:137–40 ("oppos[e] the invaders," 138); William Thompson to James Wilson, 28 June 1775, case 4, box 15, Generals of the Revolution, Gratz ("prevent"); Valentine Crawford to George Washington, 24 June 1775, ser. 4, GWP ("Leaky Boat"); petitions, Feb. 1775, PA 4:603–12; letters, May 1775, PA 4:622–29; Westmoreland County, resolutions, 16 May 1775, AA4 2:615–16; St. Clair to Penn, 25 May 1775, PA 4:628–29; "Treaty Between Virginia and the Indians," 61–63; Committee of the Western Waters of Augusta County, speeches, 26 June 1775, RVRI 3:229–30; James Wood, diary, 9 July 1775, RUO 37–38; Percy B. Caley, "The Life Adventures of Lieutenant-Colonel John Connolly: The Story of a Tory," *Western Pennsylvania Historical Magazine* 11 (1928): 99–104; James Patrick McClure, "The Ends of the American Earth: Pittsburgh and the Upper Ohio Valley to 1795" (Ph.D. diss., University of Michigan, 1983), 275–93, 325–26; Daniel P. Barr, "Contested Land: Competition and Conflict Along the Upper Ohio Frontier, 1744–1784" (Ph.D. diss., Kent State University, 2001), 300–305, 309–10.

12. Cresswell 79 ("quarreling"); Arthur St. Clair to John Penn, 15 Sept. 1775, SCP 1:361–62; Indian commissioners, report, 24 Sept. 1775, RVRI 4:140–41.

13. The documentary record reveals little about this woman, not even her name. One of Butler's allies called her a "cursed whore": Aeneas MacKay, unaddressed, 31 Oct. 1775, case 4, box 13, Generals of the Revolution, Gratz. She was likely the same woman who had visited Butler in

jail the year before, only to be "drummed all round the town" by Connolly's allies: St. Clair to Penn, 25 Aug. 1774, AA4 1:684. Given the many unknowns, perhaps the best label is the most ambiguous: she was Butler's friend.

14. The documentary record is little kinder to Susanna Connolly than to her unnamed antagonist. According to one male visitor, she had "all the gesture & conduct of a s[er]p[en]t." He added that "one S. G. was suposed to be much in her good graces": Prevost 138, 130.

15. Mackay, unaddressed, 31 Oct. 1775, case 4, box 13, Generals of the Revolution, Gratz; Mackay to James Wilson, 8 Nov. 1775, in "Notes and Queries," *Pennsylvania Magazine of History and Biography* 29, no. 3 (1905): 369–70; Ephraim Douglass to James Wilson, 21 Nov. 1775, in "Correspondence of the Revolution," *Historical Register: Notes and Queries, Historical and Genealogical, Relating to Interior Pennsylvania* 2, no. 1 (1884): 58–60; Margaret Pearson Bothwell, "Devereux Smith, Fearless Pioneer," *Western Pennsylvania Historical Magazine* 40, no. 4 (Winter 1957): 277–91.

16. D. Barr, "Contested Land," 301–5. The reciprocal arrests continued until at least June 1776: Pentecost to Committee of Safety, 4 June 1776, RVRI 7:361; Jasper Yeates to James Wilson, 30 July 1776, in "Notes and Queries," 359–60.

17. Pittsburgh traders like Butler often depended on the labor and social networks of what the missionary David McClure called a "temporary wife," most (but not all) of whom were Indian women: McClure 53–54. Colonists' description of Butler's friend as a "woman" rather than "squaw" suggests that they perceived her as white, but they might have said the same about countless light-skinned people who, thanks to intermarriage and adoption, belonged to Shawnee, Delaware, Wyandot, or Haudenosaunee families.

18. Cresswell 60 ("wilderness Country"); Crawford to Washington, 24 June 1775, GWP ("Indens towns"); treaty record, 10 Oct. 1775, RUO 99 ("our Negroes"); Nourse, "Journey to Kentucky," 256.

19. Westmoreland County, resolutions, 16 May 1775, AA4 2:615 ("military body"); Preston to William Christian, 1 May 1775, RUO 8–9 ("Just Returns"); West Augusta Committee, resolutions, 16 May 1775, RVRI 3:137–40; St. Clair to Penn, 15 Sept. 1775, SCP 1:361–62; Pentecost, letters, Nov. 1776, RUO 212–14, 219–21; John Canon to William Harrod, 7 Dec. 1776, RUO 222; McDonnell, *Politics of War*, 92–94; Francis S. Fox, "Pennsylvania's Revolutionary Militia Law: The Statute That Transformed the State," *Pennsylvania History* 80, no. 2 (Spring 2013): 204–14.

20. John Pendleton Kennedy, ed., *Journals of the House of Burgesses of Virginia, 1773–1776* (Richmond: Virginia State Library, 1905), 282–83 ("settle the Accounts"); Third Virginia Convention, Proceedings, 11 Aug. 1775, RVRI 3:418 ("poor Widows"); Report of Northern Claims Commissioners for Dunmore's War, n.d., and Edmund Pendleton to Robert Carter, 1 Dec. 1776, RVRI 5:35–36. For subsequent claims, see Proceedings of the Fifth Virginia Convention, 15, 19, and 24 June 1776, RVRI 7:512, 550, 592. For total payments, see RVRI 5:38–39n16. For itemized payments and equivalencies, compare Pittsburgh payrolls, 1775, Accession 41, RG #1, Virginia Colonial Government Records, Library of Virginia, miscellaneous reel 78, microfilm; and West Augusta public service claims, 1775, Accession 25, RG #1, Virginia Colonial Government Records, Library of Virginia, miscellaneous reel 78, microfilm.

21. Inhabitants of Grave Creek to William Harrod, and agreement to serve in the militia, 2 Jan. 1777, RUO 224–25. For Shepherd, see West Augusta public service claims, 1775, 16–17.

22. Inhabitants of Clinch River Valley, petition, [June 1776], RVRI 7:362–63. For the county committee's response, see proceedings at Fort Chiswell, 11 June 1776, RVRI 7:442.

23. Mackay to James Wilson, 20 Nov. 1776, case 4, box 13, Generals of the Revolution, Gratz

("artfull Insinuations"); Captains of Mackay's Battalion, petition, 16 Oct. 1776, Yeates ("remote"); Butler to commissioners, 7 Nov. 1776, case 4, box 11, Generals of the Revolution, Gratz ("where they Pleased"); Mackay to James Wilson, 10 Sept. 1776, "Correspondence of the Revolution," 61–63; Mackay to commissioners, 3 Nov. 1776, Society Collection, HSP; Morgan to John Hancock, Nov. 1776, Morgan 1:17–18; George Wilson to James Wilson, 5 Dec. 1776, PA2 10:657–58; Timothy Pickering, journal, 1 Mar. 1777, in *The Life of Timothy Pickering*, ed. Octavius Pickering (Boston: Little, Brown, 1867), 1:122–23.

24. Mackay to James Wilson, 20 Aug. 1776, Society Collection, HSP; Westmoreland County Committee to Committee of Safety, 23 Aug. 1775, PA 4:647–48; Preston to Fleming, 30 May 1776, RUO 156–57; John Stuart to Fleming, 3 Sept. 1776, RUO 193–95.

25. MMD 259.

26. James Wood, diary, 10 July 1775, RUO 40 ("as the White People"); MMD 265–66.

27. St. Clair to Joseph Shippen, 12 July 1775, PA 4:637 ("his Interest"); "Treaty Between Virginia and the Indians," 70, 72–75 ("King George"); Wood, diary, July 1775, RUO 38–41 ("Amply reward," 41); MMD 257, 260–61, 265–66, 275.

28. Treaty minutes, Oct. 1775, RUO 85–90, 109–10, 121, 124–25 ("Commands of our Saviour," 110; "made room," 86; "your Mothers," 89).

29. *Journals of the Continental Congress, 1774–1789*, ed. Worthington C. Ford (Washington, DC: U.S. Government Printing Office, 1904–37), 3:433, 4:208, 268–70; MMD 290; West Augusta public service claims, 1775, p. 42; Hermann Wellenreuther, "White Eyes and the Delawares' Vision of an Indian State," *Pennsylvania History* 68, no. 2 (Spring 2001): 151–52.

30. Commissioners, report, 24 Sept. 1775, RVRI 4:140–41 ("scolded"); CRBJ 30 August and 3, 5, 7, 9, and 11 Sept. 1775 ("Old love," 7 Sept.; "made us Relations," 11 Sept.); John Dodge, "A Narrative of the Capture and Treatment of John Dodge, by the English, at Detroit," *Remembrancer; or, Impartial Repository of Public Events* 8 (1779): 74.

31. MMD 306–7, 330 ("take their Scalps," 307); treaty minutes, Oct. 1775, RUO 103–6, 113–16, 123 ("the two Children," 104); Butler to James Wilson, 8 Apr. 1776, AA4 5:815–18; Devereux Smith to Wilson, 11 Apr. 1776, box 17, Miscellaneous American Papers, case 8, Gratz; Shawnees, messages to Congress, 24 and 26 Apr. 1776, AA4 6:541–42.

32. CRBJ 30 Aug. 1775 ("dogs or servants"); commissioners to Kustaloga, 23 Aug. 1776, Morgan 2:17–18 ("accidentally"); John Anderson to commissioners, 30 Aug. 1776, Yeates ("for Rum," "sensear friends"); information received at Williamsburg, 10 Feb. 1775, AA4 1:1226; "Treaty Between Virginia and the Indians," 75–76; MMD 264, 271–72, 277–78.

33. CRBJ 3, 6, and 12 Sept. 1775 ("with tears," 3 Sept., "Not bring Evil," 12 Sept.). Cf. see Richard White, *The Middle Ground: Indians, Empires, and Republics in the Great Lakes Region, 1650–1815* (New York: Cambridge University Press, 1991), 76–93.

34. CRBJ 1, 3, 5, 7, and 12 Sept. 1775 ("his blood relations," 7 Sept.; "Windots had struck," 12 Sept.); "Intelligence of Captain Pike" [Pipe], n.d., AA4 1:874; Wood, diary, July and August 1775, RUO 43–48, 49–50, 58; Elliot to commissioners, 31 Aug. 1776, Morgan 2:19–20; William Wilson to commissioners, 26 Sept. 1776, AA5 2:514; Garret Pendergrass, deposition, 20 July 1775, RVRI 3:327; the Doctor, report, Sept. 1775, RUO 67–70; Cornstalk, speech, 11 Oct. 1775, RUO 101–2; MMD 280, 354.

35. CRBJ 5 Sept. 1775 ("to suply"); Dartmouth to Guy Johnson, 24 July 1775, *Documents Relative to the Colonial History of the State of New-York*, 15 vols., ed. E. B. O'Callaghan (Albany, NY: Weed, Parsons, & Co., 1853–58), 8:596; John Caldwell to [Thomas Gage], 5 May 1775, AS 128, TGP; [Jehu Hay], journal, 5 Jan. and 20 Mar. 1776, Henry Hamilton Papers, Burton Historical

Collection, Detroit Public Library (this journal is attributed to Hamilton, but internal evidence indicates it was written by Hay); MMD 305; Robert S. Allen, *His Majesty's Indian Allies: British Indian Policy in the Defence of Canada, 1774–1815* (Toronto: Dundurn, 1992), 46.

36. Mackay to James Wilson, 15 Jan. 1776, box 13, case 4, Generals of the Revolution, Gratz ("have no hand"; "Insignificant Rascals"); [Hay], journal, 20 and 23 Mar., 13 July, and 29 Nov. 1776 ("a little meat," 20 Mar.); John Williams, report to the Transylvania proprietors, 3 Jan. 1776, *Boonesborough*, 237–38; MMD 296. By early 1776, Virginians asserted that Hamilton was paying Indians for colonists' scalps: see Williamsburg, *Virginia Gazette* (Purdie), no. 56, 23 Feb. 1776, [3]. Hay's journal and other British correspondence offer no support for this rumor.

37. Pentecost to Committee of Safety, 15 May 1776, RVRI 7:153–54 ("justly irritated"; "Vengence"); John Floyd to Preston, 1 May 1776, RUO 153 ("greatest part"); Shawnees, messages to Congress, 24 and 26 Apr. 1776, AA4 6:541 ("even though"); MMD 310.

38. Alexander Cameron to John Stuart, 9 July 1776, CO5/77 fol. 167v ("into a Hogshead"); Henry Stuart, account of proceedings with Indians, 25 Aug. 1776, CO5/77 fols. 177–78, 181–82, 187–88 (quotations 181–82); William Christie and Patrick Lockhart, unaddressed, 27 July 1776, Yeates; Gregory Evans Dowd, *A Spirited Resistance: The North American Indian Struggle for Unity, 1745–1815* (Baltimore: Johns Hopkins University Press, 1992), 48–49; Tyler Boulware, *Deconstructing the Cherokee Nation: Town, Region, and Nation Among Eighteenth-Century Cherokees* (Gainesville: University Press of Florida, 2011), 156–57. For two thousand warriors, see John Stuart to George Germaine, 23 Aug. 1776, CO5/77 fol. 128.

39. Floyd to Preston, 21 July 1776, *Boonesborough*, 249–51 ("the greater part"); William Wilson to Morgan, 6 Aug. 1776, Yeates ("aney notion"); commissioners to Committee for Indian Affairs, 30 July and 2 Aug. 1776, Morgan 2:2 ("much uneasiness"), 4; Matthew Arbuckle to Fleming, 15 Aug. 1776, RUO 186–87; intelligence from Williamsburg, 30 Aug. 1776, AA5 1:1228; Wilson to commissioners, 26 Sept. 1776, AA5 2:514; MMD 328–29; Dowd, *Spirited Resistance*, 52; Faragher, *Daniel Boone*, 131–37.

40. Henry Stuart to John Stuart, 7 May 1776, CO5/77 fols. 145–47 ("so hemmed in," 146r; "21 Horse load," 145r); Henry Stuart, account of proceedings with Indians, 25 Aug. 1776, CO5/77 fols. 182r ("supplied them") and 189r ("100 Horse load"); John Stuart to Germaine, 23 Aug. 1776, CO5/77 fol. 129r ("Kings Enemies"); Cameron to John Stuart, 9 July 1776, CO5/77 fol. 168r ("furnish"); Cameron to John Stuart, 7 May 1776, CO5/77 fol. 139r; Henry Hamilton to James Heron, 12 July 1776, Yeates.

41. Henry Hamilton to Morgan, 20 July 1776, Yeates ("ready"); William Wilson, report, 26 Sept. 1776, AA5 2:516 (quotations); John Montour, deposition, 2 Oct. 1776, Yeates; Hamilton to Dartmouth, 2 Sept. 1776, MPHS 10:268–70; MMD 335; GD 15 Sept. 1776. For Hay and Detroit merchants, see Peter E. Russell, "Hay, Jehu," in *Dictionary of Canadian Biography*, vol. 4 (University of Toronto/Université Laval, 2003), http://www.biographi.ca/en/bio/hay_jehu_4E.html; Karen Marrero, "On the Edge of the West: The Roots and Routes of Detroit's Urban Eighteenth Century," in *Frontier Cities: Encounters at the Crossroads of Empire*, ed. Jay Gitlin, Barbara Berglund, and Adam Arenson (Philadelphia: University of Pennsylvania Press), 67–86.

42. William Wilson to commissioners, 13 Aug. 1776, Yeates ("Stick their tomohawk"); Montour, deposition, 2 Oct. 1776, Yeates ("War Song," "defenceless Women"); intelligence from an Indian, 3 Sept. 1776, Yeates.

43. Henry Hamilton to Dartmouth, 2 Sept. 1776, MPHS 10:268 ("small parties"); Isaac Williams, extract from a letter to James Heron, 11 Sept. 1776, Yeates; Anderson to commissioners, 25 Sept. 1776, Yeates; John Cook to Andrew Hamilton, 2 Oct. 1776, RUO 205–6; White Mingo,

intelligence, 18 Oct. 1776, Yeates; Anderson, report, 12 Oct. 1776, Morgan 2:61–62; Pentecost to Patrick Henry, 5 Nov. 1776, RUO 212–14; Pentecost to Morgan, 19 Nov. 1776, Morgan 1:15; MMD 336–44; [Hay], journal, 21 Dec. 1776.

44. David Zeisberger to Morgan, 21 Nov. 1776, Morgan 1:18 ("to scout"); Montour, deposition, 2 Oct. 1776, Yeates; William Wilson, report, 26 Nov. 1776, AA5 2:518; MMD 344; [Hay], journal, 23 and 29 Nov. and 21 Dec. 1776 ("joking with them"); MMD 349 ("always inciting").

45. Delaware chiefs to the thirteen states, 14 Aug. 1776, Yeates ("preserv[e] the peace"); White Eyes, speech, 9 Dec. 1776, Yeates ("a strong Place"); Wilson to commissioners, 13 and 17 Aug. 1776, Yeates; Anderson to commissioners, 24–25 Sept. 1776, Yeates; commissioners to Anderson, 5 Sept. 1776, Yeates; Wilson to commissioners, 26 Sept. 1776, Morgan 2:[54]; MMD 332, 337, 343–44.

46. Council minutes, 19, 13–14, 34–35, box 204, folder 9, GCP.

47. Council minutes, 30–31. On Delaware womanhood, see Gregory Evans Dowd, *War Under Heaven: Pontiac, the Indian Nations and the British Empire* (Baltimore: Johns Hopkins University Press, 2002), 186; Gunlög Fur, *A Nation of Women: Gender and Colonial Encounters Among the Delaware Indians* (Philadelphia: University of Pennsylvania Press, 2009).

48. MMD 356.

49. Council minutes, 10, 22–24, 29–30, 37 ("the Boundary").

50. GD 17–18 Oct. 1776, 15 May 1777; MMD 259–60; Dowd, *Spirited Resistance*.

51. Zeisberger to Anderson, 8 Jan. 1777, Morgan 1:30 ("almost inclin'd"); MMD 374 ("received them"); Delaware council, speech, 26 Mar. 1777, Morgan 1:84–86. For McCormick, see Anderson to commissioners, 25 Sept. 1776, Yeates; MMD 337, 339, 350, 468–69; Alexander McCormick to Daniel Brodhead, 29 June 1779, FAUO 382–83; John Heckewelder to Brodhead, 30 June 1779, PA 7:524–26.

52. James O'Hara to Devereux Smith, 8 Apr. 1777, box 1, folder 1, Darlington Family Papers, 1753–1921, DAR.1925.01, Darlington Collection, Special Collections Department, University of Pittsburgh, http://digital.library.pitt.edu/d/darlington/index.html ("free men"); MMD 348, 352–53, 354, 358, 360 ("Detroit," 358); George Rogers Clark, diary, 25 and 29 Dec. 1776, GRC 20; Delaware Council to Morgan, 26 Feb. 1777, Morgan 1:47–49; Shawnee chiefs to United States, 28 Feb. 1777, Morgan 1:57–59; Morgan to commissioners, 9 Mar. 1777, Morgan 1:56–57.

53. Arbuckle to [John] Neville, 26 Dec. 1776, Morgan 1:32; [Hay], journal, 24 Dec. 1776 and 19 Jan. 1777.

Chapter 4

1. MMD 397, 374, 399–402, 406. For warning Virginians, see David Zeisberger to George Morgan, 7 July 1777, FDUO 18–19; Zeisberger to Edward Hand, 29 July and 22 Sept. 1777, FDUO 27–29, 93–95. I have found no letter warning of this specific attack, but Hand did order a local militia commander to reinforce the fort: David Shepherd to Hand, 22 Aug. 1777, FDUO 46–48.

2. Richard White, *The Middle Ground: Indians, Empires, and Republics in the Great Lakes Region, 1650–1815* (New York: Cambridge University Press, 1991), 366–67.

3. Henry Hamilton, extract of a Council at Detroit, 17–21 June 1777, FDUO 7–13 ("War Song," 9); Zeisberger to Morgan, 7 July 1777, FDUO 18–19.

4. George Morgan to commissioners, 9 Mar. 1777, Morgan 1:56–57; David Shepherd to Patrick Henry, 24 Mar. 1777, RUO 242–43; George Rogers Clark diary, Mar.–June 1777, GRC 8:21–22; MMD 358, 360, 368, 376, 379; William Crawford to John Hancock, 22 Apr. 1777, RUO 249–51; *Maryland Journal and Baltimore Advertiser* 4, no. 185, 20 May 1777, [3]. Both Crawford and the

Maryland Journal report that, in one attack, raiders burned to death a woman and several children. However, Zeisberger reported the arrival of a captured woman and four children, unburnt, at Lichtenau about a week later: MMD 372.

5. George Germain to Guy Carleton, 26 Mar. 1777, MPHS 9:347 ("excit[e]"); John Minor to Zackwell Morgan, 14 July 1777, Draper 1U:64; Edward Hand to Katherine Hand, 24 July and 25 Aug. 1777, box 1, folder 2, EHP; John Gibson to Edward Hand, 31 July 1777, FDUO 33–35; James Booth to Zadoc Springer, 2 Aug. 1777, Draper 4ZZ:10; Arthur Campbell to William Fleming, 11 Aug. 1777, Draper 1U:78; Samuel Moorhead to Hand, 19 Aug. 1777, FDUO 46; Clark diary, Aug. and Sept. 1777, GRC 8:23; letters to William Fleming, 11–12 Sept. 1777, FDUO 78–82; Zackwell Morgan to Hand, 18 Sept. 1777, FDUO 93; David Shepherd to Hand, 27 Sept. 1777, FDUO 106–7; John Van Metre to Edward Cook, 28 Sept. 1777, FDUO 110–11; Matthew Arbuckle to Hand, 6 Oct. 1777, FDUO 127; MMD 386, 389, 394, 395, 401, 406, 412, 414, 418, 421; Hamilton to Carleton, [15 Jan. 1778], MPHS 9:431; Hamilton to Frederick Haldimand, [Sept. 1778], MPHS 9:465; extract of a letter from Quebec, 25 Aug. 1778, *Remembrancer; or, Impartial Repository of Public Events* 7 (1778–79): 51.

6. Hamilton to Carleton, 25 Apr. 1778, MPHS 9:437 ("what Lands"); Council held at Detroit, 14 June 1778, MPHS 9:450; Ian Kenneth Steele, *Warpaths: Invasions of North America* (New York: Oxford University Press, 1994); Armstrong Starkey, *European and Native American Warfare, 1675–1815* (Norman: University of Oklahoma Press, 1998).

7. Narrative of Ansel Goodman, 1832, in *The Revolution Remembered: Eyewitness Accounts of the War for Independence*, ed. John C. Dann (Chicago: University of Chicago Press, 1999), 280–82; interview with Joseph Jackson, Apr. 1844, Draper 11C:62; Hamilton to Carleton, 25 Apr. 1778, MPHS 9:435; Linda Clark Nash, ed., *The Journals of Pierre-Louis Lorimier, 1777–1795* (Montreal: Baraka, 2012), 76; Stephen Aron, *How the West Was Lost: The Transformation of Kentucky from Daniel Boone to Henry Clay* (Baltimore: Johns Hopkins University Press, 1996), 29, 41–43; John Mack Faragher, *Daniel Boone: The Life and Legend of an American Pioneer* (New York: Holt, 1992), 153–66.

8. Germain to Carleton, 26 Mar. 1777, MPHS 9:347 ("crushing"); Hamilton, proclamation, 5 Jan. 1778, Morgan 3:24–25 ("faithfull & loyal"); Hamilton, proclamation, 24 June 1777, FDUO 14; Gibson to Hand, 31 July 1777, FDUO 33–35; Hamilton to Carleton, [15 Jan.] and 25 Apr. 1778, MPHS 9:431, 435; Arent De Peyster to Alexander McKee, 2 Nov. 1779, MPHS 10:371.

9. "Recollections of Samuel Murphy," n.d., FDUO 216–20 ("sunk [a] tomahawk," 218); Hand to Jasper Ewing, 7 Mar. 1778, FDUO 215–16 ("Savage Conduct," 216); George Morgan to White Eyes, 20 Mar. 1778, FDUO 228; Sampson Mathews et al. to White Eyes, 20 Mar. 1778, Morgan 3:13; United American States to the Delaware Council, 13 Apr. 1778, FDUO 269–70; Hamilton to Carleton, 25 Apr. 1778, MPHS 9:436; George Morgan to Board of War, 17 July 1778, FAUO 113. For the sugar-making process, see MMD 130, 438; Lucy Eldersveld Murphy, "To Live Among Us: Accommodation, Gender, and Conflict in the Western Great Lakes Region, 1760–1832," in *Contact Points: American Frontiers from the Mohawk Valley to the Mississippi, 1750–1830*, ed. Andrew R. L. Cayton and Fredrika J. Teute (Chapel Hill: University of North Carolina Press, 1998), 276–77.

10. White, *Middle Ground*, 384 (quotations); Gregory Evans Dowd, *A Spirited Resistance: The North American Indian Struggle for Unity, 1745–1815* (Baltimore: Johns Hopkins University Press, 1992), 75–76; Colin G. Calloway, *The Shawnees and the War for America* (New York: Penguin, 2007), 64–65; Patrick Griffin, *American Leviathan: Empire, Nation, and Revolutionary Frontier* (New York: Hill and Wang, 2007), 152–54.

11. George Morgan to Hancock, 15 Mar. 1777, Morgan 1:61–62 ("to massacre," "Officer"); Jasper Yeates to James Wilson, 31 Aug. 1776, in "Notes and Queries," *Pennsylvania Magazine of History and Biography* 29, no. 3 (1905): 360–61 ("no Stopping"); commissioners to Committee for Indian Affairs, 30 July 1776, Morgan 2:2 ("buying"); commissioners to Congress, 18 Aug. 1776, Morgan 2:11–12; Dorsey Pentecost to William Harrod, 12 Nov. 1776, RUO 219–20; George Morgan to Pentecost, 16 Feb. 1777, Morgan 1:35. For Morgan's land speculation, see Morgan and Robert Callender, advertisement, *Pennsylvania Journal*, no. 1715, 18 Oct. 1775, [4]; Max Savelle, *George Morgan, Colony Builder* (New York: Columbia University Press, 1932).

12. For the Lochry brothers, see Arthur St. Clair to Joseph Shippen, n.d., SCP 1:268; minutes of the Provincial Council, 11 Mar. 1771, CRP 9:730; McClure 105; paper of Pennsylvania officials, 1774, PA 4:478–80; James Smith, deposition, 14 Feb. 1775, PA 4:610; Robert Hanna et al. to John Penn, 13 Feb. 1775, AA4 1:1273–74; Commissioners for Indian Affairs to William Lochry, 8 Oct. 1776, Yeates; Minutes of the Council of Safety, 2 Dec. 1776 and 31 Jan. 1777, CRP 11:24, 110; Proctor to Council of Safety, 27 Jan. 1777, PA 5:202; minutes of the Supreme Executive Council, 4 and 21 Mar. 1777, CRP 11:173, 186–87; FDUO 39n79, 139n6. For Pentecost, see Pentecost to Committee of Safety, 4 June 1776, RVRI 7:361; James Patrick McClure, "The Ends of the American Earth: Pittsburgh and the Upper Ohio Valley to 1795" (Ph.D. diss., University of Michigan, 1983), 282–83, 329–30. For Shepherd, see court minutes, 19 Sept. 1775, in Boyd Crumrine, ed., *Virginia Court Records in Southwestern Pennsylvania: Records of the District of West Augusta and Ohio and Yohogania Counties, Virginia, 1775–1780* (Baltimore: Genealogical Publishing Company, 1974); George Morgan to David Shepherd, 29 July 1777, Draper 1SS:63–65; Abraham Shepherd to David Shepherd, 2 and 24 Nov. 1778 and 8 Jan. 1779, Draper 1SS:133–35, 137–39, 153–55. For the emergence of upper Ohio elite, see R. Eugene Harper, *The Transformation of Western Pennsylvania, 1770–1800* (Pittsburgh, PA: University of Pittsburgh Press, 1991).

13. Henry to Pentecost, 13 Dec. 1776, RUO 223 ("arms and accoutrements"); militia arrangements, Jan.–Apr. 1777, RUO 229–35; Clark diary, 1777, GRC 8:21 and 23; David Shepherd, unaddressed, 26 Mar. 1777, Draper 1SS:25; minutes of a Council of War, 16 Apr. 1777, vol. 1, p. 6, EHP; Henry to Hand, 3 July 1777, FDUO 16–18; Monongalia County Council of War, 27 June 1777, Draper 1U:60; Hand to Yeates, 10 June 1777, FDUO 6; Zackwell Morgan to Hand, 8 July 1777, Draper 1U:63. For militia laws, see Hand to Archibald Lochry, 6 July 1777, box 3, folder 47, DAF; Arthur J. Alexander, "Pennsylvania's Revolutionary Militia," *Pennsylvania Magazine of History and Biography* 69, no. 1 (1945): 15–25; Hannah Benner Roach, "The Pennsylvania Militia in 1777," *Pennsylvania Genealogical Magazine* 23, no. 3 (1964): 161–230; Francis S. Fox, "Pennsylvania's Revolutionary Militia Law: The Statute That Transformed the State," *Pennsylvania History* 80, no. 2 (Spring 2013): 204–14; Michael A. McDonnell, *The Politics of War: Race, Class, and Conflict in Revolutionary Virginia* (Chapel Hill: University of North Carolina Press, 2007), 92–93.

14. Gibson to Hand, 1 Aug. 1777, FDUO 35; David Shepherd to Hand, 22 Aug. 1777, FDUO 46–48; John Page to Hand, 17 Sept. 1777, FDUO 85–86; Morgan Jones to his parents, n.d., Draper 1U:71; MMD 385.

15. Meeting of Botetourt militia officers, 29 Aug. 1777, Draper 1U:88; Hand to Fleming, 12 Aug. 1777, Draper 1U:80; Zackwell Morgan to Hand, 15 Aug. 1777, vol. 1, p. 18, EHP; Shepherd to Hand, 22 Aug. 1777, FDUO 47; Hand to Yeates, 25 Aug. 1777, FDUO 48–49; Page to Hand, 17 Sept. 1777, FDUO 85; Abraham Smith to Hand, 21 Sept. 1777, vol. 1, p. 27, EHP; John Moore to Hand, 22 Sept. 1777, vol. 1, p. 28, EHP; John Bowyer to Fleming, 24 Sept. 1777, FDUO 104–5;

Hand to Archibald Lochry, 18 Oct. 1777, box 3, folder 52, DAF; Lochry to Hand, 2 Nov. 1777, Draper 1U:127; John Dickinson to Hand, 7 Nov. 1777, FDUO 150–51; Hand to Patrick Henry, 9 Nov. 1777, FDUO 154–55; John Stuart, narrative, n.d., FDUO 158.

16. Arbuckle to Hand, 6 Oct. 1777, FDUO 126 ("thought proper"); Arbuckle to Hand, 7 Nov. 1777, FDUO 150 ("well satisfied"); Stuart, narrative, n.d., FDUO 157–62 ("cocked," 159; "seven or eight," 160; "returned home," 162); John Anderson et al., deposition, 10 Nov. 1777, FDUO 163 ("not in his power"); Hand to Henry, 9 Dec. 1777, FDUO 177 ("would be vain"); William Preston to Fleming, 2 Dec. 1777, FDUO 168–69; MMD 417–18.

17. Hand to Ewing, 7 Mar. 1778, FDUO 215–16 (quotations); "Recollections of Samuel Murphy," 216–20.

18. Hand to Ewing, 7 Mar. 1778, FDUO 215–16 ("could not," "Savage Conduct," "Behave well"); Hand to Yeates, 2 Oct. 1777, FDUO 119 ("Murder").

19. George Rogers Clark to Hand, 30 Mar. 1778, FDUO 249 ("entirely evacuated"); John Evans to Hand, 18 Apr. 1778, FDUO 273 ("the forts"); Lochry to Thomas Wharton, 13 May 1778, PA 6:495 ("General Evacuation"); Preston to Fleming, 17 May 1778, FAUO 52 ("the People"); Hand to Horatio Gates, 14 May 1778, FAUO 50 ("whole country"); Monongalia County Council of War, 27 June 1777, Draper 1U:60; Hand to Yeates, 30 Mar. 1778, FDUO 250; Hand to Clark, 22 Apr. 1778, GRC 8:45; Hand to Gates, 24 Apr. 1778, FDUO 279; William Jack to Hand, 2 June 1778, vol. 1, p. 45, EHP; MMD 438, 440, 446.

20. Daniel Brodhead to Michael Huffnagle, 30 Apr. 1779, box 1, folder 1, DBP ("constantly calling"); Archibald Lochry to Wharton, 6 Dec. 1777, PA 6:68 ("Houses"); Campbell to Fleming, 11 Aug. 1777, Draper 1U:78; meeting of Botetourt militia officers, 29 Aug. 1777, Draper 1U:88; Van Metre to Cook, 28 Sept. 1777, FDUO 111; Hamilton to Carleton, 25 Apr. 1778, MPHS 9:435; William McKee to Hand, 21 June 1778, FAUO 98–99; John Irwin to Richard Campbell, 19 Nov. 1778, FAUO 175; Brodhead to Lochry, 28 Apr. 1779, box 1, vol. 1, DBP; Lochry to Brodhead, 1 May 1779, FAUO 299; Brodhead to George Washington, 22 May 1779, PA 12:113–15; Morgan Jones to his parents, n.d., Draper 1U:71; Eric Hinderaker, *Elusive Empires: Constructing Colonialism in the Ohio Valley, 1673–1800* (New York: Cambridge University Press, 1997), 221, 224.

21. Campbell to Fleming, 11 Aug. 1777, Draper 1U:78 ("Congress"); Henry to Preston, 27 June 1778, FAUO 100–101 ("general use"); Fleming to Henry, 19 July 1778, FAUO 115–17 ("could not"); John Campbell to Hand, 21 Sept. 1777, vol. 1, p. 26, EHP; Daniel McFarland to Hand, 14 May 1778, vol. 1, p. 43, EHP; Brodhead to Lochry, 25 Apr. 1779, box 1, vol. 1, DBP; Lochry to Joseph Reed, 1 May 1779, PA 7:362–63; Brodhead to Irwin, 7 May 1779, box 1, vol. 1, DBP; Minutes of the Supreme Executive Council, CRP 11:377, 394, 444–45, 477, 779–80, 12:372–73; Ansel Goodman, narrative, 1832, in Dann, *Revolution Remembered*, 280–82.

22. George Morgan to Hand, 15 Mar. 1778, vol. 1, p. 38, EHP; William McKee to Hand, 29 Mar. 1778, FDUO 246–48; Daniel Smith to Arthur Campbell, 19 June 1778, FAUO 96–97; Patrick Lockhart to Fleming, 13 Sept. 1778, FAUO 138; Thomas Clare to Joseph Skelton, 28 Apr. 1779, GWP; Brodhead to John Clark, 27 July 1779, box 1, vol. 1, DBP; E. Wayne Carp, *To Starve the Army at Pleasure: Continental Army Administration and American Political Culture, 1775–1783* (Chapel Hill: University of North Carolina Press, 1984).

23. Henry to Fleming, 5 May 1778, FAUO 45 ("too complex"); Buffalo Creek inhabitants, petition, 13 Aug. 1777, Draper 1U:82 ("move off"); Henry Taylor to Hand, 14 Aug. 1777, FDUO 45 ("all the Ammonition"); Devereux Smith to Hand, 11 July 1777, vol. 1, pp. 15, EHP; Abraham Hite to Hand, 5 July 1777, Draper 1U:61; Lochry to Wharton, 13 May 1778, PA 6:495; Daniel McFarland to Hand, 14 May 1778, vol. 1, p. 43, EHP; Lochry to Hand, n.d. [1778?], vol. 1, p. 34, EHP;

Albert H. Tillson, *Gentry and Common Folk: Political Culture on a Virginia Frontier, 1740–1789* (Lexington: University Press of Kentucky, 1991), 87–90.

24. George Woods and Thomas Smith to Hand, 23 Nov. 1777, Draper 1U:131 ("voluntarily formed"); Lachlan McIntosh to Board of War, 11 Jan. 1779, FAUO 199 ("much waste"); George Vallandigham to Hand, 11 Apr. 1778, Draper 2U:11; Westmoreland magistrates to McIntosh, 26 Oct. 1778, FAUO 150; William Crawford to Archibald Lochry, 29 Oct. 1778, Officers of the Revolution, case 4, box 18, Gratz; McIntosh to Lochry, 30 Oct. 1778, FAUO 155–56; reminiscences of James Powers, [1816], FAUO 199–200.

25. Robert A. Gross, *The Minutemen and Their World* (1976; New York: Hill and Wang, 2001).

26. MMD 265, 299–303, 308–12; David Edmunds, "'This Much Admired Man': Isaac Glikhikan, Moravian Delaware," in *Ethnographies and Exchanges: Native Americans, Moravians, and Catholics in Early North America*, ed. A. G. Roeber (University Park: Penn State University Press, 2008), 1–16.

27. George Croghan to Thomas Gage, 1 Jan. 1770, AS 89, TGP; council minutes, 9 Oct. 1775, RUO 86–87; MMD 275, 387, 397, 399–400, 402; Hermann Wellenreuther, "White Eyes and the Delawares' Vision of an Indian State," *Pennsylvania History* 68, no. 2 (Spring 2001): 139–61.

28. MMD 407, 409–12, 416, 440–48, 452–53 ("eradicate," 407; "were offering," 441); White Eyes and Killbuck to George Morgan, 14 Mar. 1778, Morgan 3:21 ("restore Peace"); White Eyes to Morgan, 23 Sept. 1777, FDUO 100–101; Morgan, letters to Delawares, 1 Oct. 1777, FDUO 115–18; Morgan to White Eyes, 20 Mar. 1778, FDUO 228; Zeisberger to Morgan, 6 Apr. 1778, Morgan 3:40–42; Morgan, report on meetings with Delawares, 25–26 Apr. 1778, Morgan 3:53–57. For Wandochale, see Delaware Council to Morgan, 26 Feb. 1777, Morgan 1:47–49; Morgan to John Jay, 28 May 1778, FAUO 343–44.

29. MMD 448–49, 452–53, 455–57 ("all orderly," 448); Council held at Detroit, 14–20 June 1778, MPHS 9:445 ("great distance"); Haldimand to Hamilton, 6 Aug. 1778, MPHS 9:400 ("conquer[ed]"); White Eyes and Killbuck to George Morgan, 9 June 1778, PA 6:588 ("more disposed"); Hand to White Eyes and Killbuck, 17 June 1778, PA 6:601 ("enter into friendship"); Arbuckle to Hand, 2 June 1778, FAUO 64–65.

30. Council held at Detroit, 14 June 1778, MPHS 9:442–52 ("turn[ing] [their] heads," 449); MMD 456–57 ("wanted to force," "behaved very quietly," 456); Zeisberger to George Morgan, 19 July 1778, FAUO 119 ("send an army"); Lewis to Fleming, 14 Aug. 1778, FAUO 127 ("the War be carryed"); speech of Great Lakes Indians to Delawares, 18 June 1778, FAUO 94–95; White Eyes to Morgan, 19 July 1778, FAUO 117.

31. MMD 457, 461–62, 464, 465 ("much danger," 461; "tore up," 465); Bawbee [Odingquanooron], speeches to White Eyes and George Morgan, 16 Aug. 1778, FAUO 129 ("shake hands"); Zeisberger to commissioners, 25 Aug. 1778, FAUO 132 ("no Peace"); McIntosh to Archibald Lochry, 30 Oct. 1778, box 4, folder 76, DAF ("earnestly applyed"). For Odingquanooron's name, see Articles of Peace between William Johnson and the [Wyandots], 18 July 1764, in *Documents Relative to the Colonial History of the State of New-York*, 15 vols., ed. E. B. O'Callaghan (Albany, NY: Weed, Parsons, & Co., 1853–58), 7:651.

32. John Armstrong to Congress, 1778, PA 6:614 ("immediate attack"); Edward Ward to James Wilson, 9 Mar. 1777, box 7, folder 28, DAF ("all the Lands"); Virginia Council, resolutions, 7 July 1778, FAUO 104 ("carry on"); McIntosh to Fleming, 30 Oct. 1778, FAUO 154 ("keep possession"); George Morgan to Board of War, 17 July 1778, FAUO 112–13; Armstrong to Henry Laurens, 22 July 1778, PA 6:657–58; Continental Congress, resolution, 25 July 1778, FAUO 121;

Morgan to Jay, 28 May 1778, FAUO 343–44; Randolph C. Downes, "George Morgan, Indian Agent Extraordinary, 1776–1779," *Pennsylvania History* 1, no. 4 (October 1934): 212.

33. "Treaty at Fort Pitt," 12 Sept. 1778, FAUO 138–45 ("as their own," 141); "Treaty with the Delawares, 1778," Avalon Project, Yale Law School, http://avalon.law.yale.edu/18th_century/del1778.asp (accessed 18 Sept. 2016); "Orderly book of 8th Pennsylvania regiment, 1778–1779," FAUO 433 ("Lieutenant Colonel"); MMD 465, 479.

34. MMD 469–76 ("Pardon and peace," 471); John Heckewelder to Gibson, 8 Feb. 1779, GWP ("all his Men"); Zeisberger to George Morgan, 20 Jan. 1779, FAUO 201–2; "Capt. Kilbuck & the other Chiefs of the Delawar Nation" to Pipe and Wingenum, n.d., PFH addl. mss. 21782, fols. 259–60, reel 55; Hinguapooshes to Brodhead, 13 June 1779, FAUO 361–62. Herrmann Wellenreuther finds Gelelemend's protests unconvincing: see his "White Eyes," 158–59.

35. Estate of White Eyes, 9 Nov. 1778, FAUO 168–69 ("Sundry Papers"); MMD 479 ("real peace"); George Morgan, unaddressed, 12 May 1784, frame 72, George Morgan Papers, 1775–1822, Library of Congress, microfilm, https://lccn.loc.gov/mm77033464 ("put to death"). At the time, McIntosh and his men reported that White Eyes had died of smallpox (not long after, they said the same about a Moravian Indian who died under similarly mysterious circumstances). Several years later, in a private, unaddressed, and possibly unsent letter, Morgan alleged murder. Morgan is no ideal source (he was hundreds of miles away at the time), but the timing of White Eyes's death makes the smallpox story implausible. The Moravian messengers left the army on 5 or 6 Nov., convinced that all was well. White Eyes's possessions were inventoried, in Pittsburgh, on 9 Nov. White Eyes presumably died between 6 and 8 Nov. Perhaps not coincidentally, on 7 Nov. scouts discovered the bodies, killed and scalped, of two militiamen who had slipped out of the camp to hunt: an eerie echo of Cornstalk's fate at Point Pleasant. Smallpox victims often endure several days of flu-like symptoms before developing the distinctive rash, and they typically suffer for ten or more days before death. Since White Eyes was healthy on 5 or 6 Nov., it is very unlikely that he had died of smallpox by 9 Nov. Apart from the two Indians, no one else in McIntosh's army had come down with the disease. See MMD 482; Robert McCready, "A Revolutionary Journal and Orderly Book of General Lachlan McIntosh's Expedition, 1778," *Western Pennsylvania Historical Magazine* 1, no. 1–3 (Mar.–Sept. 1960): 11–12; Stephen Burkam, recollections, [1845], FAUO 157; Downes, "George Morgan," 215–16; Elizabeth A. Fenn, *Pox Americana: The Great Smallpox Epidemic of 1775–82* (New York: Hill and Wang, 2001), 15–20. On White Eyes's attire, see Robert S. DuPlessis, *The Material Atlantic: Clothing, Commerce, and Colonization in the Atlantic World, 1650–1800* (New York: Cambridge University Press, 2015), 102–13.

36. George Morgan to Laurens, 29 Nov. 1778, Morgan 3:136; McCready, "Revolutionary Journal," 17; Delaware and Wyandot chiefs, message, 21 Dec. 1778, FAUO 187–88; Big Cat to Brodhead, 22 May 1779, FAUO 334–35; MMD 482.

37. MMD 481 ("heard and enjoyed"); McCready, "Revolutionary Journal," 16–17 (other quotations), 269–70.

38. McIntosh, speech to Delawares, 22 Nov. 1778, FAUO 178–80.

39. James Littel to William [?], 29 Jan. 1779, in McCready, "Revolutionary Journal," 162 ("fort Noncence"); McIntosh to Richard Campbell, 7 and 13 Nov. 1778, FAUO 167–68, 172–73; Burkam, recollections, FAUO 157; Henry to Fleming, 20 Nov. 1778, FAUO 177; John Dodge to Congress, 25 Jan. 1779, FAUO 206–10; Brodhead to Nathanael Greene, 26 May 1779, PA 12:118.

40. Delaware and Wyandot chiefs, message, 21 Dec. 1778, FAUO 187 ("at some distance"); Indian speeches at Detroit, 2 Jan. 1779, FAUO 192 ("all [their] might"); MMD 479, 489, 491–94, 497–99 ("many promises," 492); Gibson, letters, Jan. 1779, in *Collections of the Illinois State*

Historical Library, ed. H. W. Beckwith (Springfield: Illinois State Historical Library, 1903), 1:383–86 ("doe something," 385); Zeisberger to Morgan, 20 Jan. 1779, FAUO 201–2; Killbuck to Gibson and Morgan, 9 Feb. 1779, FAUO 223–24; Gibson to McIntosh, 13 Feb. 1779, GWP; Heckewelder and Killbuck letters, 12–13 Mar. 1779, FAUO 242–49; Mason Bolton to Haldimand, 24 Mar. 1779, MPHS 9:427–29; John Butler to Haldimand, 2 Apr. 1779, MPHS 19:383–85; Frederick Vernon to Brodhead, 29 Apr. 1779, GWP; Benjamin Biggs, recollections, [1845], FAUO 256–57.

41. Bolton to Haldimand, 24 Mar. 1779, MPHS 9:428 ("threatened their Lands"); Detroit council, 7 Feb. 1779, FAUO 220 ("smooth Tongued"); Richard B. Lernoult to Bolton, 26 Mar. 1779, MPHS 9:429 ("being not able"); Dunquat to Delawares, [Mar. 1779], FAUO 266 ("good for nothing"); Henry Bird, extracts of letters, [Mar. 1779], PFH addl. mss. 21782, fol. 222, reel 55; cf. Michael A. McDonnell, *Masters of Empire: Great Lakes Indians and the Making of America* (New York: Hill and Wang, 2015), 295–99.

42. Big Cat to Brodhead, 4 May 1779, FAUO 308–9 ("thick timber," 308); Brodhead to Washington, 14 May 1779, case 4, box 11, Generals of the Revolution, Gratz ("not hostile"); William Crawford to Washington, 12 July 1779, ser. 4, GWP ("don very Litle"); Bird to Mason Bolton, n.d., MPHS 19:413 ("Rascals or Cowards"); John Montour to John Dodge, 28 May 1779, FAUO 346–47 ("Rebbels," 346); Guillaume Monforton to Lernoult, 7 May 1779, PFH addl. mss. 21782, fols. 228–29, reel 55; Hinguapooshes to Brodhead, 22 May, 17 and 24 June 1779, FAUO 334–35, 362–63, 379–81; McKee to Lernoult, 26 May 1779, MPHS 19:423–24; Heckewelder to Brodhead, 28 May 1779, PA 7:516–18; D. Brehm to Haldimand, 28 May 1779, MPHS 9:410–12; interview with Joseph Jackson, Apr. 1844, Draper 11C:62.17–23; MMD 502. On northern Ohio terrain, see Brodhead to Heckewelder, 29 May 1779, PA 12:121; DDZ 1:19–20. One American informant, and at least one missionary, doubted the Wyandots' sincerity: McCormick to Brodhead, 29 June 1779, FAUO 382–83; Heckewelder to Brodhead, 30 June 1779, PA 7:524–26. The furious British response, however, indicates that their defection was real.

43. Hinguapooshes to Brodhead, 24 June 1779, FAUO 379–81 ("too many"); Brodhead to John Sullivan, 6 Aug. 1779, PA 12:155 ("drubbed"); Brodhead to Sullivan, 10 Oct. 1779, PA 12:165–66 ("wolves" and "quite destitute"); Brodhead to Greene, 26 May 1779, PA 12:119; Brodhead to Washington, 31 July and 16 Sept. 1779, PA 12:146–48, 155–58; Israel and Goschachgünk council to Brodhead and Gelelemend, 11 Aug. 1779, FRUO 46–47; anonymous letter, 16 Sept. 1779, FRUO 56–57; Joseph R. Fischer, *A Well-Executed Failure: The Sullivan Campaign Against the Iroquois, July–September 1779* (Columbia: University of South Carolina Press, 1997).

44. Council with Wyandots, 17 Sept. 1779, FRUO 66–70; Brodhead to Washington, 5 June and 16 Sept. 1779, PA 12:128, 155–58. In the council record (both the version printed in FRUO and a manuscript copy in PFH addl. mss. 21782, fols. 278–80, reel 55), the Wyandot speaker's name is variously spelled Noonyoondat, Nonyeondat, Doonyontat, and Dooyontat. The editors of FRUO suggest that this was Dunquat (also known as "Half-King"), but it was more likely Duyenty, known to the French as Douillanter, and elsewhere spelled Dugantait and Deuentete.

45. Council with Wyandots, 17 Sept. 1779, FRUO 70–72; Brodhead to Washington, 16 Sept. 1779, PA 12:157–58; Welapachtschiechen and Delaware council to Brodhead, 30 Mar. 1780, FRUO 157–58; Zeisberger to Brodhead, 2 Apr. 1780, FRUO 163; Sami Lakomäki, *Gathering Together: The Shawnee People Through Diaspora and Nationhood, 1600–1870* (New Haven, CT: Yale University Press, 2014), 112.

46. MMD 494, 503, 506, 514, 517, 521–22.

Chapter 5

1. Memorial of John Bull, 12 Apr. 1782, RPRG 19:656; MMD 442–45, 597; DDZ 1:367–69, 443–44.

2. Arent De Peyster to Frederick Haldimand, 17 May 1780, MPHS 10:396 ("to shun"); Haldimand to Henry Hamilton, 6 Aug. 1778, MPHS 9:399 ("back upon"); George Washington to Daniel Brodhead, 18 Oct. 1779, FRUO 100 ("laid waste").

3. Certificates issued by the commissioners for adjusting claims to unpatented lands in Monongalia, Yohogania, and Ohio counties, Dec. 1779–Feb. 1780, Draper 1SS:5–11; "Colonel William Fleming's Journal of Travels in Kentucky, 1779–1780," in *Travels in the American Colonies*, ed. Newton D. Mereness (New York: Macmillan, 1916), 615–55; Helen Hornbeck Tanner, "The Glaize in 1792: A Composite Indian Community," *Ethnohistory* 25, no. 1 (Winter 1978): 15–39; Helen Hornbeck Tanner, ed., *Atlas of Great Lakes Indian History* (Norman: University of Oklahoma Press, 1987), 79–86.

4. Predeaux Girty, reminiscences, 1863, FRUO 164 ("her waiter"); De Peyster to Haldimand, 17 May 1780, MPHS 10:396 ("daily bringing"); Brodhead to Washington, 3 June 1779, PA 12:123 ("bid farewell"); De Peyster to Alexander McKee, 22 June 1780, MPHS 10:404 ("except the aged"); Brodhead to Timothy Pickering, 3 Nov. 1779, PA 12:179–80; "Transactions of a Meeting held at Wakitamyky," 17 Jan. 1780, PFH addl. mss. 21782, fols. 303–8, reel 55; Brodhead to Richard Peters, 18 Mar. 1780, PA 12:210–11; Welapachtschiechen to Brodhead and Gelelemend, 30 Mar. 1780, FRUO 157–59; John Heckewelder to Brodhead, 30 Mar. 1780, FRUO 159; George F. Whitaker, reminiscences, 1868, FRUO 152–53. For Wryneck, see message from Delaware and Wyandot chiefs, 21 Dec. 1778, FAUO 187–88; for St. Joseph, see L. Chevallier, unaddressed, 13 Mar. 1780, MPHS 10:380–81.

5. De Peyster to Haldimand, 8 June 1780, MPHS 10:400; Haldimand to De Peyster, 6 July 1780, MPHS 10:408.

6. Chiefs and principal warriors to Richard B. Lernoult, 20 Oct. 1779, MPHS 10:365 ("protect"); Haldimand to De Peyster, 6 July 1780, MPHS 10:408 ("vast treasure"), 410 ("however they may threaten"); De Peyster to H. Watson Powell, 4 Apr. 1781, MPHS 19:615 ("fight twice"); Haldimand to De Peyster, 10 Aug. 1780, MPHS 10:416 ("most attentive"); Shawnees to Lernoult, 26 Sept. 1779, MPHS 19:468–70; De Peyster to McKee, 2 Nov. 1779, MPHS 10:370–71; De Peyster to Haldimand, 8 June 1780, MPHS 10:400; Haldimand to De Peyster, 18 June 1780, MPHS 10:402; De Peyster to Haldimand, 3 Nov. 1781, MPHS 10:536–37.

7. McKee to De Peyster, 8 July 1780, MPHS 19:541 ("naked & defenceless"); Henry Bird to De Peyster, 1 July 1780, MPHS 19:539 ("gone through"); De Peyster to Haldimand, 8 Mar. 1780, MPHS 10:378–79; extract of a letter from Bird, 21 May 1780, MPHS 9:584; De Peyster to McKee, 22 June 1780, MPHS 10:404; Michael A. McDonnell, *Masters of Empire: Great Lakes Indians and the Making of America* (New York: Hill and Wang, 2015), 304–6. Cf. Ian Kenneth Steele, *Betrayals: Fort William Henry and the Massacre* (New York: Oxford University Press, 1990).

8. Brodhead to Joseph Reed, 17 Oct. 1780, PA 8:589 ("rise in arms"); Brodhead to Col. Gaddes, 29 Oct. 1779, PA 12:178; Brodhead to Washington, 30 May 1780, PA 12:242; Archibald Lochry to Reed and John Proctor to Reed, 1 June 1780, PA 8:282–85; Reed to Lochry, 2 June 1780, PA 8:290; Brodhead, letters to Samuel Brady, 21 Sept. 1780, Uriah Springer, Sept. 1780, and Frederic Vernon, 20 Oct. 1780, box 1, vol. 1, DBP; Brodhead to Washington, 17 Oct. 1780, pp. 1–3, Daniel Brodhead, letterbook, 1780–85, Papers of Daniel Brodhead, HSP; Brodhead to Ephraim Blaine, 3 Nov. 1780, pp. 7–8, Brodhead, letterbook, 1780–85; Brodhead to William Taylor, 15 Nov. 1780,

pp. 10–11, Brodhead, letterbook, 1780–85; Daniel Brodhead to Richard Peters, 7 Dec. 1780, FRUO 301–2.

9. Reed to Lochry, 17 Mar. 1781, PA 9:18 ("loiter[ed] away"); Hand to Lochry, 4 June 1777, box 3, folder 46, DAF; Brodhead to Lochry, 30 Apr. 1779, box 1, vol. 1, DBP; Reed to Lochry, 21 May 1779, PA 7:430–32; Brodhead to Lochry, 31 May 1779, PA 12:122–23; Brodhead to Reed, 9 Oct. 1779, PA 12:163–64; Brodhead to Joseph Erwin, 13 Oct. 1779, PA 12:169–70; Reed to Brodhead, 30 Oct. 1779, PA 7:771; Thomas Campbell to Supreme Executive Council, n.d., PA 8:36; Brodhead, letters to John Clarke and Lochry, 2 Jan. 1780, PA 8:68–70; Lochry to Reed, 9 Jan. 1780, PA 8:77–78; Erwin to Reed, 10 Jan. 1780, PA 8:79–80; Brodhead to Lochry, 20 Jan. 1780, PA 12:202–3; Reed to Brodhead, 14 Feb. 1780, PA 8:109–10; Brodhead to Reed, 20 and 27 Apr. 1780, PA 8:197–99, 211; Robert Hanna and William Love to Irvine, 3 Dec. 1781, Draper 2AA:4.

10. Bird to Lernoult, 9 June 1779, MPHS 10:337 ("three or four thousand"); William Homan to Bird, 15 Aug. 1780, MPHS 10:419 ("ripping up"); Delawares and Shawnees, speech, 22 Aug. 1780, MPHS 10:420–21; De Peyster to Haldimand, 31 Aug. 1780, MPHS 10:423–24; John H. Moore, ed., "A Captive of the Shawnees, 1779–1784," *West Virginia History* 23, no. 4 (July 1962): 291–92; Tanner, *Atlas*, maps 16, 17.

11. Brodhead to Reed, 22 Jan. 1781, PA 8:707 ("to acquire"); Berkeley County militia officers to Thomas Jefferson, 25 Jan. 1781, VSP 1:461–62 ("suffer any punishment"); Brodhead to Reed, 25 Feb. 1781, PA 8:743–44; John Gibson to George Rogers Clark, 6 May, 30 May, and 5 June 1781, GRC 8:547–48, 559–61; Reed to Clark, 15 May 1781, PA 9:137; David Duncan to Gibson, 3 June 1781, PA 9:190; Thomas Stokely to Reed, 4 Aug. 1781, PA 9:330–31.

12. Christopher Hays and Thomas Scott to Reed, 15 Aug. 1781, PA 9:355 ("armed force"); Scott to Reed, 31 July 1781, PA 9:324–25 ("hyghly oppressive"); James Marshel to Reed, 27 June 1781, PA 9:233–34 ("under any government"); Hugh H. Brackenridge to Clark, 4 June 1781, GRC 8:560–61; Clark to Monongalia County inhabitants, 18 June 1781, and agreement of Monongalia County inhabitants, 19 June 1781, GRC 8:567–68; Clark to the Officers of Pennsylvania and Virginia, 23 June 1781, GRC 8:569–70; Isaac Mason to Reed, 1 July 1781, PA 9:238–39; Dorsey Pentecost to Reed, 27 July 1781, PA 9:315–19; Marshel to Reed, 8 Aug. 1781, PA 9:344–45; Archibald McClean to Reed, 13 Aug. 1781, PA 9:352–53.

13. Stokely to Reed, 4 Aug. 1781, PA 9:330–31; Clark to Reed, 4 Aug. 1781, PA 9:331–32; Lochry to Reed, 4 Aug. 1781, PA 9:333; Joseph Brant to McKee, 21 Aug. 1781, MPHS 19:655–56; Ephraim Douglass to Irvine, 29 Aug. 1781, *Pennsylvania Magazine of History and Biography* 4, no. 2 (1880): 248; Andrew Thompson and McKee to De Peyster, 29 Aug. 1781, MPHS 19:658; proceedings of Kentucky militia officers, 5–7 Sept. 1781, GRC 8:596–603; John Todd, Jr., to Thomas Nelson, 21 Oct. 1781, GRC 19:8–10; Thompson to De Peyster, 26 Sept. 1781, MPHS 10:515–16; McKee to De Peyster, 26 Sept. 1781, MPHS 10:516–18; McKee to De Peyster, 2 Nov. 1781, MPHS 10:535–36; Isaac Anderson, journal, [1781–82], PA6 2:405–6.

14. Gelelemend to Brodhead, 19 July 1780, FRUO 219 ("Virginian Devils"); Brodhead to Delaware Council, 27 May 1780, FRUO 184 ("high reward"); Brodhead to Washington, 3 May 1779, GWP; Brodhead to Capt. Biggs, 7 June 1779, box 1, vol. 1, DBP; Brodhead to Campbell, 14 July 1779, PA 12:135–36; Brodhead to Washington, 26 Oct. 1779, PA 12:177.

15. Delaware chiefs to Monsieur Gerard, 25 May 1779, FAUO 337–38; message from Cooshowking to Wakitumekie, [Aug. 1780], PFH addl. mss. 21782, fol. 384, reel 56; MMD 481–82.

16. Reed to Brodhead, [July 1779], PA 7:569 ("several Parties"); Speech of Delawares to Congress, 10 May 1779, FAUO 317–21; Brodhead to Washington, 22 May 1779, PA 12:114; Delaware

chiefs to Gerard, 25 May 1779, FAUO 337–38; Brodhead to Washington, 25 June 1779, PA 12:131–32; MMD 297–98, 314, 339, 356–58, 390–92, 408, 413, 421–22, 425, 452–53, 478–79.

17. Brodhead to Reed, 17 Oct. 1780, PA 8:589 ("neither Bread"); Brodhead to Reed, 2 Nov. 1780, PA 8:596 ("destroy," "may not"); MMD 540.

18. Gelelemend to Brodhead, 26 Feb. 1781, FRUO 339–40 ("Friends," "are getting ready," 340); MMD 549–51 ("arming themselves," 551); Brodhead, letters to Wingenund and William Penn, 2 Dec. 1780, FRUO 298–99; William Penn to Brodhead, 13 Jan. 1781, FRUO 315–16; Gelelemend to Brodhead, 15 Jan. 1781, FRUO 316–17; Heckewelder to Brodhead, 26 Feb. 1781, FRUO 337–38; De Peyster to Delawares, 12 Apr. 1781, FRUO 375–76.

19. Brodhead to Reed, 10 Mar. 1781, PA 8:766 ("general Indian war"); Brodhead to David Shepherd, 8 Mar. 1781, FRUO 342–43; Brodhead to Washington, 27 Mar. 1781, FRUO 352–53; Lochry and James Peiry to Brodhead, 2 Apr. 1781, PA 9:51–52; Indian Council, 26 Apr. 1781, MPHS 10:474; memorandum, 26 Apr. 1781, MPHS 10:476; Simon Girty to De Peyster, 4 May 1781, MPHS 10:478; Brodhead to Reed, 22 May 1781, PA 9:161; Gibson to Thomas Jefferson, May 30, 1781, FRUO 399–400; "Rolls of Coshocton Expedition," [Apr. 1781], FRUO 461–69; John Heckewelder, *Narrative of the Mission of the United Brethren Among the Delaware and Mohegan Indians* (1820; New York: Arno, 1971), 214–15; Thomas H. Johnson, "The Indian Village of 'Cush-Og-Wenk,'" *Ohio Archaeological and Historical Publications* 21 (1912): 433.

20. Brodhead to Heckewelder, 21 Jan. 1781, FRUO 321 ("much confidence"); Girty to De Peyster, 4 May 1781, MPHS 10:478 ("Beat all"); Brodhead to Reed, 22 May 1781, PA 9:161 ("killed fifteen"). For the leaders of the Erwin raid, see Brodhead to Reed, 2 Nov. 1780, PA 8:596; Minutes of the Supreme Executive Council, 13 Nov. 1780, CRP 12:539–40.

21. DDZ 1:3–6 ("behaved," 4); Zeisberger to Brodhead, 18 Aug. 1781, GWP ("wou'd prove"); C&M fols. 14–16; Zeisberger to Brodhead and Gibson, 21 Aug. 1781, GWP.

22. C&M fol. 17 ("Cousins"); Zeisberger to Brodhead, 21 Aug. 1781, GWP ("tired"); DDZ 1:4–5 ("dangerous place," "Take counsel"). For watchwords, see MMD 96n26, 117, 163n280.

23. DDZ 1:6–9 ("extreme need," 6; "leading chief," 9n1; "to dance," 7); C&M fols. 18–24.

24. Gibson to Washington, 30 Sept. 1781, GWP ("the Country"); DDZ 1:9–15, 17–18 ("the best," 14); McKee to De Peyster, 26 Sept. 1781, MPHS 10:518; C&M fols. 24–36.

25. De Peyster, conference with Pipe and Wingenum, 9 Nov. 1781, MPHS 10:538–41 ("always apprized," 539; "to instruct," 540); McKee to De Peyster, 26 Sept. 1781, MPHS 10:518; De Peyster, conference with Hurons, 21 Oct. 1781, MPHS 10:527–28; extract of a council, 11 Dec. 1781, MPHS 10:545–46; DDZ 1:15–20, 37–41; C&M fols. 41–45.

26. Speech of Delawares and Shawnese, 22 Aug. 1780, MPHS 10:420 ("destitute"); McKee to De Peyster, 22 Aug. 1780, PFH addl. mss. 21782, fols. 381–82, reel 55; McKee to De Peyster, [ca. 1 Mar. 1781], MPHS 19:597–98; Brant to Isadore Chene and Matthew Elliot, 19 May 1781, MPHS 19:634–35; Chene to De Peyster, 20 May 1781, MPHS 19:635–36; McKee to De Peyster, 15 July 1781, MPHS 19:647–48; DDZ 1:20–24, 47–48, 50–51, 60–63, 66; Sami Lakomäki, *Gathering Together: The Shawnee People Through Diaspora and Nationhood, 1600–1870* (New Haven, CT: Yale University Press, 2014), 113.

27. Extract of a council, 11 Dec. 1781, MPHS 10:545 ("starving in the woods"); De Peyster to McKee, 4 Oct. 1781, MPHS 10:522–23; De Peyster to Haldimand, 5 Oct. 1781, MPHS 10:523; DDZ 1:48, 56–57. For Welapachtschiechen, see Zeisberger to Brodhead, 18 Aug. 1781, GWP; Zeisberger to Brodhead and Gibson, 21 Aug. 1781, GWP; DDZ 1:24–25; C&M fols. 45–46.

28. DDZ 1:24–25, 29, 31, 36, 44, 47, 60, 64, 66 ("perfectly quiet," 29; "taken prisoners," 31);

C&M fols. 38–40, 45–47 ("the Americans," 47); McKee, unaddressed, 10 Apr. 1782, PFH addl. mss. 21783, fol. 140, reel 56 ("they would not"); Brodhead to John Ettwein, 23 Oct. 1781, no. 144, reel 1, Papers of John Ettwein, Archives of the Moravian Church, Bethlehem, PA, microfilm; Schebosh to Ettwein, 4–5 Nov. 1781, no. 504, reel 3, Papers of John Ettwein.

29. Scott to Reed, 19 Oct. 1781, PA 9:438 ("Commission Hunters"); Irvine to Washington, 2 Dec. 1781, ser. 4, GWP ("heap of ruins"); Gibson to Washington, 24 Aug. and 30 Sept. 1781, GWP; Gibson to Barnard Gratz and Michael Gratz, 26 Aug. 1787 [1781], case 1, box 2, Gratz; Douglass to James Irvine, 29 Aug. 1781, "Notes and Queries," *Pennsylvania Magazine of History and Biography* 4, no. 2 (1880): 247; Brodhead to Washington, 29 Aug. 1781, GWP; Gibson to Shepherd, 12 Sept. 1781, Draper 2SS:25; Washington County inhabitants to Reed, 15 Aug. 1781, PA 9:355–56; Bethlehem Township inhabitants, petition and letter to Pentecost, 26–27 Oct. 1781, RPRG 19:110–14; Hanna and Love to Irvine, 3 Dec. 1781, Draper 2AA:4; Irvine to President of Council, 3 Dec. 1781, PA 9:458–59; William Moore to Irvine, 17 Dec. 1781, PA 9:468; Scott to Moore, 2 Feb. 1782, RPRG 19:424–25; Marshel to Moore, 4 Feb. 1782, PA 9:484–85. For the harvest, see Marshel to Irvine, 4 Apr. 1782, WIC 286; McKee, unaddressed, 10 Apr. 1782, and De Peyster to [Haldimand], 14 May 1782, PFH addl. mss. 21783, fols. 139–41, 154, reel 56.

30. Minutes of Supreme Executive Council, 2 and 4 Apr. 1781, CRP 12:681–83; Marshel to Reed, 5 and 27 June and 8 Aug. 1781, PA 9:193–94, 233–34, 343; "Arrangement of Militia, 1781–82," [Aug. 1781], PA2 14:747–50; militia returns, Sept. 1781, PA6 2:132–33. For Marshel, see FAUO 258n1; WIC 277n1; and R. Eugene Harper, *The Transformation of Western Pennsylvania, 1770–1800* (Pittsburgh, PA: University of Pittsburgh Press, 1991), 77, 103–4, 146; Washington County tax list, 1781, PA3 22:743. For Pentecost, see the election results, 9 Oct. 1781, PA6 11:393; minutes of the Supreme Executive Council, 30 Nov. 1781, CRP 13:134; James Patrick McClure, "The Ends of the American Earth: Pittsburgh and the Upper Ohio Valley to 1795" (Ph.D. diss., University of Michigan, 1983), 276–79, 329–30, 403–8. For Williamson, see Washington County tax list, 1781, PA3 22:729; Virginia land entries, 1780–81, PA3:548, 552, 558; Ohio County Courts-Martial, 1779–81, FRUO 425–30; Washington County militia roll, 25 Sept. 1781, PA6 2:92. For the expedition, see Brodhead to Ettwein, 23 Oct. 1781, no. 144, reel 1, Papers of John Ettwein; Schebosh to Ettwein, 4–5 Nov. 1781, no. 504, reel 3, Papers of John Ettwein. An undated roster of fifty-seven names, labeled "Williamson's Expedition," appears twice in the published *Pennsylvania Archives*. The editors assumed that this was a partial list of participants in the March 1782 expedition, but it seems more likely to be from the smaller October 1781 venture: see PA2 14:769–70 and PA6 2:257–58. Contemporary sources do not identify the expedition's commander, but early local histories state it was Williamson: Joseph Doddridge, *Notes on the Settlement and Indian Wars of the Western Parts of Virginia and Pennsylvania, from 1763 to 1783, Inclusive*, ed. J. S. Ritenour and W. T. Lindsey (1912; Parsons, WV: McClain Printing Company, 1960), 199; Alexander Scott Withers, *Chronicles of Border Warfare*, annotated ed., ed. Reuben Gold Thwaites (1895; Parsons, WV: McClain Printing Company, 1975), 322–23.

31. Marshel to Irvine, 20 and 26 Nov. 1781, WIC 279–81 ("volunteer plans," 279); Marshel to Reed, 6 Nov. 1781, PA 9:444–45 ("in full form"); Marshel to Moore, 4 Feb. 1782, PA 9:484–85 ("a Large Mob"); Marshel to Reed, 8 Aug. 1781, PA 9:345; return of militia officers, 4 Feb. 1782, PA6 2:217–19; Washington County class rolls, [1781–82], PA6 2:7–10, 17–21, 25–28, 76–84, 91–93, 117–25, 130–34, 152–55, 163–68, 200–210. For Tenmile Creek, compare militia rolls with Washington County tax lists, 1781, PA3 22:704, 712, 721, 722, 724, 747, 748.

32. For Nonhelema, see Johann David Schoepf, *Travels in the Confederation, 1783–1784*, trans. Alfred J. Morrison (Philadelphia: W. J. Campbell, 1911), 277. For Betsey and Gibson, see

Denny 286; John Neville to Clark, 14 Apr. 1782, GRC 19:57–58; William Irvine to Ann Irvine, 12 Apr. 1782, WIC 344; Gibson to Isaac Craig, 5 Aug. 1784, box 1, folder 23, Northwest Territory Collection, Indiana Historical Society, Indianapolis. For Gelelemend's band, see orderly book, 12 Nov. 1781, Draper 2NN:188; Irvine to Washington, 7 Feb. 1782, WIC 90; court-martial, 12 Jan. 1782, Draper 2NN:206; "extract of a letter dated Chartiers," *Pennsylvania Journal* 1493, 22 May 1782, [3]; Irvine to Washington, 20 Apr. 1782, WIC 99–102; DDZ 1:85; Margaret Pearson Both-well, "Killbuck and Killbuck Island," *Western Pennsylvania Historical Magazine* 44, no. 4 (Dec. 1961): 344–45. For Irvine and Gibson, see Irvine to Washington, 2 Dec. 1781 and Feb. 1782, ser. 4, GWP; Irvine to Board of War, 13 and 14 Dec. 1781, WIC 163–65; Finley to Irvine, 2 Feb. 1782, WIC 351–53; soldiers of the 7th Virginia Regiment to Irvine, n.d., WIC 103n1; Gibson to Irvine, 13 and 15 Feb. 1782, ser. 4, GWP.

33. *Pennsylvania Packet* 872, 16 Apr. 1782, [3] ("wife and children," "called themselves"); DDZ 1:82 ("to be off"); *Pennsylvania Packet* 865, 30 Mar. 1782, [3]; Michael Huffnagle to Moore, 8 Mar. 1782, PA 9:511; C&M fols. 48–49; William M. Farrar, "The Moravian Massacre," *Ohio Archaeological and Historical Publications* 3 (1891): 287–93.

34. Irvine to Moore, May 3, 1782, WIC 239; militia returns, 9 Mar. 1782, PA6 2:31–33, 135–38; *Pennsylvania Packet* 872, 16 Apr. 1782, [3]. For ammunition, see minutes of the Supreme Executive Council, 20 Dec. 1781, CRP 13:151.

35. Leonard Sadosky, "Rethinking the Gnadenhütten Massacre: The Contest for Power in the Public World of the Revolutionary Frontier," in *The Sixty Years' War for the Great Lakes, 1754–1814,* ed. David Curtis Skaggs and Larry L. Nelson (East Lansing: Michigan State University Press, 2001), 187–214.

36. C&M fol. 50 ("good treatment"); Frederick Lineback [Leinbach], relation, [Apr. 1782], PA 9:524 ("Minister Schebosch"); DDZ 1:79–80.

37. C&M fols. 51 and 56; DDZ 1:80–81; Lineback, relation, [Apr. 1782], PA 9:524. For Thomas and family, see MMD 581, 594, 597, 599.

38. C&M fols. 52–54; DDZ 1:80; Edmund De Schweinitz, *The Life and Times of David Zeisberger: The Western Pioneer and Apostle of the Indians* (Philadelphia: Lippincott, 1871), 551–52; "Records of the Moravian Mission Among the Indians of North America: Indian Individuals Index," Primary Source Media, GALE CENGAGE Learning, http://microformguides.gale.com; MMD 563–600.

39. C&M fols. 55–56; McKee, unaddressed, 10 Apr. 1782, PFH addl. mss. 21783, fols. 139–41, reel 56 ("Speech wampum"); DDZ 1:79.

40. William Croghan to William Davies, 6 [July] 1782, GRC 19:71 ("liv[ed] with them"); C&M fol. 55 ("must Dye," "good and true," "wrung their Hands"); John Rose, "Journal of a Volunteer Expedition to Sandusky, from May 24 to June 13, 1782," *Pennsylvania Magazine of History and Biography* 18 (1894): 294 ("Bigotted notions"); Lineback, relation, PA 9:524 ("either to carry"); Pentecost to Moore, 8 May 1782, PA 9:540; *Pennsylvania Packet,* 7 Nov. 1782, [2]; Irvine to Washington, 20 Apr. 1782, ser. 4, GWP; DDZ 1:81; Doddridge, *Settlement and Indian Wars,* 199; Rob Harper, "Looking the Other Way: The Gnadenhutten Massacre and the Contextual Interpretation of Violence," *William and Mary Quarterly* 64, no. 3 (2007): 629–36.

41. C&M fols. 55–61 ("praying," 58; "condemning Party," 55; "very loving," 61); DDZ 1:79–80 ("forgive," 79); Lineback, relation, [Apr. 1782], PA 9:525 ("kept on singing"); Irvine to Washington, 20 Apr. 1782, ser. 4, GWP; William Irvine to Ann Irvine, 12 Apr. 1782, Draper 2AA:17–21.

42. C&M fols. 60–65; DDZ 1:80–82.

43. McKee, unaddressed, 10 Apr. 1782, PFH addl. mss. 21783, fols. 139–41, reel 56; William

Irvine to Ann Irvine, 12 Apr. 1782, Draper 2AA:17–21; Bull, memorial, 13 Apr. 1782, RPRG 19:656; Nevill to Clark, 14 Apr. 1782, GRC 19:58; Irvine to Washington, 20 Apr. 1782, ser. 4, GWP; "Extract of a letter dated Chartiers," *Pennsylvania Journal* 1493, 22 May 1782, [3]; DDZ 1:85; Irvine to [Isaac Craig], Sept. 1782, Draper 1AA:316–19.

44. Pentecost to Moore, 8 May 1782, PA 9:540–41 ("some condemning," "a Confusion"); DDZ 1:89–90; De Peyster to Haldimand, 13 May 1782, MPHS 10:573–74; *Pennsylvania Packet* 868, 9 Apr. 1782; *Pennsylvania Packet* 872, 16 Apr. 1782, [3]; Charles Thomson to Moore, 9 Apr. 1782, PA 9:523–24; Moore to Irvine, 13 Apr. 1782, PA 9:525; Irvine to Moore, 9 May 1782, WIC 241–45; Gibson to Nathaniel Seidel, 9 May 1782, WIC 362n; Moore to Irvine, 30 May 1782, WIC 245–46; resolution of the General Assembly, 15 Aug. 1782, WIC 246n2; Edward Cook to Moore, 2 Sept. 1782, PA 9:629; Croghan to Davies, 6 July 1782, GRC 19:57–58.

45. Harper, "Gnadenhutten Massacre," 636–40.

46. Irvine to commander of volunteers, 14 May 1782, WIC 118n ("to destroy"); De Peyster to Haldimand, 18 Aug. 1782, MPHS 10:629 ("Effegies"); Irvine to Marshel, 29 Mar. 1782, WIC 282–83; Irvine to Washington, 21 May 1782, ser. 4, GWP.

47. De Peyster to Haldimand, 13 May, 23 June, and 18 Aug. 1782, MPHS 10:573–74, 594–95, 628–29; De Peyster to Powell, 15 May 1782, MPHS 20:16; John Turney to De Peyster, 7 June 1782, MPHS 10:583; Captain Snake to De Peyster, 8 June 1782, MPHS 10:583–84; John Rose to Irvine, 13 June 1782, WIC 367–78; Powell to Haldimand, 1 July 1782, MPHS 20:28–29; Croghan to Davies, 6 July 1782, GRC 19:71–73; De Peyster to Thomas Brown, 18 July 1782, WIC 372n; De Peyster to McKee, 6 and 19 Aug. 1782, MPHS 20:37–39 and 10:630–31; extract from a speech by Chiefs of the Six Nations, 11 Dec. 1782, WIC 374n; Rose, "Expedition to Sandusky."

48. Irvine to Lincoln, 1 July 1782, WIC 175 ("Indian settlements"); letters and petitions to Irvine, 1782, WIC 298–302, 307n2, 380–84; Huffnagle to Moore, July 1782, PA 9:596; Irvine to Marshel, 10 Aug. 1782, WIC 307–8; Antoine Chesne to De Peyster, 16 Aug. 1782, MPHS 10:628; Bernard Dougherty to Moore, 19 Aug. 1782, PA 9:619–20; William Caldwell to De Peyster, 26 Aug. 1782, PFH addl. mss. 21783, fols. 231–32, reel 56; Daniel Boone to Benjamin Harrison, 30 Aug. 1782, GRC 19:98–99; John Floyd to Clark, 31 Aug. 1782, GRC 19:106; McKee to De Peyster, 28 Aug. 1782, MPHS 20:49–51; Irvine to Clark, 16 Sept. 1782, GRC 19:116–17; McDonnell, *Masters of Empire*, 308.

49. A. Dundas to Haldimand, 23 Oct. 1782, MPHS 20:68 ("approaching bands"); Haldimand to De Peyster, 21 Oct. 1782, MPHS 10:660 ("Public money"); Irvine to Benjamin Lincoln, 16 Apr. 1783, WIC 187 ("total extirpation"); De Peyster to Powell, 27 Aug. 1782, MPHS 10:633–34; Lincoln to Irvine, 27 Sept. 1782, WIC 184; Irvine to Clark, 7 Nov. 1782, GRC 19:149; McKee to De Peyster, 15 Nov. 1782, PFH addl. mss. 21783, fol. 270, reel 56; De Peyster to Allan MacLean, 7 Jan. 1783, MPHS 20:87–88; "Colonel William Fleming's Journal of Travels in Kentucky in 1783," in Mereness, *Travels in the American Colonies*, 668–72.

Chapter 6

1. Shawnees and George Walls, speeches, 9 Aug. and 11 Sept. 1783, VSP 3:521, 529–30; Arent De Peyster to Allan MacLean, 17 July 1783, MPHS 20:146; Indian council, 30 July 1783, MPHS 20:153–54.

2. W[illiam] North, unaddressed, 7 Aug. 1786, box 1, folder 26, Northwest Territory Collection, Indiana Historical Society, Indianapolis ("immortal hatred," "back woods men"); Peter Muhlenberg to Baron Steuben, 23 Apr. 1784, box 1, folder 25, Northwest Territory Collection ("proper measures"); John Fitch to Governor of Virginia, 30 Mar. 1785, VSP 4:20 ("spy out").

3. Henry Knox to Josiah Harmar, 27 June 1786, Harmar 3:66; report on Indian Affairs, 15 Oct. 1783, PA 10:119–24; Eric Hinderaker, *Elusive Empires: Constructing Colonialism in the Ohio Valley, 1673–1800* (New York: Cambridge University Press, 1997), 236.

4. "Ephraim Douglass and His Times, Including the Journal of George McCully and Various Letters of the Period," ed. Clarence M. Burton, *Magazine of History, with Notes and Queries*, extra no. 10 (1910): 50, 47, 61.

5. CRBJ 4 Sept. 1775; Delaware Council to George Morgan, 26 Feb. 1777, Morgan 1:47–49; Henry Bird to De Peyster, 21 May 1780, MPHS 19:524; Indian council, 20 Sept. 1785, MPHS 11:465–67; Helen Hornbeck Tanner, ed., *Atlas of Great Lakes Indian History* (Norman: University of Oklahoma Press, 1987), 44, 81–84, maps 9, 13, 16, 17; Richard White, *The Middle Ground: Indians, Empires, and Republics in the Great Lakes Region, 1650–1815* (New York: Cambridge University Press, 1991), 436–37; Helen Hornbeck Tanner, "Coocoochee: Mohawk Medicine Woman," *American Indian Culture and Research Journal* 3, no. 3 (1979): 26–27.

6. De Peyster to MacLean, 7 Jan. 1783, MPHS 20:87 ("dupes"); transactions at Sandusky, 6–8 Sept. 1783, MPHS 20:179–82 ("voice of the whole," 180); MacLean to Frederick Haldimand, 18 May 1783, MPHS 20:117–21; Morgan to Senecas, 14 Aug. 1783, MPHS 11:380–81; "Ephraim Douglass," 54, 58.

7. Joseph Brant, treaty proceedings, [1784], Draper 23U:4; "Treaty of Fort Stanwix, in 1784," ed. Neville B. Craig, *Olden Time* 2, no. 9 (Sept. 1847): 413–14, 418–20, 422–24 ("free and independent," 418); "Journal of Griffith Evans, 1784–1785," ed. Hallock F. Raup, *Pennsylvania Magazine of History and Biography* 65, no. 2 (Apr. 1941): 212; Pennsylvania Indian Commissioners, proceedings, 1784–85, RPRG 9:980–81; Alan Taylor, *The Divided Ground: Indians, Settlers, and the Northern Borderland of the American Revolution* (New York: Alfred A. Knopf, 2006), 157–60.

8. "Extracts from the Journal of Arthur Lee," ed. Neville B. Craig, *Olden Time* 2, no. 7–8 (July–Aug. 1847): 336; Denny 54–55; Pennsylvania Indian Commissioners, proceedings, RPRG 9:983–88.

9. Piteosawa, speech to Americans, 8 Nov. 1785, Draper 23U:30–31 ("our Chiefs"); Obadiah Robins to W. Ferguson, 29 Sept. 1786, enclosed in Ferguson to Harmar, 18 Oct. 1786, Harmar 4:43 ("must not"); Butler 516 ("broke faith"); Brant, memorandum, 6 Nov. 1784, Ayer 106, folder 1, Ayer Manuscripts, Newberry Library, Chicago; Alexander McKee to John Johnson, 2 June 1785, MPHS 11:457–58; Michael Huffnagle to Harmar, July 1785, Harmar 2:104; Indian council, 20 Sept. 1785, MPHS 11:465–67; Denny 56; "Journal of Samuel Montgomery," ed. David I. Bushnell, *Mississippi Valley Historical Review* 2, no. 2 (Sept. 1915): 263–65; Gregory Evans Dowd, *A Spirited Resistance: The North American Indian Struggle for Unity, 1745–1815* (Baltimore: Johns Hopkins University Press, 1992), 93–94; Thomas S. Abler, *Cornplanter: Chief Warrior of the Allegany Senecas* (Syracuse, NY: Syracuse University Press, 2007), 69–72; Taylor, *Divided Ground*, 246–47.

10. Ephraim Douglass to John Dickinson, 2 Feb. 1784, PA 10:553 ("authority"); Douglass to John Armstrong, 29 May 1784, PA 10:582 ("rabble"); Philip Jenkins, deposition, 7 June 1784, PA 10:595.

11. Edward Cook to William Irvine, 29 May 1782, WIC 325 ("general outcry"); Cook to Irvine, 10 June 1782, WIC 326–27 ("a prelude"); Douglass to Armstrong, 29 May 1784, PA 10:583 ("cautioned"); Dorsey Pentecost to William Moore, 18 May 1782, PA 9:545–46; John Robinson and Hugh Brackenridge, depositions, 20 June and 4 July 1782, PA 9:572–73; Alexander McClean to Moore, 27 June 1782, PA 9:564–67; William McCleery to Irvine, 30 June 1782, box 4, folder 19, INF; James Marshel to Irvine, 17 July 1782, WIC 302; Charles Campbell to Moore, Sept. 1782,

RPRG 19:1017–18; Irvine, unaddressed, Sept. 1782, Draper 1AA:316–19; Christopher Hays to Moore, 20 Sept. 1782, PA 9:637–38; James Trimble to commissioners of taxes, 28 June 1784, RPRG 21:266–67; Marshel to Dickinson, 7 July 1784, RPRG 21:292–93; Terry Bouton, "A Road Closed: Rural Insurgency in Post-Independence Pennsylvania," *Journal of American History* 87, no. 3 (2000): 855–87.

12. Robert Johnson to Patrick Henry, 5 Dec. 1786, VSP 4:191 ("cohees," "tuckyahoes"); "Diary of Major Erkuries Beatty: Paymaster of the Western Army, May 15, 1786, to June 5, 1787," *Magazine of American History with Notes and Queries* 1, no. 1, 2 (1877): 435–36 ("very superstitious," "no religion"); Richard Scott Blackburn, "A Short Journal of a Trip from Winchester in Virginia to New Orleans," 26 Apr. 1789, Clements Library, Ann Arbor, MI ("ranting"); Denny 88 ("carry on"); Stephen Aron, *How the West Was Lost: The Transformation of Kentucky from Daniel Boone to Henry Clay* (Baltimore: Johns Hopkins University Press, 1996), 70–73; Terry Bouton, *Taming Democracy: "The People," the Founders, and the Troubled Ending of the American Revolution* (New York: Oxford University Press, 2007); Honor Sachs, *Home Rule: Households, Manhood, and National Expansion on the Eighteenth-Century Kentucky Frontier* (New Haven, CT: Yale University Press, 2015).

13. William Croghan to Pentecost, 28 Apr. 1782, Draper 30J:41 ("to go Settle"); Irvine to George Washington, 20 Apr. 1782, ser. 4, GWP ("a new state"); McKee to Johnson, 9 Sept. 1783, MPHS 20:183 ("before their great People"); Jonathan Heart to William Judd, 8 Jan. and 4 June 1786, William Judd Papers, 1786–1797, collection no. 80327, Connecticut Historical Society ("Federal territory"); transactions at Sandusky, 31 Aug. 1783, MPHS 20:175 ("to encroach"); Irvine to Moore, 9 May 1782, WIC 244; Armstrong to Harmar, 13 Apr. 1785, Harmar 2:56; Irvine to Harmar, 31 May 1785, Harmar 2:77; Ebenezer Denny, "Report after Destroying the Cabbins of the Intruders upon the Lands of the United States," 23 Aug. 1785, Harmar 2:110; "Petition of the Intruders on the lands of the United States," 30 Aug. 1785, Harmar 2:116.

14. Bethlehem Township inhabitants, petition, 26 Oct. 1781, RPRG 19:110–11; Pittsburgh inhabitants, petition, 1 Aug. 1782, RPRG 19:936–38; Joseph McGarraugh to Isaac Mason, 14 Dec. 1784, RPRG 21:948; Hays to Dickinson, 12 May 1784, PA 10:264–65; memorial from Fayette County, 15 June 1784, PA 10:280–81; McClean to Dickinson, 16 July 1784, PA 10:293–94; John Allen and James Finley to Supreme Executive Council, 21 Apr. 1785, RPRG 22:56; Douglass to Dickinson, 5 Aug. 1785, RPRG 22:344–45; Somerset Township inhabitants, petitions, [28 June and 3 Sept. 1788], RPRG 24:192–93, 346–50; William Parker to Benjamin Franklin, 3 Sept. 1788, RPRG 24:351; minutes of the Supreme Executive Council, 21 Nov. 1781, 9 Aug. 1782, 5 Feb. 1785, 27 Aug. 1785, and 30 June 1788, CRP 13:122, 351; 14:346, 526; 15:483.

15. William Finley to Irvine, 13 May 1784, box 5, folder 22, INF; Finley to Irvine, 30 Jan. 1785, box 5, folder 24, INF; Irvine to Harmar, 31 May 1785, Harmar 2:77; Thomas Wilkins to David Duncan et al., 20 July 1785, and James McLelland to Duncan, 24 July 1785, reel 1, Isaac Craig Papers, Carnegie Library of Pittsburgh, microfilm; Finley to Irvine, 27 Feb. 1786, box 6, folder 4, INF; Duncan to Harmar, 28 Mar. 1786, Harmar 3:22; Duncan to Harmar, enclosing deposition of John Leith, 16 May 1786, Harmar 3:48–49; Armstrong to Harmar, [May 1786], box 1, folder 18, John Armstrong Papers, 1772–1950, Indiana Historical Society, Indianapolis; Irvine to Isaac Craig and John Finley, 22 July 1786, box 6, folder 5, INF; Duncan to Irvine, 1 Dec. 1786, box 6, folder 5, INF; letters to Irvine, Jan. 1787, box 6, folder 6, INF; Duncan to Irvine, 10 Feb. 1787, box 6, folder 7, INF; Duncan to Harmar, 17 June 1787, Harmar 6:2; Duncan to Irvine, 7 Dec. 1787, box 6, folder 11, INF; Duncan to Irvine, 23 Mar. 1788, box 6, folder 14, INF; *Journals of the Continental Congress, 1774–1789*, ed. Worthington C. Ford (Washington, DC: U.S. Government Printing

Office, 1904–37), 28:488n. On the importance of salt springs, see Johann David Schoepf, *Travels in the Confederation, 1783–1784*, trans. Alfred J. Morrison (Philadelphia: W. J. Campbell, 1911), 254–56; Sachs, *Home Rule*, 46–51.

16. Harmar to Irvine, 10 Dec. 1786, box 6, folder 5, INF; Denny 132, 133–34; Duncan to Harmar, 28 Mar. 1786, Harmar 3:22.

17. James Tucker and Aaron Gregg, depositions, 31 Jan. 1782, RPRG 19:417–18; David Enoch and Daniel Leet, petition, 2 Feb. 1782, RPRG 19:426–28; Thomas Scott to Timothy Matlack, 15 Feb. 1782, RPRG 19:466; James Brison to Charles Biddle, 22 Apr. 1790, RPRG 25:198; CRP 13:38.

18. Douglass to Dickinson, 5 Aug. 1785, RPRG 22:344–45; inhabitants of Washington town, petition, [23 Sept. 1785], RPRG 22:437–39; certificates for division of townships, 1786–89, RPRG 22:1098, 23:768, and 24:731–33.

19. Butler 454–56 (quotations 454).

20. Butler 456–58, 488–490, 500.

21. Indian council, 18 May 1785, MPHS 25:691–93; Robins to Harmar, 17 May 1785, Harmar 2:66. Captain Wolf may have been a Shawnee, also known as Biaseka, the son of Cornstalk: Sami Lakomäki, *Gathering Together: The Shawnee People Through Diaspora and Nationhood, 1600–1870* (New Haven, CT: Yale University Press, 2014), 115.

22. John H. Moore, ed., "A Captive of the Shawnees, 1779–1784," *West Virginia History* 23, no. 4 (July 1962): 294–95 ("not a slave," 294); McKee, letters to De Peyster and Walls, 29 May 1783, MPHS 20:125–26; Walls to James Sherlock, 10 Apr. 1784, VSP 3:574; Butler 444, 460; Anne Crabb, "'What Shall I Do Now?': The Story of the Indian Captivities of Margaret Paulee, Jones Hoy, and Jack Callaway, 1779–ca. 1789," *Filson Club History Quarterly* 70, no. 4 (Oct. 1996): 392–95; Aron, *How the West Was Lost*, 53–56.

23. Robert Petterson to [Walter Finney], 12 July 1786, enclosed in Finney to Harmar, 22 July 1786, Harmar 3:80 ("Banditty"); CRBJ 30 Aug. 1775; Butler 445–47; Richard Butler to William Grayson, 31 May 1785, Draper 3U:600–601; Butler to Irvine, 26 Aug. 1787, box 6, folder 9, INF; Butler, petition, 31 Aug. 1788, RPRG 24:340–42; *Life and Letters of Samuel Holden Parsons*, ed. Charles S. Hall (Binghamton, NY: Otsiningo Publishing Company, 1905), 581; Parsons to his children, 7 Jan. 1786, *Life and Letters of Samuel Holden Parsons*, 480–82; Heart to Judd, 8 Jan. 1786, Judd Papers; Heart to Jeremiah Wadsworth, 22 Jan. 1785 [1786], *Life and Letters of Samuel Holden Parsons*, 486–87; Evans, "Journal of Griffith Evans, 1784–1785," 231–32; Henry Innes to John Brown, 4 Apr. 1788, box 2, pp. 10–13, Innes Papers, no. 439, Ayer Manuscripts; David Andrew Nichols, *Red Gentlemen and White Savages: Indians, Federalists, and the Search for Order on the American Frontier* (Charlottesville: University of Virginia Press, 2008), 39.

24. Butler 520, 522–24 ("every one," 520; "God gave us," 522; "the destruction," 524); Denny 73.

25. Speech of Maloontha, Shade, and Painted Pole, [1786], Draper Manuscripts, 23U:33–34 ("striving"); Thomas Hutchins to John Francis Hamtramck, 27 Aug. 1786, enclosed in Hamtramck to Harmar, 1 Sept. 1786, Harmar 4:14 ("firm peace"); Heart to Judd, 4 June 1786, Judd Papers ("a few Banditi"); Duncan to Harmar, 28 Mar. 1786, Harmar 3:22; Denny 81–84, 87–88, 93; John Hart to John Doughty, 27 Apr. 1786, box 1, folder 17, Armstrong Papers; Major Ancrum, letter, 8 May 1786, MPHS 11:488–89; Duncan to Harmar, 16 May 1786, Harmar 3:48; "Diary of Major Erkuries Beatty," 177–78; Beatty to Armstrong, 14 June 1786, box 1, folder 18, Armstrong Papers; Captain Taeenica, information, 6 July 1786, Harmar 3:75; Philip Leibert, report, 20 July 1786, Harmar 3:85; Joseph Saunders, report, 24 July 1786, Harmar 3:96; Half King, speech, 2 Sept. 1786, and Jacob Springer to Hutchins, 13 Sept. 1786, Harmar 4:27; George Brickell and Thomas Girty, depositions, and anonymous report, 13 and 14 Sept. 1786, enclosed in Ferguson to

Harmar, 16 Sept. 1786, Harmar 4:28–29; speech of the Wyandots and Delawares, 23 Sept. 1786, and Robins to Ferguson, 29 Sept. 1786, both enclosed in Ferguson to Harmar, 18 Oct. 1786, Harmar 4:38, 43; Dowd, *Spirited Resistance*, 13–16.

26. George Rogers Clark to John Wyllys, 25 June 1786, Harmar 3:64 ("chastise"); Knox to Harmar, 27 June 1786, Harmar 3:66 ("unprovoked aggression"); Henry to Virginia delegates, 5 July 1786, *Patrick Henry: Life, Correspondence and Speeches*, 3 vols., ed. William Wirt Henry (New York: Charles Scribner's Sons, 1891), 3:363 ("attacking"); Ebenezer Denny to Harmar, 15 June 1786, Denny 88; Levi Todd to Henry, 22 June and 12 July 1786, VSP 4:151, 155; Henry to Samuel Brown, 11 Aug. 1785, *Patrick Henry*, 3:313; John May to Henry, 19 Apr. and 14 July 1786, VSP 4:119–20, 204–5; Henry to Virginia delegates, 16 May 1786, *Patrick Henry*, 3:350; Henry to Annie Christian, 20 Oct. 1786, *Patrick Henry*, 3:379–80. On Blue Licks, see Levi Todd to Robert Todd, 26 Aug. 1782, VSP 3:333–34.

27. Finney to Harmar, 22 July 1786, Harmar 3:92 ("Conviction"); Harmar to Finney, 11 Oct. 1786, letterbook A, 28:166, Harmar ("co-operate"); Articles of Confederation, 1 Mar. 1781, article VI, par. 5 ("certain advice"); Henry to Virginia delegates, 16 May 1786, *Patrick Henry*, 3:350–52; Finney to Harmar, 3 July 1786, Harmar 3:72; Harmar to Finney, 27 July 1786, letterbook A, 28:141–43, Harmar; Levi Todd to Henry, 29 Aug. 1786, VSP 4:166; letters to Henry, 7 Dec. 1786, and judges' opinion, 15 May 1786, VSP 4:191–95; Knox to Harmar, 22 Jan. 1787, Harmar 5:9–12.

28. Depositions, 29 Nov. 1786, VSP 4:186–89 ("Beef," "a gun," 188; "Arbitrary power," 187); Levi Todd, letters to Robert Patterson, n.d., Draper 1MM:166–67; acting magistrates of Fayette County to Henry, 7 Dec. 1786, Draper 1MM:171.

29. Finney to Harmar, 31 Oct. 1786, Harmar 4:73 ("turn'd back"); L. C. Helderman, "The Northwest Expedition of George Rogers Clark, 1786–1787," *Mississippi Valley Historical Review* 25, no. 3 (Dec. 1938): 326–31 ("who's for home," 327); L. Todd to Henry, 29 Aug. 1786, VSP 4:166; Caleb Wallace to William Fleming, 23 Oct. 1786, Draper 9J:244; Andrew R. L. Cayton, *Frontier Indiana* (Bloomington: Indiana University Press, 1996), 95–96.

30. Benjamin Logan to Edmund Randolph, 17 Dec. 1786, and resolutions, 13 Sept. 1786, VSP 4:204–5 ("Delinquents," 205); L. Todd to Henry, 29 Aug. 1786, VSP 4:166; Robins to Ferguson, 29 Sept. 1786, enclosed in Ferguson to Harmar, 18 Oct. 1786, Harmar 4:43; anonymous letter to Henry, 7 Dec. 1786, VSP 4:192; Finney to Harmar, 31 Oct. 1786, Harmar 4:73; Lewis Wetsell, information, 14 Nov. 1786, Harmar 4:88; [McKee], report on Logan expedition, n.d., Draper 23U:38; Denny 93–94; William Lytle, narrative, *Historical Collections of Ohio*, ed. Henry Howe (Cincinnati, OH: Derby, Bradley & Co., 1848), 299–301.

31. Harmar to Knox, 14 May 1787, letterbook B, 28:79–82, Harmar ("plundering"); Finney to Harmar, 8 Dec. 1786, Harmar 4:99 ("Partial strokes"); Duncan to Harmar, 17 June 1787, Harmar 6:2 ("Dont mean"); Abraham Coon [Kuhn] and Massayeh Haire to Butler, 28 Oct. 1786, Harmar 4:66 ("keep back"); Butler to Harmar, 13 Feb. 1787, Harmar 5:37; John Finley to Harmar, 16 Apr. 1787, Harmar 5:61; Daniel Brodhead to Daniel Britt & Co., 16 May 1787, Isaac Craig Papers; Innes to Brown, 4 Apr. 1788, box 2, pp. 10–13, Innes Papers, Ayer Manuscripts 439, Newberry Library, Chicago; Wyllys to Harmar, 12 May 1788, Harmar 7:83; *Kentucke Gazette* 1–2 (1787–88), photostat (Ann Arbor: University of Michigan, 1918), 15 Dec. 1787, [2], 9 Feb. 1788, [2], 23 Feb. 1788, [2], 31 May 1788, [2], and 16 Aug. 1788, [2].

32. Logan to Shawnees, [9 Oct. 1786], Draper 23U:38–39 ("proportionable"); "Diary of Major Erkuries Beatty," 437 ("good deal"); general court-martial, 21 Mar. 1787, VSP 4:258–59; Harmar to Knox, 14 May 1787, letterbook B, 28:76–82, Harmar; Logan to Randolph, 17 May and

24 Sept. 1787, VSP 4:286–87, 344; Captain Johnny, speech, 20 Aug. 1787, *Kentucke Gazette*, 1:3, 25 Aug. 1787, [3–4]; [Patterson] to McKee, n.d., Draper 2MM:9; Tanner, "Coocoochee," 27–28.

33. *Journals of the Continental Congress*, 28:487–88, 34:536; Tanner, *Atlas*, 87. For Nonhelema, see Charles A. Hanna, *The Wilderness Trail*, 2 vols. (New York: Knickerbocker, 1911), 2:388; Louise Phelps Kellogg, "Non-hel-e-ma, Shawnee Princess," in *Old Chillicothe: Shawnee and Pioneer History*, ed. William Albert Galloway (Xenia, OH: Buckeye, 1934), 285–88; DHDW 308n25; Henry to William Fleming, 19 Feb. 1778, FDUO 209; Matthew Arbuckle to Fleming, 26 July 1777, FDUO 25–27; William McKee to Edward Hand, 31 Dec. 1777, FDUO 195; William Preston and Fleming to Henry, 14 Mar. 1778, FDUO 225; Preston and Fleming to Shawnees, 3 Apr. 1778, FDUO 261; "Attack on Fort Donnally," FAUO 69; Col. De la Balme to le Chavalier de la Luzerne, in *Kaskaskia Records: 1778–1790*, ed. Clarence Walworth Alvord, Collections of the Illinois State Historical Library, vol. 5 (Springfield: Illinois State Historical Library, 1909), 166; Schoepf, *Travels in the Confederation*, 277; Benjamin Harrison to Clark, 9 Apr. 1783, GRC 19:223; Clark and Butler to the President of Congress, 22 June 1785, and petition of Katharine, alias Grenadier, n.d., Draper 14S:157–60.

34. Heart to Harmar, 2 Feb. 1788, Harmar 7:20 ("strongest Marks"); Heart to Harmar, 12 May and 1 June 1787, Harmar 5:83, 106–8; Heart to Judd, 5 June and 8 July 1787, Judd Papers; Heart, "Part of the State of Pennsylvania," [Spring 1787], Maps 6-C-8, Harmar.

35. North to [Harmar], 29 July 1786, Harmar 3:98; David Luckett to Harmar, 10 July 1785, Harmar 2:97; Huffnagle to Harmar, July 1785, Harmar 2:104; George Brickell, deposition, 13 Sept. 1786, Harmar 4:28–29; Ferguson to Harmar, 16 Sept. 1786, Harmar 4:30; Conference of William Butler and Cornplanter, 10 Sept. 1786, Harmar 4:24; Nichols, *Red Gentlemen*, 129; Taylor, *Divided Ground*, 158–60, 246. For Buffalo Creek, see Alyssa Mt. Pleasant, "After the Whirlwind: Maintaining a Haudenosaunee Place at Buffalo Creek, 1780–1825" (Ph.D. diss., Cornell University, 2007).

36. Heart to Harmar, 26 Aug. 1787, Harmar 6:67 ("Humanity compells"); Heart to Judd, 30 Oct. 1787, Judd Papers ("continually killing"); Harmar to Knox, 15 June 1788, SCP 2:46 ("no officer"); Duncan to Harmar, 11 Sept. 1787, Harmar 6:72; Heart to Harmar, 2 Feb. 1788, Harmar 7:20; John Jeffers to Harmar, 5 Oct. 1789, Harmar 11:50.

37. Heart, letters to Judd, 1786–90, Judd Papers ("proprietor," 4 June 1786; "my Friends," 15 Nov. 1786; "sufficient Influence," 21 July 1787); Heart to Wadsworth, 22 Jan. 1785 [1786], *Life and Letters of Samuel Holden Parsons*, 486–87; Parsons, letters, 1 and 7 Nov. 1789, *Life and Letters of Samuel Holden Parsons*, 567–68. For Heart's cartographic skill, see Heart, "Part of the State of Pennsylvania," and other holdings of the William L. Clements library.

38. Minutes of the Supreme Executive Council, 29–30 Oct. 1790, CRP 16:501–4, 508 ("fine prime goods," 502; "moth eaton," 504); "Treaty with the Six Nations, 1789," Avalon Project at Yale Law School, http://avalon.law.yale.edu/18th_century/six1789.asp (accessed 28 Sept. 2016); agreement between the Six Nations and commissioners for lands on Lake Erie, &c., 9 Jan. 1789, PA 11:529–33; Jeffers to Harmar, 8 Sept. 1790, Harmar 13:85; Brackenridge to Thomas Mifflin, 4 Oct. 1790, PA 11:732–33; Jacob Slough to Butler, 28 June 1791, Richard Butler Papers, Burton Historical Collection, Detroit Public Library; Jeffers to Craig, 30 Dec. 1791, Isaac Craig Papers; Nichols, *Red Gentlemen*, 131–33; Taylor, *Divided Ground*, 246–49.

39. Hutchins to Harmar, 30 Sept. 1786, Harmar 4:45; Hutchins, unaddressed, 10 Jan. 1788, box 3, folder 18, Thomas Hutchins Papers, 1759–1807, Collection 308, HSP; Hutchins, unaddressed, 23 Apr. 1788, box 3, folder 20, Hutchins Papers, HSP; Peter S. Onuf, *Statehood and Union: A History of the Northwest Ordinance* (Bloomington: Indiana University Press, 1987);

Andrew R. L. Cayton, *The Frontier Republic: Ideology and Politics in the Ohio Country, 1780–1825* (Kent, OH: Kent State University Press, 1986); White, *Middle Ground*, 445–48; Nichols, *Red Gentlemen*, 88–92; Patrick Griffin, "Reconsidering the Ideological Origins of Indian Removal: The Case of the Big Bottom 'Massacre,'" in *The Center of a Great Empire: The Ohio Country in the Early Republic*, ed. Andrew R. L. Cayton and Stuart D. Hobbs (Athens: Ohio University Press, 2005), 14–18.

40. Thomas P. Slaughter, *The Whiskey Rebellion: Frontier Epilogue to the American Revolution* (New York: Oxford University Press, 1986); R. Eugene Harper, *The Transformation of Western Pennsylvania, 1770–1800* (Pittsburgh, PA: University of Pittsburgh Press, 1991); Aron, *How the West Was Lost*; Bouton, *Taming Democracy*; Woody Holton, *Unruly Americans and the Origins of the Constitution* (New York: Hill and Wang, 2007); Sachs, *Home Rule*.

41. The best account of the St. Clair campaign is Colin G. Calloway, *The Victory with No Name: The Native American Defeat of the First American Army* (New York: Oxford University Press, 2014). See also Isabel Thompson Kelsay, *Joseph Brant, 1743–1807: Man of Two Worlds* (Syracuse, NY: Syracuse University Press, 1984); White, *Middle Ground*, 454–65; Dowd, *Spirited Resistance*, 99–108; Cayton, *Frontier Indiana*, 146–63; Larry L. Nelson, *A Man of Distinction Among Them: Alexander McKee and the Ohio Country Frontier, 1754–1799* (Kent, OH: Kent State University Press, 1999); John Sugden, *Blue Jacket: Warrior of the Shawnees* (Lincoln: University of Nebraska Press, 2000); Helen Hornbeck Tanner, "The Glaize in 1792: A Composite Indian Community," *Ethnohistory* 25, no. 1 (Winter 1978): 15–39.

42. Jonathan Cass to Craig, 1 Apr. 1792, Isaac Craig Papers; Jeffers to Harmar, 1 May and 1 June 1790, Harmar 12:95, 120; Jeffers to Isaac Craig, 22 Nov. 1791, Isaac Craig Papers; Nichols, *Red Gentlemen*, 141, 166–69; Taylor, *Divided Ground*, 288–93; Michael Leroy Oberg, *Peacemakers: The Iroquois, the United States, and the Treaty of Canandaigua, 1794* (New York: Oxford University Press, 2016).

43. Treaty of Greenville, 3 Aug, 1795, Avalon Project, Yale Law School, http://avalon.law. yale.edu/18th_century/greenvil.asp (accessed 2 Oct. 2016); Dowd, *Spirited Resistance*, 111–15; White, *Middle Ground*, 466–73; Calloway, *Victory with No Name*, 142–52; Andrew R. L. Cayton, "'Noble Actors' Upon 'the Theatre of Honour': Power and Civility at the Treaty of Greenville," in *Contact Points: American Frontiers from the Mohawk Valley to the Mississippi, 1750–1830*, ed. Andrew R. L. Cayton and Fredrika J. Teute (Chapel Hill: University of North Carolina Press, 1998), 235–69.

44. White, *Middle Ground*, 493–502; Joy A. Bilharz, *The Allegany Senecas and Kinzua Dam: Forced Relocation Through Two Generations* (Lincoln: University of Nebraska Press, 1998); Taylor, *Divided Ground*, 313–15; Oberg, *Peacemakers*, 138–43.

45. David Andrew Nichols, *Engines of Diplomacy: Indian Trading Factories and the Negotiation of American Empire* (Chapel Hill: University of North Carolina Press, 2016); Lawrence B. A. Hatter, *Citizens of Convenience: The Imperial Origins of American Nationhood on the U.S.-Canadian Border* (Charlottesville: University of Virginia Press, 2017); Susan Gaunt Stearns, "Streams of Interest: The Mississippi River and the Political Economy of the Early Republic, 1783–1803" (Ph.D. diss., University of Chicago, 2011).

Conclusion

1. John Emerson [Amberson], "Advertisement," 12 Mar. 1785, in *Ohio in the Time of the Confederation*, ed. Archer Butler Hulbert (Marietta, OH: Marietta Historical Commission, 1918), 98–99; Frederick Jackson Turner, "Contributions of the West to American Democracy

(1903)," in *Rereading Frederick Jackson Turner: "The Significance of the Frontier in American History" and Other Essays*, ed. John Mack Faragher (New York: Henry Holt, 1994), 86; Charles Theodore Greve, *Centennial History of Cincinnati and Representative Citizens* (Chicago: Biographical Publishing Company, 1904), 94.

2. John Armstrong to Josiah Harmar, 13 Apr. 1785, Harmar 2:56. In the upper Ohio Valley, secessionist murmurings surfaced periodically but rarely amounted to much: James Patrick McClure, "The Ends of the American Earth: Pittsburgh and the Upper Ohio Valley to 1795" (Ph.D. diss., University of Michigan, 1983), 330, 401–2, 628–29. Such movements were stronger in Kentucky and the abortive state of Franklin, but even there they proved short-lived: Thomas P. Slaughter, *The Whiskey Rebellion: Frontier Epilogue to the American Revolution* (New York: Oxford University Press, 1986), chs. 2–3.

3. Richard White, *The Middle Ground: Indians, Empires, and Republics in the Great Lakes Region, 1650–1815* (New York: Cambridge University Press, 1991), 443–68; Gregory Evans Dowd, *A Spirited Resistance: The North American Indian Struggle for Unity, 1745–1815* (Baltimore: Johns Hopkins University Press, 1992), 99–115.

4. Jonathan Heart to William Judd, 20 June 1790, William Judd Papers, 1786–1797, collection no. 80327, Connecticut Historical Society.

5. Patricia Nelson Limerick, *The Legacy of Conquest: The Unbroken Past of the American West* (New York: W. W. Norton, 1987); Richard White, *"It's Your Misfortune and None of My Own": A History of the American West* (Norman: University of Oklahoma Press, 1991); Jeffrey Ostler, *The Plains Sioux and U.S. Colonialism from Lewis and Clark to Wounded Knee* (Cambridge: Cambridge University Press, 2004); Benjamin Madley, *An American Genocide: The United States and the California Indian Catastrophe, 1846–1873* (New Haven, CT: Yale University Press, 2016).

6. Rosalva Aída Hernández Castillo and Mariana Mora, "Ayotzinapa: ¿Fue el estado? Reflexiones desde la antropología política en Guerrero," *LASA Forum* 46, no. 1 (Winter 2015): 28–34. After months of investigation, an Inter-American Commission on Human Rights panel refuted much of the official story, finding that federal police and military personnel were present during the attack and kidnapping: Interdisciplinary Group of Independent Experts, Ayotzinapa Reports I and II (2015–16), http://prensagieiayotzi.wixsite.com/giei-ayotzinapa/informe- (accessed 2 Oct. 2016).

BIBLIOGRAPHY

Archival and Digital Primary Sources

American Archives: Consisting of a Collection of Authentick Records, State Papers, Debates, and Letters. 4th and 5th ser. Washington, DC, 1837. http://dig.lib.niu.edu/amarch/.

Archives of the Moravian Church. Bethlehem, PA. Microfilm.

Avalon Project at Yale Law School. http://avalon.law.yale.edu.

Burton Historical Collection. Detroit Public Library.

Carnegie Library of Pittsburgh.

Colonial Office. CO5: America and West Indies, Original Correspondence, Etc., 1606–1807. 119 microfilm reels. Public Records of Great Britain, ser. 4. White Plains, NY: Kraus-Thompson, 1987.

Darlington Collection. Special Collections Department, University of Pittsburgh. http://digital .library.pitt.edu/d/darlington/index.html.

George Morgan Papers, 1775–1822. Library of Congress. Microfilm.

George Washington Papers. Library of Congress. https://www.loc.gov/collections/george-wash ington-papers/.

Haldimand, Frederick. Unpublished Papers and Correspondence, 1758–1784. London: World Microfilm, 1977.

Historical Society of Pennsylvania.

Hutchins, Thomas. "A New Map of the Western Parts of Virginia, Pennsylvania, Maryland and North Carolina." London, 1778.

Indiana Historical Society, Indianapolis.

Kentucke Gazette 1–2 (1787–88). University of Michigan, Ann Arbor, 1918. Photostat.

Lyman C. Draper Manuscripts. Wisconsin Historical Society, Madison.

Maryland Journal and Baltimore Advertiser. Newsbank/Readex, America's Historical Newspapers. http://www.readex.com/content/americas-historical-newspapers.

Papers relating to Indians, 1750–1775. George Chalmers Papers, 1606–1812. New York Public Library. Microfilm.

Pennsylvania Journal (1772). Newsbank/Readex, America's Historical Newspapers. http://www .readex.com/content/americas-historical-newspapers.

Pennsylvania Packet 865, 872 (1782). Microfilm.

Records of Pennsylvania's Revolutionary Governments, 1775–90. RG 27. Pennsylvania State Archives, Harrisburg. Microfilm.

Records of the Land Office. Pennsylvania State Archives.

The Remembrancer; or, Impartial Repository of Public Events 7 (1778–79).

Thomas Jefferson Papers. Library of Congress. https://www.loc.gov/collections/thomas-jefferson
-papers/.
Virginia Colonial Government Records. Library of Virginia. Miscellaneous reel 78,
microfilm.
Virginia Gazette (Dixon and Hunter; Purdie and Dixon; Rind). 1772–76. Newsbank/Readex, Amer-
ica's Historical Newspapers. http://www.readex.com/content/americas-historical-newspapers.
William Judd Papers, 1786–1797. Collection no. 80327. Connecticut Historical Society.
William L. Clements Library, University of Michigan, Ann Arbor.

Primary Sources in Print

Beatty, Charles. *The Journal of a Two Months Tour . . . to the Westward of the Alegh-Geny Mountains.* London: William Davenhill and George Pearch, 1768.
Beatty, Erkuries. "Diary of Major Erkuries Beatty: Paymaster of the Western Army, May 15, 1786,
to June 5, 1787." *Magazine of American History with Notes and Queries* 1, no. 1, 2 (1877): 175–
79, 235–43, 309–15, 380–84, 432–38.
Bliss, Eugene F., ed. and trans. *Diary of David Zeisberger a Moravian Missionary Among the In-
dians of Ohio.* 2 vols. 1885; St. Clair Shores, MI: Scholarly Press, 1972.
Burton, Clarence M., ed. "Ephraim Douglass and His Times, Including the Journal of George
McCully and Various Letters of the Period." *Magazine of History, with Notes and Queries,*
extra no. 10 (1910).
Butterfield, C. W., ed. *Washington-Irvine Correspondence.* Madison, WI: David Atwood, 1882.
Collections of the Illinois State Historical Library. 20 vols. Springfield: Illinois State Historical
Library, 1903–24.
Colonial Records of Pennsylvania. 16 vols. Harrisburg, PA: Theo. Fenn & Co., 1838–53.
Connolly, John. "A Narrative of the Transactions, Imprisonment, and Sufferings of John Con-
nolly, an American Loyalist." *Pennsylvania Magazine of History and Biography* 12, no. 3, 4
(1888): 310–24, 407–20.
"Correspondence of the Revolution." *Historical Register: Notes and Queries, Historical and Gene-
alogical, Relating to Interior Pennsylvania* 2, no. 1 (1884): 58–66.
Craig, Neville B., ed. *The Olden Time* 1 and 2. 1846–47.
Crumrine, Boyd, ed. *Virginia Court Records in Southwestern Pennsylvania: Records of the District of West Augusta and Ohio and Yohogania Counties, Virginia, 1775–1780.* Baltimore: Ge-
nealogical Publishing Company, 1974.
Dann, John C., ed. *The Revolution Remembered: Eyewitness Accounts of the War for Indepen-
dence.* Chicago: University of Chicago Press, 1999.
Denny, Ebenezer. *Military Journal of Major Ebenezer Denny, an Officer in the Revolutionary and In-
dian Wars.* Edited by William H. Denny. Philadelphia: Historical Society of Pennsylvania, 1859.
Doddridge, Joseph. *Notes on the Settlement and Indian Wars of the Western Parts of Virginia and
Pennsylvania, from 1763 to 1783, Inclusive.* Edited by J. S. Ritenour and W. T. Lindsey. 1912;
Parsons, WV: McClain, 1960.
Evans, Griffith. "Journal of Griffith Evans, 1784–1785." Edited by Hallock F. Raup. *Pennsylvania
Magazine of History and Biography* 65, no. 2 (Apr. 1941): 202–33.
Ford, Worthington C., ed. *Journals of the Continental Congress, 1774–1789.* Washington, DC:
U.S. Government Printing Office, 1904–37.
Gill, Harold B., Jr., and George M. Curtis III, eds. *A Man Apart: The Journal of Nicholas Cress-
well, 1774–1781.* Lanham, MD: Lexington, 2009.

Hall, Charles S., ed. *Life and Letters of Samuel Holden Parsons*. Binghamton, NY: Otsiningo Publishing Company, 1905.

Hanna, Charles A. *The Wilderness Trail*. 2 vols. New York: Knickerbocker, 1911.

Hazard, Samuel, ed. *Pennsylvania Archives*. 12 vols. Philadelphia: Joseph Severns & Co., 1852–56.

Heckewelder, John. *Narrative of the Mission of the United Brethren Among the Delaware and Mohegan Indians*. 1820; New York: Arno, 1971.

Henry, William Wirt, ed. *Patrick Henry: Life, Correspondence and Speeches*. 3 vols. New York: Charles Scribner's Sons, 1891.

Historical Collections: Collections and Researches Made by the Michigan Pioneer and Historical Society. 40 vols. Lansing, MI: Wynkoop, Hallenbeck, & Crawford Co., 1874–1929.

History of the Dividing Line and Other Tracts. 2 vols. Richmond, VA, 1866.

Howe, Henry, ed. *Historical Collections of Ohio*. Cincinnati, OH: Derby, Bradley & Co., 1848.

Hulbert, Archer Butler, ed. *Ohio in the Time of the Confederation*. Marietta, OH: Marietta Historical Commission, 1918.

Jackson, Donald, and Dorothy Twohig, eds. *The Diaries of George Washington*. 6 vols. Charlottesville: University Press of Virginia, 1976–79.

Jefferson, Thomas. *Jefferson's Notes, on the State of Virginia; with the Appendixes—Complete*. Appendix 4, 29–53. Baltimore: W. Pechin, 1800. Eighteenth Century Collections Online, Gale Group. http://galenet.galegroup.com/servlet/ECCO.

Jones, David. *A Journal of Two Visits Made to Some Nations of Indians on the West Side of the River Ohio in the Years 1772 and 1773*. 1774; New York: Arno, 1971.

Jordan, John W., ed. "James Kenny's 'Journal to Ye Westward,' 1758–59." *Pennsylvania Magazine of History and Biography* 37, no. 4 (1913): 395–449.

———, ed. "Journal of James Kenny, 1761–63." *Pennsylvania Magazine of History and Biography* 37, no. 1–2 (1913): 1–47, 152–201.

Kellogg, Louise Phelps, ed. *Frontier Advance on the Upper Ohio, 1778–1779*. Publications of the State Historical Society of Wisconsin, vol. 23. Madison: State Historical Society of Wisconsin, 1916.

———, ed. *Frontier Retreat on the Upper Ohio*. Publications of the State Historical Society of Wisconsin, vol. 24. Madison: State Historical Society of Wisconsin, 1917.

Kennedy, John Pendleton, ed. *Journals of the House of Burgesses of Virginia, 1773–1776*. Richmond: Virginia State Library, 1905.

Lacey, John. "Journal of a Mission to the Indians in Ohio, July–September, 1773." *Historical Magazine, and Notes and Queries Concerning the Antiquities, History, and Biography of America*, 2nd ser., 7, no. 2 (1870): 103–10.

"Letters of Colonel George Croghan." *Pennsylvania Magazine of History and Biography* 15, no. 4 (1891): 429–39.

McClure, David. *Diary of David McClure, Doctor of Divinity, 1748–1820*. Edited by Franklin B. Dexter. New York: Knickerbocker, 1899.

McCready, Robert. "A Revolutionary Journal and Orderly Book of General Lachlan McIntosh's Expedition, 1778." *Western Pennsylvania Historical Magazine* 1, no. 1–3 (Mar.–Sept. 1960): 1–17, 157–77, 267–88.

Mereness, Newton D., ed. *Travels in the American Colonies*. New York: Macmillan, 1916.

Minutes of Conferences, Held at Fort Pitt, in April and May, 1768. Philadelphia: William Goddard, 1769.

Montgomery, Samuel. "Journal of Samuel Montgomery." Edited by David I. Bushnell. *Mississippi Valley Historical Review* 2, no. 2 (Sept. 1915): 262–73.

Moore, John H., ed. "A Captive of the Shawnees, 1779–1784." *West Virginia History* 23, no. 4 (July 1962): 287–96.

Mulkearn, Lois, ed. *George Mercer Papers: Relating to the Ohio Company of Virginia.* Pittsburgh, PA: University of Pittsburgh Press, 1954.

Nash, Linda Clark, ed. *The Journals of Pierre-Louis Lorimier, 1777–1795.* Montreal: Baraka, 2012.

"Notes and Queries." *Pennsylvania Magazine of History and Biography* 4, no. 2 (1880): 247–60.

"Notes and Queries." *Pennsylvania Magazine of History and Biography* 29, no. 3 (1905): 359–80.

Nourse, James. "Journey to Kentucky in 1775." *Journal of American History* 19, no. 2–4 (1925): 121–39, 251–60, 351–64.

O'Callaghan, E. B., ed. *The Documentary History of the State of New York.* 4 vols. Albany, NY: Weed, Parsons, & Co., 1850–51.

———, ed. *Documents Relative to the Colonial History of the State of New-York.* 15 vols. Albany, NY: Weed, Parsons, & Co., 1853–58.

Palmer, William P., ed. *Calendar of Virginia State Papers and Other Manuscripts.* 11 vols. Richmond, VA: R. U. Derr, 1875–93.

The Papers of Sir William Johnson. 12 vols. Albany: State University of New York, 1921–63.

Parrish, John. "Extracts from the Journal of John Parrish, 1773." *Pennsylvania Magazine of History and Biography* 16, no. 4 (1893): 443–48.

Pickering, Octavius, ed. *The Life of Timothy Pickering.* Boston: Little, Brown, 1867.

Ranck, George W., ed. *Boonesborough: Its Founding, Pioneer Struggles, Indian Experiences, Transylvania Days, and Revolutionary Annals.* Filson Club Publications No. 16. Louisville, KY: Filson Club, 1901.

Reese, George, ed. *The Official Papers of Francis Fauquier, Lieutenant Governor of Virginia, 1758–1768.* 3 vols. Charlottesville: University Press of Virginia, 1981–83.

Rose, John. "Journal of a Volunteer Expedition to Sandusky, from May 24 to June 13, 1782." *Pennsylvania Magazine of History and Biography* 18 (1894): 129–57, 293–328.

Saunders, William L., ed. *Colonial and State Records of North Carolina.* Raleigh, NC: P. M. Hale, 1886–1907. Documenting the American South. http://docsouth.unc.edu/csr/index.html.

Schoepf, Johann David. *Travels in the Confederation, 1783–1784.* Translated by Alfred J. Morrison. Philadelphia: W. J. Campbell, 1911.

Smith, Gerald H., ed. *Bedford County, Pennsylvania: Quarter Sessions, 1771–1801.* Westminster, MD: Heritage, 2010.

Smith, James. *An Account of the Remarkable Occurrences in the Life and Travels of Col. James Smith.* Lexington, KY: John Bradford, 1799.

Smith, William Henry, ed. *The St. Clair Papers: The Life and Public Services of Arthur St. Clair.* 2 vols. Cincinnati, OH: Robert Clarke & Co., 1882.

Stevens, Sylvester K., and Donald H. Kent, eds. *The Papers of Col. Henry Bouquet.* Northwestern Pennsylvania Historical Series. Harrisburg: Pennsylvania Historical Commission, 1940–43.

Stuart, John. "Narrative by Captain John Stuart of General Andrew Lewis' Expedition." *Magazine of American History with Notes and Queries* 1, no. 11, 12 (1877): 668–79, 740–50.

Thwaites, Reuben Gold, and Louise Phelps Kellogg, eds. *Documentary History of Dunmore's War, 1774*. Madison: Wisconsin Historical Society, 1905.

——, eds. *Frontier Defense on the Upper Ohio, 1777–1778*. 1912; Millwood, NY: Kraus Reprint, 1973.

——, eds. *The Revolution on the Upper Ohio, 1775–1777*. Madison: Wisconsin Historical Society, 1908.

"Treaty Between Virginia and the Indians at Fort Dunmore (Pittsburg) June, 1775." *Virginia Magazine of History and Biography* 14, no. 1 (July 1906): 54–79.

Van Schreeven, William J., Robert L. Scribner, and Brent Tarter, eds. *Revolutionary Virginia: The Road to Independence*. 7 vols. Charlottesville: University Press of Virginia, 1973–83.

Wainwright, Nicholas B., ed. "George Croghan's Journal: April 3, 1759 to April [30], 1763." *Pennsylvania Magazine of History and Biography* 71, no. 4 (Oct. 1947): 313–444.

——, ed. "Turmoil at Pittsburgh: Diary of Augustine Prevost, 1774." *Pennsylvania Magazine of History and Biography* 85, no. 2 (1961): 111–62.

Wellenreuther, Hermann, and Carola Wessel, eds. *The Moravian Mission Diaries of David Zeisberger, 1772–1781*. Translated by Julie Tomberlin Weber. University Park: Pennsylvania State University Press, 2005.

Withers, Alexander Scott. *Chronicles of Border Warfare*. Annotated ed. Edited by Reuben Gold Thwaites. 1895; Parsons, WV: McClain, 1975.

Woods, Neander M., ed. *The Woods-McAfee Memorial*. Louisville, KY: Courier-Journal, 1905.

Secondary Sources

Abernethy, Thomas Perkins. *Western Lands and the American Revolution*. New York: Russell and Russell, 1959.

Abler, Thomas S. *Cornplanter: Chief Warrior of the Allegany Senecas*. Syracuse, NY: Syracuse University Press, 2007.

——. "Kayahsota." In *Dictionary of Canadian Biography*, vol. 4. University of Toronto/Université Laval, 2003. http://www.biographi.ca/en/bio/kayahsota_4E.html.

Abrams, Marc D., and Gregory J. Nowacki. "Native Americans as Active and Passive Promoters of Mast and Fruit Trees in the Eastern USA." *Holocene* 18, no. 7 (2008): 1123–37.

Adelman, Jeremy, and Stephen Aron. "From Borderlands to Borders: Empires, Nation-States, and the Peoples in Between in North American History." *American Historical Review* 104, no. 3 (1999): 814–41.

Alexander, Arthur J. "Pennsylvania's Revolutionary Militia." *Pennsylvania Magazine of History and Biography* 69, no. 1 (1945): 15–25.

Allen, Robert S. *His Majesty's Indian Allies: British Indian Policy in the Defence of Canada, 1774–1815*. Toronto: Dundurn, 1992.

Anderson, Fred. *The Crucible of War: The Seven Years' War and the Fate of Empire in British North America, 1754–1766*. New York: Alfred A. Knopf, 2000.

Aron, Stephen. *How the West Was Lost: The Transformation of Kentucky from Daniel Boone to Henry Clay*. Baltimore: Johns Hopkins University Press, 1996.

Barr, Daniel P. "Contested Land: Competition and Conflict Along the Upper Ohio Frontier, 1744–1784." Ph.D. diss., Kent State University, 2001.

Barr, Juliana. "Geographies of Power: Mapping Indian Borders in the 'Borderlands' of the Early Southwest." *William and Mary Quarterly* 68, no. 1 (Jan. 2011): 5–46.

Beauchamp, W. M. "Shikellimy and His Son Logan." In *Twenty-First Annual Report of the American Scenic and Historic Preservation Society*, 599–611. New York, 1916.

Beeman, Richard R. "Deference, Republicanism, and the Emergence of Popular Politics in Eighteenth-Century America." *William and Mary Quarterly* 49, no. 3 (1992): 401–30.

Belich, James. *Replenishing the Earth: The Settler Revolution and the Rise of the Angloworld, 1783–1939*. New York: Oxford University Press, 2009.

Benton, Lauren. "Colonial Law and Cultural Difference: Jurisdictional Politics and the Formation of the Colonial State." *Comparative Studies in Society and History* 41, no. 3 (July 1999): 563–88.

———. *Law and Colonial Cultures: Legal Regimes in World History, 1400–1900*. Cambridge: Cambridge University Press, 2001.

Bilharz, Joy A. *The Allegany Senecas and Kinzua Dam: Forced Relocation Through Two Generations*. Lincoln: University of Nebraska Press, 1998.

Blackhawk, Ned. "The Displacement of Violence: Ute Diplomacy and the Making of New Mexico's Eighteenth-Century Northern Borderlands." *Ethnohistory* 54, no. 4 (2007): 723–55.

Block, Sharon. *Rape and Sexual Power in Early America*. Chapel Hill: University of North Carolina Press, 2006.

Blockmans, Wim, André Holenstein, and Jon Mathieu, eds. *Empowering Interactions: Political Cultures and the Emergence of the State in Europe 1300–1900*. Farnham, UK: Ashgate, 2009.

Bohaker, Heidi. "*Nindoodemag*: The Significance of Algonquian Kinship Networks in the Eastern Great Lakes Region, 1600–1701." *William and Mary Quarterly* 63, no. 1 (Jan. 2006): 23–52.

Boissevain, Jeremy. *Friends of Friends: Networks, Manipulators and Coalitions*. Oxford: Basil Blackwell, 1974.

Bothwell, Margaret Pearson. "Devereux Smith, Fearless Pioneer." *Western Pennsylvania Historical Magazine* 40, no. 4 (Winter 1957): 277–91.

———. "Edward Ward: Trail Blazing Pioneer." *Western Pennsylvania Historical Magazine* 43, no. 2 (1960): 99–127.

———. "Killbuck and Killbuck Island." *Western Pennsylvania Historical Magazine* 44, no. 4 (Dec. 1961): 343–60.

Boulware, Tyler. *Deconstructing the Cherokee Nation: Town, Region, and Nation Among Eighteenth-Century Cherokees*. Gainesville: University Press of Florida, 2011.

Bouton, Terry. "A Road Closed: Rural Insurgency in Post-Independence Pennsylvania." *Journal of American History* 87, no. 3 (2000): 855–87.

———. *Taming Democracy: "The People," the Founders, and the Troubled Ending of the American Revolution*. New York: Oxford University Press, 2007.

Braddick, Michael J. *State Formation in Early Modern England c. 1550–1700*. Cambridge: Cambridge University Press, 2000.

Browning, Christopher R. *Ordinary Men: Reserve Police Battalion 101 and the Final Solution in Poland*. 2nd ed. New York: HarperCollins, 1998.

Brubaker, Rogers, and Frederick Cooper. "Beyond 'Identity.'" *Theory and Society* 29, no. 1 (2000): 1–47.

Caley, Percy B. "The Life Adventures of Lieutenant-Colonel John Connolly: The Story of a Tory." *Western Pennsylvania Historical Magazine* 11 (1928): 10–49, 76–111, 144–79, 225–59.

Calloway, Colin G. *The American Revolution in Indian Country: Crisis and Diversity in Native American Communities*. Cambridge: Cambridge University Press, 1995.

——. *The Shawnees and the War for America*. New York: Penguin, 2007.

——. *The Victory with No Name: The Native American Defeat of the First American Army*. New York: Oxford University Press, 2014.

Campbell, William J. *Speculators in Empire: Iroquoia and the 1768 Treaty of Fort Stanwix*. Norman: University of Oklahoma Press, 2012.

Carp, E. Wayne. *To Starve the Army at Pleasure: Continental Army Administration and American Political Culture, 1775–1783*. Chapel Hill: University of North Carolina Press, 1984.

Cayton, Andrew R. L. *Frontier Indiana*. Bloomington: Indiana University Press, 1996.

——. *The Frontier Republic: Ideology and Politics in the Ohio Country, 1780–1825*. Kent, OH: Kent State University Press, 1986.

——. "'Noble Actors' Upon 'the Theatre of Honour': Power and Civility at the Treaty of Greenville." In *Contact Points: American Frontiers from the Mohawk Valley to the Mississippi, 1750–1830*, edited by Andrew R. L. Cayton and Fredrika J. Teute, 235–69. Chapel Hill: University of North Carolina Press, 1998.

Converse, Harriet Maxwell. *Myths and Legends of the New York State Iroquois*. Museum Bulletin no. 125. Edited by Arthur Caswell Parker. Albany: University of the State of New York, 1908.

Crabb, Anne. "'What Shall I Do Now?': The Story of the Indian Captivities of Margaret Paulee, Jones Hoy, and Jack Callaway, 1779–ca. 1789." *Filson Club History Quarterly* 70, no. 4 (Oct. 1996): 363–404.

Cronon, William, George A. Miles, and Jay Gitlin, eds. *Under an Open Sky: Rethinking America's Western Past*. New York: W. W. Norton, 1992.

David, James Corbett. *Dunmore's New World: The Extraordinary Life of a Royal Governor in Revolutionary America*. Charlottesville: University of Virginia Press, 2013.

De Schweinitz, Edmund. *The Life and Times of David Zeisberger: The Western Pioneer and Apostle of the Indians*. Philadelphia: Lippincott, 1871.

Dowd, Gregory Evans. *A Spirited Resistance: The North American Indian Struggle for Unity, 1745–1815*. Baltimore: Johns Hopkins University Press, 1992.

——. *War Under Heaven: Pontiac, the Indian Nations and the British Empire*. Baltimore: Johns Hopkins University Press, 2002.

Downes, Randolph C. *Council Fires on the Upper Ohio: A Narrative of Indian Affairs in the Upper Ohio Valley Until 1795*. Pittsburgh, PA: University of Pittsburgh Press, 1940.

——. "George Morgan, Indian Agent Extraordinary, 1776–1779." *Pennsylvania History* 1, no. 4 (Oct. 1934): 202–16.

Drinnon, Richard. *Facing West: The Metaphysics of Indian-Hating and Empire-Building*. Minneapolis: University of Minnesota Press, 1980.

DuPlessis, Robert S. *The Material Atlantic: Clothing, Commerce, and Colonization in the Atlantic World, 1650–1800*. New York: Cambridge University Press, 2015.

DuVal, Kathleen. *Independence Lost: Lives on the Edge of the American Revolution*. New York: Random House, 2015.

——. *The Native Ground: Indians and Colonists in the Heart of the Continent*. Philadelphia: University of Pennsylvania Press, 2007.

Edmunds, David. "'This Much Admired Man': Isaac Glikhikan, Moravian Delaware." In *Ethnographies and Exchanges: Native Americans, Moravians, and Catholics in Early North America*, edited by A. G. Roeber, 1–16. University Park: Penn State University Press, 2008.

Elbourne, Elizabeth. "The Sin of the Settler: The 1835–36 Select Committee on Aborigines and

Debates over Virtue and Conquest in the Early Nineteenth-Century British White Settler Empire." *Journal of Colonialism and Colonial History* 4, no. 3 (2003): 1–49.

Faragher, John Mack. *Daniel Boone: The Life and Legend of an American Pioneer*. New York: Holt, 1992.

Farrar, William M. "The Moravian Massacre." *Ohio Archaeological and Historical Publications* 3 (1891): 276–300.

Fearon, James D., and David D. Laitin. "Explaining Interethnic Cooperation." *American Political Science Review* 90 (1996): 715–35.

Fenn, Elizabeth A. *Pox Americana: The Great Smallpox Epidemic of 1775–82*. New York: Hill and Wang, 2001.

Ferguson, R. Brian, and Neil L. Whitehead, eds. *War in the Tribal Zone: Expanding States and Indigenous Warfare*. Santa Fe, NM: School of American Research Press, 2000. ACLS Humanities E-Book. http://hdl.handle.net/2027/heb.03246.

Fischer, Joseph R. *A Well-Executed Failure: The Sullivan Campaign Against the Iroquois, July–September 1779*. Columbia: University of South Carolina Press, 1997.

Ford, Lisa. *Settler Sovereignty: Jurisdiction and Indigenous People in America and Australia, 1788–1836*. Cambridge, MA: Harvard University Press, 2011.

Fox, Francis S. "Pennsylvania's Revolutionary Militia Law: The Statute That Transformed the State." *Pennsylvania History* 80, no. 2 (Spring 2013): 204–14.

———. "The Prothonotary: Linchpin of Provincial and State Government in Eighteenth-Century Pennsylvania." *Pennsylvania History* 59, no. 1 (Jan. 1992): 41–53.

Fur, Gunlög. *A Nation of Women: Gender and Colonial Encounters Among the Delaware Indians*. Philadelphia: University of Pennsylvania Press, 2009.

Gerlach, Christian. "Extremely Violent Societies: An Alternative to the Concept of Genocide." *Journal of Genocide Research* 8, no. 4 (2006): 455–71.

Gorn, Elliott J. " 'Gouge and Bite, Pull Hair and Scratch': The Social Significance of Fighting in the Southern Backcountry." *American Historical Review* 90, no. 1 (Feb. 1985): 18–43.

Gould, Eliga H. *Among the Powers of the Earth: The American Revolution and the Making of a New World Empire*. Cambridge, MA: Harvard University Press, 2012.

Gould, Roger V. "Patron-Client Ties, State Centralization, and the Whiskey Rebellion." *American Journal of Sociology* 102, no. 2 (Sept. 1996): 400–429.

———. "Political Networks and the Local/National Boundary in the Whiskey Rebellion." In *Challenging Authority: The Historical Study of Contentious Politics*, edited by Michael P. Hanagan, Leslie Page Moch, and Wayne T. Brake, 36–53. Minneapolis: University of Minnesota Press, 1998.

Greene, Jack P. "Colonial History and National History: Reflections on a Continuing Problem." *William and Mary Quarterly* 64, no. 2 (2007): 235––50.

Greve, Charles Theodore. *Centennial History of Cincinnati and Representative Citizens*. Chicago: Biographical Publishing Company, 1904.

Griffin, Patrick. *American Leviathan: Empire, Nation, and Revolutionary Frontier*. New York: Hill and Wang, 2007.

———. "Reconsidering the Ideological Origins of Indian Removal: The Case of the Big Bottom 'Massacre.'" In *The Center of a Great Empire: The Ohio Country in the Early Republic*, edited by Andrew R. L. Cayton and Stuart D. Hobbs, 11–35. Athens: Ohio University Press, 2005.

Gross, Robert A. *The Minutemen and Their World*. 1976; New York: Hill and Wang, 2001.

Grumet, Robert S. *The Munsee Indians: A History*. Norman: University of Oklahoma Press, 2009.

Hallenberg, Mats, Johan Holm, and Dan Johansson. "Organization, Legitimation, Participation: State Formation as a Dynamic Process—the Swedish Example, c. 1523–1680." *Scandinavian Journal of History* 33, no. 3 (Sept. 2008): 247–68.

Harper, John Robinson (Rob). "Revolution and Conquest: Politics, Violence, and Social Change in the Ohio Valley, 1765–1795." Ph.D. diss., University of Wisconsin–Madison, 2008.

Harper, R. Eugene. *The Transformation of Western Pennsylvania, 1770–1800*. Pittsburgh, PA: University of Pittsburgh Press, 1991.

Harper, Rob. "Looking the Other Way: The Gnadenhutten Massacre and the Contextual Interpretation of Violence." *William and Mary Quarterly* 64, no. 3 (2007): 621–44.

Hatter, Lawrence B. A. *Citizens of Convenience: The Imperial Origins of American Nationhood on the U.S.-Canadian Border*. Charlottesville: University of Virginia Press, 2017.

Helderman, L. C. "The Northwest Expedition of George Rogers Clark, 1786–1787." *Mississippi Valley Historical Review* 25, no. 3 (Dec. 1938): 317–34.

Hernández Castillo, Rosalva Aída, and Mariana Mora. "Ayotzinapa: ¿Fue el estado? Reflexiones desde la antropología política en guerrero." *LASA Forum* 46, no. 1 (Winter 2015): 28–34.

Hinderaker, Eric. *Elusive Empires: Constructing Colonialism in the Ohio Valley, 1673–1800*. New York: Cambridge University Press, 1997.

Hindle, Steve. *The State and Social Change in Early Modern England, c. 1550–1640*. Basingstoke, UK: Palgrave, 2000.

Hixson, Walter L. *American Settler Colonialism: A History*. New York: Palgrave Macmillan, 2013.

Hofstra, Warren R. *The Planting of New Virginia: Settlement and Landscape in the Shenandoah Valley*. Baltimore: Johns Hopkins University Press, 2005.

Hofstra, Warren R., and Robert D. Mitchell. "Town and Country in Backcountry Virginia: Winchester and the Shenandoah Valley, 1730–1800." *Journal of Southern History* 59, no. 4 (1993): 619–46.

Hogue, Michel. *Metis and the Medicine Line: Creating a Border and Dividing a People*. Chapel Hill: University of North Carolina Press, 2015.

Holton, Woody. *Forced Founders: Indians, Debtors, Slaves, and the Making of the American Revolution in Virginia*. Chapel Hill: University of North Carolina Press, 1999.

———. *Unruly Americans and the Origins of the Constitution*. New York: Hill and Wang, 2007.

Hulsebosch, Daniel J. *Constituting Empire: New York and the Transformation of Constitutionalism in the Atlantic World, 1664–1830*. Chapel Hill: University of North Carolina Press, 2005.

Interdisciplinary Group of Independent Experts. Ayotzinapa Reports I and II, 2015–16. http://prensagieiayotzi.wixsite.com/giei-ayotzinapa/informe-.

James, Alfred Proctor. *The Ohio Company: Its Inner History*. Pittsburgh, PA: University of Pittsburgh Press, 1959.

Johnson, Thomas H. "The Indian Village of 'Cush-Og-Wenk.'" *Ohio Archaeological and Historical Publications* 21 (1912): 432–35.

Joseph, G. M., and Daniel Nugent, eds. *Everyday Forms of State Formation: Revolution and the Negotiation of Rule in Modern Mexico*. Durham, NC: Duke University Press, 1994.

Karsten, Peter. *Between Law and Custom: "High" and "Low" Legal Cultures in the Lands of the British Diaspora—the United States, Canada, Australia, and New Zealand, 1600–1900*. Cambridge: Cambridge University Press, 2002.

Kellogg, Louise Phelps. "Non-hel-e-ma, Shawnee Princess." In *Old Chillicothe: Shawnee and Pioneer History*, edited by William Albert Galloway, 283–95. Xenia, OH: Buckeye, 1934.

Kelsay, Isabel Thompson. *Joseph Brant, 1743–1807: Man of Two Worlds*. Syracuse, NY: Syracuse University Press, 1984.

Kidwell, Clara Sue. "Indian Women as Cultural Mediators." *Ethnohistory* 39, no. 2 (1992): 97–107.

Kimmerer, R. W., and F. K. Lake. "The Role of Indigenous Burning in Land Management." *Journal of Forestry* 99, no. 11 (1 Nov. 2001): 36–41.

Lakomäki, Sami. *Gathering Together: The Shawnee People Through Diaspora and Nationhood, 1600–1870*. New Haven, CT: Yale University Press, 2014.

Lee, Wayne E. *Crowds and Soldiers in Revolutionary North Carolina: The Culture of Violence in Riot and War*. Gainesville: University Press of Florida, 2001.

Lester, Alan. *Imperial Networks: Creating Identities in Nineteenth Century South Africa and Britain*. New York: Routledge, 2001.

Limerick, Patricia Nelson. *The Legacy of Conquest: The Unbroken Past of the American West*. New York: W. W. Norton, 1987.

Loveman, Mara. "The Modern State and the Primitive Accumulation of Symbolic Power." *American Journal of Sociology* 110, no. 6 (May 2005): 1651–83.

MacLeitch, Gail D. *Imperial Entanglements: Iroquois Change and Persistence on the Frontiers of Empire*. Philadelphia: University of Pennsylvania Press, 2011.

Madley, Benjamin. *An American Genocide: The United States and the California Indian Catastrophe, 1846–1873*. New Haven, CT: Yale University Press, 2016.

Mallon, Florencia E. *Peasant and Nation: The Making of Postcolonial Mexico and Peru*. Berkeley: University of California Press, 1994.

Mancall, Peter C. *Deadly Medicine: Indians and Alcohol in Early America*. Ithaca, NY: Cornell University Press, 1995.

———. *Valley of Opportunity: Economic Culture Along the Upper Susquehanna, 1700–1800*. Ithaca, NY: Cornell University Press, 1991.

Marrero, Karen. "On the Edge of the West: The Roots and Routes of Detroit's Urban Eighteenth Century." In *Frontier Cities: Encounters at the Crossroads of Empire*, edited by Jay Gitlin, Barbara Berglund, and Adam Arenson, 67–86. Philadelphia: University of Pennsylvania Press, 2012.

McClure, James Patrick. "The Ends of the American Earth: Pittsburgh and the Upper Ohio Valley to 1795." Ph.D. diss., University of Michigan, 1983.

McConnell, Michael N. *A Country Between: The Upper Ohio Valley and Its Peoples, 1724–1774*. Lincoln: University of Nebraska Press, 1992.

McDonnell, Michael A. *The Politics of War: Race, Class, and Conflict in Revolutionary Virginia*. Chapel Hill: University of North Carolina Press, 2007.

McDonnell, Michael A. *Masters of Empire: Great Lakes Indians and the Making of America*. New York: Hill and Wang, 2015.

McElwain, Thomas. "'Then I Thought I Must Kill Too': Logan's Lament: A 'Mingo' Perspective." In *Native American Speakers of the Eastern Woodlands: Selected Speeches and Critical Analyses*, edited by Barbara Alice Mann, 107–21. Westport, CT: Greenwood, 2001.

Merrell, James H. *Into the American Woods: Negotiators on the Pennsylvania Frontier*. New York: W. W. Norton, 1999.

———. "Second Thoughts on Colonial Historians and American Indians." *William and Mary Quarterly* 69, no. 3 (July 2012): 451–512.

Merritt, Jane T. *At the Crossroads: Indians and Empires on a Mid-Atlantic Frontier, 1700–1763.* Chapel Hill: University of North Carolina Press, 2003.

Miller, Cary. *Ogimaag: Anishinaabeg Leadership, 1760–1845.* Lincoln: University of Nebraska Press, 2010.

Montoya, María E. *Translating Property: The Maxwell Land Grant and the Conflict over Land in the American West, 1840–1900.* Berkeley: University of California Press, 2002.

Morrissey, Robert Michael. *Empire by Collaboration: Indians, Colonists, and Governments in Colonial Illinois Country.* Philadelphia: University of Pennsylvania Press, 2015.

Moses, A. Dirk, ed. *Genocide and Settler Society: Frontier Violence and Stolen Indigenous Children in Australian History.* New York: Berghahn, 2004.

Moyer, Paul B. *Wild Yankees: The Struggle for Independence Along Pennsylvania's Revolutionary Frontier.* Ithaca, NY: Cornell University Press, 2007.

Mt. Pleasant, Alyssa. "After the Whirlwind: Maintaining a Haudenosaunee Place at Buffalo Creek, 1780–1825." Ph.D. diss., Cornell University, 2007.

———. "Independence for Whom?: Expansion and Conflict in the Northeast and Northwest." In *The World of the Revolutionary American Republic: Land, Labor, and the Conflict for a Continent,* edited by Andrew Shankman, 116–33. New York: Routledge, 2014.

Munger, Donna B. *Pennsylvania Land Records: A History and Guide for Research.* Wilmington, DE: Scholarly Resources, 1991.

Murphy, Lucy Eldersveld. *A Gathering of Rivers: Indians, Métis, and Mining in the Western Great Lakes, 1737–1832.* Lincoln: University of Nebraska Press, 2000.

———. "To Live Among Us: Accommodation, Gender, and Conflict in the Western Great Lakes Region, 1760–1832." In *Contact Points: American Frontiers from the Mohawk Valley to the Mississippi, 1750–1830,* edited by Andrew R. L. Cayton and Fredrika J. Teute, 270–303. Chapel Hill: University of North Carolina Press, 1998.

Nelson, Larry L. *A Man of Distinction Among Them: Alexander McKee and the Ohio Country Frontier, 1754–1799.* Kent, OH: Kent State University Press, 1999.

Nichols, David Andrew. *Engines of Diplomacy: Indian Trading Factories and the Negotiation of American Empire.* Chapel Hill: University of North Carolina Press, 2016.

———. *Red Gentlemen and White Savages: Indians, Federalists, and the Search for Order on the American Frontier.* Charlottesville: University of Virginia Press, 2008.

Novak, William J. "The Myth of the 'Weak' American State." *American Historical Review* 113, no. 3 (June 2008): 752–72.

Oberg, Michael Leroy. *Peacemakers: The Iroquois, the United States, and the Treaty of Canandaigua, 1794.* New York: Oxford University Press, 2016.

Olmstead, Earl P. *David Zeisberger: A Life Among the Indians.* Kent, OH: Kent State University Press, 1997.

Onuf, Peter S. *Statehood and Union: A History of the Northwest Ordinance.* Bloomington: Indiana University Press, 1987.

Ostler, Jeffrey. *The Plains Sioux and U.S. Colonialism from Lewis and Clark to Wounded Knee.* Cambridge: Cambridge University Press, 2004.

Ostrom, Elinor. *Governing the Commons: The Evolution of Institutions for Collective Action.* Cambridge: Cambridge University Press, 1990.

Palmer, Alison. *Colonial Genocide*. Adelaide, Australia: Crawford House, 2000.

Preston, David L. *Braddock's Defeat: The Battle of the Monongahela and the Road to Revolution*. New York: Oxford University Press, 2015.

——. *The Texture of Contact: European and Indian Settler Communities on the Frontiers of Iroquoia, 1667–1783*. Lincoln: University of Nebraska Press, 2009.

Richter, Daniel K. *Before the Revolution: America's Ancient Pasts*. Cambridge, MA: Harvard University Press, 2011.

——. "Cultural Brokers and Intercultural Politics: New York-Iroquois Relations, 1664–1701." *Journal of American History* 75, no. 1 (1988): 40–67.

——. *The Ordeal of the Longhouse: The Peoples of the Iroquois League in the Era of European Colonization*. Chapel Hill: University of North Carolina Press, 1992.

——. "War and Culture: The Iroquois Experience." *William and Mary Quarterly* 40, no. 4 (Oct. 1983): 528–59.

Roach, Hannah Benner. "The Pennsylvania Militia in 1777." *Pennsylvania Genealogical Magazine* 23, no. 3 (1964): 161–230.

Rushforth, Brett. "Slavery, the Fox Wars, and the Limits of Alliance." *William and Mary Quarterly* 63, no. 1 (2006): 53–80.

Russell, Lynette, ed. *Colonial Frontiers: Indigenous-European Encounters in Settler Societies*. Manchester: Manchester University Press, 2001.

Russell, Peter E. "Hay, Jehu." In *Dictionary of Canadian Biography*, vol. 4. University of Toronto/Université Laval, 2003. http://www.biographi.ca/en/bio/hay_jehu_4E.html.

Sachs, Honor. *Home Rule: Households, Manhood, and National Expansion on the Eighteenth-Century Kentucky Frontier*. New Haven, CT: Yale University Press, 2015.

Sadosky, Leonard. "Rethinking the Gnadenhütten Massacre: The Contest for Power in the Public World of the Revolutionary Frontier." In *The Sixty Years' War for the Great Lakes, 1754–1814*, edited by David Curtis Skaggs and Larry L. Nelson, 187–214. East Lansing: Michigan State University Press, 2001.

Saler, Bethel. *The Settlers' Empire: Colonialism and State Formation in America's Old Northwest*. Philadelphia: University of Pennsylvania Press, 2014.

Saunt, Claudio. *West of the Revolution: An Uncommon History of 1776*. New York: W. W. Norton, 2014.

Savelle, Max. *George Morgan, Colony Builder*. New York: Columbia University Press, 1932.

Scheidley, Nathaniel. "Hunting and the Politics of Masculinity in Cherokee Treaty-Making, 1763–75." In *Empire and Others: British Encounters with Indigenous Peoples, 1600–1850*, edited by Martin Daunton and Rick Halpern, 167–85. Philadelphia: University of Pennsylvania Press, 1999.

Schutt, Amy C. *Peoples of the River Valleys: The Odyssey of the Delaware Indians*. Philadelphia: University of Pennsylvania Press, 2007.

Seeman, Erik R. *The Huron-Wendat Feast of the Dead: Indian-European Encounters in Early North America*. Baltimore: Johns Hopkins University Press, 2011.

Silver, Peter. *Our Savage Neighbors: How Indian War Transformed Early America*. New York: W. W. Norton, 2008.

Slaughter, Thomas P. *The Whiskey Rebellion: Frontier Epilogue to the American Revolution*. New York: Oxford University Press, 1986.

Sleeper-Smith, Susan. *Indian Women and French Men: Rethinking Cultural Encounter in the Western Great Lakes*. Amherst: University of Massachusetts Press, 2001.

Slotkin, Richard. *Regeneration Through Violence: The Mythology of the American Frontier, 1600–1860*. Middletown, CT: Wesleyan University Press, 1973.

Smith, Stacey L. *Freedom's Frontier: California and the Struggle over Unfree Labor, Emancipation, and Reconstruction*. Chapel Hill: University of North Carolina Press, 2013.

Snyder, Christina. *Slavery in Indian Country: The Changing Face of Captivity in Early America*. Cambridge, MA: Harvard University Press, 2010.

Starkey, Armstrong. *European and Native American Warfare, 1675–1815*. Norman: University of Oklahoma Press, 1998.

Stasiulis, Daiva, and Nira Yuval-Davis, eds. *Unsettling Settler Societies: Articulations of Gender, Race, Ethnicity and Class*. London: Sage, 1995.

Stearns, Susan Gaunt. "Streams of Interest: The Mississippi River and the Political Economy of the Early Republic, 1783–1803." Ph.D. diss., University of Chicago, 2011.

Steckley, John L. *The Eighteenth-Century Wyandot: A Clan-Based Study*. Waterloo, Ontario: Wilfrid Laurier University Press, 2014.

Steele, Ian Kenneth. *Betrayals: Fort William Henry and the Massacre*. New York: Oxford University Press, 1990.

———. *Warpaths: Invasions of North America*. New York: Oxford University Press, 1994.

Sugden, John. *Blue Jacket: Warrior of the Shawnees*. Lincoln: University of Nebraska Press, 2000.

Tanner, Helen Hornbeck, ed. *Atlas of Great Lakes Indian History*. Norman: University of Oklahoma Press, 1987.

———. "Coocoochee: Mohawk Medicine Woman." *American Indian Culture and Research Journal* 3, no. 3 (1979): 23–41.

———. "The Glaize in 1792: A Composite Indian Community." *Ethnohistory* 25, no. 1 (Winter 1978): 15–39.

Taylor, Alan. *The Divided Ground: Indians, Settlers, and the Northern Borderland of the American Revolution*. New York: Alfred A. Knopf, 2006.

Thrush, Coll. *Indigenous London: Native Travelers at the Heart of Empire*. New Haven, CT: Yale University Press, 2017.

Tillson, Albert H. *Gentry and Common Folk: Political Culture on a Virginia Frontier, 1740–1789*. Lexington: University Press of Kentucky, 1991.

Tilly, Charles. *The Politics of Collective Violence*. Cambridge: Cambridge University Press, 2003.

Turner, Frederick Jackson. "Contributions of the West to American Democracy (1903)." In *Rereading Frederick Jackson Turner: "The Significance of the Frontier in American History" and Other Essays*, edited by John Mack Faragher, 31–60. New York: Henry Holt, 1994.

Van Kirk, Sylvia. *Many Tender Ties: Women in Fur-Trade Society, 1670–1870*. Norman: University of Oklahoma Press, 1980.

Vaughan, Alden T. "Frontier Banditti and the Indians: The Paxton Boys' Legacy." *Pennsylvania History* 51, no. 1 (1984): 1–29.

———. *Transatlantic Encounters: American Indians in Britain, 1500–1776*. Cambridge: Cambridge University Press, 2008.

Wainwright, Nicholas B. *George Croghan: Wilderness Diplomat*. Chapel Hill: University of North Carolina Press, 1959.

Warren, Stephen. *The Worlds the Shawnees Made: Migration and Violence in Early America*. Chapel Hill: University of North Carolina Press, 2014.

Weaver, John C. *The Great Land Rush and the Making of the Modern World: 1650–1800*. Montreal: McGill-Queen's University Press, 2003.

Wellenreuther, Hermann. "White Eyes and the Delawares' Vision of an Indian State." *Pennsylvania History* 68, no. 2 (Spring 2001): 139–61.

White, Richard. *"It's Your Misfortune and None of My Own": A History of the American West.* Norman: University of Oklahoma Press, 1991.

———. *The Middle Ground: Indians, Empires, and Republics in the Great Lakes Region, 1650–1815.* New York: Cambridge University Press, 1991.

Witgen, Michael. *An Infinity of Nations: How the Native New World Shaped Early America.* Philadelphia: University of Pennsylvania Press, 2012.

Wolfe, Patrick. "Settler Colonialism and the Elimination of the Native." *Journal of Genocide Research* 8, no. 4 (2006): 387–409.

INDEX

ACKNOWLEDGMENTS

────────

This book exists because many, many people and institutions have given me their time, encouragement, advice, criticism, friendship, money, and love. Much of what may be praiseworthy in these pages can be attributed to them; all errors and omissions are my own. Expressed in full, my gratitude would add a chapter to the text. A few pages must suffice.

The project germinated in the late 1990s, when I moved to Columbus, Ohio, and house-sat for my great-aunt, Dorothy Robinson Schaffner, who had recently moved into a nursing home. Dorothy had researched our family history for decades, and I was eager to learn. While combing through her notes, and peppering her with questions, I noticed that our ancestors' migrations into and across Ohio corresponded closely with the United States' displacement of native nations from their land. I began to wonder about what brought about that transformation. A few years later I began studying early American history—a field I knew almost nothing about—with a vague notion of researching eighteenth-century Ohio. For nudging me down this long road, I first thank, and honor the memory of, Aunt Dorothy.

The late Jeanne Boydston made this project possible. I will always be grateful for her keen criticism, boundless curiosity, exacting standards, and steady encouragement. I strive, throughout my professional life, to live up to the standard she set.

Among so much else, Jeanne advised me to read the work of, and later make the acquaintance of, Drew Cayton, a founder of the subfield I had so unreadily entered. Drew encouraged me to write the book and offered invaluable suggestions for improvement. In the years that followed, he continued to challenge me to think more creatively about both eighteenth-century Ohio and the larger enterprise of writing history. His scholarly accomplishments were paired with kindness, humility, and generosity toward his colleagues. Like Jeanne, we lost Drew far too soon. His influence permeates this book.

Throughout this project, I have enjoyed exceptionally generous financial support. The U.S. Department of Education's Jacob K. Javits Fellowships Program funded four years of research and writing. The Andrew W. Mellon Foundation and the American Council of Learned Societies awarded me two year-long fellowships, enabling me to turn a mare's nest of research notes into the beginnings of a book. I was fortunate to spend the latter fellowship year in residence at the Institute for Research in the Humanities at the University of Wisconsin–Madison (UW). I am grateful to Susan Friedman and the community of IRH fellows who welcomed and encouraged me throughout that year. I completed most of the remaining research, and drafted much of the final text, during a year-long National Endowment for the Humanities fellowship at the Huntington Library. I am immensely grateful to the Huntington staff for their hospitality and support. I thank the research director, Steve Hindle, for his interest in and feedback on my work, and his dedication to nurturing a supportive and inspiring scholarly community. I and my book benefited immensely from formal and informal conversations among a wonderfully collegial cohort of Huntington fellows. I am especially grateful to Matt Babcock, Alison Games, Fred Hoxie, Jacob Lee, Samantha Seeley, Isaac Stephens, and Valerie Traub for their thoughtful comments on my work, and to Matt, Sarah Grossman, Aurelio Hinarejos Rojo, Julie Orlemanski, and Sandra Rebok for our magnificent hikes in the San Gabriel and Santa Monica mountains.

At Madison, I enjoyed the support of an outstanding group of scholars, including Chuck Cohen, Susan Johnson, Ned Blackhawk, and the late Neil Whitehead. I am especially grateful to Chuck and Susan for their detailed feedback on my writing and their ongoing support of me and my work after Jeanne's passing. The UW History Department collectively taught me the interdependence of methodological rigor, conceptual sophistication, and clear, effective writing. I owe particular thanks to the late Paul Boyer, Bill Cronon, Suzanne Desan, Colleen Dunlavy, Steve Kantrowitz, Florencia Mallon, James Schlender Jr., Steve Stern, and Thongchai Winichakul. At UW, I was also able to participate in the activities of the Committee on Institutional Cooperation's American Indian Studies Consortium (CIC-AISC), which gave me an invaluable introduction to that field. I thank Lucy Murphy and John Sanchez for the chance to take their respective CIC-AISC seminars at the Newberry Library's D'Arcy McNickle Center.

I conducted research for this book at the Carnegie Library of Pittsburgh, the Darlington Memorial Library, the Filson Historical Society, the Historical

Society of Pennsylvania, the Huntington Library, the Indiana Historical Society, the Library Company of Philadelphia, the Newberry Library, the William L. Clements Library, and the Wisconsin Historical Society. I owe more than I can say to the many librarians, archivists, and other staff who helped me find my way through these rich collections. For funding my research travel, I thank the Clements, the CIC-AISC and the McNickle Center, the Filson, the Mellon Foundation, UW, the University of Wisconsin–Stevens Point (UWSP), and the Wisconsin chapter of the National Society of Colonial Dames of America.

I am grateful for the opportunity to try out arguments and receive feedback at scholarly conferences and seminars hosted by the American Society for Ethnohistory, the CIC-AISC, the McNickle Center, the Filson Institute, the Historical Society of Pennsylvania, the McNeil Center for Early American Studies, the Omohundro Institute for Early American History and Culture, the Society for Historians of the Early American Republic, the Tanner Humanities Center, and the Western Historical Society. I thank these organizations, the conference organizers, the commentators, and my co-panelists for making these experiences possible.

While working on this project, I published related articles in the *William and Mary Quarterly* and the *Journal for Genocide Research*. I thank their editors and staff and the anonymous reviewers for their feedback and support. I also thank both journals for permission to include some content from these articles in this book. Portions of Chapters 1 and 2 will appear in a chapter of *Borderland Narratives: Exploring North America's Contested Spaces, 1500–1850*, edited by Glenn Crothers and Andrew Frank, forthcoming from the University Press of Florida. Many thanks to Glenn and Andrew for this opportunity and to Eric Hinderaker for his feedback on the chapter.

In January 2010, I had lunch with Dan Richter and Bob Lockhart to discuss whether my project would be suitable for publication by the University of Pennsylvania Press. I am grateful for their initial interest in the project, and much more so for their advice, encouragement, and patience during the many years since. Both read early draft chapters and helped me refine the book's argument and organization. Bob's editorial input has been insightful, considerate, candid, and always focused on producing the best possible book. I also thank the press's anonymous reviewers and the faculty editorial board for their fruitful suggestions, as well as Paul Dangel for creating the maps and Alexander Trotter for compiling the index.

I owe a great deal to my students and colleagues at UWSP. I am very grateful for the help and support of library staff there. My colleagues in the Department of History and International Studies released me from teaching responsibilities during two year-long fellowships, and they supported my work in countless other ways. I particularly thank Tobias Barske, Valerie Barske, Susan Brewer, Mike Demchik, Gar Francis, Brian Hale, Jerry Jessee, Theresa Kaminski, Nancy Lopatin-Lummis, Brad Mapes-Martin, Kate Moran, Camarin Porter, Neil Prendergast, Greg Summers, and Lee Willis for their advice and their encouragement of my research and writing. I am grateful to the late Sally Kent for her unwavering willingness to pop into my office to chat about ethnic cleansing and genocide. For indexing, I received financial support from the University Personnel Development Committee's Publication Fund Program and from my department's Faculty Development Fund. I am especially grateful for the opportunity to work with UWSP students, who challenge and inspire me daily. I owe particular thanks to veterans of my research methods seminar, from whom I have learned at least as much as they have from me, and those in my Fall 2015 Revolutionary America course, who read and provided feedback on two chapter drafts.

This book would not have been possible without the support and encouragement of a long list of friends and colleagues. In addition to those mentioned above, I thank Miriam Axel-Lute, Jenne Bergstrom, Rebecca Brannon, Rebecca Bryan Tell, Joanne Budzien, Greg Dowd, Lisa Ford, Michael Goode, John Hall, Lawrence Hatter, Jennifer Holland, Jennifer Hull, Jill Kapla, Sami Lakomäki, Dee Lawrence, Jacob Lee, Wayne Lee, Gladys McCormick, Rebekah Mergenthal, Alyssa Mt. Pleasant, Elizabeth Dilkes Mullins, Nick Mullins, David Nichols, Hannah Nyala, Lindsay O'Neill, Michelle Orihel, David Preston, Honor Sachs, Bethel Saler, Susan Sleeper-Smith, Stacey Smith, John Smolenski, Susan Gaunt Stearns, Kathryn Tomasek, Stewart West, and the late Helen Tanner. I am particularly grateful to Steve Volk for introducing me to academic history and encouraging me to pursue this career.

Above all, I thank the Robinson and Harper families, and particularly Molly Harper, Katie Harper Jerstad, and Peder Jerstad, for their lifelong love and support. I owe the greatest debts to my parents, Gordon and Jill Harper, and my grandparents, the late Les Harper, Marjorie Harper, John Robinson, and Pauline Robinson. This book is for them.

www.ingramcontent.com/pod-product-compliance
Lightning Source LLC
Chambersburg PA
CBHW030940150426
42812CB00064B/3074/J